W9-AGN-721

MARION GORMAN

EDITOR: CHARLES GERRAS

BOOK DESIGN: JOAN PECKOLICK

Rodale Press, Emmaus, Pa.

Printed in the United States of America on recycled paper containing a high percentage of de-inked fiber.

Photography by Jim Freeman, North Light Photography.

Photographs on pages 64-65, 145, and 181 by Christie C. Tito.

Photographs on pages 103 and 127 courtesy of the Blue Goose, Inc., Hagerstown, Maryland.

Library of Congress Cataloging in Publication Data

Gorman, Marion.
Cooking with fruit.

Includes index.
1. Cookery (Fruit) I. Gerras, Charles. II. Title.
TX811.G67 641.6′4 82-21493
ISBN 0-87857-414-X hardcover

2 4 6 8 10 9 7 5 3 1 hardcover

To my parents
PHILLIP and MARIA (BESSIE) FRISCH
and my sisters
KATHRYN HRYWNAK and HELEN WOLINSKI
who shared with me
the first course of my feast of fruit.

CONTENTS

CONTENTS

PART II

Fruit Medley

PART III

Basics

PART IV

Holding Fruits for the Future

INVITATION TO THE FEAST

During a recent trip to the supermarket I saw a young mother and daughter scouting the produce counter. They came to a small bin of luscious-looking fruit. "What are they?" asked the child. "Mangoes, I think," said the mother. "Can we buy some?" "I don't think so, honey. I wouldn't know what to do with them," the mother replied.

A lot of strange fruits are showing up at our markets, and many people are stymied about how to use them. But, really, these fruits aren't strange. Somewhere, each species abounds and is as familiar to its area as the apple is to us. To gain familiarity, we simply have to try eating them in preparations or out of hand.

Getting to know these exotic fruits and discovering more exotic uses for our common fruits can brighten a dim menu and add a sense of adventure to our meals and snacks. At this very moment, during a brutal cold wave in New York, I am feasting on a big box of sunshiny oranges sent to me by friends in Florida – oranges with soup, with scrambled eggs, with sole, adding juice and rind to bran muffins, and organizing a dinner party just to serve my favorite orange roast duck with orange potatoes.

As I work with food and write about it, so many ideas seem to come from experiences that are remembered because of the impression of fruit. I dream of the mornings when I sat in the lean-to kitchen in Tres Palos, Mexico, waiting for Miguel to fetch my horse while I watched his wife, Fujencia, feed breakfast to the children . . . breakfast of papaya, mango, pineapple, or watermelon, with tortillas and *cafe con leche* . . . everyday fruits picked from the yard and nearby fields, which were devoured with smiles and happiness. Later, during our ride, I would probably enjoy a refreshing drink of cool, exquisite, jellylike flesh and water of a baby coconut felled from a tree by Miguel's machete.

In my thoughts I continually roam Mexican markets pungently perfumed with the profusion of tropical fruits which the *campesino* vendors like to arrange artistically, like a Gauguin painting come to life – fruits that are today making their way to northern markets. Our farm in Tuscany is another fantasy of fruit. Felipe and I must go there this summer to take care of repairs, but at the top of my mind, I am looking forward to gathering the little strawberries called *fraises de bois,* the sweet cherries, our *white* peaches, wild raspberries, and luscious fresh figs.

As a youngster in Michigan, I feasted on a cornucopia of homegrowns – literally wallowing in red raspberries as I picked them from the bushes into a lard pail tied around my waist (a rapturous way of earning summer money) – on Mother's *apfel kuchen*, complaining only when the dough rose too high (we preferred it thin and soaked with juice) – on blueberries in the bog by Saginaw Bay, which we gathered on family outings – and on baskets and baskets of strawberries-cherries-gooseberries-peaches-plums-grapes-crabapples-apples, which we helped Mother can into rows and rows of colorful, gleaming mason jars, always certain of a blue ribbon or two at the county fair.

From my French cooking teachers, especially my mentor Dione Lucas, I learned that fruit is the cook's palette from which endless picture-perfect temptations of color, texture, and flavor can be created – like the pinwheel pattern of fresh fruit on top of a cream-filled tart, glistening with the glaze of apricot or currant syrup. Wherever I go I am hopelessly seduced when a main dish has been fashioned with fruit, be it fish, poultry, or meat – an ancient idea whose time has come, a way of adding instant glamour, since fruit ought to be cooked little, if at all.

A piece of perfectly ripe fruit, plain and simple, is still the fastest fast food in the world – the way I tote a couple of bananas, nectarines, or pears for eating under the hair dryer or on a shuttle flight. And I wholeheartedly agree with writer/connoisseur M. F. K. Fisher that "winter or summer, I think the best dessert in the world, after no matter how plain or elaborate a meal, is what is at its peak of ripening from the fields and orchards" – the way folks in the tropics eat fruits most of the time.

Fruit is the most sensuous of foods. It is beguiling and so willing. It promises, and gives, instant pleasure and satisfaction. It is never boring. This book presents a feast of more than 50 kinds of fruit – a fantasia of magical colors, succulent textures, heady nectars, and ravishing taste sensations . . . ready to eat.

The Art of Cooking with Fruit

In this paean to cooking with fruit, we prefer to begin with fresh fruit in season, hopefully at ideal ripeness. Fruits are the foods that, in their natural state, are endowed with the most color, flavor, texture, and cooking versatility, offering a kaleidoscope of eating excitement. The recipes in this book aim to bring out and emphasize these natural assets. Heat cooking, if required, is minimal. Addition of seasonings and flavor accents is discreet. Salt and alcohol are not specified. When necessary, light honey instead of sugar is used for sweetening.

Sweet Seduction in Variety and Versatility

Ever since the Garden of Eden, we know that fruit just naturally provokes our senses to tingling anticipations of sweet seduction, and it continues to do so with a tour de force of limitless variety and versatility.

(continued on page xiv)

THE VERSATILE FRUITS

TYPE OF FRUIT	Edible Raw	Beverage	Appetizer	Salad	Soup	Fish/Shellfish	Poultry	Red Meats	Grain, Vegetable, Egg Main Dish or Accompaniment	Breads, Muffins, Coffee Cake	Desserts, Cakes, Pies	Garnishes, Sauces	Dried Fruit, Confections	Canning
Apples	•	•	•	•	•	•	•	•	•	•	•	•	•	•
Apple-Pears	•		•	•		•	•	•	•	•	•	•	•	•
Apricots	•	•	•	•	•		•	•	•	•	•	•	•	•
Avocados	•	•	•	•	•	•	•	•	•		•	•		
Bananas	•	•	•	•	•	•	•	•	•	•	•	•	•	
Blackberries (also Boysenberries, Dewberries, Loganberries, Mulberries)	•	•			•						•	•		•
Blueberries (also Huckleberries)	•									•	•	•	•	•
Breadfruit	•			•	•			•	•					
Carambolas	•	•	•	•	•	•					•	•	•	•
Carob		•								•	•	•	•	
Cashew Apples	•													
Cherimoyas (also Custard Apples, Ilamas, Soursops, Sugar Apples)	•	•									•			
Cherries (Sweet, Sour)	•	•	•		•		•				•	•	•	•
Coconuts	•	•	•	•		•	•		•	•	•	•	•	
Crabapples							•	•				•		•
Cranberries	•	•		•	•		•	•	•	•	•	•		•
Dried Currants	•		•							•	•	•		
Currants (Black, Red, White)		•								•	•	•		•
Dates	•		•	•						•	•	•	•	
Figs	•		•	•			•		•	•	•	•	•	•
Gooseberries	•					•	•	•			•	•		•
Grapefruit	•	•	•	•		•	•				•	•	•	
Grapes	•	•	•	•	•	•	•				•	•		•
Guavas	•	•		•	•	•	•	•	•		•	•	•	•
Kiwi Fruit	•		•	•		•	•	•	•		•	•	•	
Kumquats	•		•	•		•	•	•			•	•	•	•
Lemons	•	•	•	•	•	•	•	•	•	•	•	•	•	•
Limes	•	•	•	•	•	•	•	•	•	•	•	•	•	•

THE VERSATILE FRUITS — continued

TYPE OF FRUIT	Edible Raw	Beverage	Appetizer	Salad	Soup	Fish/Shellfish	Poultry	Red Meats	Grain, Vegetable, Egg Main Dish or Accompaniment	Breads, Muffins, Coffee Cake	Desserts, Cakes, Pies	Garnishes, Sauces	Dried Fruit, Confections	Canning
Loquats	•		•	•							•	•		•
Lychees	•		•	•			•				•	•	•	•
Mameys	•		•	•			•				•	•		
Mandarins (Tangerines, Tangelos, Clementines, other zipper-skins)	•	•	•	•	•	•	•	•	•	•	•	•	•	•
Mangoes	•	•	•	•	•	•	•	•	•	•	•	•	•	•
Melons (Muskmelons, Watermelons)	•	•	•	•	•	•	•				•	•		•
Oranges	•	•	•	•	•	•	•	•	•	•	•	•	•	•
Papaws	•													
Papayas	•	•	•	•	•	•	•	•	•		•	•		•
Passion Fruit	•	•									•	•		
Peaches (also Nectarines)	•	•	•	•	•		•	•	•		•	•	•	•
Pears	•	•	•	•	•		•	•	•		•	•	•	•
Persimmons	•			•							•	•		
Pineapples	•	•	•	•		•	•	•	•	•	•	•	•	•
Plantains						•	•	•	•					
Plums	•	•	•	•			•	•	•		•	•	•	•
Pomegranates	•	•		•			•	•	•		•	•		
Prickly Pears	•												•	
Prunes	•	•	•	•			•	•	•	•	•	•	•	
Quinces														•
Raisins	•		•	•					•	•	•	•	•	
Raspberries (Black, Red, White)	•	•			•			•			•	•		•
Rhubarb		•			•						•	•		•
Sapodillas	•										•			
Sapotes		•									•			
Star Apples	•										•	•		
Strawberries	•	•	•	•	•						•	•	•	•
Tamarinds		•									•	•		•
Ugli Fruit	•	•	•	•							•	•	•	

INVITATION TO THE FEAST

THE PARAMETERS OF "FRUIT" IN THIS BOOK: Botanically speaking, a fruit is the ovary of the plant, the product that contains its reproductive seed, surrounded by pulp and skin. Tomatoes, eggplants, cucumbers, olives, nuts, and legumes are all fruits. In this book, however, we are featuring fruits that are usually eaten for their sweet or sweetened pulp. (Thus, in this interpretation, rhubarb – not a fruit, but a vegetable – is included.)

The Sweet We Ought to Eat

Fruit is a self-contained, natural, multinutrient capsule, the best and tastiest kind. It is the sweet we are encouraged to eat more of – naturally occurring sugars (glucose and fructose) accompanied by a variety of vitamins, minerals, and fiber. Fruits, vegetables, and grains are the foods with a high vitamin, mineral, and fiber content. Fruits are particularly famous for their generous supplies of vitamins A and C. They also contain some of the B vitamins and a range of minerals, notably iron and calcium. Of interest for special diets, most fruits have low sodium content, and, except for avocados and coconuts, contain almost no fat. Gram for gram, we can eat more fruit for fewer calories.

Picking The Best

Choosing properly ripe fruit is where connoisseurship really counts. I have never seen more careful examination and selection or rejection of fruit for its state of ripeness than by the Mexicans. They simply won't touch a fruit until it is absolutely ready to eat.

Many favorite fruits are now available year-round, because modern agriculture has developed hybrids with different seasons and refrigerated shipping methods especially for putting picked fruit in a "holding pattern" until it reaches the consumer. Selective picking and controlled, refrigerated shipping have also made it possible for more kinds of tropical fruits to make the trip north in good condition.

With an ever-increasing variety of fruits available, it is important for the consumer to know the signs of true ripeness of different fruits. And they differ! Some fruits, such as pineapples, must be picked when fully ripe because they will not continue to ripen off the plant. Others, such as pears, are best when picked at a stage called "proper maturity," which is not quite ripe enough for eating, because they best complete their ripening process *after* removal from the plant. Fruits of this type are held in correct refrigeration to temporarily suspend the ripening process. When such fruit is allowed to stand at room temperature, or placed in a brown paper bag, or a plastic bag with a few holes, or a fruit ripener bowl, the ethylene gas exuded from the fruit will surround it and complete the ripening, usually in one to four days. In this book, tips for recognizing proper ripeness are presented for each fruit.

STORAGE OF FRUIT: Ideally, fresh, properly ripe fruit should be refrigerated for maximum keeping time in the home. If fruit is to be eaten within a day or two, it is lovely to arrange it in a bowl as a centerpiece on the dining table, coffee table, or sideboard.

When you have large quantities of certain fruits, like apples, they can be stored for indefinite periods. It is best to consult technical manuals for correct conditions and temperatures for different fruits.

PRESERVATION OF FRUIT: Many fruits can be suitably kept for longer periods than refrigeration allows by dehydration and freezing (see the section on holding fruits for the future) and by canning. The USDA Agriculture Information Bulletin 410 (*Canning, Freezing, and Storing Garden Produce*) is a particularly good manual for the technicalities of home canning.

Fruits Make a Beautiful Impression

Fruits Glorify the Cook Fruits are preeminent among all foods in richness of color, texture, and ready-to-eat flavor. They are the cook's delight.

Fresh fruits have fascinating shapes, colors, textures and sheens, and leaves. They are pictures in themselves, as many fine paintings attest. I enjoy composing all kinds of arrangements with fruits for centerpieces, from a simple monotone arrangement to an elaborate tiered epergne piled with lady apples and pears and dripping with grapes. I shall never forget the time we entertained food and wine writer/author Doris Tobias at lunch in our apartment. I filled a virescent Royal Copenhagen bowl with lemons, only lemons, and tucked a few fresh lemon leaves (from the local florist) in the crevices. I thought the arrangement was quite dramatic on the bare mahogany table. Doris was ecstatic! I had no idea that she was a lemon fanatic and had just finished writing a whole cookbook dedicated to lemons. When there's no time to prepare a tray of appetizers, my favorite fallback is to run out to the greengrocer and pick out the most luscious-looking bunches of grapes. They are served on a silver plate, accompanied by a dish of raw cashew nuts. Guests seem to find the offering irresistible.

Fruit Centerpieces Start with a fruit bowl. Its eye appeal is irresistible. I don't think I have ever visited a Mexican home, from the most modest to the grandest, where there has not been a ravishing assortment of fresh fruits on the table or sideboard. Often, when we dined, guests declined the prepared dessert but succumbed to a piece of fresh fruit. The *haut gourmand* demands a fruit centerpiece instead of flowers. In the tropics, people just think fruit decorations are beautiful and quite a matter of course; they love to arrange them.

Some of the most beautiful centerpieces I have seen are the fruit arrangements that graced the table in the executive dining room of Lic. Ernesto Robles Leon in Mexico City. I had the pleasure of dining there several times; each was an education, a tasting choice from masses of exotic tropical fruits. At the Club Industriales in Mexico City, the beautiful free-form centerpieces of fresh fruits are arranged on the bare red tablecloths, in monolithic fashion, both on the buffet table and in smaller groupings on the dining tables.

In tropical countries everywhere, the dining decor is accented with arrangements often combining fruit, flowers, and leaves – in Bermuda, Florida, California, the Caribbean, Mexico. My Acapulco cateress friend, Susana Palazeulos, offers these ideas:

- For a party buffet centerpiece, create huge masses of "grapes," actually constructing guavas to look like bunches of grapes by sticking them together with toothpicks or skewers, ensconced in fresh lemon leaves. (Toothpicks or skewers can be used to hold fruit arrangements together in other compositions.)
- Use upright pineapple shells as vases for flowers and leaves (candles, too) on individual tables. Cut one-third off the top of a pineapple; cut out the flesh for cooking use. Fill the hollowed shell with a flower arrangement.

Fruit centerpieces are exciting, colorful, and enduring, and many guests enjoy taking a piece of fresh fruit after a party meal.

Fruit Serving Decorations Fruits are also a favorite media for serving decorations, which seem to be the special expertise of the French, Japanese, and Mexicans. The simple addition of lemon slices on a fish or burnished pineapple rings surrounding roast pork guarantees instant glamour and piques the appetite. Even a scoop of cottage cheese can be converted from common to elegant with a melon fan or an orange loop.

Fresh fruits, whole or cut in various shapes, are made-to-order media for decorating platters or individual serving plates. The *nouvelle cuisine* chefs probably thrust fruit decorating to new heights with their precise still-life plate arrangements, such as a serving of pate garnished with a slice of kiwi with a slightly overlapping slice of carrot, relieved with two spreading tarragon leaves, balanced by a row of skinny green beans and a halved cherry tomato on the opposite side of the plate.

This Oriental exoticism – patterned arrangements of garnishes on the serving plate – has captivated today's chefs and home hobby cooks. A three-star example is this fruit dessert served at the L'Archestrate restaurant in Paris: "a whole green roasted fig was sliced in half and filled with tiny red *fraises de bois* [wild strawberries], served lukewarm with a scoop of fresh pistachio ice cream on the side, all in a pool of strawberry puree." The same reporter also disclosed chef Alain Senderens's discovery and apparent passion for passion fruit – with a specialty of passion fruit soup garnished with kiwi, mango, pineapple, and nefle (a crabapplelike fruit of the Japanese medlar tree) served in a soup bowl with lots of juice, like an exotic fruit salad.

The Mexicans, the French, and the Japanese have always shown a special talent for beautiful, often simple, fruit decorations. The following are a few basic fruit garnish ideas which can be used on appetizer, salad, main dish, or dessert servings:

Orange Loops: Cut orange slices 3/8 inch thick. Cut each slice in half. Make a cut between skin and flesh to within 1 inch from the end. Curl skin under uncut portion.

Melon Fans: Cut cantaloupe into 1-inch-thick rounds. Cut the rounds into thirds. Remove seeds from center with small round cookie cutter (for neat round shape). Cut away rind, leaving three fan shapes from one slice. On surface of each fan shape, make four or five wedge-shaped cuts about 1/4 inch deep and remove wedge pieces. The fan shape should now have fan ridges (like accordion pleats).

Citrus Fruit Star Cut: See instructions in the section on oranges. This can be done with grapefruit, lemons, limes, and oranges – and cucumbers.

Red and Green Lemon Slices: Cut thin slices of lemon. On a plate, place separate mounds of paprika and very finely chopped fresh parsley. Press half of a lemon slice on paprika and the other half on parsley. (These are attractive surrounding a cold fish platter.)

Lemon Spirals: Cut a thin lemon slice horizontally. Make 1 radial cut (to center only). Twist in spiral shape.

Most fruits lend themselves beautifully for decoration with the dish in which they are featured, as described in many of the recipes in this book.

As shown in the preceding chart, fruits can be used in all kinds of cooking preparations. They can be featured in or accompany any course, savory or sweet, in all kinds of meals. Actually, it is only our Western idea that sweet foods should come at the end of a meal. As we continue to internationalize our cooking, our notions about fruit are being liberated.

Fruits have special attraction for the time-conscious cook. Guests are always impressed when a main dish is garnished with fruit. The chef's secret is that fruit is a quick trick, since a fruit garnish should be raw or barely cooked. Too much cooking would disintegrate most fruits.

Obviously the fruit feaster believes, with author-epicure Richard Condon, that "fruit is an aphrodisiac which excites the passion for living. It courts, seduces, ravishes, then cherishes all of the senses (as well as the sense of most worthy accomplishment) by treating each as if it existed alone, as if all satisfaction were dependent on this one sense, while it orchestrates all five into complex permutations of sensations." (*The Mexican Stove*, Doubleday, 1973.)

PART I

Those Fabulous Fruits

APPLES

If the Great Depression deprived some of us of nickles and dimes to spend in the corner candy store, it caused me to be raised on that all-American food, the apple. Every autumn Father frugally gathered bushels of apples from our own backyard trees and added to them with one or two Sunday journeys to the orchards of Benton Harbor. We stored them carefully in the cellar, enough to last through the winter and the following spring, for school lunch boxes, fast-food snacks whenever we were hungry – and home-baked *apfel kuchen* on the breakfast table *every* day. "Bessie's *apfel kuchen*" was unique and renowned in our town – thin sheets of yeast-risen coffee cake dough covered with rows of juicy apple slices glazed with honey syrup. Mother's specialty evolved as we persuaded her to make the *kuchen* thinner and the rows of apple slices tighter so that it became thoroughly saturated with apple juice as it baked. One large pan of *apfel kuchen* was taken to Grandfather every Sunday afternoon when we called for him in the Model A for his weekly ride through the county farm roads. (It was during these rides that he and Father prognosticated the future of Saginaw County agriculture.)

Americans still eat more apples than any other fruit. Apples are found almost everywhere in the world and are especially bountiful in America – over 500 varieties. There are eating and cooking apples, the majority being dual purpose, with varying harvest times, providing a year-round, all-around healthy food. No one description fits all apples except that they grow on trees. Apples come in different colors – red, green, golden, mottled or striped; they brag different flavors – tart, sweet, or mellow; and they present different textures – crisp, hard, juicy, or snappy.

Apples contain a modest assortment of vitamins and minerals, and it is important to remember that most of their vitamin C is lodged just under the skin. The apple skin, besides being temptingly beautiful and appetite arousing, is high-grade dietary fiber and a very effective toothbrush.

Nowhere is the old adage "beauty is only skin deep" more true than in selecting apples. There are times when picture-perfect apples and larger sizes are essential. But when the purpose is not for show, most other apples are as good and more economical. Good apples should look fresh and reasonably unblemished. They should be firm, unbruised, not wilted or punctured, and of good color for the variety. Immature apples often lack color and are usually

COOKING ASPECTS OF SOME POPULAR VARIETIES OF APPLES

Variety	Harvest and Market Period	Flavor and Texture	Best Use	Freezability (slices)
SUMMER				
Beacon	Aug. – Sept.	mild, mellow	cooking & raw	fair
Early McIntosh	Aug.	slightly tart, tender	raw	good
Fenton	Aug. – Sept.	mild, mellow	raw	fair
Granny Smith	Apr. – July	tart, crisp	cooking & raw	very good
Gravenstein	July – Sept.	tart, crisp	cooking & raw	good
Lodi	July – Aug.	tart, soft	cooking	good
FALL				
Cortland	Oct. – Jan.	mild, tender	cooking & raw	very good
Delicious, Golden	Sept. – May	sweet, semifirm	cooking & raw	very good
Delicious, Red	Sept. – June	sweet, mellow	raw	fair
Empire	Oct. – Apr.	slightly tart, firm	cooking & raw	good
Greening, Rhode Island and Northwest	Oct. – Mar.	slightly tart, crisp	cooking	excellent
Idared	Oct. – June	slightly tart, firm	cooking & raw	good
Jonathan	Sept. – Jan.	tart, tender	cooking & raw	very good
McIntosh	Sept. – Jan.	slightly tart, tender	cooking & raw	good
Newtown Pippin	Sept. – June	slightly tart, firm	cooking & raw	excellent
Northern Spy	Oct.	slightly tart, crisp	cooking & raw	excellent
Paulared	Sept. – Oct.	tart, crisp	raw	good
Rome Beauty (Red Rome)	Oct. – June	slightly tart, firm	cooking & raw	very good
Stayman	Oct. – Mar.	tart, semifirm	cooking & raw	good
Winesap	Oct. – June	slightly tart, firm	cooking & raw	very good
York Imperial	Oct. – Apr.	tart, firm	cooking	good

poor in flavor. Overripe apples yield to slight pressure and the flesh is usually soft, mealy, and lacking in flavor. Apples grown in more humid parts of our country, with greater rainfall and fewer days of bright sunlight, tend to have a little more russet and other "weather marks" on the skin; they may not be quite as brightly colored and smooth as those grown in more arid parts of the country, but these traits do not affect the quality and flavor of the apples in any way.

About three medium-size apples represent a pound. One pound of unpeeled apples yields about three cups of peeled, sliced, or diced fruit. To keep peeled apples from discoloring, sprinkle generously with fresh lemon juice or place them in a pan of cold water with lemon juice.

The list of apple's temptations reads like the Garden of Eden cookbook – apple sauce, apple pie, apple butter, apple cider, apple *kuchen*, apple strudel, apple turnovers, apple fritters, apple pancakes, steamed apple pudding, apple pandowdy, apple brown betty, apple charlotte, apple upside-down cake, baked apples, the Waldorf salad, dried apple rings and chips. As our desire for the original fruit runs unabated, apples continue to inspire more gustatory delights, in any type of meal or course – soup, salad, with main-dish poultry, meats and grains, in desserts, with cheese – perfection.

Lady apple is a tiny jewel of an apple. Its dainty perfection is treasured by connoisseurs as a tempting decoration, certain to be plucked for a delectable moment of eating out of hand. Lady apples are about 1½ inches in diameter, usually with a yellow-green skin, brightly rouged on one side. They have a crisp, juicy pulp with a fine concentrated apple flavor. They are ancient fruits, long prized in France, but the species has always been rare. A few orchards of lady apple trees are now cultivated in the United States, mainly in Missouri, Ohio, and Washington. The fruit is available in the late fall and winter months.

APPLE BREAD

DO-AHEAD TIP: *This bread can be stored in freezer.*

- **8 tablespoons unsalted butter**
- **¼ cup light honey**
- **2 eggs, beaten**
- **1 cup ground cooking apples (put unpeeled, cored apples through fine meat grinder or process to ground stage in food processor)**
- **2 cups whole wheat pastry flour**
- **1½ teaspoons baking soda**
- **1½ tablespoons sour cream**
- **½ cup chopped walnuts or pecans**
- **1 teaspoon grated orange rind**
- **1 teaspoon vanilla extract**

Preheat oven to 350°F. Oil an 8-inch loaf pan (1½-quart capacity), line with waxed paper, and oil paper lining. Dust lining lightly with flour.

In mixer, beat butter until light and creamy. Add honey and beat again. Add beaten eggs and mix. Then add apples. In separate bowl, sift flour with soda. Add flour mixture gradually to wet ingredients, beating briefly after each addition. Add sour cream, nuts, orange rind, and vanilla. Operate mixer only until batter is well mixed.

Pour batter into prepared pan and bake 50 to 60 minutes, or until top rebounds to touch. Turn apple bread out of pan immediately and peel off waxed paper. Serve hot or cold.

Makes 1 loaf

APPLE AND CELERY SOUP

Potage de Pomme et Celeri

This soup can be served hot or cold.

DO-AHEAD TIP: *This soup can be frozen. Thaw at room temperature, or faster in covered heavy pot over low heat. Add garnish choice at serving time.*

SOUP

- 3 tablespoons light vegetable oil (e.g., safflower)
- 3 large celery ribs, sliced
- 1 large yellow onion, sliced
- 1 large carrot, sliced
- 7 medium-size apples, peeled, cored and sliced
- 3 cups stock (e.g., chicken, vegetable, or soy—3 cups water with 4 teaspoons tamari soy sauce)
- 2 teaspoons meat flavoring (e.g., Marmite brewer's yeast extract or vegetable paste)

CHOICE OF GARNISH

fried apple rings (for hot soup)

- 1 apple, cored, but not peeled, cut into 6 round slices, each ½ inch thick
- 2 tablespoons light vegetable oil

¾ cup thick sour cream (for hot or cold soup)

SOUP: In deep, heavy 6- to 8-quart pot, combine oil, celery, onion, and carrot. Cook over moderate heat 3 minutes, stirring occasionally. Add apples and cook mixture over high heat until apples are soft. Stir in stock and meat flavoring, bring soup to a boil, and simmer until all vegetables are soft. Puree soup in food processor or blender, or rub through fine vegetable strainer. Return to pot and reheat for hot serving. Chill for cold serving.

GARNISH: To make fried apple rings, heat oil in saute pan and quickly brown apple slices on both sides.

PRESENTATION: Float apple ring on top of individual serving of hot soup. Or, drop a spoonful of sour cream on top of hot or cold serving.

4 to 6 servings

APPLE CREPE CAKE WITH APRICOT SAUCE

Apple puree is sandwiched between layers of thin crepes, like a cake, and covered with zesty apricot glaze.

DO-AHEAD TIP: *Crepes can be prepared anytime and stored in freezer. Cake can be assembled and sauce prepared a day ahead and refrigerated.*

CREPES
10 to 12 6-inch Basic Crepes (see Index)

APPLE PUREE (about 4 cups)
8 medium-size cooking apples, cored, peeled, and thickly sliced

grated rind of 1 lemon

1½ cups apricot jam

½ teaspoon freshly grated nutmeg

¼ cup light honey

APRICOT SAUCE
1 cup apricot jam

1 tablespoon fresh lemon juice

½ cup shredded blanched almonds, toasted

APPLE PUREE: In deep, heavy pot, combine apples and lemon rind. Cover and cook over low heat until apples are soft, stirring occasionally. Continue cooking until almost all liquid has evaporated. Add jam, nutmeg, and honey. Cook over low heat 2 or 3 minutes to blend all ingredients. Set aside to cool slightly.

APRICOT SAUCE: Combine jam and lemon juice in saucepan and stir over low heat until jam is dissolved. Strain through wire strainer. Return to pan and add only enough water to bring to medium syrup consistency. Reheat.

PRESENTATION: Place 1 crepe on serving plate and spread with apple puree. Cover with another crepe and spread with apple puree. Continue to stack crepes sandwiched with apple puree in this manner, but do not spread puree on top of last crepe. Spread top crepe with thin glaze of apricot sauce and sprinkle with almonds. Pour remaining apricot sauce on plate around cake. Refrigerate until ready to serve.

4 to 6 servings

APPLE CREPES WITH SOUR CREAM SAUCE OR YOGURT SAUCE

DO-AHEAD TIP: *Stuffed crepes and sauce can be prepared a day ahead and refrigerated. At serving time, brush with melted butter and brown under broiler.*

8 to 12 6-inch Basic Crepes (see Index)

4 cups Apple Puree (see Apple Crepe Cake in this section)

4 tablespoons unsalted butter, melted

2 cups Sour Cream Dessert Sauce or Yogurt Dessert Sauce (see Index)

Spread underside (the side cooked last) of crepes with puree, roll them up like cigars, and arrange in a row on shallow, heatproof serving plate. Brush tops with melted butter and brown lightly under broiler. Serve with separate bowl of cold sour cream sauce or yogurt sauce.

4 to 6 servings

APPLES

BESSIE'S *APFEL KUCHEN*

A very thin sheet of yeast kuchen *dough is spread in a jelly roll pan and covered with rows of sliced apples glazed with buttered honey syrup. This* kuchen *can be made with the original light coffee cake dough (using whole wheat pastry flour and butter) or a roll-type dough (using whole wheat bread flour and vegetable oil). The latter will yield a somewhat sturdier product when baked.*

DO-AHEAD TIP: *Either type of dough can be prepared 2 or 3 days before baking and stored in the freezer.* Kuchen *can be baked a day or two ahead of serving; in fact, it will keep for about a week, covered with aluminum foil.*

COFFEE CAKE DOUGH

- 1 tablespoon active dry yeast
- ¼ cup lukewarm water
- 2 cups whole wheat pastry flour
- 10 tablespoons unsalted butter
- 3 large eggs
- 1 tablespoon light honey

APPLE TOPPING

- 5 to 6 large cooking apples (e.g., Granny Smith or Northern Spy), cored, peeled, and cut into quarters, then cut into slices no more than 3/16 inch thick
- 3 tablespoons unsalted butter
- ½ cup light honey
- 1 teaspoon ground cinnamon

COFFEE CAKE DOUGH: Dissolve yeast in water. Place ½ cup flour in small bowl. Add dissolved yeast and stir until a firm ball forms. Turn ball of dough out onto lightly floured work surface and knead a little until bottom is smooth. Cut a cross on the surface. Drop ball of dough (cut side up) into small bowl half filled with lukewarm water and let stand until it rises to top of water.

Meanwhile, beat butter in mixer until light and creamy. Remove butter and set aside in separate dish. (It is not necessary to clean mixer bowl for next step.) Place 1½ cups flour in mixer bowl. Add eggs and honey and beat well. Add creamed butter and beat again. Lift yeast ball out of water with your hand so that it drains through fingers and add to mixer bowl. Beat dough thoroughly.

Wipe inside of large bowl with damp cloth and dust lightly with flour. Transfer dough to this bowl. Cover with plastic wrap and cloth. Let dough stand in warm place (80° to 85°F. – such as oven set to 140°F. with door ajar) until it doubles in bulk.

When dough has risen, place dough in bowl in freezer. (Do not break the rise.) After dough has become *firm* in freezer, it is best to transfer it to refrigerator and let it rest for about 6 hours or overnight. Or, chilled dough can be prepared for baking immediately, but one must work very quickly when rolling it out.

Preheat oven to 375°F. Have ready well-oiled 18 × 12-inch jelly roll pan. Turn well-chilled dough out onto floured work surface. *Quickly* roll dough out to thin sheet the size of the pan. Lay dough over rolling pin lengthwise, like a tent, and transfer to pan. Using your fingers, spread dough evenly over bottom and into corners of pan.

BESSIE'S *APFEL KUCHEN*—continued

APPLE TOPPING: Place lengthwise rows of apple slices, all going in the same direction, on top of dough. As each slice is added, place it in back of preceding slice, pushing it slightly under the slice in front and pressing it gently into the dough. Continue to make even rows, touching each other, until dough is covered. If there is space on the side of the pan that is not wide enough for another row of apples, cover this area with slices placed sideways. Stand pan in warm place and allow dough to rise again.

Combine butter, honey, and cinnamon in small saucepan and stir over low heat until mixture is blended. Gently and generously brush mixture all over apples and dough. Bake 25 to 30 minutes, or until edges of dough are slightly tinged with brown. Remove from oven but leave in pan until serving. To serve, cut in strips about 2 inches wide by 4 or 5 inches long.

Makes 1 kuchen

NOTE: When peaches or plums are in abundance, use fresh peaches (peeled, pitted, and cut into ½-inch-thick slices) or fresh sweet plums (pitted and cut into ¼-inch-thick slices) instead of apples.

BESSIE'S *APFEL KUCHEN* WITH ROLL-TYPE DOUGH

- 1 cup milk, scalded and cooled
- ¼ cup lukewarm water
- 1 tablespoon active dry yeast
- ⅓ cup light vegetable oil (e.g., safflower)
- ¼ cup light honey
- 1 egg
- 3 cups whole wheat bread flour
- 3 tablespoons unsalted butter, melted
- Apple Topping (see recipe above)

Dissolve yeast in water. In mixer, combine dissolved yeast, milk, oil, honey, and egg. Mix at low speed about 6 minutes. Add flour a little at a time, beating after each addition. Dough should leave sides of bowl. Add a little more flour if necessary. Turn dough out onto floured work surface and knead until smooth and elastic. Let dough rest 10 minutes.

Have ready well-oiled 18 × 12-inch jelly roll pan. Roll dough out to a sheet large enough to cover bottom of pan. Shape dough into corners with fingers. Lightly brush top of dough with melted butter.

Preheat oven to 400°F. Cover dough with rows of apple slices as described above. Place preparation in warm place and allow to rise until dough is doubled in height. Then brush topping with butter-honey-cinnamon mixture. Bake 30 to 40 minutes, until edges of dough and apples are slightly browned.

Makes 1 kuchen

APPLE TARTLETS

DO-AHEAD TIP: *Tartlets can be made a day ahead and refrigerated.*

TARTLET SHELLS
- 12 baked 3½- or 4-inch tartlet shells (in baking tins) of Plain Whole Wheat Short Pastry 1 or 2 (see Index)
- 3 tablespoons fine whole wheat bread crumbs or graham cracker crumbs
- 1 teaspoon ground cardamom

FILLING
- 6 large, firm, tart apples
- 4 tablespoons fresh lemon juice
- ½ cup apricot preserve
- 1 tablespoon grated lemon rind
- 1 tablespoon light honey
- 1 tablespoon unsalted butter

GLAZE
- ½ cup apricot preserve
- 1 tablespoon lemon juice

TARTLET SHELLS: Mix crumbs and cardamom and sprinkle a little of this mixture in each tartlet shell.

FILLING: Preheat oven to 375°F. Peel and core apples. Dice 3 apples and sprinkle with 2 tablespoons lemon juice. Cut 3 apples into very thin slices and sprinkle with 2 tablespoons lemon juice. Mix diced apple with apricot preserve and lemon rind. Fill tartlet shells with diced apple mixture. On top of mixture, arrange sliced apples in pinwheel pattern. Combine honey and butter in small saucepan and stir over low heat until blended. Brush a little of mixture on sliced apple toppings. Place tartlets on jelly roll pan and bake 25 minutes. Place under broiler for a moment to singe edges of sliced apples.

GLAZE: Combine apricot preserve and lemon juice in small saucepan and stir over low heat until dissolved. Brush tartlets with glaze. Cool tartlets in tins.

Makes 12 tartlets

NORMANDY STYLE CHICKEN OR PHEASANT
Poulet ou Faisan Normande

Sauteed chicken or pheasant in an unforgettable sauce of pureed apple, celery, and cream. The presentation is garnished with the flavors of the sauce: bundles of celery sticks stuck through sauteed apple rings, and accompanied by Parisienne Potatoes.

DO-AHEAD TIP: *This dish can be cooked a day ahead. At serving time, cover with foil and rewarm in 300°F. oven. Brown briefly under broiler and add garnishes.*

POULTRY
- 1 3½- to 4½-pound whole dressed chicken or 2 small chickens or pheasants
- ½ lemon

POULTRY: Preheat oven to 350°F. Dry chicken or pheasant inside and out and rub all over with cut side of lemon. Insert in cavity 1 tablespoon oil, liver, and celery leaf. Tie poultry neatly. Heat 2 tablespoons oil in deep, heavy pot and brown poultry lightly all over. Remove from pot and set aside.

NORMANDY STYLE CHICKEN OR PHEASANT—continued

- 3 tablespoons light vegetable oil (e.g., safflower)
- 1 poultry liver
- sprig celery leaf
- 1 apple, cored and sliced but not peeled
- 1 large yellow onion, sliced
- ¾ cup sliced celery
- ½ teaspoon meat flavoring (e.g., Marmite brewer's yeast extract, vegetable paste, or meat glaze)
- 2 tablespoons whole wheat pastry flour
- 1½ cups stock (e.g., chicken, vegetable, or soy—1½ cups water with 1½ teaspoons tamari soy sauce)
- ¾ cup heavy cream, whipped
- 3 tablespoons freshly grated Parmesan cheese

GARNISH

- 2 large celery ribs, cut into matchstick-size strips
- 1 large apple, peeled, cut into 4 round slices, each ½ inch thick, and neatly cored with 1-inch-round cutter (soak apple slices in cold water with a little lemon juice until ready to cook)
- 2 tablespoons light vegetable oil

Add to pot apple, onion, and celery. Cover pot and cook over moderate heat until ingredients are tender. Remove from heat and stir in meat flavoring and flour. Add stock and stir over moderate heat until mixture boils. Transfer mixture to food processor or blender and puree.

Return pureed sauce to pot. Carve poultry into serving pieces and place in pot. Spoon some sauce over poultry. Cook in oven, uncovered, about 30 minutes, or until meat is tender.

Remove poultry from pot, carefully scraping off sauce. Arrange poultry on hot au gratin dish or serving platter and keep warm. Place pot with sauce over low heat on top of stove. With whisk, beat in whipped cream, a spoonful at a time. Spoon sauce over poultry and sprinkle grated cheese on top. Dot with a few drops of oil.

GARNISH: Divide celery matchsticks into 4 equal groups and tie into bundles with kitchen string. Place in pot and just cover with cold water. Bring water to a boil slowly and remove celery at once, setting bundles aside. Dry apple rings between paper towels. Heat oil in saute pan and fry apple slices over high heat until golden brown on both sides. Remove from pan and carefully slip bundles of celery sticks through holes in apple rings. Remove strings.

PRESENTATION: Place poultry preparation under broiler to lightly brown top. Place pile of Parisienne potatoes on opposite ends of dish. Arrange apple and celery garnish on two sides of dish. Serve at once.

4 to 6 servings

PARISIENNE POTATOES

- 3 large all-purpose or baking potatoes, pared
- 2 tablespoons light vegetable oil (e.g., safflower)
- 1 tablespoon finely chopped fresh parsley

Using small melon scoop (¾-inch diameter), cut out balls of potato. Put potato balls in pot and barely cover with cold water. Bring to a boil slowly and drain immediately. Dry potato balls between paper towels.

Heat oil in saute pan. Add potato balls and cover pan. Shake over moderate heat until potato balls are golden brown all over. At this point they should be tender. Sprinkle with parsley and remove with slotted spoon to small dish.

4 to 6 servings

WALDORF SALAD ASPIC WITH WALNUT MAYONNAISE

An elegant new act for an old classic. A juice extractor is required for this recipe.

DO-AHEAD TIP: *This salad should be prepared a day in advance in order for aspic to become well set.*

ASPIC
- 1½ cups carrot juice
- 1½ cups celery juice
- 3 tablespoons unflavored gelatin
- 6 tablespoons water
- 1 tablespoon fresh lemon juice
- ½ cup finely chopped celery
- 1½ cups chopped peeled apples

WALNUT MAYONNAISE
- 1 cup Basic Mayonnaise (see Index)
- ½ cup heavy cream, whipped
- ½ cup coarsely chopped English walnuts

- 1 small head Boston lettuce

ASPIC: Combine carrot and celery juices in bowl. Combine gelatin and water in small saucepan and dissolve over low heat. When mixture has cooled a little, add to carrot and celery juices, beating vigorously with whisk to blend thoroughly. Add lemon juice. Stand mixture in freezer for 10 minutes or so – only until aspic begins to set. Then fold in celery and apple. Pour into 5- or 6-cup mold and refrigerate until aspic is firmly set.

WALNUT MAYONNAISE: Fold mayonnaise and whipped cream together, then fold in walnuts.

PRESENTATION: Have ready chilled serving platter. To turn aspic out of mold, slide thin knife around edge of aspic. Hold mold in larger bowl of hot water for 1 minute. Place serving plate bottom side up on top of mold, invert, and remove mold. Cut lettuce into fine shreds and arrange as border around aspic. Serve walnut mayonnaise in separate bowl.

4 to 6 servings

APPLE CHARLOTTE

Charlotte aux Pommes

The tall, cylindrical charlotte mold is lined with crisp, fried bread strips, the center is filled with zesty, spicy apple sauce, and it is baked. It is served warm or cold, with a dollop of creme fraiche.

DO-AHEAD TIP: *Apple charlotte can be prepared a day ahead.*

- **12 tablespoons unsalted butter**
- **1 loaf whole wheat bread**
- **3 tablespoons plus 1/4 cup light honey**
- **4 pounds tart cooking apples, peeled, cored, and cut into thick slices**
- **grated rind of 2 lemons**
- **1 1/2 cups apricot preserve**
- **1/2 teaspoon freshly grated nutmeg**
- **1/2 teaspoon ground ginger**
- **1 1/2 cups Creme Fraiche (see Index)**

Generously butter 2-quart charlotte mold (or 7-inch springform cake pan or other straight-sided mold) and place it in refrigerator. Trim crusts from bread. Cut each slice into 3 equal strips.

Heat 3 tablespoons butter and 1 tablespoon honey in saute pan. Saute strips of bread on one side only. Drain bread strips on paper towels, sauteed side up. Add more butter and honey to pan (3 tablespoons butter to 1 tablespoon honey) as necessary to saute all strips of bread. Line bottom of mold with bread strips in a spoke pattern, cutting them to form points at the center. Line sides of mold snugly with vertical strips of bread. There should be about one-fourth of the bread strips remaining, which will be used to cover the top after the mold is filled with apple mixture.

Preheat oven to 375°F. Place apples in heavy pot, sprinkle with a little water, cover, and cook until they are tender but not mushy. Add lemon rind, preserve, 4 tablespoons butter, nutmeg, ginger, and 1/4 cup honey. Mix well and continue cooking over low heat until mixture is well blended but apples are still a bit crunchy. Spoon mixture into the bread-lined mold. Cover top with reserved bread strips (in any fashion; when the mold is turned out, this topping will be on the bottom of the serving plate). Place mold on baking sheet and bake for 40 minutes.

To serve the apple charlotte (either warm or at room temperature), let it stand for awhile after removing from oven. (Or, it may be chilled.) Slide a knife around inside of mold to loosen, place a serving plate bottom side up on top of mold, invert assembly, and lift mold away from apple charlotte. (The sides of the apple charlotte will bulge when mold is removed.) Serve with separate bowl of creme fraiche.

6 to 8 servings

POACHED APPLES WITH VANILLA PASTRY CREAM, APRICOT SAUCE, AND ALMONDS

DO-AHEAD TIP: *Apples and pastry cream can be prepared a day ahead and refrigerated. At serving time, fill apples with pastry cream, coat with sauce, and sprinkle with almonds.*

- **6** tablespoons apricot jam
- grated rind of ½ orange
- **⅓** cup light honey
- **½** cup water
- **4 to 6** large apples, cored but not peeled
- **2** cups Vanilla Pastry Cream (see Index)
- **½** cup shredded blanched almonds, toasted

Combine jam, orange rind, honey, and water in deep, heavy pot, large enough to stand all of the apples on the bottom. Stir mixture over moderate heat until it comes to a boil. Simmer to light syrup consistency. Stand apples in syrup and poach, uncovered, over low heat until just tender. Using large slotted spoon, carefully transfer apples to serving dish and chill in refrigerator. Reserve syrup.

PRESENTATION: Put pastry cream into pastry bag fitted with large star tube (#8 or #9). Pipe pastry cream into center of each apple, ending with rosette on top. Rewarm syrup if it has thickened, adding another tablespoon or two of water, if necessary. Spoon a little sauce on top of each apple and sprinkle with almonds.

4 to 6 servings

More Apple Recipes

See Index for the following recipes:

APPETIZER: *Pico de Gallo;* MAIN DISHES: Poached Chicken Hawaiian, Potato Pancakes with Fruit Sauce; SALADS: Cabbage and Fruit Salad with Honey Dressing, *Salade Provencale,* Tossed Greens Salad with Fruit; DESSERTS: Cobbler, *Dulce de Camote,* Fruit Fritters, *Le Clafouti, Macedoine de Fruits;* SAUCE: Apple Sauce.

APRICOTS

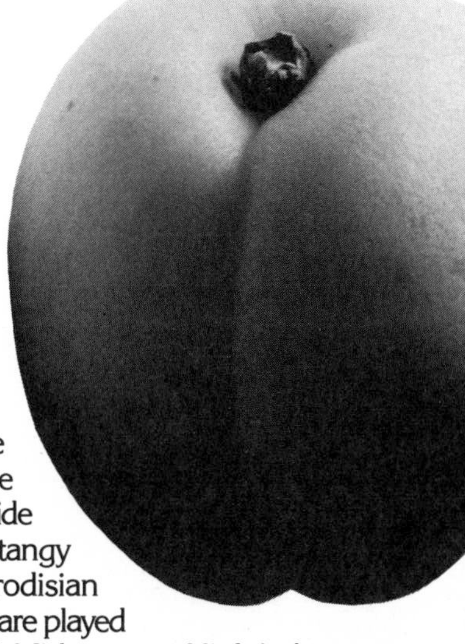

Apricots (preferably pronounced with the hard ā) may look like dainty miniature peaches, but inside they're a pent-up explosion of tangy flavor. Is this the brew of aphrodisian power? Even William Shakespeare played with their legendary fantasy in *A Midsummer Night's Dream*, as the Queen of the Fairies plied her erstwhile lover with "apricocks."

Another aficionado of the siren fruit is my natural foods collaborator, Felipe de Alba. Each year we celebrate his birthday, April 9, with the feast of Felipe's choice. Aren't all men like little boys when they can choose a whole meal of their most favorite foods? For Felipe, delicately poached sole Duglere (veloute sauce with shreds of fresh tomato and mushroom, and duchess potato garnish) is de rigueur, and. . . apricots. . . always apricots.

Early April is not quite the season for fresh apricots, but dried ones, too, are bright and tasty. Fresh or dried, this punchy-flavored fruit is a versatile standout in many preparations; yet, for this occasion, I wanted to create the femme fatale of desserts for this impassioned apricot lover. That evening, in the candlelight, after the ecstasy of the sole, I brought to the guest of honor a big, brilliant sunburst of bright, beaming apricots – framed in a border of crunchy chopped almonds, atop rich vanilla pastry cream, in crisp, buttery whole wheat pastry. The Sunburst Apricot Tart bowled him over. It is permanently *the* birthday tart.

In classical patisserie the apricot is the magical touch on many masterpieces – the golden glaze on fancy cakes, pastry creams, mousses, and light-colored fruit tarts (a standard technique: a gentle brushing of apricot syrup made by dissolving apricot jam with a few drops of lemon juice and straining the mixture). It is a nice, tingly sauce with dessert dumplings, crepes, and puddings. When apricot jam is mixed with cooked apples or apple sauce, apple's more reticent flavor comes alive. Apricot's resilient color and zest in cooking make it a compatible and lovely garnish with hot and cold poultry and meat dishes, too.

One of the first harbingers of spring is the budding, blossoming apricot tree, and it delivers its ripened fruit fairly early – from May to August. Softly blushing without, toothsome and perfumed within, the fruits achieve their best flavor when tree ripened. Unlike many other fruits, apricots picked semiripe do not develop satisfactorily. That is why we find few, if any, fresh apricots in the market beyond their season. But we can enjoy dried apricots year-round – almost a different, but equally glorious fruit with flavor and nutrients still intact. Apricots also make excellent preserves, which find many uses, as professional chefs have long known. Although the apricot tree can be grown in the north temperate zone, as early plantings in Colonial Virginia attest, most of our supply today comes from California.

About 12 medium-size fresh apricots represent a pound. For most preparations, the thin, barely velvety skin is not removed. If you wish to peel apricots, immerse them in boiling water for 20 to 30 seconds, plunge them into cold water, and slip off the skins.

Fresh or dried apricots can be eaten out of hand as snacks or served from fruit centerpieces. They can be stewed (as my father loved them on hot cereal); used in pies, tarts, and cakes, shortbreads and muffins, mousses and souffles; as decorations, garnishes, toppings, and lively sauces. Use fresh apricots or nectar (puree with a little water added) in drinks and cold soups. In season, fresh apricot halves are a special treat in tossed green salads and mixed fruit bowls.

APRICOT MOUSSE

DO-AHEAD TIP: *Mousse should be prepared several hours to 1 day ahead in order to chill and set.*

- 2 cups water
- grated rind of 1 lemon
- 1 tablespoon fresh lemon juice
- ⅓ cup plus 2 tablespoons light honey
- 1 pound dried apricots
- 1 tablespoon unflavored gelatin
- 3 egg whites
- 1½ cups heavy cream
- 1 teaspoon vanilla extract
- ½ cup coarsely shaved carob bar

Combine 1½ cups water, lemon rind, lemon juice, and ⅓ cup honey in deep, heavy pot and stir over moderate heat until mixture boils. Add apricots and simmer until tender. Transfer apricots and cooking syrup to food processor or blender and puree.

Combine gelatin and ½ cup water in small saucepan, and stir over low heat until dissolved. Add slowly to apricot puree, beating constantly. Let puree cool just to point of setting. Beat egg whites to soft peaks, add apricot puree, and fold together smoothly. Beat heavy cream over bowl of ice. When almost stiff, add 2 tablespoons honey and vanilla. Continue beating until cream holds shape. Fold one-third of whipped cream into apricot mixture. Spoon mousse into dessert serving bowl and place in refrigerator to set.

PRESENTATION: Put remaining whipped cream into pastry bag fitted with medium star tube (#6 or #7). Pipe rosettes all over top of mousse. Scatter shaved carob on top of whipped cream. Refrigerate until serving time.

4 to 6 servings

APRICOTS *A L'IMPERATRICE*

A lovely dessert rice ring with apricots and almonds.

DO-AHEAD TIP: *This dish should be prepared a day ahead and refrigerated in order to set.*

RICE RING

- 4 tablespoons short grain brown rice (the fluffier, stickier character of short grain rice is preferred for dessert use)
- 2 cups milk
- 1/4 cup light honey
- 2 tablespoons unflavored gelatin
- 1/4 cup hot water
- 2 teaspoons vanilla extract
- 2 eggs, separated
- 1 cup heavy cream, whipped

GLAZE

- 3/4 cup apricot jam
- 1 tablespoon fresh lemon juice
- 1/4 cup water

APRICOTS

- 9 ripe whole apricots, or 18 canned unsweetened apricot halves, or 18 dried apricot halves, soaked
- 18 whole blanched almonds

RICE RING: Have ready a lightly oiled round layer cake pan (8- or 9-inch diameter). Combine rice and milk in deep, heavy pot and cook over very low heat until rice absorbs all of the milk and is tender. Stir occasionally to prevent scorching. If necessary, add more milk. When rice is cooked, add honey.

Soften gelatin in water and stir into rice. Transfer rice mixture to metal bowl or saucepan and place over bowl of ice. Stir until mixture is nearly cool. Add vanilla and egg yolks. Beat egg whites to soft peaks and fold gently and smoothly into rice mixture. Then fold in whipped cream. Fill pan with rice mixture and place in refrigerator until firmly set.

GLAZE: Combine jam, lemon juice, and water in saucepan and stir over low heat until jam is dissolved. Rub through wire strainer. Set aside.

APRICOTS: If fresh apricots are used, peel them, cut in half and remove stones. Arrange apricot halves on plate cut side up, pour apricot glaze over all, and chill.

PRESENTATION: When rice mold is set, turn out onto flat serving plate. (To turn out, slide thin knife around edge of rice. Hold mold in bowl of hot water 1 minute. Place serving plate bottom side up on top of mold, invert, and remove mold.) Arrange apricot halves around rice, cut side up, and spoon a little excess glaze into the hollows. Place a blanched almond in the center of each apricot half. Refrigerate until serving time.

6 to 8 servings

APRICOT WHIP WITH CINNAMON-CAROB SHARDS

A dramatic presentation delivers an interesting flavor combination: tangy apricot whip with cold, crisp cinnamon-carob shards stuck into whipped cream rosettes. For an even more impressive presentation, serve apricot whip in Cinnamon-Carob Cups.

DO-AHEAD TIP: *This dessert can be prepared and assembled a day ahead and refrigerated.*

APRICOT WHIP
- 1 pound dried apricots
- 2 cups water
- 2 tablespoons fresh lemon juice
- 6 egg whites

CINNAMON-CAROB SHARDS
- 3 ounces carob bar or nuggets
- ½ teaspoon ground cinnamon
- 1 cup heavy cream, whipped

APRICOT WHIP: Cook apricots in water until soft. Drain well and puree with lemon juice in food processor or rub through strainer and let cool. Beat egg whites to soft peaks. Using rubber scraper, fold apricot puree lightly and evenly into egg whites. Pile up in serving bowl or spoon into Cinnamon-Carob Cups.

CINNAMON-CAROB SHARDS: Cut 12 to 18 narrow triangles of waxed paper, about 3 inches long. Have ready a baking sheet of a size that will fit on freezer shelf. If carob bar is used, cut into nugget-size pieces. Put carob and cinnamon in small, heatproof bowl and stand in saute pan half filled with simmering water. Stir mixture with small wooden spatula or rubber scraper until dissolved and smooth. Let stand over barely simmering water.

Spread 12-inch piece of waxed paper on work surface near stove. Place waxed paper triangle on large waxed paper and spread triangle with thin coating of dissolved carob. Place carob-coated waxed paper on baking sheet. Coat all waxed paper triangles in this manner. Place in freezer to harden.

PRESENTATION: Put whipped cream into pastry bag fitted with star tube and pipe rosettes on top of apricot whip. Remove waxed paper from cinnamon-carob triangles and stick them into rosettes. Refrigerate until serving time.

6 to 8 servings

CINNAMON-CAROB CUPS

DO-AHEAD TIP: *These cups can be prepared at any time and stored in freezer.*

- 8 ounces carob bar or nuggets
- 1½ teaspoons ground cinnamon
- 8 cupcake paper cases

If carob bar is used, cut into nugget-size pieces. Combine carob and cinnamon in heatproof bowl. Stand bowl in saute pan half filled with simmering water. Stir over low heat until mixture is completely dissolved and smooth.

Using small spatula or butter knife, completely coat insides of paper cases with mixture. Place cases on baking sheet and put in freezer to set. When cinnamon-carob cups have hardened, carefully peel off paper.

PRESENTATION: To serve with apricot whip, fill each cinnamon-carob cup with apricot whip. Top with whipped cream rosette. Stick cinnamon-carob shard into rosette.

Makes 8 cinnamon-carob cups

APRICOT AND RICE STUFFING

Use this tangy stuffing in domestic or game fowl or in pork or veal pockets.

DO-AHEAD TIP: *Stuffing can be prepared a day ahead and refrigerated.*

- 2 tablespoons light vegetable oil (e.g., safflower)
- 1 small yellow onion, chopped
- 1 tablespoon finely chopped fresh parsley
- 1 cup chopped celery and celery leaf
- 2 teaspoons tamari soy sauce
- ½ teaspoon dried savory
- ¼ pound dried apricots
- 3 cups Plain-Cooked Brown Rice (see Index)

Heat oil in saute pan. Add onion, parsley and celery and stir over moderate heat 3 minutes. Add tamari and savory. Cut apricots in strips with kitchen shears. Combine all ingredients with rice in mixing bowl and mix with wooden spoon.

Yields 4 to 5 cups

VEAL CHOPS MARINA

This recipe calls for fresh apricots, but it can also be made with dried apricots.

DO-AHEAD TIP: *Ingredients can be readied several hours ahead. Cook at serving time.*

- 4 tablespoons unsalted butter
- 6 veal chops, 3/4 to 1 inch thick
- 2 teaspoons fresh thyme, or 1/2 teaspoon dried thyme
- 1/8 teaspoon freshly grated nutmeg
- freshly ground white pepper
- 1 cup stock (e.g., chicken, vegetable, or soy—1 cup water with 1 teaspoon tamari soy sauce), plus extra to thin sauce, if necessary
- 1/2 teaspoon dry mustard
- 12 to 16 fresh apricots, peeled and pitted, or 1 pound dried apricots, soaked or simmered

Puree enough apricots to yield 2/3 cup puree. Reserve 12 to 16 nice halves.

Heat butter in large saute pan and brown chops on both sides. Sprinkle with thyme, nutmeg, and pepper. Add stock, cover, and simmer 10 to 15 minutes, or until meat is very tender, turning chops occasionally. Add more stock, if necessary, to keep meat moist. Remove chops from pan and set aside.

Mix apricot puree with dry mustard and add to saute pan. Add just enough stock to make thick sauce. Cook until blended. Add apricot halves, coat with sauce, and cook 1 to 2 minutes, or until warmed. Return chops to saute pan and turn to coat with sauce. Simmer over very low heat 2 to 3 minutes.

PRESENTATION: Arrange chops on warm serving platter. Garnish with apricot halves and coat with sauce.

6 servings

DEEP-FRIED STUFFED APRICOTS WITH APRICOT SAUCE

DO-AHEAD TIP: *Apricots can be stuffed and sauce prepared a day ahead. Coat and deep-fry at serving time.*

- 12 fresh apricots
- ¾ cup water
- ¾ cup light honey
- 1 vanilla bean (scraping and pod)
- 12 toasted almond slivers
- 12 pitted dates
- 1 cup apricot preserve
- 2 teaspoons fresh lemon juice
- 1 egg
- 1 tablespoon unsalted butter, melted
- ¾ cup dry whole wheat bread crumbs
- about 2 cups light vegetable oil (e.g., safflower)

Peel apricots by immersing them in boiling water for 20 to 30 seconds, then plunging them in cold water and slipping off the skins.

Combine water, honey, and vanilla bean in heavy pot large enough to hold all of the apricots on the bottom. Stir over moderate heat until syrup comes to a boil. Reduce heat to simmer and add apricots. Poach apricots gently about 5 minutes. (They should not become soft or lose their shape.) Drain apricots and chill them.

Insert 1 almond sliver in each date and close tightly. Cut a slit down the side of each apricot, carefully remove the pits without tearing the apricots, replace each pit with a stuffed date, and close the apricot.

Combine apricot preserve and lemon juice in a small saucepan and stir over low heat until preserve is dissolved. Rub through fine wire strainer. Transfer to sauce bowl.

Combine egg and cool melted butter in small bowl and beat well. Dip apricots in egg mixture and then roll them in bread crumbs.

Heat vegetable oil in deep fryer to 375°F, using a deep-fry thermometer. Fry coated apricots in hot oil until golden brown and remove at once. Drain on paper towels. Arrange fried stuffed apricots on doily on serving plate. Serve with separate bowl of apricot sauce.

4 to 6 servings

APRICOTS

THE SUNBURST APRICOT TART

Create a brilliant sunburst any time of the year with bright, beaming apricots atop vanilla pastry cream in a crisp, flavorful whole wheat pastry shell.

DO-AHEAD TIP: *This tart can be prepared a day ahead and refrigerated.*

TART

- 2 cups Vanilla Pastry Cream (see Index)
- 1 baked 11- or 12-inch pastry shell of Plain Whole Wheat Short Pastry 1 or 2 (see Index)

TOPPING

- 1½ pounds fresh apricots, peeled and halved, or 1 pound dried apricots
- 1 cup apricot preserve
- 2 tablespoons fresh lemon juice
- ½ cup chopped almonds or walnuts

TART: Spread pastry cream in baked pastry shell.

TOPPING: If dried apricots are used, place them in heavy pot with 1½ cups water and ¼ cup honey and cook over low heat until apricots are tender but still firm and shapely. Remove from heat and chill in syrup. Then drain and blot dry between paper towels.

Arrange apricot halves, round side up, neatly in concentric circles on top of pastry cream. Dissolve preserve with lemon juice in small saucepan. Let cool to room temperature. Brush apricots gently and evenly with preserve. Using teaspoon, sprinkle 1-inch border of chopped nuts around edge of tart. Refrigerate until serving time.

8 to 10 servings

More Apricot Recipes

See Index for the following recipes:

APPETIZER OR CONFECTION: Apricot-Coconut Balls; MAIN DISH: *Chiles Rellenos*; SALADS: Cabbage and Fruit Salad with Honey Dressing, Tossed Greens Salad with Fruit; DESSERTS: Beignets Souffles with Fresh Fruit Sauce, *Dulce de Camote*; Fresh Fruit Ice Cream, Frozen Fruit Yogurt, Fruit Fritters, Fruit Sherbet, Hearts of Avocado Cream with Apricot Sauce, *Le Clafouti*, *Macedoine de Fruits*, Refrigerator Cheesecake with Fresh Fruit Topping; BEVERAGES: Apricot Nectar with Buttermilk or Yogurt, Papaya, Peaches, Nectarines, or Apricots with Buttermilk or Yogurt; SAUCES: Fresh Fruit Sauce, Fruit Syrup.

AVOCADOS

"Avocado Love Feast" was the title of an assignment that I received from a national magazine to create a story and all kinds of ways to eat avocado. For an old aficionado of the unctuous fruit, this was truly a labor of love. Boxes of avocados were delivered to my kitchen, which inspired fantasies and feasts for every eating excuse. At the appointed due date, I presented copy and recipes enough for a book. Four or five months later, however long it takes for copy to get published in magazines, I was gratified, if not a bit stunned in this instance, to see that my avocado recipes had apparently tested successfully. In print, in big letters and full color, the editors had subtitled my "Avocado Love Feast" with "Who Needs Aphrodisiacs? Avocados Taste Better!"

That avocado is a love fruit there is no doubt, and it is an all-around good fruit to love. When Cortes and his band of conquistadores came to the New World, they were captivated by the strange green fruit that was considered sacred and amorously potent by Moctezuma's people. They rushed galleons of the fruit back to Europe, where it was welcomed with joy. The name avocado derives from its Aztec name, *Ahuaca Cuahuitl,* meaning "tree of testicles," the natives' forthright description of the avocado tree laden with its sac-shaped fruit.

Even earlier, the Mayas knew of the avocado's "powers" and told the tale of the Indian, Seiokai, who was able to trace his unfaithful wife to the end of the world by following the avocado trees which sprang from the seeds her lover discarded. As you can see on any clear night, his pursuit continues, for *he* is the constellation Orion, his wife the star cluster Pleiades, her lover Hyades. And for many generations to follow, young señoritas in Mexico were forbidden to venture out of their huts during the height of the avocado season.

But as Orion is constant, so is the avocado – it knows no season. Winter and summer varieties are harvested practically back to back. The most familiar winter avocado comes in a smooth green skin, the summer variety in a pebbled dark skin, ranging in color from bright (avocado) green through black. Inside, the qualities are the same: buttery smooth pulp, with dramatic coloration from bright green under the skin to rich yellow at the center around the big seed, and a subtle, nutty flavor. About 75 percent of our avocados come from California and most of the rest from Florida. Summer's dark beauties make their entrance in May. In November, the smooth green winter variety takes over.

Avocados are best when perfectly ripe. Cradle one in your hand; it should be just soft to the touch. Most avocados are picked when a little underripe and still hard so they don't come to market in an overripe state. They continue to ripen naturally, off the tree. You can speed ripening by wrapping avocados in brown paper or foil, or by placing them in a plastic fruit ripener. Ripe avocados keep well in the refrigerator, but do not freeze them.

There is no limit to the ways of preparing avocado once it is fully ripe. To open, just halve the avocado lengthwise and twist gently to separate. Whack a sharp knife directly into the seed and twist to lift it out. To peel the two half shells, just place the cut side down in the palm of your hand and pull the skin back. To slice, place peeled halves cut side down on a cutting board and cut lengthwise or crosswise into crescents. Lengthwise slices may be diced or cut into cubes. If you are not going to use the peeled avocado immediately, bathe it in lemon or lime juice or cover it securely with plastic wrap so it won't discolor. If it has been pureed, embed the seed in it.

Anytime is the right time to eat avocado – breakfast, lunch, or dinner. Carry it with you in a brown bag with a spoon for lunch or a snack. It is a natural and healthy fast food. Feast on avocado. It is the course victorious in any kind of meal. Although it is a fruit that is not usually prepared as a dessert in this country (as it is in Brazil), that is rank oversight. A little culinary adventure will disclose a world of new dessert surprises that are sensational. Try our recipe for hearts of avocado cream in a pool of red raspberry or golden apricot sauce, or Frozen Avocado-Lime Souffle.

You can give in to the charisma of the avocado with a clear conscience. In proportion, it is low in calories and loaded with nutrients, making it a good slimming food. Compare its calorie content with the examples of typical lunchtime foods given in the table below.

The avocado nourishes with a rare and rich formula. It is composed of 1.9 percent protein, 14.8 percent fat, 5.7 percent carbohydrate, 2.4 percent fiber, and 74 percent water. Like all plant foods, it contains no cholesterol, and its fat is the desirable kind – unsaturated (87 percent). Avocado is the butter of the plant kingdom.

It is a life-giving food, packed with rich deposits of 11 vitamins and 8 minerals. Half an avocado (80.8 grams) contains only 132 calories, yet it is a concentrate of vitamins A, C, and E, and potassium, with almost no sodium.

Enjoy the fantasy of avocado. It is one of our most perfect foods, ready-cooked by nature and abundant throughout the year.

Food	Serving Size	Calories
Avocado	½ shell (approx. 87 grams)	138
Yogurt	1 cup (245 grams)	152
Gelatin dessert, plain	1 cup (240 grams)	142
Gelatin dessert, with 2 tablespoons heavy cream	1 cup (240 grams)	248
Hamburger patty (no bun)	3 ounces (85 grams)	186
Cottage cheese	½ cup (105 grams)	112
Split pea soup	1 cup (255 grams)	301
Tuna salad	½ cup (102 grams)	175

AVOCADO AND CRAB TROPICALE

An exotic first course or light main dish featuring avocado and crab meat, briefly baked and served in individual crab or scallop shells.

DO-AHEAD TIP: *The mixture can be readied about 8 hours ahead. Bake at serving time.*

- 1 ripe avocado, peeled and coarsely chopped
- ⅔ to 1 pound lump crab meat
- 2 medium-size ripe tomatoes, peeled, seeded, and coarsely chopped
- 4 tablespoons dry whole wheat bread crumbs
- 4 tablespoons light vegetable oil (e.g., safflower)
- 4 pearl onions, finely chopped (about ½ cup)
- ⅓ cup freshly grated Parmesan cheese
- 1 teaspoon curry powder
- freshly ground white pepper
- 1 tablespoon tamari soy sauce
- ½ cup sour cream
- 2 tablespoons finely chopped fresh chives or parsley

Preheat oven to 350°F. In mixing bowl, combine avocado, crab meat, tomato, 2 tablespoons bread crumbs, 3 tablespoons oil, onions, 2 tablespoons cheese, curry powder, pepper to taste, and tamari. Toss together lightly.

Divide mixture into crab or scallop shells, 4 to 6 inches in diameter, or similar size individual baking dishes. Sprinkle remaining bread crumbs, cheese, and a few drops of oil over tops. Bake until tops are slightly browned. Warm sour cream in small saucepan, add chives or parsley, and pour some sauce over each serving.

4 to 6 servings

AVOCADOS

APHRODITE'S SALAD

This lovely salad uses artichoke heart, avocado, two kinds of endive, and aromatic dill.

DO-AHEAD TIP: *Dressing and the two endives can be put in salad bowl a day ahead and chilled. At serving time, add artichoke, avocado, and dill.*

- ½ cup Basic Vinaigrette Dressing (see Index)
- 1 bunch curly endive (chicory), washed, dried, and crisped
- 2 to 3 large heads Belgian endive, thinly sliced on the diagonal
- 1 ripe avocado
- 6 plain-cooked artichoke bottoms, cubed
- 4 tablespoons chopped fresh dill, or 1 tablespoon dried dillweed

Pour vinaigrette dressing on bottom of serving bowl. Cut curly endive into bite-size pieces and drop lightly on top of dressing. Then add Belgian endive. Cover with plastic wrap and refrigerate until ready to serve.

At serving time, peel and cube avocado. Then scatter avocado and artichoke cubes on top of endive. Sprinkle dill over top. Then toss with dressing that is on bottom of bowl.

4 to 6 servings

AVOCADO DREAM FISH

Cold poached fish covered with avocado and dill sauce, garnished with tomato and egg sections.

DO-AHEAD TIP: *Fish can be poached and sauce prepared a day ahead. Embed avocado seed in sauce to avoid discoloration. Refrigerate preparations and assemble at serving time.*

FISH

- 1 3- to 4-pound whole fish (e.g., sea trout, bass, pike, or section of salmon), boned and skinned (there should be 2 long boneless and skinless sides of fish)
- about 4 tablespoons fresh lemon juice

FISH: Preheat oven to 350°F. Wash fish in lemon juice and cold water and pat dry between paper towels.

AVOCADO DREAM FISH—continued

COURT-BOUILLON

- 1 tablespoon light vegetable oil (e.g., safflower)
- 1 or 2 fresh mushrooms, sliced
- ½ cup mixed sliced carrots, celery, and onions
- 1½ cups water
- 1 bay leaf
- 2 sprigs parsley, thyme, or celery leaf
- 6 peppercorns

SAUCE

- 1 ripe avocado (about 7 ounces)
- 1 tablespoon fresh lemon juice
- about 4 tablespoons light vegetable oil
- 2 tablespoons finely chopped fresh dill, or 2 teaspoons dried dillweed
- ½ teaspoon tamari soy sauce
- cayenne pepper

GARNISH

- 1 small head Boston lettuce, crisped and cut into fine shreds
- 2 hard-cooked eggs, quartered
- 2 small ripe tomatoes, quartered

COURT-BOUILLON: This is a seasoned liquid for cooking fish and shellfish when prepared fish stock is not available. (After seafood has been cooked in court-bouillon [pronounced coor-boo-yoh] it is very good fish stock because it contains the juices from the seafood; it should be reserved for future use.) Put oil and mushroom slices in 1-quart saucepan and saute 1 minute. Add mixed vegetables and saute 2 minutes. Add water, bay leaf, herb, and peppercorns. Slowly bring liquid to a boil. Remove from heat and set aside.

To poach fish, place both fish fillets on oblong baking dish, such as Pyrex. Pour all of court-bouillon mixture, including vegetables, over fish. Cover fish with sheet of waxed paper. Cook in oven only until flesh becomes firm and opaque, about 12 minutes. Remove fish from oven at once and chill in cooking liquid.

SAUCE: Cut avocado in half lengthwise and peel. In food processor, combine avocado, lemon juice, oil, dill, tamari, and a dash of cayenne pepper. Puree until mixture is smooth. If too stiff for coating consistency, add another 1 or 2 tablespoons oil.

PRESENTATION: When fish is cold, carefully transfer fillets to serving platter. (Strain liquid and store for future use as fish stock.) Surround fish with border of crisp shredded lettuce. On top of lettuce, arrange alternating wedges of hard-cooked egg and tomato, encircling fish. When ready to serve, coat fish fillets with avocado and dill sauce. Or, sauce may be served separately.

4 to 6 servings as main course or 8 as appetizer

BREAST OF CHICKEN STUFFED WITH AVOCADO ON TOMATO FONDUE

Avocado puree is sandwiched between split, boned breasts of chicken, roasted, coated with crumbs, and served on a sauce of fresh tomatoes and herbs.

DO-AHEAD TIP: *Tomato fondue can be made a day ahead. Near serving time, sandwich avocado puree in breasts of chicken and cook them. Cooking time is only 25 minutes.*

FONDUE

- 1 tablespoon light vegetable oil (e.g., safflower)
- 1 teaspoon finely chopped fresh garlic
- 4 to 6 medium-size ripe tomatoes, peeled and coarsely chopped
- 4 tablespoons tomato paste
- 1 tablespoon fresh thyme, or 1 teaspoon dried thyme
- 1 tablespoon finely chopped chives
- 1 tablespoon tamari soy sauce
- freshly ground black pepper

CHICKEN AND STUFFING

- 2 ripe avocados (about 7 ounces each)
- 4 small pearl onions, finely chopped
- 4 tablespoons finely chopped fresh parsley
- 2 tablespoons fresh lemon juice
- 1 teaspoon tamari soy sauce
- cayenne pepper
- 6 half breasts of chicken, skinned and boned

FONDUE: Over moderate heat, cook oil and garlic in 2-quart saucepan 1 minute. Add tomatoes, tomato paste, thyme, and chives. Cook over low heat until tomatoes break down and become a thick sauce. Add tamari and pepper. Set aside.

CHICKEN AND STUFFING: Preheat oven to 350°F. Peel avocados and puree in food processor. Add onions, parsley, lemon juice, tamari, and dash of cayenne pepper. Blend well.

Place a skinned, boned half breast of chicken on cutting board. Using a straight-bladed chef's knife, slice lengthwise, like a hot dog bun – almost but not quite through, leaving a connection on one side. Spread avocado mixture generously between the two layers of chicken breast and close neatly. Prepare all chicken breasts in this manner.

Have ready an oiled oblong roasting pan. Carefully place stuffed chicken breasts in pan. Pour ½ cup water on bottom of pan and place in oven for 15 minutes.

BREAST OF CHICKEN STUFFED WITH AVOCADO – continued

COATING

6 tablespoons dry whole wheat bread crumbs

6 tablespoons finely chopped fresh parsley

2 teaspoons finely chopped fresh thyme, or ½ teaspoon dried thyme

2 teaspoons finely chopped fresh garlic

· bunch of crisp fresh parsley

COATING: Meanwhile, mix all herb and crumb coating ingredients together on a plate. When chicken breasts have been in oven 15 minutes, remove them but leave oven on. Carefully take each stuffed chicken breast in your hands, coat both sides with herb and crumb mixture, place chicken breasts back in pan, and return to oven to cook another 10 minutes.

PRESENTATION: Spread tomato fondue on bottom of hot serving platter. Arrange stuffed chicken breasts in row on top of tomato fondue and garnish with parsley.

6 servings

AVOCADO-LEMON SOUP

A hot avocado soup without cream. It is exquisitely light and is loveliest when served in its pristine simplicity, with no garnish. If desired, pass a plate of cheese straws.

DO-AHEAD TIP: *This soup can be prepared in minutes and should be made just prior to serving.*

4 cups strong chicken stock

2 eggs

1 ripe avocado (about 7 ounces)

4 tablespoons fresh lemon juice

Pour stock into heavy pot and bring to a boil. Beat eggs in food processor or blender. Peel avocado. Add avocado and lemon juice to beaten eggs and process until mixture is completely blended. Add ½ cup hot stock to egg and avocado mixture and blend. Add another ½ cup stock and blend again. Pour this mixture into remaining stock in pot, stirring constantly. Warm soup over low heat, but do not boil or egg will curdle.

4 to 6 servings

AVOCADOS

AVOCADO AND RADISH MOUSSE WITH RADISH POM-POMS

DO-AHEAD TIP: *This dish should be prepared 8 hours to 1 day ahead and refrigerated in order to allow gelatin to set.*

MOUSSE
- 2 ripe avocados (about 7 ounces each)
- ½ cup Basic Mayonnaise (see Index)
- 3 tablespoons fresh lemon juice
- 1 teaspoon tamari soy sauce
- cayenne pepper
- ¼ cup plus 2 tablespoons water
- 3 tablespoons unflavored gelatin
- 1 cup shredded red radish
- 4 egg whites

GARNISH
- 4 to 6 medium-size red radish pom-poms
- 4 to 6 sprigs watercress

MOUSSE: Oil 1½-quart ring mold (or 6 ramekins or custard cups, 6 to 8 ounces each). Invert on paper towels and set aside to drain.

Peel avocados and puree in food processor. Add mayonnaise, 2 tablespoons lemon juice, tamari, and a dash of cayenne pepper, and mix well. Set aside.

Combine water, gelatin, and 1 tablespoon lemon juice in small saucepan and cook over moderate heat, stirring constantly, until gelatin is dissolved. Remove from heat and let cool slightly. Add gelatin mixture to avocado puree, a little at a time, blending constantly.

Pat shredded radish dry between paper towels and set aside. Beat egg whites in large bowl until soft peaks form. Carefully fold avocado mixture into egg whites. Stir in shredded radish. Fill mold(s) with mousse. Refrigerate at least 8 hours or overnight.

GARNISH: To make radish pom-poms, cut root and stem from each radish. Thinly slice each radish lengthwise from root end *almost* through to stem end. Slice again at opposite angle from root end *almost* through to stem end. Transfer radishes to bowl of ice and refrigerate.

PRESENTATION: Just before serving, pat pom-poms dry with paper towels. Slide small, thin knife around edge of mold(s). Set mousse in bowl of hot water briefly to loosen, then invert mold(s) onto serving platter. Garnish with radish pom-poms and watercress sprigs.

4 to 6 servings

CURRIED AVOCADO-TOMATO SOUP

Serve this soup hot or cold.

DO-AHEAD TIP: *Soup can be prepared ahead and frozen. Thaw at room temperature and reblend in food processor. To serve, briefly rechill or rewarm, as desired.*

SOUP

- 3 tablespoons light vegetable oil (e.g., safflower)
- 3 small yellow onions, chopped
- 1 teaspoon finely chopped fresh garlic
- 1½ tablespoons curry powder
- 1 teaspoon dry mustard
- 1 tablespoon tamari soy sauce
- 1 tablespoon whole wheat pastry flour
- 1½ tablespoons tomato paste
- 6 medium-size ripe tomatoes, peeled and sliced
- 3 cups strong stock (e.g., chicken, vegetable, or soy—3 cups water with 4 teaspoons tamari soy sauce)
- 2 ripe avocados (about 7 ounces each)

GARNISH

- ½ cup finely shredded carrots
- 2 tablespoons finely chopped fresh parsley

SOUP: Combine oil, onions, and garlic in deep, heavy 4-quart pot. Stir over moderate heat about 2 minutes, or until onions are soft but not browned. Add curry powder, mustard, tamari, flour, and tomato paste and mix well. Stir over low heat 1 minute. Add tomatoes and cook over moderate heat 3 minutes. Add stock and stir mixture over moderate heat until it boils. Reduce heat and simmer 5 minutes.

Peel avocados and puree in food processor. Remove and set aside. When soup is cooked, puree it in processor until smooth. Return soup to pot and stir in avocado puree. Use whisk to blend thoroughly. Rewarm over low heat for hot serving. Chill thoroughly for cold serving.

PRESENTATION: Garnish servings of hot or cold soup with a sprinkling of shredded carrot and chopped parsley.

6 to 8 servings

MEXICAN GUACAMOLE SAUCE OR DIP

This is the authentic Mexican way of preparing this famous sauce, whether it is made at the elegant Club Industriales in Mexico City, the colonial Restaurant Tlaquepaque in Acapulco, or anywhere else that serves genuine Mexican food. It is actually a very simple, quickly assembled sauce of chopped— not pureed— ingredients. Serve with chips and dunkables.

DO-AHEAD TIP: *If sauce must be made in advance, embed the avocado seed in it to avoid discoloration.*

1 ripe avocado, peeled and chopped

2 tablespoons chopped fresh cilantro (fresh coriander leaf or Chinese parsley)

1 medium-size ripe tomato, peeled and chopped

2 teaspoons chopped serrano chili (fresh or canned)

2 teaspoons fresh lemon juice

Combine all ingredients in bowl and mix well.

Yields about 1 cup

HEARTS OF AVOCADO CREAM WITH RASPBERRY OR APRICOT SAUCE

These little hearts of avocado cream served in a pool of red raspberry or golden apricot sauce are lovely to look at and delicious to eat. This recipe requires 6 individual-size china or wicker coeur a la creme *molds (3 inches each) that are available in most cookware shops.*

DO-AHEAD TIP: *The hearts of avocado cream should be allowed to stand in the refrigerator at least 8 hours or overnight.*

AVOCADO CREAM
- 1½ ripe avocado (about 10½ ounces total)
- 6 ounces cream cheese
- ½ cup light honey
- 1½ teaspoons vanilla extract
- 1½ cups heavy cream, whipped

RASPBERRY SAUCE
- ¾ cup seedless red or black raspberry jam
- 1 tablespoon fresh lemon juice
- ⅓ cup water

APRICOT SAUCE
- ¾ cup apricot jam
- 1 tablespoon fresh lemon juice
- ⅓ cup water

To prepare lining for molds, combine 2 cups iced water, a pinch of baking soda, and 2 tablespoons lemon juice in small bowl and soak 6 squares of 4 thicknesses of cheesecloth, 6 inches each, in the mixture until molds are ready to be filled.

AVOCADO CREAM: Cut avocados in halves and peel. Puree 3 halves in food processor or rub through fine strainer. In food processor or mixer, beat avocado puree and cream cheese together until blended. Add honey and beat well. Add vanilla and beat again. *Fold* this mixture into whipped cream.

Wring squares of cheesecloth damp-dry and line molds, leaving 2-inch overhang all around. Fill molds with avocado cream and wrap extra cheesecloth over tops. Place filled molds on cake pan and chill in refrigerator at least 8 hours.

RASPBERRY SAUCE: Combine raspberry jam, lemon juice, and water in small saucepan. Stir over low heat until jam is dissolved. Consistency should be that of a thin pouring sauce. If too thick, add another 1 or 2 tablespoons water and reheat for a moment.

APRICOT SAUCE: Combine apricot jam, lemon juice, and water in small saucepan. Stir over low heat until jam is dissolved. Rub sauce through small wire strainer. Consistency should be that of a thin pouring sauce. If too thick, add another 1 or 2 tablespoons water and reheat for a moment.

PRESENTATION: Pour a shallow pool of raspberry or apricot sauce (about 3 tablespoons) on individual dessert plate. (Plain white plates are attractive with color contrast of avocado cream heart and sauce.) Unmold heart of avocado cream on center of pool of sauce. Prepare all servings in this manner. Do not pour sauce over heart. The avocado green heart should stand in the middle of a pool of red or golden sauce.

6 servings

FROZEN AVOCADO-LIME SOUFFLE

DO-AHEAD TIP: *This dish can be prepared and stored in freezer at 0°F. for about a week prior to serving.*

SOUFFLE
- 1 ripe avocado
- 2 tablespoons grated lime rind
- 6 tablespoons fresh lime juice
- 4 egg yolks
- 2 whole eggs
- ½ cup light honey
- 2 cups heavy cream, whipped

CHOICE OF DECORATION
- if in season, 18 to 24 fresh violets
- if in season, 18 to 24 fresh red raspberries
- ¼ cup chopped pistachios or toasted shredded almonds

SOUFFLE: In order to show part of frozen souffle mixture "rising" above the top of the dish in souffle style, use no larger than 1-quart souffle dish or straight-sided glass serving bowl. Fasten collar around dish to contain mixture that will be above top of dish: Tear off length of aluminum foil or waxed paper 1½ times the outer girth of dish. Fold in half lengthwise. Wrap foil or waxed paper around outside of dish and fasten with masking tape or kitchen string. Set dish aside.

Peel avocado and puree in food processor or rub through fine strainer. Add lime rind and lime juice and beat thoroughly. Set mixture aside.

In mixer, beat egg yolks, whole eggs, and honey until mixture is light and thick. Using rubber scraper, fold two-thirds of whipped cream into egg mixture. Then fold in avocado mixture. Spoon preparation into prepared souffle dish and freeze at 0°F.

PRESENTATION: At serving time, remove collar from dish and spread remaining whipped cream on top of souffle. Arrange row of fresh violets (edible) or raspberries around edge. Or, sprinkle top with chopped nuts. Serve frozen souffle in its dish on serving tray.

6 to 8 servings

More Avocado Recipes

See Index for the following recipes:

MAIN DISH: Fruit Omelet; SALAD: Tossed Greens Salad with Fruit.

BANANAS

Nothing Marina Polvay does should surprise me. "Marina, what are you doing?" I exclaimed as I walked into the Forge Restaurant in Miami Beach one midafternoon, to find her straddling a banana tree. There, in that elegant dining room, this petite, effervescent lady, one of the most imaginative of food impresarios, dressed in jeans and a pullover, was, with some helpers, literally building a banana plantation and fruiting it with bunches of fresh, ripe bananas – the tiny ones called *dominicos.*

"We're setting up the dessert for tonight's dinner," cried Marina. That evening, when dessert time arrived, guests in formal regalia, gathered for a grand banquet to honor the national president of the Chaine des Rotisseurs, Roger Yaseen, picked their own fresh bananas from the trees and took them to the cooks at the *gueridons,* who dunked them in hot orange sauce and draped them over scoops of homemade custard ice cream – the debut of Bananas Forge.

Barely a hundred years ago, most Americans had never tasted bananas. They became an everyday fruit only after late nineteenth-century entrepreneurs, working with the knowledge that bananas actually ripen best when picked green and allowed to mature off the tree, designed special railroad cars and the famed banana boats, each with controlled-climate interiors sympathetic to completing the banana's ripening. Thus, in a period of 10 to 20 days, bananas could be picked green, shipped several thousand miles while ripening en route, and distributed ready to eat in thousands of United States markets. It still seems incredible that this strictly tropical fruit could be made so plentiful everywhere merely by coordinating distribution with its natural cycle.

We Americans welcomed the banana into our lives as though it were as common as the apple. In fact, we have become quite dependent on it, regarding it as a security symbol in the kitchen. We buy three, four, or a half dozen without any special plan for bananas in the menu, just to have on hand – for a snack, to add to a dish of yogurt or cottage cheese, or perhaps to saute and serve with a piece of broiled chicken or a kebab. When my associate Felipe is staying at the studio, it seems that my life is dominated by bananas. Felipe eats two or three every day, and they must be of a precise ripeness. On top of the refrigerator, we maintain a trove of three groups of three or four bananas each, each group on the tray at a different stage of ripeness – greenish, as they are usually found in the market; yellow, beginning to brown; and some with brown specks all over. The latter is this native Mexican's idea of a perfect banana, which he eats with his meal, takes to his room for a midnight snack, carries in his pocket to meetings, movies, and concerts, and uses to fortify himself during travel.

In addition to the yellow bananas, there are red bananas, green bananas, and miniature bananas – bunches of fruits literally the size of the human finger, the *dominicos.* These latter types are common in the tropics and southern Florida. They are delicious. I have always been enchanted with the little *dominicos* and love using them in fruit centerpieces and party dishes in Mexico. I wish some enterprising produce importer would bring them north, so we could have them at least for festive treats.

I first met the red banana during one of my early sojourns in Acapulco, while staying in a complex of cottages near the Cultural Center. I was fascinated with the banana tree in the yard, especially because its ripening fruit was plump and red instead of slender and yellow. One day, the charming pregnant lady who supervised the cottages came to my door and presented me with a white cloth bundle – inside, a cluster of these bananas with burnished red skins. The flesh was sweet nectar with a vibrant banana flavor.

The term "plantain" may refer to a particular large type of banana or to any green banana that is used as a vegetable. When the banana is green it contains a lot of starch and either type is eaten as a staple food, like potatoes, in the tropics. (See the section on plantains.)

Botanically, the banana fruit is considered a berry – a simple fruit with a pulpy or fleshy wall and one or more seeds but no true stone. The banana plant is an herb – a large-leafed plant, often of tree height, which blossoms and develops those familiar many-fingered "stems," as the fully fruited shoots on the tree are called. (When they are detached, a "hand" has eight or more fingers; a "cluster" has three or more fingers.) The banana plant bears fruit just once, then it is cut down and is replaced by a sucker (little plant shoot) that has formed at the base of the previous plant.

The banana connoisseur wants a banana that is plump, unblemished, firm and bright in appearance. Its exact color is not a quality factor. A greenish banana may be of just as good quality as a yellow one, but not yet at the eating stage. The banana flesh contains starch that will convert to sugar, or ripen, when held at room temperature. Some people, like Felipe, want bananas fully ripened, with brown-flecked skin; some prefer them at the all-yellow stage, or even with a green tip. When bananas are at the desired stage of ripeness, reserve supplies can be refrigerated. They will keep for several days with continued good-quality flesh, but the skins may turn brown.

On the other hand, the quality of a green banana will be damaged by ordinary refrigeration. Once its ripening process has been interrupted by cold, the banana does not resume normal ripening when the temperature is raised. So keep it out of the refrigerator until it has ripened the way you like it. Also, avoid bananas that are soft or otherwise show bruising by considerable discoloration. One pound of bananas represents about three of medium size, or slightly more than two cups sliced.

This luscious *paradisiaca* of the tropics, as it has been referred to by poets and adventurers, combines well with many foods and enhances all cuisines. In New York, a dinner invitation from ethnic cooking expert Copeland Marks means either Indonesian or Guatemalan food, his two main specialties. Definitely, bananas will be on either menu. If the meal is Indonesian, we will have banana fritters, which always accompany the Balinese main course, in addition to whatever else is being served. If the fare is Guatemalan, we will begin the meal by munching on homemade banana chips (the kind you can make in a home dehydrator, or deep-fry).

One of my favorite fruit combinations is a simple and elegant dessert often served by Susana Palazuelos, caterer of many of Acapulco's beautiful parties: scoops of homemade banana ice cream piled in a fresh pineapple shell. A flavor marriage made in heaven! Any non-cook can become a super-chef merely by peeling and slicing a banana and letting imagination roam:

For an appetizer, cut one-inch slices, scoop out a hollow with a melon baller, and fill with seasoned cream cheese. Bananas in salads and fruit bowls are naturals. Whole wheat bread sandwiches with peanut butter and sliced bananas, perhaps with shredded raw carrot, are terrific. Savory sauces and gravies with banana puree and a touch of curry powder are exotic. Fold chunks of banana into hot rice for an Oriental pilaff. In the tropics, bananas with beans, chicken, turkey, or meat is common practice. (There they also use the wide banana leaves to enclose mixtures and bake them, much the way we do in parchment or foil.) Banana is a very compatible fruit. It has been mainly the American and French cooks who invented the various ways of using bananas in breads, muffins, cakes, cream pies, tarts, souffles, puddings and turnovers.

For special diets – low fat, low sodium – and for infants and the elderly, the banana is unbeatable. It is wonderfully satisfying, yet one medium-size banana, weighing about 175 grams, contains only 101 calories and 0.2 percent fat. Three-fourths of the banana is moisture and 21 percent natural sugars (dextrose, levulose, and sucrose) with a wide range of vitamins and minerals, but almost no sodium.

BALI-STYLE BANANA FRITTERS

Pisang Goreng

According to Indonesian cooking expert Copeland Marks, banana fritters are ubiquitous in Balinese meals. Plain banana fritters accompany the main course, be it fish, poultry, or meat. They may also be served as dessert with a little hot honey and butter syrup drizzled over them.

DO-AHEAD TIP: *Bananas and batter can be readied a few hours ahead. Fry at serving time.*

FRITTERS
1 egg, beaten

1 tablespoon milk

1 tablespoon light honey

6 tablespoons whole wheat pastry flour

1 pound bananas (about 3 medium-size)

¼ cup light vegetable oil (e.g., safflower)

SAUCE (optional)
¼ cup light honey

2 tablespoons unsalted butter

FRITTERS: Mix egg, milk, honey, and flour to a smooth batter. Cut each banana into 3 pieces diagonally. Heat oil in saute pan until medium hot (when a drop of water sizzles). Coat banana pieces with batter and fry on one side until light brown. Turn and brown on the other side. Remove and drain on paper towels.

SAUCE: Combine honey and butter in small saucepan and stir until mixture is blended. Serve sauce separately or pour over dessert banana fritters.

6 servings as accompaniment or 4 as dessert

BANANAS

BANANA PILAFF

DO-AHEAD TIP: *Pilaff can be cooked a few hours ahead and held at room temperature. At serving time, rewarm in 300° F. oven. Transfer to a hot serving dish and sprinkle with grated cheese.*

- 3 tablespoons light vegetable oil (e.g., safflower)
- 4 bananas, slightly green, cut into 1-inch-thick slices
- 2 tablespoons chopped yellow or white onions
- 1 cup long grain brown rice
- 1 egg, beaten
- 2½ cups stock (e.g., chicken, vegetable, or soy—2½ cups water with 3 teaspoons tamari soy sauce) or water
- 1 teaspoon curry powder
- ¼ cup freshly grated Parmesan cheese

Preheat oven to 350°F. Heat oil in saute pan. Add bananas and onions and cook over moderate heat 3 minutes. Set aside.

Combine rice and egg in deep, heavy pot. Stir over moderate heat until all rice kernels are dry and separate. Add stock (or water) and curry powder, and bring to a boil. Add banana and onion mixture. Cover pot with firm-fitting lid and cook in oven 45 minutes without disturbing rice.

PRESENTATION: When rice is cooked, fluff with 2 forks and transfer to warm serving dish. Sprinkle grated cheese on top.

Yields about 5 cups

BANANA ICE CREAM IN PINEAPPLE BOATS

Banana and pineapple are a fabulous flavor combination. This is a pretty but simple way to serve them.

DO-AHEAD TIP: *Banana ice cream can be stored in freezer for about a week. Assemble in pineapple halves at serving time.*

- 1 ripe pineapple
- 2 quarts Banana Ice Cream (see Index—Fresh Fruit Ice Cream)

Cut pineapple in half lengthwise, through the leaves. Cut out centers, removing most of the pulp but leaving a sturdy shell with the crown intact. Cut core from pulp and chop pulp. Chill pineapple shells thoroughly.

PRESENTATION: Arrange 2 pineapple shells with leaves intact on serving tray. Fill with scoops of banana ice cream. Serve chopped pulp in separate bowl.

8 to 10 servings

BANANA BRAN MUFFINS

DO-AHEAD TIP: *Baked muffins can be stored in freezer in a sealed plastic bag.*

- 1 cup sifted whole wheat pastry flour
- ½ teaspoon baking soda
- 1 teaspoon baking powder (without aluminum salts)
- 2 tablespoons unsalted butter
- ⅓ cup light honey
- 1 egg, beaten
- 1 cup miller's bran
- 2 cups thinly sliced bananas
- ¼ cup chopped walnuts (optional)

Preheat oven to 375°F. Have ready 12 oiled muffin tins. Sift flour, soda, and baking powder together. Beat butter in mixer. Add honey and beat again. Add egg and bran and mix. Add bananas and mix well. Add dry ingredients and beat only until mixed. Add nuts, if desired. Divide batter evenly in muffin tins. Bake 20 to 30 minutes, or until tops rebound to touch.

Makes 12 muffins

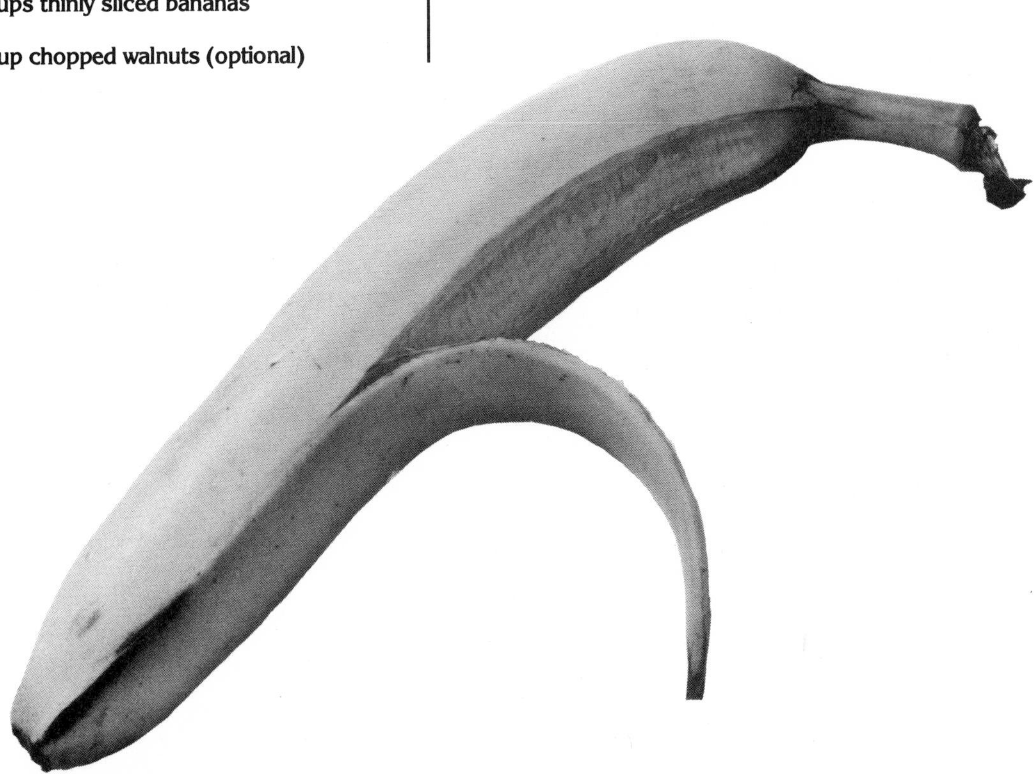

BANANA MOUSSE MARLBOROUGH

A glittering dome of banana mousse covered with a mosaic of banana slices and chopped pistachios set in tart lemon jelly.

DO-AHEAD TIP: *This dessert should be prepared a day ahead in order for mold to be firmly set.*

COATING
- 4 tablespoons unflavored gelatin
- 4 cups cold water
- 2/3 cup light honey
- 3/4 cup fresh lemon juice
- 4 2-inch strips pared lemon rind
- 2 or 3 medium-size bananas (not too ripe)
- 1/2 cup chopped pistachios

BANANA MOUSSE
- 3 whole eggs
- 3 egg yolks
- 1/3 cup light honey
- 2 tablespoons unflavored gelatin
- 1/4 cup cold water
- 2 teaspoons fresh lemon juice
- 2 cups mashed ripe bananas (about 4 medium-size)
- 1 1/2 cups heavy cream, whipped

COATING: Soak gelatin in 1/2 cup cold water. In saucepan combine soaked gelatin, 3 1/2 cups water, honey, lemon juice, and lemon rind. Stir over low heat until mixture boils and gelatin is dissolved. Remove from heat.

Have ready 2 1/2- or 3-quart plain dome mold, such as a metal mixing bowl, that has been chilled in the freezer. Place this mold over a larger bowl of crushed ice. Pour two-thirds of lemon jelly mixture into the mold and slowly turn over ice until a 3/16-inch-thick jelly coating forms all over. Pour out excess jelly. Refrigerate mold until jelly is very stiff.

Cut 2 or 3 bananas into 3/16-inch-thick slices. If remaining jelly has set, rewarm to liquefy; then stir over ice to point of setting. Dip each banana slice in lemon jelly and stick to jelly coating in mold. Completely cover sides and bottom of mold with banana slices. Between bananas sprinkle chopped pistachios. Using a small spoon, pour a little more jelly at point of setting over pistachios. Return mold to refrigerator.

BANANA MOUSSE: Combine eggs, egg yolks, and honey in mixer and beat until light and thick. Soak gelatin in water and lemon juice in small saucepan. Then stir over low heat until gelatin is dissolved. Let cool until lukewarm and pour into egg mixture, beating constantly. Add mashed bananas and fold in lightly and evenly. Fold in one-third of whipped cream.

Fill jelly-lined mold with banana mousse. Return to refrigerator to set. Rewarm remaining jelly to liquefy and chill to point of setting. Pour over top of mold and return it to refrigerator. Allow to chill at least 8 hours or overnight.

PRESENTATION: Have chilled serving platter ready. To loosen mousse, slide a small, thin knife around the edge. Hold mold in bowl of hot water 1 minute. Place serving platter bottom side up on top of mold. Carefully invert assembly and remove mold. Put remaining whipped cream in pastry bag fitted with star tube and pipe rosettes around bottom of dome. Chill.

6 to 8 servings

BANANA NUT MAYONNAISE

Banana-nut mayonnaise goes well with any fruit or shellfish salad.

DO-AHEAD TIP: *This mayonnaise will keep for a week or so in refrigerator.*

- 1 egg yolk
- ½ teaspoon dry mustard
- 1 tablespoon fresh lemon juice
- ¾ cup light vegetable oil (e.g., safflower)
- 2 tablespoons peanut butter
- 1 medium-size banana, mashed

Combine egg yolk and mustard in food processor or mixer and blend well. Add lemon juice and blend again. Continue blending while *very slowly* adding oil. Add peanut butter and blend. Transfer to mixing bowl. Using rubber scraper, fold in mashed banana lightly and evenly.

Yields 1½ cups

BANANAS FORGE

DO-AHEAD TIP: *Homemade vanilla ice cream can be prepared several days ahead.*

- 8 tablespoons unsalted butter
- ¾ cup light honey
- 6 ounces (half of 12-ounce container) frozen orange juice concentrate (do not thaw)
- grated rind of 1 orange
- ¼ cup fresh orange juice
- ⅛ teaspoon ground cinnamon
- ⅛ teaspoon freshly grated nutmeg
- 12 *dominicos* (miniature bananas), halved lengthwise, or 6 large bananas, halved horizontally and then halved lengthwise
- 1½ quarts Basic Vanilla Ice Cream (see Index)

In large saute pan, combine butter and honey and cook over low heat until dissolved and blended. Add frozen orange juice, orange rind, fresh orange juice, cinnamon, and nutmeg. Cook over very low heat, stirring frequently, until syrup thickens (about 15 minutes). Place bananas in sauce and cook 2 minutes. Spoon bananas and sauce over individual servings of vanilla ice cream.

6 servings

BANANAS

COLD BANANA SOUFFLE

DO-AHEAD TIP: *This dessert should be prepared a day ahead in order for souffle to be firmly set.*

SOUFFLE
Banana Mousse (see Banana Mousse Marlborough in this section)

DECORATION
1/4 cup chopped pistachios

1 banana, thinly sliced

SOUFFLE: Tear off length of aluminum foil or waxed paper 1½ times the outer girth of 3-cup (#5) souffle dish. Fold in half lengthwise and brush with oil. Wrap around souffle dish and fasten with masking tape or string.

Pour mousse mixture into prepared souffle dish and let stand in refrigerator until firmly set.

PRESENTATION: When souffle is set, carefully remove paper collar. Stick chopped pistachios around sides of souffle. Spread half of remaining whipped cream (see mousse recipe) on top. Cover top with banana slices. Put rest of whipped cream in pastry bag fitted with small star tube (#3 or #4) and pipe little rosettes around top edge. Refrigerate until serving time.

4 to 6 servings

More Banana Recipes

See Index for the following recipes:

DESSERTS: Cranberry-Banana Tartlets, French Fruit Tart and Tartlets, Fresh Fruit Ice Cream, Frozen Fruit Yogurt, Fruit Fritters, Fruit Omelet; *Macedoine de Fruits;* BEVERAGE: Banana with Buttermilk or Yogurt.

BLACKBERRIES

If you live in the country or go to the country on holiday, chances are you've had the happy experience of gathering a mess of wild blackberries. Even if only a handful, how good they taste – warm, sun-sweetened, a slight crunch of little seeds – no matter the snags, scratches, and gnat bites you also collected if you were not properly outfitted for berrying among the briers.

When I was a child, berrying was a serious (and fun) foray for the whole family on a Saturday or Sunday in the brush around Chesaning. There we also acquired berries from a few Indian families who lived deep in the thicket, far off the road. At the behest of Aunt Tillie, who was for many years the commissioner of education for Saginaw County and constantly distressed that these Indian children did not attend school because their clothes were so shabby, my sister and I took them clothes we and our friends had outgrown. In return they gave us choice blackberries they had gathered and pretty little decorative baskets of vivid colors and patterns that they had woven. (The reeds were from surrounding brush; the bright colors from pigments of blackberries and other wild berries and leaves.) Blackberries were a favorite fruit for jam and sauces used in rich, purply-black pie fillings and cobblers to brighten the long Michigan winters.

Dewberries, boysenberries, loganberries, and mulberries all resemble the blackberry in appearance – an oblong berry composed of many pulp-enclosed seeds called drupelets. Blackberries and dewberries are bright black. Boysenberries and loganberries are dark red to red-black. Mulberries range in color from white to red to black. The main differences are the plants on which they grow and where they grow. Blackberries grow erect, and wild patches may be found in every state of the Union, including Alaska and Hawaii, while cultivated blackberry plants prefer the northern sections. Dewberries (also called groundberries), boysenberries, and loganberries grow on plants which trail on the ground and prosper better in the South and West. Mulberries are of a different genus (*Morus*, of Oriental origin) than the blackberry (*Rubus*), but look like small blackberries. They grow on trees, and are found throughout the country. One name – blackberries – will do for all in recipes for cooking and eating.

Blackberries generally are a sweet-flavored fruit, although dewberries, boysenberries, and loganberries may be slightly tart. The ground types are usually larger than blackberries, often nearly an inch long and about as wide, generally rounder and juicier looking. In contrast, blackberries are narrower, oblong or conical in shape, and often twice as long as they are broad.

BLACKBERRIES

You can "berry" in the country or at your local fruit market from June to September. If you buy your blackberries, good-quality berries are plump and have a bright, clean, fresh appearance. Overripe berries are dull in color, soft, and sometimes leaky. Blackberries are particularly rich in magnesium and vitamin C, and count their many seeds as good dietary fiber.

These tempting, glossy drupelets are impossible to resist eating out of hand and – as soon as possible – in a bowl with fresh cream. With a little more kitchen time, they can become a divine cobbler or flummery, pancakes or pie, mousse, ice cream or sherbet, shortcake or topping on cheesecake, fresh or canned sauce to serve with custard-type desserts, and that delicious jam.

Any type of blackberries may be used in the following recipes.

BLACKBERRY MOUSSE

Raspberry Mousse 1 (see Index), with 1½ cups strained blackberry pulp instead of raspberries

2 tablespoons light honey

3 tablespoons water

thinly shredded rind of 1 lemon

1 cup heavy cream, whipped

½ cup cleaned whole blackberries

In small saucepan, combine honey and water and bring to a boil over low heat. Add lemon rind and let barely simmer until rind is translucent. Drain on paper towel.

PRESENTATION: Put whipped cream in pastry bag fitted with medium star tube (#6 or #7). Pipe rosettes all over top of mousse and top each with whole blackberry. Sprinkle border of lemon rind around edge of dish. Refrigerate until ready to serve.

8 servings

MINTED, JELLIED BLACKBERRY SOUP

DO-AHEAD TIP: *Soup can be prepared a day or two ahead and refrigerated.*

- 1 quart ripe blackberries, picked over and cleaned
- 1/3 cup light honey
- 1 quart white grape juice, apple juice, or light lemonade
- 1/2 stick cinnamon bark
- 3 whole cloves
- 12 mint leaves
- 1 1/2 tablespoons unflavored gelatin
- 1/4 cup cold water
- 6 mint sprigs

Crush blackberries lightly in food processor or with potato masher. In 2-quart saucepan, combine berry pulp, honey, juice, cinnamon, cloves, and mint leaves. Bring mixture to a boil slowly, remove from heat, and strain. Return to pan. Soak gelatin in water and add to soup. Stir over low heat until gelatin is dissolved and blended with soup. Chill soup. It will be a light jelly, barely set.

PRESENTATION: Serve in chilled crystal soup or dessert bowls. Garnish each serving with a sprig of mint.

4 to 6 servings

More Blackberry Recipes

See Index for the following recipes:

DESSERTS: Cobbler, Flummery, Fresh Fruit Ice Cream, Frozen Fruit Yogurt, Fruit Sherbet, Fruit Shortcake, *Macedoine de Fruits*, Refrigerator Cheesecake with Fresh Fruit Topping; SAUCE: Fresh Fruit Sauce.

BLUEBERRIES

Another summertime excursion for the feast of fruit was blueberry picking. For this specialty, we packed our pails and picnic lunches and headed for the marshlands along Saginaw Bay and Lake Huron. It is recorded that in 1616 an explorer found the Indians gathering blueberries at this same Lake Huron. For them, these abundant wild fruits were a sustenance food – they ate them fresh, and they dried them in the sun for use during the winter in soups and with meats. As we picked the sky-blue berries covered with powdery, pearly bloom, we were occasionally reminded of the Indians who once roamed these shores, for it was not uncommon only three or four decades ago to find a stray stone arrowhead in the sandy soil. Today Michigan is one of the foremost sources of cultivated blueberries. I hope some of those wild bushes are still there, too.

Gathering wild blueberries was fiercely competitive. We tried hard to arrive ahead of other groups, to search out the best bushes and stake out our territory. Mother supervised the quality of our picking – no leaves, twigs, or green berries – as we emptied our waist-tied pails (formerly lard pails) into larger pails that were the measure of her supply, enough to merit putting up a batch of jam or sauce. She smiled as she observed her own little Indians with blue-stained faces, hands, and clothes.

Blueberries grow almost everywhere in the world and thrive all over the United States and Canada. One of the most perfect meals I can remember was in the countryside near Gloucester, Massachusetts, where we were vacationing. There, hard against the rocky coast of the roaring Atlantic, we came upon a roadside stand with a couple of plank tables and benches and several huge steaming drums. The fare, eaten there: steamed lobsters and sweet corn on the cob, thick slices of tomato, and blueberries and cream – all local, brought in that morning. A fine backyard feast even if you don't live next to the Atlantic.

The blueberry bush, which varies in height from a few inches to 10 to 15 feet and is extant south to north in the United States, bears fruit from May through September. The berries may be syrupy sweet to tart, and may range in size from ⅛ inch to more than 1 inch in diameter. The average blueberry may contain as many as 65 seeds, which do not deter from its luscious palatability. Most berries have blue-black skin but are covered with a light-colored bloom that is a natural protective wax.

The name blueberry and huckleberry are used interchangeably, although each is of a different genus. The huckleberry, which only grows wild, has ten large seeds, each of which is surrounded by a bony covering or pit.

BLUEBERRIES

Cultivated blueberries are generally sold according to size, the larger berries being more expensive. Size is based on the number of berries required to fill a half-pint measure (90 or less, 90-130, 130-190, and over 190). Berries should be plump, fresh in appearance, dry, and with full color, which may be anything from light blue to dark blue to blue-black. Overripe fruit has a dull, lifeless appearance and is often soft and watery. Properly cared for, good blueberries will last up to two weeks under home refrigeration. Frozen blueberries held at 0°F. will retain their taste and quality for more than two years.

There is something enigmatic about blueberries. They are titillating while seeming as basic as home and the flag. They excite even the bleary-eyed at breakfast when added to hot or cold cereal or used in muffins, biscuits, pancakes, and waffles. They're a sure hit in pies and tarts, crumb cakes, shortcakes, and biscuit-covered cobblers; in fruit soup and fritters; and as sauces for custards and puddings. As jam and jelly, they are unsurpassed. Blueberries become sprightly polka dots in a mixed fruit bowl; they win fame as the topping on New York-style cheesecake, not to mention the New England specialty, blueberry grunt – hot blueberry dumplings with blueberry sauce and thick cream.

With all of their appetite appeal, blueberries are a healthy food and a convenience food. They require no pitting or peeling and there is no waste. Just rinse, eat, and enjoy.

BLUEBERRY GRUNT

DO-AHEAD TIP: *Dumpling dough, sauce, and whipped cream can be prepared a few hours ahead. Heat sauce and cook dumplings at serving time.*

DUMPLINGS
- 1 cup whole wheat pastry flour
- 2 teaspoons baking powder (without aluminum salts)
- ½ cup light cream

SAUCE
- 2 cups cleaned ripe blueberries
- ½ cup light honey
- ¾ cup water
- 2 teaspoons fresh lemon juice

- 1 cup heavy cream, plain or whipped, or Creme Fraiche (see Index)

DUMPLINGS: Sift flour and baking powder together. Combine in mixing bowl with light cream and stir only until batter is smooth.

SAUCE: Combine blueberries, honey, water, and lemon juice in deep, heavy pot. Bring to a boil slowly and simmer 3 minutes, stirring occasionally. Using a tablespoon, drop batter into hot blueberry sauce, keeping dumplings separate so they do not stick together. Cover pot with firm-fitting lid and simmer over low heat 20 minutes, or until dumplings puff and toothpick inserted in center comes out clean.

PRESENTATION: Have ready 4 to 6 warm dessert or cereal bowls. With slotted spoon, transfer dumplings to bowls. Spoon sauce around dumplings. Serve heavy cream or creme fraiche in separate bowl.

6 servings

BLUEBERRY SOUFFLE WITH BLUEBERRY SAUCE

This is a style of baked souffle prepared without flour and egg yolks.

DO-AHEAD TIP: *Blueberries can be pureed, syrup prepared, souffle dish readied, and sauce prepared a day ahead. Near serving time, rewarm syrup and proceed with souffle mixture and baking.*

SOUFFLE
- **3 cups cleaned blueberries**
- **1 tablespoon fresh lime or lemon juice**
- **3/4 cup light honey**
- **1/4 cup water**
- **1 tablespoon cornstarch or potato flour**
- **1 teaspoon grated lemon rind**
- **8 egg whites**
- **1/2 cup slivered almonds**

SAUCE
- **1 cup blueberry jam**
- **2 teaspoons fresh lemon juice**
- **1 cup cleaned blueberries**

SOUFFLE: Prepare 1 1/2-quart souffle dish by tearing off length of aluminum foil or waxed paper 1 1/2 times the outer girth of dish. Fold in half lengthwise. Brush lightly with oil. Wrap paper collar around outside of dish and fasten with kitchen string or masking tape.

Puree blueberries with lime or lemon juice in food processor or blender. Combine honey and water in small saucepan and stir over low heat until mixture boils. Add syrup to blueberry puree.

In separate small bowl, mix 2 or 3 tablespoons blueberry mixture with cornstarch or potato flour; then add this mixture to rest of blueberry puree. Pour blueberry mixture into saucepan and stir over low heat until it thickens. Add lemon rind, remove from heat, and chill.

Preheat oven to 375°F. Beat egg whites to soft peaks and gently fold into cooled blueberry mixture. Spoon mixture into prepared souffle dish. Bake 50 minutes to 1 hour. About 10 minutes before souffle is finished baking, have slivered almonds at hand. Quickly open oven door and sprinkle them on top of souffle.

SAUCE: Strain jam and combine with lemon juice in small saucepan. Stir over low heat until mixture boils. Add blueberries and remove from heat. (Sauce may be served hot or cold.)

PRESENTATION: When souffle is baked, gently place on serving plate and carefully remove collar. Serve at once with separate bowl of sauce.

4 to 6 servings

BLUEBERRY PIE

DO-AHEAD TIP: *Pie can be baked a day ahead and refrigerated.*

PASTRY
1½ quantity of dough for Plain Whole Wheat Short Pastry 1 (see Index)

FILLING
1 tablespoon cornstarch or potato flour
2 tablespoons water
¾ cup light honey
1 quart blueberries, picked over and cleaned
1 tablespoon fresh lemon juice
1 egg, beaten

PASTRY: Preheat oven to 350°F. Spread length of waxed paper on work surface and dust with flour. Place a ball of two-thirds of dough in center and sprinkle with a little more flour. Flatten ball a little with rolling pin and cover with another sheet of waxed paper. Roll dough between 2 sheets of waxed paper to a round large enough to line 9- or10-inch pie plate. Shape dough firmly against the inside. Run rolling pin over rim to trim off excess dough. Prick bottom of dough with fork in several places. Place sheet of waxed paper on top of dough and cover with dried beans or raw rice to hold paper down. Bake 20 minutes. Remove weight and waxed paper. Leave oven set at 350°F.

FILLING: Mix cornstarch or potato flour and water in a cup and stir until smooth. Combine with honey in small saucepan. Stir over low heat until mixture is just blended and thickened. Remove from heat and mix with blueberries. Add lemon juice. Pour blueberry mixture into pastry shell.

Roll out remaining dough into long strip between sheets of waxed paper. Cut into ½-inch-wide strips long enough to cover pie. Arrange strips on top of blueberry filling in lattice pattern and press edges to bottom pastry. Brush pastry with beaten egg. Place pie on baking sheet and bake 20 to 30 minutes, until top is lightly browned.

6 to 8 servings

More Blueberry Recipes

See Index for the following recipes:

DESSERTS: Cobbler, French Fruit Tart and Tartlets, Fresh Fruit Ice Cream, Frozen Fresh Fruit Souffle, Fruit Sherbet, Fruit Shortcake, *Macedoine de Fruits*, Refrigerator Cheesecake with Fresh Fruit Topping; SAUCE: Fresh Fruit Sauce.

CAROB

A cooking demonstration I especially enjoy doing is to prepare Dione Lucas's celebrated chocolate mousse recipe – with the promise of only half the calories, no saturated fat or caffeine, and almost no sodium – using carob instead of chocolate. First I pass around to the audience samples of dried whole carob pods and some pods chopped into kibbles which members are invited to nibble. Even people in the group who are adventuresome and informed about foods are being exposed for the first time to this ancient food of the Middle East, known long before chocolate was discovered in the New World. They are surprised and delighted with its taste and color (similar to chocolate) and its natural sweetness. Yes, when you chew a piece of carob pod, it is sweet; it is 46 percent natural sugar. (Chocolate, which is comparatively much higher in calories because it is more than 50 percent fat, is naturally bitter and must have sugar – more calories – added to be edible.)

It's the fleshy pod, the fruit of the carob tree, which grows all over the world, that is used for food. In some places carob pods are referred to as St. John's bread or locust bread, because it is said that they are actually the "locusts" named in the Bible as John the Baptist's food during his sojourn in the wilderness. (The hard beans or seeds within are called carats, which since biblical times have been the basis for measuring the weight of gold and gems.)

For today's cooking needs, the thick, flat, leathery, chocolate-colored pods, 3 to 12 inches in length, are partially dried and chopped into kibbles, which are then roasted, ground, and blended into a fine, flavorful powder. This brown powder is processed in the same forms as chocolate – powder (like cocoa), bars, and nuggets. These products are available nationally in specialty foods stores and many supermarkets.

My own discovery of carob is fairly recent (perhaps eight years ago), and I have had a love affair with it since. Fully ten years before that I had been sternly advised by a distinguished (and expensive) dermatologist to avoid chocolate. I followed that counsel faithfully, even while teaching others how to prepare those irresistible French chocolate delights. For the likes of me, carob became the yes-yes instead of no-no answer to a world of favorite desserts.

Perhaps it's time for modern cooks and gastro-

nomes to discover carob for its own fine, natural flavor. It has pleased the human palate for thousands of years. Its rather mild "chocolatelike" flavor (for lack of a more relative description) perks up with such flavorings as a touch of cinnamon, or orange, vanilla, almond, or mint concentrate.

To replace cocoa ingredient: Use an equal amount of carob powder instead of cocoa.

To replace solid chocolate ingredient: Use three tablespoons of carob powder plus one tablespoon of water in place of one ounce or one square of baking chocolate. Carob in a solid bar or nuggets can be used ounce for ounce in place of sweet or semisweet chocolate.

CAROB CREPES WITH CREAM CHEESE

DO-AHEAD TIP: *Crepes can be made ahead and stored in freezer. Filling can be prepared a day ahead. Assemble crepes at serving time.*

CREPES
16 6-inch Carob Crepes (see Index)

FILLING
8 ounces cream cheese

¼ cup light honey

1 teaspoon carob powder

2 tablespoons grated orange rind

1 cup heavy cream, whipped

GLAZE
¼ cup orange marmalade

2 tablespoons unsalted butter

FILLING: Beat cream cheese in mixer until creamy. Add honey, carob powder, and orange rind, and beat again. Add cream cheese mixture to whipped cream and fold together lightly with rubber spatula.

GLAZE: Combine orange marmalade and butter in a small saucepan and stir over low heat until mixture is dissolved and blended.

PRESENTATION: Spread underside (the side cooked last) of each crepe with 3 tablespoons cream cheese mixture. Roll up lightly and place on individual serving plates. Brush a little glaze over each stuffed crepe.

8 servings

CAROB MOUSSE

DO-AHEAD TIP: *This mousse keeps well in the freezer for 2 or 3 days. Before serving, let stand at room temperature for about 5 minutes.*

MOUSSE
16 tablespoons (1 cup) carob powder

1 teaspoon vanilla extract or orange flavoring, or ¼ teaspoon mint flavoring

Have serving container(s) ready. They may be 6 individual custard cups or small ramekins, or a 1½- to 2-quart serving bowl.

MOUSSE: Combine carob powder, vanilla or orange or mint flavoring, cinnamon, honey, and water in saucepan and stir over low heat until mixture is smooth and shiny. Remove from heat and beat in egg yolks with small wire whisk, 1 at a time. Set mixture aside.

CAROB MOUSSE—continued

1 teaspoon ground cinnamon

2 tablespoons light honey

½ cup hot water

5 large eggs, separated

DECORATION (optional)
1 cup heavy cream, whipped

1 tablespoon carob powder

Beat egg whites to soft peaks. Add carob mixture to egg whites and stir vigorously with whisk until mixture is well blended, frothy, and shiny. Pour mixture into 1-quart measuring pitcher and then into individual serving containers or large serving bowl. Place mousse in freezer to set.

PRESENTATION: Serve mousse plain or decorate with whipped cream rosettes, if desired. Put whipped cream in pastry bag fitted with large star tube (#8 or #9). Pipe large rosette on top of each individual serving or all over top of large serving. Put carob powder in shaker or small wire strainer and top each serving with light sprinkle of powder.

6 servings

CAROB NAPOLEON

Fine French patisserie au naturel: *layers of crisp, flaky whole wheat puff pastry sandwiched with carob pastry cream and topped with carob coating and chopped almonds.*

DO-AHEAD TIP: *Baked puff pastry strips and pastry cream can be made a day ahead. On day of serving, assemble presentation and refrigerate.*

1 pound Whole Wheat Puff Pastry (see Index)

4 cups Carob Pastry Cream (see Index)

¾ cup Coating Carob (see Index)

½ cup coarsely ground (not pulverized) toasted almonds

Roll out pastry into 12 by 16-inch rectangle on lightly floured surface. Cut rectangle into 4 12 by 4-inch strips. Transfer strips and leftover scraps of dough to dampened baking sheet(s) and place in freezer until strips are frozen solid. (Puff pastry bakes best when it is put into oven while frozen.)

Preheat oven to 400°F. Bake strips and scraps until puffed and lightly browned (about 30 to 40 minutes). Loosen gently with spatula and let stand on baking sheet(s) until cool.

PRESENTATION: To assemble, place 1 puff pastry strip on serving platter and spread with ½ cup carob pastry cream. Place second pastry strip on top of first and spread with pastry cream. Repeat with remaining pastry strips and pastry cream. (Do not spread pastry cream on top.) Use remaining pastry cream to coat sides. If necessary, thin coating carob to spreadable consistency with a few drops of hot water. Spread coating carob on top of assembly and sprinkle with ground almonds.

6 servings

CAROB

GATEAU FAVORI DIONE LUCAS
Dione Lucas's Favorite Cake

A glorious company dessert is this large cream puff ring filled with mounds of carob pastry cream and whipped cream. The top is encrusted with toasted almond slivers.

DO-AHEAD TIP: Gateau favori *can be prepared a day ahead and refrigerated.*

quantity of 1 recipe for unbaked Basic Chou Paste (see Index)

1 **cup slivered blanched almonds**

2 **cups Carob Pastry Cream (see Index)**

2 **cups Creme Chantilly (see Index)**

Preheat oven to 375°F. Using 7- or 8-inch plate as a stencil, mark a circle on dry baking sheet with ice pick or other sharp pointed tool. Put chou paste in pastry bag fitted with large plain tube (#8 or #9) and pipe a ring of dough on the circle. Carefully pipe another ring on top of the first one. Gently brush top of dough with remaining beaten egg (see dough recipe), and sprinkle generously with slivered almonds. Let dough stand at room temperature 30 minutes. Then bake 45 minutes. Reduce oven temperature to 350°F. and bake another 15 minutes. Remove from oven and let cool.

PRESENTATION: Carefully cut cream puff ring in half horizontally. Place bottom half on doily on serving plate. Fill one pastry bag fitted with large *plain* tube (#8 or #9) with carob pastry cream. Fill another pastry bag fitted with medium *star* tube (#6 or #7) with creme chantilly. On bottom half of cream puff ring, pipe 2-inch-high mounds of pastry cream all around the circle. Between mounds of pastry cream, pipe rosettes of creme chantilly. Carefully place top of cream puff ring on top of filling. (Filling should be visible from sides.) Refrigerate until serving time.

6 to 8 servings

RED MOLE WITH CHICKEN, TURKEY, OR PORK
Mole Rojo con Pollo, Pavo o Puerco

In Mexican cooking, the word mole *(pronounced mo-leh) means a sauce with chili (pepper). There are many kinds of chilies that can be combined in many ways in sauces, at which Mexican cooks are masters. As noted in this recipe, not all chilies are hot, nor are all chilies compatible with each other. This red* mole *recipe is Pepe Santiago's version of* Mole Poblano, *famous for its inclusion of chocolate (semisweet). As an aficionado of Mexican cuisine, I was happy to discover that carob can be a satisfactory alternative to chocolate in Pepe's tasty recipe.*

RED MOLE WITH CHICKEN, TURKEY, OR PORK—continued

DO-AHEAD TIP: *Meat and sauce can be prepared 2 to 3 days ahead and refrigerated. Combine and warm at serving time.*

MEAT

1 4-pound chicken, or 2 small chickens, or equivalent section of turkey, cut into small serving pieces; or 3 to 4 pounds stewing pork (depending on quantity of bones), cut into 2-inch cubes

2 large celery ribs, sliced

1 large yellow onion, sliced

4 cups cold water

MOLE BASE

6 ancho chilies (dried Poblano chilies, dark reddish-brown, about 5 inches by 3 inches, mild to piquant in flavor)

3 guajillo chilies (dried, reddish-brown, slender, 4½ inches by 1½ inches, very hot), or 3 pasillo chilies (brownish-black, about 6 inches by 1 inch, very hot)

RED MOLE SAUCE

3 tablespoons light vegetable oil (e.g., safflower)

¾ teaspoon finely chopped fresh garlic

1 cup chopped Bermuda onion

2 teaspoons meat flavoring (e.g., Marmite brewer's yeast extract, vegetable paste, or meat glaze)

4 to 5 tablespoons Mole Base or to taste

4½ tablespoons carob powder

3 cups stock reserved from poaching meat

4 to 6 cups hot Plain-Cooked Brown Rice (see Index)

MEAT: Put meat in deep, heavy pot with celery and onion. Add water and bring to a boil. Reduce heat to low, cover pot, and simmer until meat is tender. Remove meat; strain and reserve stock.

MOLE BASE: In blender, combine ancho and guajillo or pasillo chilies with a little water and blend until smooth.

RED MOLE SAUCE: In the pot in which meat was cooked, combine oil, garlic, and onion. Stir over low heat until onion is translucent. Add meat flavoring, mole base to taste, and carob. Stir until mixture is blended. Add stock. Bring to a boil and simmer about 10 minutes, or until flavors are blended.

PRESENTATION: Add cooked meat to sauce in pot and rewarm together. Transfer to warm casserole or platter and serve, accompanied by separate bowl of hot brown rice.

6 servings

NOTE: The dried chilies are available in the West and Southwest and in cities where there are Spanish markets. Bottled red *mole* paste (Tia Maria brand) can be substituted.

COLLECTION OF CAROB COOKIES OR *PETITS FOURS SECS*

DO-AHEAD TIP: *Cookies can be stored in covered container in freezer.*

PINWHEELS

LIGHT DOUGH
- 1¼ cups whole wheat pastry flour
- grated rind of 1 lemon
- 4 tablespoons unsalted butter
- 1½ egg yolks
- 2 tablespoons light honey

CAROB DOUGH
- 1¼ cups whole wheat pastry flour
- 2 tablespoons carob powder
- ½ teaspoon ground cinnamon
- 4 tablespoons unsalted butter
- 1½ egg yolks
- 2 tablespoons light honey
- 1 teaspoon vanilla extract
- egg wash (1 egg yolk mixed with 1 teaspoon water)

LIGHT DOUGH: In food processor, combine flour, lemon rind, and butter. Process only to the texture of coarse meal. In small bowl, mix egg yolks and honey. Add to flour mixture and process until blended but still crumbly. Stop processor, gather mixture with your hand, and transfer to work surface. Form a ball. Set aside.

CAROB DOUGH: In food processor, combine flour, carob powder, cinnamon, and butter. Process only to the texture of coarse meal. In small bowl, mix egg yolks, honey, and vanilla. Add to flour mixture and process until blended but still crumbly. Stop processor, gather mixture with your hand, and transfer to work surface. Form a ball.

Place light dough between floured sheets of waxed paper, roll to 3/16-inch thickness, and set aside. Also roll carob dough between floured sheets of waxed paper to 3/16-inch thickness. Remove top paper from white dough and brush with egg wash. Remove top paper from carob dough and turn this dough out on top of light dough. Remove sheet of waxed paper that is on top. Carefully roll two layers of dough up tightly, like a jelly roll. Wrap in waxed paper and chill in freezer or refrigerator until firm.

Preheat oven to 350°F. Line baking sheet with waxed paper (do not oil). Cut roll of dough into ¼-inch-thick slices and place on baking sheet. Bake 15 to 20 minutes.

Makes 4 to 5 dozen cookies

VANILLA AND CAROB ALMOND CRESCENTS

Serve a mixture of vanilla and carob almond crescents, the tips of both types coated with carob.

VANILLA ALMOND CRESCENTS
- 5 tablespoons unsalted butter
- 1 ½ tablespoons light honey
- ¼ cup blanched almonds, pulverized
- 1 cup sifted whole wheat pastry flour
- 1 teaspoon vanilla extract
- about ¼ cup Coating Carob (see Index)

CAROB ALMOND CRESCENTS
- ingredients for Vanilla Almond Crescents, plus 1 ½ tablespoons carob powder

VANILLA ALMOND CRESCENTS: Preheat oven to 300°F. In mixer, beat butter until light and creamy. Add honey and beat. Add almonds and beat. Stir in flour and vanilla and mix with wooden spoon.

Dust damp baking sheet with flour. Take a small handful of dough and roll a little between your hands to the shape of a short rod. Place on bare work surface and roll into long strip, about ⅜ inch thick. Cut in 2-inch strips. Place pieces of dough on baking sheet, curling them like half-moons. Bake 20 to 25 minutes, depending on size of cookies. (They should not brown.) Let cool. To coat tips, dip 1 tip of each crescent in coating carob. Place on cooled baking sheet in freezer until carob hardens. Then place crescents in storage container.

CAROB ALMOND CRESCENTS: Follow recipe for Vanilla Almond Crescents, but add carob powder to flour. Bake as directed.

Dip 1 tip of each crescent in coating carob.

Makes about 3 dozen vanilla and 3 dozen carob cookies

CAROB-COATED FRUIT STICKS

- 4 egg yolks
- ¼ cup light honey
- 2 teaspoons vanilla extract
- ¾ cup sifted whole wheat pastry flour
- ½ cup chopped walnuts
- ½ cup raisins
- ½ cup chopped apricots or dates
- about ¼ cup Coating Carob (see Index)

Preheat oven to 300°F. Line baking sheet with waxed paper and oil waxed paper. In mixer, beat egg yolks until foamy. Add honey and beat until frothy. Add vanilla. Fold in flour. Fold in nuts and fruits. Put mixture in pastry bag with ½- to ¾-inch opening *without* tube. Pipe strips of dough full width of baking sheet, with strips about 4 inches apart. Bake about 30 minutes, depending on thickness of strips.

When strips are cool, spread top of strips with coating carob. Cut strips in 2-inch lengths. Place on cooled baking sheet in freezer until carob hardens. Then place fruit sticks in storage container.

Makes 3 to 4 dozen sticks

(continued)

COLLECTION OF CAROB COOKIES—continued

CAROB-CINNAMON BITES

COOKIES
- 1¼ cups whole wheat pastry flour
- 3 tablespoons carob powder
- ½ teaspoon ground cinnamon
- 4 tablespoons unsalted butter
- 1½ egg yolks
- 2 tablespoons light honey
- 1 teaspoon vanilla extract

FILLING
- ¼ cup seedless red or black raspberry jam or apricot jam
- 1 teaspoon fresh lemon juice

COOKIES: Preheat oven to 350°F. In food processor, combine flour, carob, and cinnamon, and process until mixed. Add butter and process only to the texture of coarse meal. In small bowl, mix egg yolks, honey, and vanilla. Add to flour mixture and process until blended but still crumbly. Stop processor, gather mixture with your hand, and transfer to work surface. Form a ball.

Line baking sheet with waxed paper (do not oil). Place ball between sheets of waxed paper on work surface and roll out to 3/16-inch thickness. Remove top waxed paper and cut dough into rounds with 1-inch cutter. Place rounds on baking sheet. Reroll remaining dough and cut more rounds. Bake about 15 minutes. Let cool.

FILLING: Combine jam and lemon juice in small saucepan and stir over moderate heat until jam is dissolved. (Strain warm apricot jam through wire strainer.) Let cool to room temperature. Sandwich jam between cookies and chill in freezer until jam is set. Then place cookies in storage container.

Makes 1½ to 2 dozen sandwiched cookies

More Carob Recipes

See Index for the following recipes:

DESSERTS: Carob Ice Cream, Cold Lemon-Carob Layered Souffle, Frozen Fresh Fruit Souffle, Lime and Carob Tart in Coconut-Crumb Crust, *Poires Belle Helene a la Caroube;* BEVERAGES: Coco-Carob, Frosted Carob; SAUCE: Carob Sauce.

CHERRIES

The entrance to our centuries-old country house in Cortona, set within the geography of the immortalized beauty of Italy's Tuscan hills, is graced with a big spreading cherry tree. The sight of that tree when it is heavily hung with shining ripe fruit – usually in June – makes me feel as though I had walked straight into the mouth-watering freshness of a scene painted by Lippi or Botticelli.

Our property, which the Cortonese refer to as "*Il Mulinaccio*," the mill, is a natural treasure of trees, bushes, flowers, fruits, and vegetables, wild and cultivated, all lovingly cared for by old Guido and Angiola. I have a passion for filling the house with arrangements of wild flowers and leaves. One day on a walk along one of the five terraces that rise above the noisy little river filled with rocks and rapids, I counted 33 different blooms! In a surge of sentiment, I brought one of each back to New York to dry and remember.

Our Italian cherry tree is a huge old affair and, probably because of Guido's instinctive agricultural expertise, still delivers an abundant harvest each year. *Il Mulinaccio*'s cherries are peach colored with a red blush, and sweet. When the fruit on the tree is "ready," Guido climbs around on the branches and shakes them to release their fruit, while Angiola and I hastily pick them off the ground. Commercial pickers might frown at this tactic, but the ripe cherries fall on a soft carpet of thick grass and are not bruised. At least this way we win some of our share of the luscious fruit from the competing birds.

Most of *Il Mulinaccio*'s cherries are consumed fresh, European style – whole cherries with stems, served in a bowl buried in crushed ice, to be eaten out of hand, even as dessert at table. When cherry season is on, the French and Italians prefer to eat cherries this way. Fine restaurants, such as Maxim's in Paris and La Mere Bise in Lyon, even the dining room in the Rome airport and the dessert cart aboard Swissair, display fresh cherries in baskets and offer individual servings in small bowls (about the size of a cream soup bowl) with ice.

Although I was raised in cherry-land (annually we made the trip to the Cherry Festival in Traverse City, Michigan – not unlike the cherry fairs of the late Middle Ages), most of the American harvest seems to go into cooking and preserving. It is curious that we Americans have never extensively adopted the simple European way of serving the pretty raw fruit at table. Yet, nothing seems to please my guests more than a frosty silver bowl of fresh cherries embedded in chipped ice – as an appetizer with cocktails or as the perfect dessert on a warm summer day.

No one knows how old *Il Mulinaccio*'s cherry tree

is, but cherries are known to have been cultivated since ancient times, all over the world. Their growth and propagation was duly recorded by Theophrastus, the Greek "Father of Botany," and it is said that General Lucullus introduced the cherry to Rome. England's first Elizabeth adored the fruit, and a gift of cherries was a popular ploy to gain her favor. The cherry was one of the first fruits cultivated by colonists in North America, from Canada to Florida. Today the cherry blossom is our national herald of spring, when the media announce the annual blooming of the famous orchard surrounding the Washington Monument.

Being a fleshy, one-seeded fruit, or drupe, the cherry is related to the peach, plum, almond, etc. There are many species of cherries, but for cooking and eating purposes, they are divided into two main groups: sweet and sour.

Sweet cherries, of which the Bing and Lambert varieties may be the most popular, are usually dark red to black, with firm flesh, about one inch in diameter. There are some light colored and white varieties. Today most of the sweet cherry crop comes from our Western states, mainly from May to August.

Sour or tart cherries are light to dark red in color when ripe, a little juicier than sweet cherries, and about 3/4 inch in diameter. Most of them are grown in the Midwest and East, predominantly the Montmorency variety. Some tart cherries when ripe are sweet enough for eating out of hand, but most are cooked. The fresh season for sour cherries is from June to August.

Our return trips from the Traverse City Cherry Festival were always enriched with a couple of bushels of cherries for canning. My sister and I became proficient cherry pitters, among other mother's helper chores. In those days Father fashioned a wire loop that worked rather well to neatly and quickly extract the pits. Today commercially designed cherry pitters are available in kitchen gadget departments. One style, around $5, pits one cherry at a time; another feeds in and pits two at a time and costs about $15. Had my young mind been more entrepreneurially directed as I picked and pitted, I should have concentrated on such an invention!

The cherries Mother canned went into sauce for fruit compotes, pies and puddings, and jam and jelly. Much of the jam was used as filling in favorite breakfast rolls and coffee cakes, which she baked weekly. I like to use fresh cherries in salads, pies, tarts, cakes, shortcake, ice cream, fruit bowls, and fruit sauces. Sweet or tart cherries are a delicious and glamorous garnish with such fat-rich meats as duck and pork. The recipe is not complicated. Just add some cherries and juice to a clear brown gravy. When there is an overabundance, sweet and sour cherries can be frozen – whole, crushed, or juiced.

A word about maraschino cherries: These are a commercial product made from sweet cherries which are bleached, pitted, and steeped in syrup with a little almond oil and food coloring. The idea seems to have originated in Italy about 300 years ago. At that time white sweet cherries were soaked in a liqueur called maraschino, which was made from marasca cherries.

CHICKEN OR PHEASANT WITH SOUR CREAM SAUCE AND CHERRIES

Poulet ou Faisan aux Cerises

This recipe calls for a whole chicken or pheasant. Another alternative is to use 4 to 6 half breasts of chicken, skinned and boned. With chicken breasts, the recipe can be prepared in a large saute pan on top of the stove, with a cooking time of 15 to 20 minutes.

DO-AHEAD TIP: *Complete recipe can be prepared a day ahead and rewarmed at serving time.*

- **1 3- to 4-pound whole dressed chicken, or 3- to 3½-pound whole dressed pheasant**
- **2 tablespoons light vegetable oil (e.g., safflower)**
- **2 tablespoons unsalted butter**
- **¼ pound firm mushrooms, finely chopped**
- **¼ teaspoon finely chopped fresh garlic**
- **½ teaspoon tomato paste**
- **1 teaspoon meat flavoring (e.g., Marmite brewer's yeast extract, vegetable paste, or meat glaze)**
- **1 tablespoon cornstarch or potato flour**
- **1 cup stock (e.g., chicken, vegetable, or soy—1 cup water with 2 teaspoons tamari soy sauce)**
- **1 cup sour cream**
- **1 cup pitted fresh sweet cherries or canned unsweetened water-packed black cherries**

Preheat oven to 350°F. Dry chicken or pheasant inside and out and tie snugly. Heat oil and 1 tablespoon butter in deep, heavy pot. Add poultry and slowly brown on all sides, turning over and over until skin is translucent and golden. Remove poultry while preparing sauce.

Add to pot 1 tablespoon butter, mushrooms, and garlic, and stir over moderate heat 1 minute. Remove from heat and add tomato paste, meat flavoring, and cornstarch or potato flour, and blend. Add stock and stir over moderate heat until sauce comes to a boil. Using metal whisk, stir in sour cream, spoonful by spoonful.

Carve poultry into serving pieces and add to sauce in pot. Cover pot and cook in oven 35 to 40 minutes, or until poultry is tender.

PRESENTATION: Arrange pieces of poultry on warm heatproof serving platter. Add cherries to sauce in pot and warm over low heat. Spoon sauce over chicken and lightly brown top under broiler.

4 to 6 servings

CHERRIES

SWEET-SOUR CHERRIES

Marinate sour cherries in a spicy honey and vinegar syrup and serve them as a cold hors d'oeuvre, as a condiment with hot or cold serving of pork, veal, turkey, or other poultry, or add some to a brown gravy.

DO-AHEAD TIP: *Cherries must marinate 2 weeks before use and will keep well in refrigerator for 4 to 6 weeks after that.*

- **1 quart (1 ½ to 2 pounds) ripe sour cherries, washed and stemmed but not pitted**
- **1 ½ cups vinegar (plain or cider)**
- **3 whole cloves**
- **¼ teaspoon freshly grated nutmeg**
- **½ stick cinnamon bark**
- **1 bay leaf**
- **¾ cup light honey**

Prick each cherry in 2 or 3 places with ice pick and set aside. Combine vinegar, cloves, nutmeg, cinnamon, bay leaf, and honey in deep, heavy 2-quart pot. Bring mixture to a boil over low heat and simmer 3 minutes to fuse flavors. Add cherries and slowly bring syrup back to a boil. Remove from heat at once and let cool to room temperature. Transfer to 1- or 1½-quart glass jar, cover, and let stand 2 weeks before using. To serve, drain most of syrup from cherries.

Yields 1 quart cherries

SOUR CHERRY PIE

DO-AHEAD TIP: *This pie can be prepared a day ahead.*

PASTRY

- 1½ quantity of dough for Plain Whole Wheat Short Pastry 1 (see Index), with iced orange juice instead of iced water
- 2 tablespoons dry whole wheat bread crumbs
- 2 tablespoons ground almonds

FILLING

- ½ cup light honey
- ¾ cup red currant jelly
- ½ tablespoon cornstarch
- 1 tablespoon orange juice
- 5 cups pitted fresh sour cherries
- 1 egg, beaten

PASTRY: Preheat oven to 375°F. Divide dough into thirds. Refrigerate one-third of dough. Roll two-thirds of dough out to ⅛-inch thickness on lightly floured surface. Line 10- or 11-inch tart pan with dough. Cover pastry with waxed paper and fill with dried beans or raw rice to hold down paper and dough. Bake 25 minutes. Remove weight and waxed paper. Mix bread crumbs and almonds together and spread over surface of pastry shell.

FILLING: Reset oven to 350°F. Combine honey and jelly in 2-quart saucepan and stir over moderate heat until dissolved. Remove from heat. Mix cornstarch with orange juice and stir into honey and jelly mixture. Return pan to moderate heat and stir until sauce becomes thick and clear. Remove from heat and add cherries. Spoon filling into pastry shell.

Roll remaining dough out to ⅛-inch thickness on lightly floured surface. Brush edge of pastry shell with some of beaten egg. Cover pie with dough and trim edges, allowing 1-inch overlap. Press edges together and trim off overlap. Crimp all around with pastry pincers. Make 3 or 4 gashes on top of pastry with sharp knife. Cut small hole in center to allow steam to escape. Roll extra dough out and cut into petal shapes, using pinking shears or knife. Brush with water and arrange in flower pattern around hole in center of pie. Brush top of pie with remaining beaten egg. Bake until golden brown, about 45 to 50 minutes. If necessary, increase oven temperature to 400°F. to brown top.

8 to 10 servings

LE CLAFOUTI

Le clafouti *is an easy-to-prepare and awfully good dessert that originated in the Limousin farm country of France as a large baked pancake with cherries in it (traditionally, the pits were left in the cherries; some claim the pits add flavor). The idea of the* clafouti *also invites the use of other fruits. A shallow baking dish is filled with fruit, crepe batter is poured over it, and the preparation is baked until it becomes a custardlike consistency and the top is browned.*

DO-AHEAD TIP: *The* clafouti *can be prepared a day ahead.*

- **5 tablespoons fine, dry whole wheat bread crumbs**
- **¼ teaspoon ground cardamom**
- **2 to 3 cups pitted or unpitted sweet cherries (or substitute 2 to 3 cups peeled, halved, and pitted fresh apricots, seedless white grapes, halved and pitted Italian prune plums, sliced fresh peaches, sliced fresh pears; or 1½ cups pitted prunes, commercially pitted; not soaked)**
- **3 eggs**
- **5 tablespoons sifted whole wheat pastry flour**
- **2 cups milk or light cream**
- **¼ cup light honey**
- **2 cups Creme Fraiche or Creme Chantilly (optional; see Index)**

Preheat oven to 375°F. Grease 11- to 12-inch shallow round baking dish or pie pan with butter or oil. Mix bread crumbs with cardamom and dust inside of baking dish with mixture. Spread fruit over bottom of dish.

Beat eggs in mixer. Add flour and mix well. Add milk or cream and beat 3 minutes. Add honey and beat 2 minutes. Pour this mixture over fruit in baking dish. Bake 40 to 45 minutes, until top is lightly browned and puffy. Let *clafouti* cool to room temperature or chill it. (Top will deflate.) To serve, cut in wedges. Top each wedge with spoonful of creme fraiche or creme chantilly, if desired.

6 to 8 servings

More Cherry Recipes

See Index for the following recipes:

SOUP: Iced Fruit Soup; DESSERTS: Cobbler, Fruit Fritters, Fruit Shortcake, *Macedoine de Fruits.*

COCONUTS

In Mexico, especially in the state of Guerrero on the Pacific coast (where I have spent a great deal of time in the villages and mountains as well as in Acapulco), *coco*, as the coconut is called in Spanish, conjures up images of large expanses of tall, waving palm trees laden with big and little husk-covered fruits clustered high in the sky just below the fronds. There, through the mountains and coastlands, I love to ride my spirited Pajarito, for a whole day, sometimes two. I am always accompanied by Miguel, my guide and friend, an invaluable help in cutting our passage through thick tropical growth. When we are thirsty, if there is a nearby coconut palm, Miguel will kick off his *huaraches* and, with the grip of his bare feet and hands, climb it – all the way to the top. Soon the sounds of several dull thuds announce the drop of some baby *cocos*. After his descent, Miguel holds a *coco* on its side, raises his machete in his right hand above his shoulder, and, with one swift stroke, slashes off the top quarter of husk and hard shell. Now we are provided with an opening from which to drink cool water and delicate, almost-liquid jelly, which has not yet matured into the familiar, solid, white coconut meat. The ecstasy of this naturally cool, memorably flavorful drink under the steamy hot tropical sun is beyond description.

Local hosts in the area serve whole baby *cocos* in other ways. They are excellent poolside drinks mixed with fresh fruit juices and ice cubes. When dosed with spirit, they become the notorious *coco loco,* or "crazy coconut." Another local specialty, created by a renowned native chef, Leonora, was first served to me at the magnificent Schoenborn estate (the only private home on the Acapulco beach) where she worked. I would like to describe it to you, because it is a perfect example of how cooking is best when it meets nature on the spot. Again, the chef was using the whole baby coconut – in its husk, with top third trimly slashed off. (Native boys are very good at this.) Leonora filled the coconut with her special curry of local fish and shrimp, which was then baked in the husk, mixing with the delicate coconut jelly (the sauce sublime!).

In the serving of it, Leonora had orchestrated an ensemble of Mexican art: natural individual casseroles – whole husk-enclosed coconuts filled with fresh-caught seafood, on handsome hand-painted Tlaquepaque plates lined with banana leaf and garnished with hibiscus flowers, laid with museum-quality Spratling silver flatware. This, on a magnificent outdoor patio overlooking the horizonless Pacific, was a feast made in heaven. Leonora's creation has since been copied by other tropical chefs. My frustration is that it cannot be enjoyed in the United States as long as shippers do not send us baby coconuts in husks. Unfortunately, the coconut palm does not thrive above the southern tip of Florida.

While living in the tropics, one discovers other delicious ways to eat coconut besides the coconut chiffon pie/divinity frosting syndrome. Rich, thick coconut milk (not to be confused with the water that you hear swishing around inside the coconut) can be made from coconuts as sold in the United States. It is the flavorful moisture extracted from the coconut meat – a simple preparation – and is used as a delicious and elegant "cream" topping on tropical fruits in particular, or to enrich and flavor curry sauce. *Cocada* (Mexican coconut custard), coconut ice cream made with coconut milk instead of grated coconut, and rice cooked in coconut water with toasted shredded coconut over the top are other local favorites.

Actually, the coconut is not a nut at all. It is a drupe type of fruit, those that have one large seed in the center, like the peach. The whole coconut fruit consists of an exterior fibrous husk (green colored when young; brown when mature), elliptical in shape, 8 to 12 inches long, which encloses the hard brown shell, which in turn encloses one very large hollow seed of whitish, oily, edible flesh. In the young fruit, this white matter is jelly, which gradually becomes firm. The large central cavity contains about ¼ cup of a watery liquid called coconut water.

Rarely, if ever, are whole coconut fruits shipped to this country. To reduce shipping bulk, the coconut husks are removed in the villages where they are harvested. Often the same workers are engaged to remove the hard shells as well. When passing through these villages, one must circumnavigate mountains of *cocos* that have been unloaded in front of the houses of workers who are employed to prepare them for market. Commercially, the white part is called copra. It has a very high fat content (the plant oil highest in saturated fat) and is used for the manufacture of cooking oil and soaps. In the tropics every part of the coconut tree is used – trunk, bark, leaves, husks, and meat. The roof of Miguel's house in Tres Palos and the sunblinds on the sides of the veranda are of thatched coconut palm fronds, probably from trees only a few yards away. (In Mexico, many *palapas* dot the beaches. *Palapa* means a cabana that has a thatched roof of palm fronds.)

In the United States we are limited to buying coconut either in the hard shell or already grated, usually presweetened, in cans. Coconut in the shell is freshest, and don't be put off, thinking that it is too much trouble. Removing the shell and grating the meat can be simple and quick:

Easy way to remove coconut shell: There are three soft spots in the top of the hard shell. (They resemble a monkeylike face, which is how the "coco-nut" got its name.) Pierce these spots with an ice pick or a screwdriver and drain the water into a container. Place the coconut in a 425°F. oven for 20 to 30 minutes. The hard shell will crack and draw away from the meat. (If you do not have the time to heat the coconut, tap it all over with a hammer until the shell cracks and falls off.) Using a paring knife or peeler, peel the inner brown skin off the white meat. Rinse the meat.

Quick way to grate coconut: Cut the peeled coconut meat into chunks and process in a food processor until finely grated. *To shred coconut,* you must use a shredder. Grated and shredded coconut keep well in the freezer.

AMBROSIA

The name of this classic American dish translates to fruit salad "with coconut." Ambrosia is a must on many Thanksgiving, Christmas, and family party tables.

DO-AHEAD TIP: *Orange, pineapple, and coconut can be readied a day ahead. Add bananas and sour cream at serving time.*

1 cup mandarin orange sections, well drained (navel orange sections can be substituted)

1 cup pineapple chunks, well drained

1 cup sliced bananas, not too ripe (3/8-inch-thick slices)

1 cup shredded fresh coconut, loosely packed

1 cup thick sour cream, or 3/4 cup yogurt blended with 1/2 cup nonfat dry milk

At serving time, combine all ingredients and mix gently with rubber spatula. Serve in large bowl or on lettuce leaves on individual salad plates.

6 servings

COCONUT CONFECTIONS

DO-AHEAD TIP: *These confections keep well in refrigerator or freezer.*

APRICOT-COCONUT BALLS

- ½ cup sour cream
- 2 tablespoons light honey
- 1½ pounds dried apricots
- ½ pound grated coconut
- ½ cup grated coconut or finely chopped toasted almonds, for coating

Mix sour cream and honey until blended and set aside. Chop apricots finely in food processor. Add coconut and sour cream and honey mixture, and process until mixed. With floured hands, roll mixture into little balls, about the size of walnuts. Then roll in coconut or almonds. Store in refrigerator or freezer. Serve in little paper candy cases.

Makes about 32 balls

COCONUT-MOLASSES CHEWS

- ¼ cup light honey
- ½ cup molasses
- 1 tablespoon white or cider vinegar
- 2 tablespoons unsalted butter
- 2 cups shredded coconut

Combine honey, molasses, vinegar, and butter in 3-cup saucepan and stir over low heat until mixture boils. Insert candy thermometer and continue boiling to 240°F. Remove from heat and add coconut. Drop from two forks on greased baking sheet. Freeze. Serve in individual paper candy cases.

Makes about 36 pieces

COCONUT CURLS

Serve these crisp, toasted, curly strips of fresh coconut in little nut dishes as an unusual and delicious snack or hors d'oeuvre. Also, they are dramatic as garnish with cold and hot fish, shellfish, poultry dishes, and salads and as decoration on all kinds of desserts, including fruit and ice cream. Coconut curls will keep several weeks in closed, airtight jar.

1 coconut

Preheat oven to 350°F. Remove coconut pulp from shell in as large pieces as possible. Peel off brown skin. Take a chunk of pulp and, using peeler, pare off thin strips of pulp 2 to 4 inches long. (They come away as curls.) Pare as much pulp as possible into curls. (Remaining small pieces of pulp can be put in food processor and grated for other use.)

Spread coconut curls on baking sheet or jelly roll pan lined with aluminum foil. Toast until golden brown, turning curls occasionally with wooden spoon. Let cool.

COCONUT MILK
Leche de Coco

DO-AHEAD TIP: *Coconut milk keeps well in refrigerator for about a week.*

1 coconut

1 cup boiling water

Remove coconut water (about 1/4 cup) and coconut meat from shell. Peel coconut meat and cut into chunks. Process meat in food processor until very finely grated. Add coconut water and process again.

To make thick coconut milk, put grated coconut in damp cloth over bowl. Twist cloth tightly to squeeze out as much liquid as possible. (This is a very rich and creamy coconut extract, a great treat spooned over fresh tropical fruits such as papayas, mangoes, mameys, bananas, guavas, oranges, and fruit puddings.)

To make light coconut milk, after extracting thick coconut milk, transfer grated coconut from cloth to empty bowl and mix with water. Let stand 30 minutes. Again pour through damp cloth, squeezing out as much liquid as possible. Combine with thick coconut milk in screwtop jar and shake well. Discard grated coconut (which is now too dry for most purposes), or use in place of bran in muffins. (Light coconut milk also has a rich coconut flavor. For more coconut accent in custard, ice cream, curry sauce, pastry cream, and the like, use it as all or part of the liquid ingredient.

Yields 1/3 to 1/2 cup thick coconut milk or 1 to 1 1/2 cups light coconut milk

COCONUT-FRIED SHRIMP WITH CURRY DIPPING SAUCE

Not the least attraction of this novel appetizer or main dish is the speed and convenience of its preparation. No batter to prepare; just coat the shrimp with coconut when convenient. Curry dipping sauce is made quickly in the blender or food processor. When shrimp coated with shreds of coconut are deep-fried, they look as though they were covered with crisp, crunchy cactus needles.

DO-AHEAD TIP: *Coconut-coated shrimp can be frozen or refrigerated. Sauce can be prepared a day ahead. Deep-fry shrimp at serving time.*

SHRIMP

1 pound raw shrimp, shelled and deveined, with tails on (for appetizer, use medium-size shrimp—about 40 to 1 pound; for main dish, use jumbo shrimp—about 24 to 1 pound)

about ½ cup whole wheat pastry flour

1 egg, beaten

1 cup shredded coconut

CURRY DIPPING SAUCE

2 tablespoons coconut butter or unsalted butter

½ cup finely chopped yellow onions

½ cup chopped peeled apples

1 medium-size banana, chopped

3 tablespoons mango chutney

2 teaspoons curry powder

1 teaspoon tamari soy sauce

cayenne pepper

½ cup stock (e.g., chicken, vegetable, or soy—1 cup water with 1 teaspoon tamari soy sauce)

½ cup Coconut Milk (see recipe in this section), or additional stock

SHRIMP: Arrange shrimp, flour, egg, and coconut on work surface. Dust each shrimp lightly with flour, dip in egg, and pat generously with coconut.

Heat oil in deep fryer to 350°F., using deep-fry thermometer. Fry coconut-coated shrimp until golden brown. Carefully remove with slotted spoon onto paper towels to drain. (Try to avoid breaking the crisp coconut shreds.)

CURRY DIPPING SAUCE: Melt butter in 1-quart saucepan. Add onions, apples, banana, chutney, curry powder, tamari, and a dash of cayenne pepper. Stir mixture over moderate heat 3 minutes, or until onions and apples are soft. Add stock and coconut milk and bring sauce to a boil. Simmer 2 minutes.

Puree sauce in food processor or blender. Return sauce to pan over low heat. Barely simmer 30 minutes.

PRESENTATION: For appetizer or main course serving, arrange shrimp in a circle on a warm napkin on serving tray. Place small bowl of sauce in center.

6 servings as main dish or 20 as appetizer

COCADA
Mexican Coconut Custard

DO-AHEAD TIP: Cocada *should be prepared a day ahead in order for custard to chill and set.*

- 3 cups light cream
- ½ cup light honey
- 1 cup finely grated fresh coconut
- 2 whole eggs
- 4 egg yolks
- 1 teaspoon almond extract
- 2 tablespoons slivered or sliced blanched almonds

In deep, heavy 2-quart pot, combine cream and honey and stir over low heat until mixture is blended. Add coconut, reduce heat to *very low*, and cook until coconut becomes translucent. Stir occasionally to avoid scorching. Remove from heat.

In small bowl, combine whole eggs, egg yolks, and almond extract. Add about 4 tablespoons cream mixture. Stir cream and egg mixture into remaining cream mixture in pot. Return pot to low heat and stir with wire whisk until mixture thickens and coats the back of a spoon, but do not boil or custard will curdle.

PRESENTATION: Transfer custard to individual ramekins or heatproof serving dish. Refrigerate until chilled and set. At serving time, sprinkle almonds on top and brown under broiler.

6 servings

More Coconut Recipes

See Index for the following recipes:

DESSERTS: Coconut-Crumb Crust, Fig-Honey Cookies, Rich Coconut Ice Cream; BEVERAGES: Coco-Carob, Coco-Limon, Coco-Piña.

CRANBERRIES

The recent wave of "cooking liberation," born under the banner of "*la nouvelle cuisine*," can take credit for stirring new excitement into this native American fruit, too long relegated to a few traditional holiday uses. Today professional chefs and cooks at home are brightening menus with cranberry soup, cranberry sauces for fish and meat as well as poultry, cranberry salad, cranberry souffle, plus pudding, sherbet, and ice cream featuring cranberries. At the same time, cranberry's classic relishes and jellies remain as firmly entrenched on our appetites as ever.

In America, the Indians, early explorers, and colonists ate cranberries as a food and for health. Then, as now, wild cranberries existed throughout the continent. The Indians cooked them with honey and maple syrup and dried them for winter use. A staple of their diet was *pemmican*, a combination of mashed cranberries and dried and pounded meat of bison, deer, or other wild game mixed with animal fat, a portable food they carried on their hunting forays, much as today's hikers and skiers tote their gorp on the trails.

The white settlers called these ruby red berries which they found in marshlands "*craneberries*" (perhaps because the blossom on its slender curved stem resembled the neck of a crane), which eventually contracted to "*cranberry*." But the Indians called the fruit by names reflecting its acid taste. The Pequots on Cape Cod called it *i-bimi* or "bitter fruit." The Narragansetts used the name *sassamesh*, meaning a sharp and cooling fruit. The Algonquins in Wisconsin called it *atoqua*, the Chippewas, *A-nibibim*. Even the old Latin generic name *oxycoccus* means sour berry.

The New Englanders liked the cranberry's keeping quality and discovered that the ground-hugging vine could be cultivated easily in the presence of a good water supply. They had developed the cranberry into an industry by the nineteenth century, and many clipper ships leaving New England ports stowed a supply of cranberries to provide fresh food for long days at sea. It seemed to ward off the dreaded scurvy. (As we now know, the cranberry contains a fair amount of scurvy-fighting vitamin C.)

Our use of cranberries as a year-round, versatile food is long overdue. The fruit has many cooking advantages. Cranberries are colorful and flavorful in all sorts of preparations; they are highly nutritious; and they keep well in the refrigerator and the freezer. Cranberries contain most vitamins and minerals, notably iron and potassium as well as vitamin C, with a low level of sodium. (One cup of cranberries contains 46 milligrams of vitamin C, which is comparable to the value in one orange or half a grapefruit.) They are rich in pectin, which is why they jell when cooked with sugar or honey. Their fresh season is from

CRANBERRIES

September to January, but they can be refrigerated for about a month, and when properly bagged (whole, plain – without sugar – or in syrup), they will keep in the freezer for about a year. (For cooking, it is not necessary to thaw frozen cranberries.)

Most of our cranberry supply comes from commercial sources. For good quality, look for berries that are plump, firm, and shiny. When preparing them for use, pick them over and discard dark and soft berries, wash, and drain well. Until a couple of years ago, the standard commercial package contained one pound of fruit, measuring four cups, which would yield one quart of whole or jellied sauce. Recently, cranberries have been sold in 12-ounce packages (three cups of berries). Be sure to note the weight of the package you buy.

Americans are adamant about their favorite style of cranberry sauce or relish with Thanksgiving dinner. I am downright addicted to raw cranberry and orange relish and always prepare extra to eat with leftover turkey. A delicious way to eat leftover cranberry sauce (the cooked kind) is on pancakes, with sour cream, the way the Swedes serve their lingonberry sauce. (Lingonberries are of the cranberry family.) Actually, there are species of cranberries in Europe and Asia as well as in America. It's the big berry that was discovered in America that has captured the cook's fancy, because it's fleshy and sweet with the right touch of tart.

CRANBERRY-BANANA TARTLETS

DO-AHEAD TIP: *Tartlets can be refrigerated for a day or two.*

8 baked 3½- or 4-inch tartlet shells of Plain Whole Wheat Short Pastry 1 or 2 (see Index)

4 bananas, thinly sliced

2 cups strained Cranberry Sauce or Cranberry Jelly (see recipes in this section)

1 cup heavy cream, whipped (optional)

Fill tartlet shells with sliced bananas. Rewarm cranberry sauce or jelly, let cool to room temperature, and spoon over bananas. Chill tartlets. If desired, put whipped cream in pastry bag fitted with small star tube (#3 or #4) and pipe border around each tartlet.

Makes 8 tartlets

CRANBERRY DRESSING

This poultry dressing can be baked separately or stuffed in fowl.

DO-AHEAD TIP: *Mixture can be made a day ahead. Cook at serving time.*

- **10 cups soft whole wheat bread cubes**
- **1 cup strong stock (e.g., chicken, vegetable, or soy—1 cup water with 2 teaspoons tamari soy sauce)**

Put bread cubes in large mixing bowl. Warm stock and pour over bread cubes. Let soak for a moment.

- **½ cup water**
- **¼ cup light honey**
- **2 cups firm fresh cranberries**

Combine water and honey in 1-quart pot and bring to a boil. Add cranberries, cover, and cook until skins burst. Set aside.

- **4 tablespoons light vegetable oil (e.g., safflower)**
- **1½ cups finely chopped yellow onions**
- **1 cup finely chopped celery**
- **1 teaspoon tamari soy sauce**
- **¾ cup finely chopped fresh parsley**
- **1 tablespoon dried sage**
- **freshly ground black pepper**

Combine oil, onions, and celery in saute pan and cook over moderate heat until onions are soft but not browned. (Celery should still be crunchy.) Add tamari, parsley, sage, and pepper.

- **2 eggs, beaten**

Add cranberry mixture, onion and celery mixture, and beaten eggs to soaked bread. Mix lightly with wooden spoon. Stuff into fowl or bake separately.

To bake dressing separately, preheat oven to 325°F. and put dressing in oiled baking dish. If roasting juices of fowl are available, drizzle them over dressing. Bake 35 to 40 minutes, or until heated through and cooked a little.

Yields about 8 cups (8 to 10 servings)

CRANBERRIES

CRANBERRY-ORANGE RELISH

DO-AHEAD TIP: *This relish should be made at least a day ahead to let flavors marry. It will keep in refrigerator up to a week.*

3 cups firm fresh cranberries

2 small or medium-size oranges (preferably seedless), quartered

⅔ cup light honey

Put cranberries and orange sections through coarse blade of food grinder, then into glass or earthenware bowl. Add honey and mix well. Cover with plastic wrap and let relish stand in refrigerator at least 24 hours before serving.

PRESENTATION: Serve in relish bowl. To garnish turkey, serve in star-cut orange cups (see the section on oranges).

Yields 4 to 5 cups

CRANBERRY JELLY

DO-AHEAD TIP: *Cranberry jelly will keep in refrigerator for about a week.*

- 3 cups firm fresh cranberries
- ⅔ cup water
- ⅔ cup light honey
- 2 teaspoons grated orange rind
- 1 tablespoon unflavored gelatin
- 2 tablespoons orange juice

Put berries in saucepan and add water. Bring to a boil, cover, and cook until skins burst. Rub through strainer and return strained puree to pan. Add honey and orange rind and cook over low heat 10 minutes. Mix gelatin with orange juice and add to cranberry puree. Stir over low heat until gelatin is dissolved. Let cool to room temperature. Pour into serving dish and chill.

Yields about 4 cups

CRANBERRY SAUCE

DO-AHEAD TIP: *Cranberry sauce will keep for about a week in refrigerator.*

- 3 cups firm fresh cranberries
- ⅔ cup water
- ⅔ cup light honey
- 2 teaspoons grated orange rind

Put berries in saucepan and add water. Bring to a boil, cover, and cook until skins burst. Add honey and orange rind, and cook 5 minutes. Chill.

Yields about 4 cups

More Cranberry Recipes

See Index for the following recipes:

DESSERT: Cranberry-Lime Sublime; BEVERAGE: Cran-Raspberry Froth.

CURRANTS

Being an incurable romantic, the sight of fresh red currants always suggests to me a brooch of rubies on a spray of jade. In practice, chefs do regard currants as the rubies of their art. They consider them essential for adding color and sparkle to fruit sauces, as glaze over red or dark fruits on open-face tarts (the way apricot syrup is used over light fruits), and as toppings on all manner of puddings, souffles, and cookies. They are favored as a filling and as a glaze for cakes, useful for making decorative red patterns on fancy pastries, and they serve as the perfect "piquante" with game.

The English are surely the most avid connoisseurs of currants. Mrs. Beeton's cookbook not only gives recipes for puddings, dumplings, tarts, jams, and jellies, but also a passionate discussion of currants' curative powers. Her discourse goes on to delineate the distinctions of the different species: "White flesh-coloured currants, with the exception of the fullness of flavor, in every respect have the same qualities as the red . . . Both white and red currants are pleasant additions to the dessert, but the black variety is mostly for culinary and medicinal purposes, especially in the form of jelly for quinseys [sore throat]. The leaves of the black currant make pleasant tea."

When I spy fresh currants in the market, which could be anytime from June to August, I buy a supply and organize my annual salute to this marvelous little berry. Fresh red currants call for English summer pudding, traditionally a mold filled with layers of stale bread soaked overnight with red currant and raspberry juices, accompanied by a bowl of creamy English custard sauce. I use Dione Lucas's mother's recipe, and old-fashioned though it is, the dish is fit for company. I also like to freeze some currant sauce – one of the mandatory accompaniments with Scottish roast pheasant (the others are bread sauce and fried bread crumbs) – or to serve with any plain-roasted poultry, lamb, or veal.

In classical cooking, currant jelly is called for often as syrup or sauce, which is made by merely warming and dissolving the jelly. It is brushed over fruit toppings, cakes, and pastries. In the recipe for *Riz a l'Imperatrice*, whole strawberries are dipped in currant jelly syrup for a shiny red glaze and dropped on clouds of fluffy rice custard. For a Sunday brunch special, pour currant jelly syrup over buckwheat or whole wheat pancakes with a dab of sour cream or creme fraiche. For a quickie dessert, swirl currant syrup through banana ice cream or sherbet – a divine combination of tart and bland. White currants seem to be as rare as white truffles. If you should find some, show them off simply by strewing them over a fresh salad or fruit cup.

CURRANT AND GREEN TOMATO CHUTNEY

1½ cups cleaned fresh red currants

2¼ cups chopped green tomatoes

2¼ cups chopped peeled tart apples

1 lemon, quartered, seeds removed, thinly sliced

1 cup finely chopped onions

1 teaspoon finely chopped fresh garlic

½ cup light honey

½ cup white or cider vinegar

½ cup water

1 tablespoon mustard seeds

¼ teaspoon cayenne pepper

1 teaspoon ground ginger

Combine all ingredients in deep, heavy pot. Simmer 20 minutes, or until fruit is soft. Pack into sterilized jars, leaving ¼ inch headspace. Adjust caps and process 5 minutes in boiling water bath.

Yields 2 pints

ENGLISH SUMMER PUDDING

Currants and raspberries are the traditional fruits for this pudding, but other available juicy berry fruit can also be used, such as strawberries, blackberries, or blueberries.

DO-AHEAD TIP: *This dessert should be prepared at least a day before serving to allow it to become thoroughly soaked with fruit juice, chilled, and set. Custard sauce should also be made a day ahead in order to chill.*

3/4 cup light honey

1/4 cup water

4 cups cleaned fresh red currants

4 cups cleaned fresh raspberries

about 2 loaves whole wheat bread, sliced

English Custard Sauce (see Index)

Put honey and water in 3-quart heavy pot and warm over low heat until mixed. Add currants and raspberries and cook about 5 minutes over low heat, until currants are tender. Stir mixture gently; do not break fruit too much. Taste and add more honey, if necessary.

Trim crusts from bread. Completely line 2-quart round bowl or springform mold with bread, using about one-fourth of bread. Spoon some fruit and syrup over bread, then add another layer of bread. Continue to alternate fruit and bread layers until all ingredients are used, ending with bread layer. Cover pudding with double piece of waxed paper and a flat plate that will fit inside the mold on top of pudding. Place a heavy weight, like a brick, on the plate and let pudding stand in refrigerator overnight.

PRESENTATION: Remove weight, plate, and waxed paper from pudding. Place serving plate on top of mold, invert, and turn out pudding. Serve chilled custard sauce in separate bowl.

8 to 10 servings

CURRANTS

FRESH CURRANT SAUCE

This is a very utilitarian sauce. Serve it with roast poultry and meats and with sweets such as pancakes, fresh fruit or fruit compote, ice cream, or custard; or use it for a sherbet base.

DO-AHEAD TIP: *Currant sauce keeps well in freezer.*

- **3/4 cup water**
- **3/4 cup light honey**
- **4 cups cleaned fresh red currants**
- **1 tablespoon fresh lemon juice**

Combine water and honey in saucepan and warm over low heat until blended. Add currants and lemon juice and bring to a boil. Reduce heat to low and simmer 5 minutes, or until currants are tender. Rub mixture through fine strainer. Let cool.

Yields 4 cups

FRESH CURRANT SHERBET

DO-AHEAD TIP: *Sherbet will keep well in freezer for 2 or 3 days. After that it will tend to become icy.*

- **2 teaspoons unflavored gelatin**
- **3 tablespoons orange juice**
- **4 cups Fresh Currant Sauce (see recipe in this section)**

Combine gelatin and orange juice in small saucepan and stir over low heat until dissolved. Stir into currant sauce. Pour mixture into drum of electric freezer and process according to manufacturer's instructions until sherbet is firm.

Yields about 4 cups

DATES

Soaring date palms with their spiring fronds and hanging clusters of golden fruits are ubiquitous in scenes of North African countries. When we traveled the length of Tunisia, there they were – everywhere! They provided a cool and serene presence in a searing sea of sand. In Monastir, they provided a majestic canopy over the ranging landscape of the presidential summer palace. They seem to stand guard at the entrance of every mosque. When the time came for us to depart the town of Sousse, Bouden Abderrazak, a camel boy from the nearby village of Kalaä Kebira, who was learning French in school and had become our self-appointed guide and friend, presented us with a gift "from the house of my father": It was a sack containing fresh dates, hard-cooked eggs, and a bottle of green olive oil made by his mother. This, he explained, was to sustain us on our long journey back to America. In fact, these foods represented the staples of the desert diet.

In this land of antiquity, the people eat mostly fresh dates, plain – as they come from the tree. Even modern hotels and restaurants in the area usually serve them that way, and rarely in preparations. Although dates are a relatively new crop in the United States, we Americans have invented all kinds of ways to eat dates, and we devour them with a passion, on cereal, in hors d'oeuvres, salads, breads and muffins, cakes, cookies and bars, pies, pudding, ice cream, frozen yogurt, dessert fillings, and after-dinner sweets.

Since the date tree can survive only in dry tropical climates, its existence in the United States is limited to the desert areas of California and Arizona, where date farming has become a thriving industry. It is useful to consumers to be familiar with the three general types of dates: soft, semisoft, and dry or bread dates. The soft are lowest in sugar and most perishable; they must be kept in cold storage. The semisoft have a high sugar content and will keep in a plastic container in the refrigerator for months. The dry also have a high sugar content and a dry, hard flesh that has limited their popularity with consumers.

Most of the dates sold in this country are the semisoft type, and they in turn can be classified by type of sugar. The Deglet Noor (meaning "date of light" in Arabic) contains sucrose or cane-type sugar. The Halawy, Zahidi, and Khadrawy contain invert sugar – a natural sugar like honey, composed of dextrose and levulose. Packaged "date sugar" is pulverized dates. It is excellent as topping over cereal and fruit, but it is not satisfactory for cooking or baking because it does not dissolve.

Indeed, dates are high concentrates of sugar – 60 to 65 percent, qualifying them as nature's candies or good quick energy food. Thus, they are high in calories, 274 in 100 grams, mostly carbohydrate with a good supply of iron and copper.

Few of us are likely to have a date palm in the backyard or to have the opportunity of seeing fresh-growing dates. Consequently, one of the fascinations of my tour through Tunisia was a close-up view of producing date palms. The fruit starts out a greenish-yellow to lemon color. When it reaches its maximum size, it is coral red or apricot orange. When it begins to soften at the tip, and until it is cured, it is amber. When it begins to dry, it is light brown or straw colored (as one finds it in the markets in Tunisia). When it is fully dried, it is a slightly deeper brown, as we know it in packages stocked by most stores.

Although dates are available in supermarkets year-round, the main marketing season is September to May, with the peak in November. Ideally, they should be stored in refrigeration at a temperature between 30° and 40°F. The lower the temperature, the longer they will retain their original quality. Dates should not be stored near flour or cereal or any other items that might be infested, nor should they be stored near onions, fish, or other odorous items, since dates tend to absorb such odors. Many recipes call for chopped dates; today this chore can be accomplished quickly in the food processor.

STUFFED DATE HORS D'OEUVRES

BROILED STUFFED DATES

DO-AHEAD TIP: *Dates can be stuffed a day ahead. Heat at serving time.*

- **24 blanched almonds**
- **24 pitted dates**
- **1 teaspoon freshly ground white pepper**
- **½ teaspoon freshly grated nutmeg**
- **2 teaspoons dry mustard**
- **2 teaspoons tamari soy sauce**
- **1 teaspoon light vegetable oil (e.g., safflower)**

Stuff almonds into dates and reshape. In small mixing bowl, combine pepper, nutmeg, mustard, tamari, and oil and mix well. Add stuffed dates, turn them to coat evenly with mixture, and allow to marinate 3 hours, or longer.

At serving time, preheat oven to 350°F. Arrange stuffed dates on baking sheet and place in oven until heated through.

PRESENTATION: An attractive way to serve the stuffed dates is to insert a cocktail pick into each one and stick them into a head of red or green cabbage on serving tray. Serve hot.

Makes 24 pieces

STUFFED DATE HORS D'OEUVRES – continued

PEANUT BUTTER STUFFED DATES

Serve these as a cold hors d'oeuvre.

pitted dates

peanut butter

horseradish

Fill dates with peanut butter mixed with a small amount of horseradish.

DATE AND ORANGE SALAD

DO-AHEAD TIP: *Ingredients can be prepared a day ahead. Arrange on salad plates at serving time.*

SALAD
- 6 large, crisp lettuce leaves
- 36 orange sections
- 18 pitted dates
- 18 walnut or pecan halves

DRESSING
- 3 ounces cream cheese, or ½ cup Basic Mayonnaise (see Index)
- ½ cup heavy cream, whipped

SALAD: Place a lettuce leaf on each of 6 individual serving plates. Arrange 6 orange sections on each plate, in a circle like spokes of a wheel. Close to center, between orange sections, put alternating pieces of dates and nuts.

DRESSING: If cream cheese is used, beat in mixer until creamy. Add creamed cheese or mayonnaise to whipped cream and fold together with rubber spatula. Put spoonful of dressing in center of each arrangement.

6 servings

DATE-NUT BARS

DO-AHEAD TIP: *Date-nut bars will keep well for several weeks in airtight container or freezer.*

- **6 eggs**
- **¾ cup light honey**
- **1½ cups sifted whole wheat pastry flour**
- **1½ teaspoons baking powder (without aluminum salts)**
- **2 cups walnuts, coarsely chopped, or pecans**
- **1 cup pitted dates, chopped**

Preheat oven to 350°F. Brush 11 by 17-inch jelly roll pan with oil, line with waxed paper, and brush with oil again.

Combine eggs and honey in mixer and beat until light and foamy. Sift flour and baking powder together. Add to egg and honey mixture and mix only until well blended. Add nuts and dates and mix. Spread mixture in prepared pan. Bake about 30 minutes, or until cake rebounds to touch. To turn out of pan, run sharp knife around edge of cake to loosen. Lay 2 sheets of waxed paper on top of cake, invert pan onto work surface, and lift away pan. Quickly remove waxed paper that is now on top. With large French knife, cut into 1 by 3-inch bars.

Makes about 48 bars

More Date Recipes

See Index for the following recipes:

DESSERTS: Date-Nut Ice Cream, *Dulce de Camote.*

FIGS

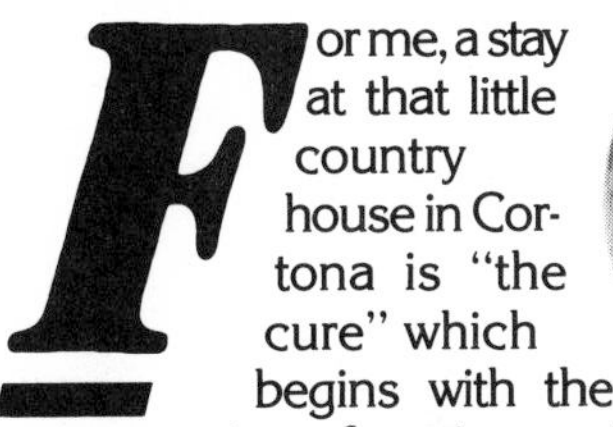

For me, a stay at that little country house in Cortona is "the cure" which begins with the mere routine of getting up in the morning, opening the shutters and heavy double doors to let the sunshine in, to see the closeup trees, the overhead arbors, and the flowers all around. Truly, a "born again" feeling! During the late summer, on the old millstone by the front door, there will be a dozen or so fresh figs (*ficos*, in Italian), picked by Angiola or Guido that morning, for our breakfast. Fresh figs from our own trees – with yogurt, or cream, or a squeeze of orange juice! (I used to be embarrassed to think of these elderly caretakers of our land having walked the five miles or so from the hill town of Cortona and already tending to their chores by 7:30. Now I regard them as inspiration. Angiola and Guido are handsome examples of how to age happily and healthily.)

The fig tree is a fascinating plant. Its large, flat, wavy leaves look as though they had been cut out in arts and crafts class. The fruit grows directly from the branches of the tree, like a series of shoots, each one a stem ending in a bulbous pod. In fact, what we call the fig is actually a fleshy pod containing many fruits, or seeds. (Each fig contains about 1,600 edible seeds.) I think it is a pretty tree and a fine shade tree to have in the yard; or, maybe that is due to Guido's pruning.

Fig trees can thrive in most climates with a bit of special care during the cold season. For commercial production, figs are grown in more arid areas, such as the desert regions of California, where the fruit can be left on the tree without deterioration until it is ripe enough to drop of its own accord. (For fresh fruit shipment, however, the figs are never allowed to drop.)

Dried figs and preserved figs are fine for certain uses, especially during the off-season, but fresh figs are an entirely different character of fruit and they have a reasonably long market period, from June to November. Figs must be tree ripened to reach their full sugar content and best eating quality. When ripe, they are soft and vary in color according to type. Remember that fresh figs are sensitive to weather; they spoil more quickly in damp, muggy, rainy weather than when it is bright and clear.

Better than half of the figs in this country are Calimyrna. These are large with golden yellow skin, amber pulp, and excellent flavor. Mission, or Black Mission, got its name from the Spanish mission gardens of California. Its skin is purplish-black, and it is medium to large when harvested in the early summer and medium to small when harvested in the late summer. The Kadota fig (or Dottato,

which we have in Italy) is medium to large with yellowish-green skin and amber or violet pulp. It ripens in the late summer or fall. In America, dried figs are usually Calimyrna or Mission type, and the canned are Kadota.

Serve fresh figs whole, halved, quartered, or sliced. If the skin is thin, it need not be peeled. Should you wish to peel a fig, begin at the stem, pull the skin off in strips, and scoop out the seeds and flesh with a spoon. Fresh figs are good in fruit salad (a lovely combination is fresh figs, blueberries, shredded coconut, banana slices, and cantaloupe chunks). You can also enjoy figs as appetizers stuffed with cheese; as garnish with braised beef, pork, poultry, or game; stewed or baked and topped with thick cream or coconut milk or custard; or pureed for use in puddings, pies, or parfaits. Dried figs can be used in batter breads, cakes, cookies, dessert fillings, and as quick-energy snacks.

DUCK BRAISED WITH FRESH FIGS

DO-AHEAD TIP: *Duck and figs can be cooked a day ahead. At serving time, cook vegetables, rewarm duck, and assemble dish.*

DUCK

- **2 4-pound whole dressed ducks**
- **freshly ground black pepper**
- **2 small oranges, quartered**
- **2 small onions, quartered**
- **1 garlic clove, halved**
- **24 fresh figs**

BROWN SAUCE

- **4 tablespoons unsalted butter**
- **1 cup mixed sliced onions, carrots, celery, and leeks**
- **1 tablespoon cornstarch or potato flour**
- **2 teaspoons tomato paste**
- **2 teaspoons meat flavoring (e.g., Marmite brewer's yeast extract, vegetable paste, or meat glaze)**
- **½ cup chopped mushrooms**
- **1 medium-size ripe tomato, not peeled, cut into eighths**

DUCK: Preheat oven to 375°F. Dry ducks inside and out with paper towels. Season cavities with pepper and insert oranges, onions, and garlic. Tie ducks snugly. Prick skin all over to release fat. Place on rack in roasting pan. Pour ½ cup water in pan and roast 20 minutes. Reduce oven temperature to 350°F. and roast duck another 30 minutes. Remove from oven and let cool a little. Leave oven set at 350°F.

BROWN SAUCE: Melt butter in 1-quart saucepan. Add mixed vegetables and cook over moderate heat about 3 minutes. Remove from heat and add cornstarch or potato flour, tomato paste, meat flavoring, mushrooms, and tomato. Add stock and stir over moderate heat until sauce comes to a boil. Reduce heat to low and let sauce barely simmer about 5 minutes.

Cut legs off ducks, cut them into drumsticks and thighs, and place in large casserole. Cut figs in quarters and place on top of duck legs. Cut breast halves in whole pieces away from bone and slice lengthwise. Arrange breast slices, overlapping on top of figs. Strain brown sauce, add chopped truffle, if desired, and pour sauce over duck. Cover casserole with waxed paper and lid, and cook in oven 30 to 45 minutes, or until duck is tender.

CROUTONS: Trim crusts from bread. Cut each slice in half diagonally to make 12 triangular croutons. Fry in butter or oil until golden brown on both sides.

DUCK BRAISED WITH FRESH FIGS—continued

2 cups stock (e.g., chicken, vegetable, or soy—2 cups water with 3 teaspoons tamari soy sauce)

1 black truffle, finely chopped (optional)

CROUTONS
6 slices bread

VEGETABLES
2 cups diced raw green beans

2 cups diced carrots

2 cups diced turnips

VEGETABLES: Cook green beans, carrots, and turnips together (in steamer or boiling water) until just tender.

PRESENTATION: Arrange bed of diced vegetables on warm serving platter. Arrange leg pieces of duck on vegetables in center. Around side, spread layer of figs, and on top of them arrange breast slices. Spoon sauce over duck. Stick fried croutons like points around dish.

6 to 8 servings

FIG-HONEY COOKIES

For milk-and-cookies break or tiny petits fours secs.

DO-AHEAD TIP: *Cookies can be stored for several weeks in airtight container or freezer.*

1 cup dried figs

½ cup unsalted butter

2 eggs

¾ cup light honey

2 tablespoons milk

3 cups sifted whole wheat pastry flour

3 teaspoons baking powder (without aluminum salts)

½ cup grated or shredded coconut

1 teaspoon lemon flavoring

3 tablespoons grated orange rind

Preheat oven to 400°F. Line baking sheet with waxed paper and oil waxed paper. Put figs in heavy pot and cover with cold water. Bring to a boil and simmer 10 minutes. Drain figs and cut into small dice.

In mixer, beat butter until light and creamy; remove from bowl and set aside. Beat eggs and honey in mixer until light and thick. Add butter and beat again. Then add milk and beat until well mixed.

Sift flour and baking powder together and add to batter. Add figs, coconut, lemon flavoring, and orange rind. Drop dabs of dough from teaspoon onto baking sheet (heaping for large cookies: ¾ inch for petits fours). Bake 12 to 20 minutes, depending on size of drops.

Makes about 2 dozen drops, 1½ inches each, or 4 dozen petits fours, ¾ inch each

FIGS

FIG AND TOMATO SALAD

DO-AHEAD TIP: *Ingredients can be readied a day ahead. Arrange salad at serving time.*

- 6 large lettuce leaves
- 6 large ripe figs, quartered
- 6 small ripe tomatoes, quartered
- ½ cup Basic Mayonnaise (see Index)
- 2 tablespoons chopped walnuts or pecans

Place a lettuce leaf on each of 6 individual salad plates. On each, arrange circle of alternating wedges of figs and tomatoes. Put spoonful of mayonnaise in center. Sprinkle with nuts.

6 servings

STUFFED FIG HORS D'OEUVRE

DO-AHEAD TIP: *Figs can be stuffed a day ahead and refrigerated.*

- 4 ounces goat cheese or cream cheese
- 12 small fresh or dried figs

Beat cheese in mixer until creamy. Cut small slits in side of figs and stuff with cheese. Chill in refrigerator.

Makes 12 pieces

More Fig Recipes

See Index for the following recipes:

SALAD: Tossed Greens Salad with Fruit; DESSERT: *Macedoine de Fruits.*

GRAPEFRUIT

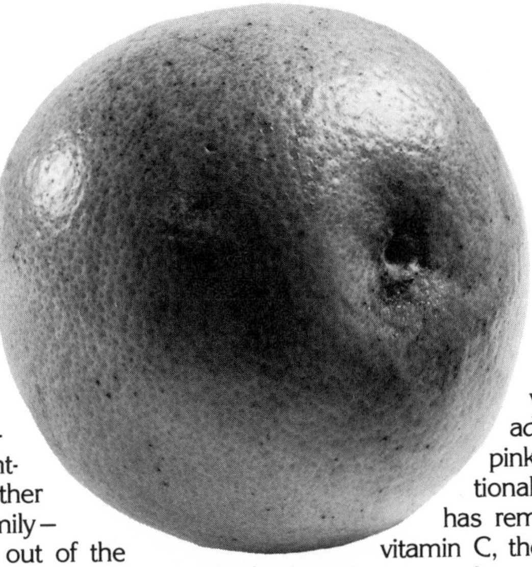

Our American grapefruit is a good 'n' genuine miracle of modern agriculture, which recently added yet another wonder to this favorite fruit family – a beautiful Star Ruby rising out of the Lone Star State. This new variety of grapefruit is instantly recognizable by its reddish-gold skin, with flesh a deeper red than that of the pinks, and a flavor that suggests overtones of apple and strawberry – a taste so perfectly balanced that it welcomes eating out of hand!

Before the end of the last century, most Americans had never even heard of the grapefruit, let alone eaten it. Its antecedent, the *pomelo*, is a fruit long rooted in the tropics (probably native to Asia). The Spaniards apparently planted the *pomelo* tree in the West Indies, where it was also called "shaddock," but gradually came to be called "grapefruit." The plant did not hit United States soil until 1823, in Florida. Then the grapefruit was a smallish, stringy fruit with many seeds and little juice, and not very much production. Then, around 1880, refrigerated shipping made it possible to transport the fruit long distances.

Fade . . . dissolve . . . 100 years later – today . . . grapefruit is a year-round food all over America, quite economical, and very much taken for granted. The grapefruit has become an important nutritional constituent in the American diet for its high vitamin C and low calorie content. One-half grapefruit contains 1½ times the daily requirement of vitamin C and a generous selection of other vitamins and minerals, while adding only 72 calories. The pink grapefruit provides additional vitamin A. Fresh grapefruit has remarkably good retention of vitamin C, the most fragile of vitamins. Freshly squeezed grapefruit juice stored at 40°F. has been shown to retain 98 percent of its vitamin C for a week.

The tangy, exhilarating flavor of grapefruit juice (three-fourths of the total fruit) provides one of our most popular morning eye-openers and all-day thirst quenchers. For the perfect half-grapefruit serving, there are knives specially designed to cut the sections neatly and completely away from the pith and special narrow spoons for efficiently extracting the bites of fruit without risking a squirt of ascorbic acid in the eye. Folks on weight-control diets eat their grapefruit halves plain or topped with a scoop of cottage cheese. Others like them broiled with a little honey and butter. It's a delicious dessert topped with various-flavored sherbets, and we have a particular favorite – with chestnuts. Imaginative cooks find ways to use zesty grapefruit sections and juice in every course of the meal – in fruit salad, seafood salad, or with tossed greens; with seafood and poultry dishes; in tarts, cakes, frostings, sherbet, and ice cream; as the mainstay in fruit bowls; and in a noble variation of crepes suzette.

Good-quality grapefruits are firm but springy to the touch. They are not soft, wilted, or flabby, but well shaped and heavy for their size. Grapefruits heavy for their size are usually thin-skinned and contain more juice than those that have a coarse skin or are puffy and spongy. Imperfections on the skin affect only the appearance, not the eating quality.

GRAPEFRUIT CREPES SUZETTE

Crepes Suzette Pamplemousse

DO-AHEAD TIP: *Crepes, grapefruit butter, and sauce can be prepared a week ahead and stored in freezer.*

CREPES

18 6-inch Basic Crepes (see Index)

GRAPEFRUIT BUTTER

6 tablespoons unsalted butter

4 tablespoons light honey

grated rind of 1 grapefruit

1 teaspoon grated lemon rind

SAUCE

6 tablespoons unsalted butter

juice of 2 grapefruit

finely shredded rind of 1 grapefruit

6 tablespoons light honey

1 tablespoon fresh lemon juice

skinned sections of 3 grapefruit

GRAPEFRUIT BUTTER: Beat butter in mixer until creamy. Add honey and beat until thoroughly incorporated and creamy. Add grapefruit and lemon rinds and beat again. Spread this butter on underside (the side cooked last) of each crepe. Fold crepes in half, then in half again.

SAUCE: In large saute pan, combine butter, grapefruit juice, rind, honey, and lemon juice. Stir mixture over low heat until rind becomes translucent. Let sauce barely simmer 5 minutes. Add grapefruit sections and warm them briefly in sauce over low heat.

PRESENTATION: Arrange folded crepes, overlapping, on warm serving platter or individual plates. Spoon sauce and grapefruit sections over crepes. Serve warm.

6 servings

FISH AND GRAPEFRUIT SALAD IN CUCUMBER BOATS

Acapulco's redoubtable style setter, Baron Jay de Laval, believes in entertaining the easy way. For luncheon, in the heat of the day, he keeps his cool and livens guests' appetites with a main dish salad inspired with a dash of imagination . . . like this one.

DO-AHEAD TIP: *Salad can be assembled a day ahead. Coat with mayonnaise and garnish at serving time.*

- 2 cucumbers (6 to 7 inches long), peeled
- freshly ground white pepper
- 1 pound sole fillets, or any skinned and boned fish, steamed and chilled
- 2 tablespoons fresh lemon juice
- skinned sections of 2 grapefruit, drained
- crisp leaves of Boston or romaine lettuce
- 1 cup Basic Mayonnaise (see Index)
- ½ cup heavy cream, whipped
- 2 yolks of hard-cooked eggs, rubbed through fine strainer
- 2 tablespoons finely chopped fresh parsley

Cut cucumbers in halves lengthwise and scoop out all the seeds. Put in pot, cover with water, bring slowly to a boil, and drain at once. Chill. Sprinkle hollows with a little pepper. Cut chilled, cooked fish in bite-size chunks, sprinkle with lemon juice, and put in cucumber boats. Lay 4 or 5 grapefruit sections diagonally on top of fish.

PRESENTATION: Place cucumber boats on lettuce leaves on individual serving plates. Fold mayonnaise with whipped cream. Cover stuffed cucumber boats completely with mayonnaise. Sprinkle with sieved egg yolk and chopped parsley. Serve at once.

4 servings as main dish

GRAPEFRUIT

GRAPEFRUIT DRESSING

Use with any combination of fresh fruit and salad greens.

DO-AHEAD TIP: *Dressing will keep for about a week in refrigerator.*

- 1 teaspoon dry mustard
- ¼ teaspoon finely chopped fresh garlic
- ½ teaspoon finely ground white pepper
- ¼ teaspoon celery seeds (optional)
- 1 tablespoon fresh lemon juice, or 1 teaspoon grated lemon rind
- ½ cup grapefruit juice
- ½ cup light vegetable oil (e.g., safflower)
- 1 egg

Combine all ingredients in screwtop jar and shake well.

Yields about 1 cup

RIZ A L'IMPERATRICE

Rice Custard with Grapefruit and Strawberries

DO-AHEAD TIP: *This dessert can be prepared a day ahead and refrigerated.*

RICE CUSTARD

- 4 cups milk or reconstituted nonfat dry milk (possibly more)
- ½ cup short grain brown rice
- ½ vanilla bean (scraping and pod)
- 3 egg yolks
- ¾ cup light honey
- 2 tablespoons unflavored gelatin
- 1 tablespoon fresh lemon juice

RICE CUSTARD: Combine milk, rice, and vanilla bean pod in large, heavy pot. Bring to a boil slowly and cook over very low heat, uncovered, stirring occasionally to prevent scorching, until rice has absorbed milk and is tender. If rice absorbs milk before it is soft, add more milk.

In mixer, beat egg yolks with honey and vanilla bean scraping until mixture is thick. In small saucepan, combine gelatin, lemon juice, and water, and stir over low heat until gelatin is dissolved. Add to egg yolk mixture and beat thoroughly.

When rice is tender, put in bowl and stand over container of ice. Add egg yolk mixture and stir until cool. Beat egg whites to soft peaks and fold into rice mixture. Fold in whipped

RIZ A L'IMPERATRICE—continued

- 1/4 cup water
- 2 egg whites
- 1 1/2 cups heavy cream, whipped
- 1 cup grapefruit sections, well drained

DECORATION

- 8 to 12 large, choice strawberries (with stems, if possible)
- 1/2 cup red currant jelly (optional)

cream, spoonful by spoonful. Dry grapefruit sections between paper towels and fold into rice mixture. Transfer to serving bowl and chill.

GARNISH: Whole strawberries can be glazed with currant jelly if desired, or used plain. To coat with jelly, dissolve jelly in small saucepan. Let cool a little at room temperature and dip strawberries into it. Arrange whole strawberries on top of rice.

6 to 8 servings

GRAPEFRUIT *EN SURPRISE*

Large oranges can be used in this recipe instead of grapefruit.

DO-AHEAD TIP: *Grapefruit sections can be cut and meringue prepared a few hours ahead. Assemble with sherbet at serving time.*

- 3 grapefruit
- 2/3 cup light honey or maple syrup
- 3 egg whites
- 3 cups Lemon Sherbet or Lime Sherbet (see Index), frozen firm

Cut grapefruit in halves and cut around each section with small, sharp knife. Remove center core. Refrigerate grapefruit until ready to assemble and serve.

To make meringue, put honey or maple syrup in small saucepan and bring slowly to a boil. In mixer, beat egg whites to soft peaks. Continue beating while very slowly adding hot honey or syrup (in very thin stream). Beat until meringue is shiny and holds its shape.

PRESENTATION: Arrange grapefruit halves on broiler tray or heatproof serving platter. Put scoop of sherbet in center of each grapefruit half. Put meringue in pastry bag fitted with large star tube (#8 or #9) and pipe swirls of meringue to completely cover tops of grapefruit. Place grapefruit under broiler briefly, just to etch meringue with brown. Serve at once.

6 servings

GRAPEFRUIT

GRAPEFRUIT HALVES WITH CHESTNUTS

DO-AHEAD TIP: *Ingredients can be prepared a day ahead. Assemble at serving time.*

- **1 pound chestnuts in shells**
- **3 grapefruit**
- **6 tablespoons sliced blanched almonds, toasted**
- **½ cup plus 1 tablespoon light honey**
- **1 cup heavy cream**
- **1 teaspoon vanilla extract**

To cook chestnuts, cut slit in flat side of each chestnut with small, pointed knife. Put chestnuts in pot, cover with water, and bring to a boil. Continue boiling 4 to 5 minutes to soften shells. Let chestnuts stand in hot water as you remove them one by one to cut away outer shell and inner skin. Discard original cooking water and return chestnuts to pot. Add more water, or half water and half milk, to cover chestnuts and simmer until chestnuts are just tender.

Cut grapefruit in halves and cut around each section to loosen. Place grapefruit sections in bowl. Pull membrane out of each grapefruit half.

Reserve 6 whole chestnuts. Cut rest of chestnuts into chunks and add to grapefruit sections. Also add almonds and ½ cup honey, and stir gently.

PRESENTATION: Fill grapefruit shells with grapefruit-chestnut-almond mixture. Beat heavy cream until thick. Add vanilla and 1 tablespoon honey, and beat until stiff. Put whipped cream in pastry bag fitted with large star tube (#8 or #9) and pipe large rosette on top of each grapefruit serving. Top with whole chestnut.

6 servings

More Grapefruit Recipes

See Index for the following recipes:

SALAD: Tossed Greens Salad with Fruit; DESSERTS: Fresh Fruit Tart and Tartlets, Grapefruit Sherbet, *Macedoine de Fruits;* BEVERAGES: Citrus Combo, Pink Pearl.

GRAPES

Let us toast the eating grape, the unfermented grape: To all of the grape-garnished dishes called Veronique, to grape sauces, grape jellies, grape tarts; to all of the ravishing clusters of luscious berries and to the glorious ways of serving them!

Since antiquity, grapes have been probably the most profound of fruit, from imparting the utmost gastronomic ecstasy to the offering of sacramental rebirth. To the painter and poet, they are the symbol of pleasure and plenty. To the gastronome, they represent three quite different foods: table grapes, raisins, and wine. Here we are concerned with table grapes. Raisins are discussed separately (see the section on raisins). In the United States most of our table grapes come from California and the East; a few from the South and Midwest.

Lief Erickson discovered grapes growing in North America. In fact, they were so abundant that the Norsemen called this land Vinland (vineland). (The grape is the berry of the Vita [vine] family.) The grapes they found, which still today are the informing grapes of the East, are called *Vitis labrusca*, and have distinct characteristics: The skin separates easily from the pulp, while the seeds are difficult to pry away from the meat. The three most popular labrusca grapes are the black Concord, the red Catawba, and the white Niagara. They might not be as sweet as the California types, but they are still awfully good to eat out of hand, especially when you give an extra squeeze to the skin to release the syrup just underneath. Eastern-type grapes are available only in the autumn, from September to November.

The Spanish mission priests introduced grapes to California soil with plantings of the European-type grape, the *Vitis vinifera*. Their characteristics are the direct opposites of those of the Eastern: The skin of California grapes adheres tightly to the pulp, the seeds are easily removed, and generally, they are sweeter. The most prominent varieties of the white are Thompson seedless, Calmeria, Lady Finger, and Perlette; of the red, Cardinal, Emperor, and Tokay; and of the purple, Ribier. Actually, there are so many California grape varieties with different harvest periods that the market season stretches throughout the year.

Grapes must ripen on the vine. They do not improve in color, sugar, flavor, or quality in any aspect after they have been picked. Once picked, they are highly perishable. Store grapes unwashed and uncovered in the refrigerator and use within three to five days. To serve, wash grapes just before using. Use kitchen shears to cut in halves and snip out the seeds. If you grow your own grapes, surplus production can be frozen – plain unsweetened, in syrup pack, or as juice.

There's a small vineyard on our place in Tuscany with the typical white Trebbiano grapes, which are sent each harvest to the wine cooperative. (Grapes, olives, and some of the produce help to defray the upkeep.) Adjoining two sides of the old stone mill-house are carefully maintained arbors of the same grapes. It is a spiritually moving sight to walk beneath them and see streaks of sun gleaming through the leaves and bunches of ripening fruit, giving them a certain ethereal translucence. Not only do I pick the ripe bunches for the table, but I also select large leaves to stuff with rice or to use as liners (natural doilies) on dessert plates. (I wish florists or green-grocers in this country would stock fresh grape leaves in season. They are pretty and edible.)

To me, the finest way to serve grapes is on the bunch, with a pair of silver grape shears – if you have them. Such was the dessert for the luncheon given some years ago for the King and Queen of Spain at the prestigious Windows on the World restaurant in New York. A plate of fresh grapes with a dish of unsalted cashews and walnuts are the quintescence of an appropriate before-dinner appetizer. Fresh grapes with cheese – perfect to start or end a meal.

Grapes are a versatile fruit. Grape jelly! I remember the slow, measured drips of juice from the big flannel jelly bag in the basement and Mother's repeated warnings not to touch the bag or the jelly would not be clear. She took special pride in her crystal-clear, burgundy red jelly. We were also fond of grape jam, even though it made our teeth and mouths blue for a while. I remember, too, one hot Sunday afternoon in Dione Lucas's kitchen, helping her prepare the favorite recipes of President Thomas Jefferson for *The First Ladies' Cookbook* (published by *Parents'* magazine). One of his specialties was a mold of grape jelly garnished with clusters of red and white grapes. I think President Jefferson, whom history credits as being quite a gourmand, would have been pleased with the grand presentation Dione created for the photograph. *Veronique* in classical French cooking denotes the presence of white grapes in savory dishes, such as quail with grapes in aspic, or fish or chicken with grapes in veloute sauce. Grapes add a festive note in salads of all sorts, in fruit bowls, on an open-face tart, in sherbet, and in frosty drinks. A simple but always pleasing dessert is a stem glass filled with white grapes mixed with sour cream or yogurt and honey.

FILETS DE SOLES VERONIQUE

Poached Fillets of Sole with White Grapes and Veloute Sauce

DO-AHEAD TIP: *This recipe can be prepared ahead. To rewarm, cover with aluminum foil and heat in 300° F. oven.*

FILLETS

- 6 fillets of sole
- 2 tablespoons plus ½ teaspoon fresh lemon juice
- 2 tablespoons unsalted butter
- 2 firm mushrooms, sliced
- 1 small onion, sliced

FILLETS: Preheat oven to 350°F. Wash fish in cold water and 2 tablespoons lemon juice. Dry fillets between paper towels and fold lengthwise with bone side out. Place on oiled baking dish.

Prepare court-bouillon as follows: Melt butter in 3-cup saucepan and add mushrooms, onion, ½ teaspoon lemon juice, and pepper. Cook over high heat 1 minute. Add water and bring to boil slowly. Spoon this mixture over fish fillets. Cover with oiled sheet of waxed paper. Poach 15 minutes in oven.

FILETS DE SOLES VERONIQUE—continued

freshly ground white pepper

1 cup water

VELOUTE SAUCE

2 tablespoons unsalted butter

1½ tablespoons whole wheat pastry flour

cayenne pepper

strained stock reserved from cooking fish

⅔ cup light cream

2 egg yolks

1 tablespoon fresh lemon juice

2 tablespoons heavy cream

⅓ cup light vegetable oil (e.g., safflower)

GARNISH

1 tablespoon unsalted butter

1 cup skinned and seeded fresh white grapes

2 tablespoons finely chopped fresh parsley

freshly ground white pepper

Remove from oven, arrange fish on serving platter, and keep warm. Strain stock (cooking liquid) and reserve.

VELOUTE SAUCE: Melt butter in 1-quart saucepan. Remove from heat and add flour and a few grains cayenne pepper and blend. Add reserved stock. Stir over moderate heat until mixture boils. Add cream and let sauce barely simmer 5 minutes.

Meanwhile, in small bowl, combine egg yolks, lemon juice, and heavy cream. Stand bowl in saute pan half filled with hot water over low heat. Beat mixture with small wire whisk until thick. Continue beating while slowly adding oil (in a very thin stream). Fold egg sauce into veloute sauce and set aside.

GARNISH: Melt butter in small pan and add grapes, parsley, and a little pepper. Warm over low heat.

PRESENTATION: Scatter grapes over fish. Spoon sauce evenly over dish. Brown top lightly under broiler.

6 servings

CONCORD GRAPE PIE

Out of this world! Those luscious slip-skin Concord grapes are strictly American and are around only a short while, usually from late August to October. Be their season ever so brief, America's "total woman," Marabel Morgan, captures their secret in this gorgeous, delicious, purple-colored pie. Topped with ice cream, it belongs in the same league as apple pie and strawberry shortcake. An important Morgan family activity is cooking together, which is how the goodness of Concord grape pie happened to be discovered.

DO-AHEAD TIP: *Pie can be baked a day ahead and refrigerated.*

PASTRY

- 1½ quantity of dough for Plain Whole Wheat Short Pastry 1 (see Index)

FILLING

- 5½ cups ripe Concord grapes (Concord variety is imperative for the slip-skin factor and its more tender skins)
- ⅔ cup light honey
- 4 tablespoons cornstarch
- 3 tablespoons water
- 1 tablespoon fresh lemon juice
- 1 tablespoon grated orange rind
- 1½ tablespoons unsalted butter
- 1 egg, beaten
- 1 quart Basic Vanilla Ice Cream (see Index)

PASTRY: Preheat oven to 350°F. Spread length of waxed paper on work surface and dust with flour. Place ball of two-thirds of dough in center and sprinkle with a little more flour. Flatten ball a little with rolling pin and cover with another sheet of waxed paper. Roll dough between two sheets of waxed paper to a round large enough to line 9- or 10-inch pie pan. Shape dough firmly against the inside. Run rolling pin over rim to trim off excess dough. Place sheet of waxed paper on top of dough and cover with dried beans or raw rice to hold dough down while baking. Bake 20 minutes. Remove from oven and remove weight and paper. Reset oven to 375°F.

FILLING: Slip Concord grape pulp out of skins and set skins aside. Put pulp in saucepan with no water and bring to rolling boil. While hot, rub pulp through strainer into mixing bowl to remove seeds. Combine strained pulp, skins, and honey, and stir well.

In small bowl, combine cornstarch, water, and lemon juice, and stir until smooth. Add cornstarch mixture and orange rind to grape mixture. Spoon mixture into pastry shell. Dot with butter.

Roll out remaining dough into long strip between sheets of waxed paper. Brush lightly with egg and cut into ½-inch-wide strips, long enough to arrange in lattice pattern on top of pie. Place pie on baking sheet and bake 40 to 45 minutes. Let cool. Add scoop of vanilla ice cream to top of each serving.

8 servings

SUPREMES DE VOLAILLES SAUTE VERONIQUE

Sauteed Breasts of Chicken (or Duck) with Grapes, with Brown Sauce

DO-AHEAD TIP: *Assembled dish (on heatproof platter) can be prepared a day ahead. At serving time, cover with aluminum foil and rewarm in 300° F. oven.*

CHICKEN BREASTS AND SAUCE

- 2 tablespoons unsalted butter
- 1 tablespoon light vegetable oil (e.g., safflower)
- 8 half breasts of chicken, skinned and boned
- ½ teaspoon finely chopped fresh garlic
- 1 teaspoon meat flavoring (e.g., Marmite brewer's yeast extract, vegetable paste or meat glaze)
- 1½ cups stock (e.g., chicken, vegetable, or soy—1½ cups water with 3 teaspoons tamari soy sauce)
- 2 teaspoons cornstarch or potato flour
- freshly ground white pepper
- 1 cup skinned seedless white grapes
- 2 tablespoons finely chopped fresh parsley

VEGETABLES (optional)

- 4 small zucchini (about 1 pound), cut into ⅛-inch-thick slices
- 2 tablespoons unsalted butter
- freshly ground white pepper
- 1 garlic clove, finely chopped
- 4 medium-size ripe tomatoes, skinned and cut into small wedges

CHICKEN BREASTS AND SAUCE: Heat butter and oil in large saute pan. Brown chicken breasts quickly on both sides and remove. Remove pan from heat and add garlic, meat flavoring, and cornstarch or potato flour, and blend. Add stock and stir over moderate heat until mixture boils. Reduce heat to low, add pepper, and put chicken back in pan. Cover and simmer slowly (about 30 minutes) until chicken is tender. Add grapes and parsley and continue cooking only until grapes are warm.

VEGETABLES: While chicken is cooking, prepare vegetable accompaniment, if desired. Place zucchini in heavy pot, cover with water, and bring slowly to a boil. Drain at once. Melt butter in same pot and add zucchini, pepper, and garlic. Cook over low heat until tender (only a few minutes). Add tomatoes and cook until they are warm.

PRESENTATION: Spread a bed of vegetables along the center of warm serving platter. Arrange chicken breasts on top and cover with sauce.

8 servings

ROAST CHICKEN WITH MEATBALLS AND BLACK GRAPES

Here's how to stretch 1 chicken to serve 4 to 6 people with class: Add savory meatballs and sauce with grapes.

DO-AHEAD TIP: *Sauce and meatball mixture can be made a day ahead. At serving time, roast chicken, fry meatballs, rewarm sauce, and assemble dish.*

CHICKEN

- 1 3½- to 4-pound whole dressed chicken
- 1 tablespoon unsalted butter
- 1 garlic clove, halved
- ½ teaspoon freshly ground white pepper
- 1 sprig fresh tarragon or celery leaf

SAUCE

- 1 tablespoon unsalted butter
- 1 chicken liver
- ½ teaspoon finely chopped fresh garlic
- 1 teaspoon meat flavoring (e.g., Marmite brewer's yeast extract, vegetable paste, or meat glaze)
- 1 teaspoon tomato paste
- 2 teaspoons cornstarch or potato flour
- 1 cup stock (e.g., chicken, vegetable, or soy—1 cup water with 1½ teaspoons tamari soy sauce)
- 1 teaspoon grape jelly
- freshly ground white pepper
- ½ cup sour cream
- 1 cup skinned and seeded black grapes

CHICKEN: Preheat oven to 300°F. Dry chicken inside and out. In cavity, insert butter, garlic, pepper, and tarragon or celery leaf. Tie chicken snugly and place on rack in roasting pan. Brush chicken all over with oil. Pour about ½ cup water on bottom of pan. Insert meat thermometer into thickest part of the thigh, not touching the bone. Roast until thermometer registers 180°F. (about 2 hours).

SAUCE: Heat butter in 1½-quart saucepan and brown chicken liver. Remove liver. Remove pan from heat and add garlic, meat flavoring, tomato paste, and cornstarch or potato flour, and blend. Add stock and stir over moderate heat until sauce comes to a boil. Add jelly and pepper, and let sauce simmer about 5 minutes. With small wire whisk, beat in sour cream, a spoonful at a time. Add grapes and warm in sauce.

ROAST CHICKEN WITH MEATBALLS—continued

MEATBALLS

½ pound ground beef

¼ pound fresh pork sausage

2 mushrooms, chopped

2 chicken livers, chopped

1 medium-size yellow onion, chopped

½ teaspoon finely chopped fresh garlic

2 tablespoons finely chopped fresh green herb (any kind)

3 tablespoons sour cream

1 egg white

freshly ground black pepper

¼ teaspoon dry mustard

2 tablespoons light vegetable oil (e.g., safflower)

any choice of vegetable (e.g., plain-cooked green beans, carrots, Brussels sprouts; braised celery; broiled tomatoes; sauteed mushrooms)

MEATBALLS: Combine all ingredients in food processor or mixer and beat only until well mixed. Form into small balls (about 1 inch diameter). Heat oil in saute pan and fry meatballs until golden brown all over.

PRESENTATION: Carve chicken into serving pieces and arrange in center of warm serving platter. Pour sauce over chicken. Surround with little piles of meatballs and vegetables.

4 to 6 servings

RICE-STUFFED GRAPE LEAVES

These stuffed grape leaves are a lovely cold hors d'oeuvre.

DO-AHEAD TIP: *This dish should be prepared a day ahead in order to chill.*

STUFFING

- 1 cup brown rice
- 1 egg, beaten
- 2½ cups stock (e.g., chicken, vegetable, or soy—2½ cups water with 3 teaspoons tamari soy sauce)
- 1 tablespoon virgin olive oil
- ½ cup chopped onions
- 2 tablespoons chopped fresh dill, or 2 teaspoons dried dillweed
- ¼ cup dried currants
- freshly ground white pepper
- ¼ teaspoon ground cinnamon
- ¼ teaspoon ground allspice

GRAPE LEAVES

- 40 grape leaves
- 2 cups water
- 2 tablespoons virgin olive oil
- 3 tablespoons fresh lemon juice
- 1 lemon, cut into small wedges

STUFFING: Preheat oven to 350°F. Put rice in deep, heavy 1-quart pot. Add egg and stir over moderate heat until all rice kernels are dry and separate. Add stock, olive oil, onions, dill, currants, pepper, cinnamon, and allspice. Stir over moderate heat until mixture boils. Cover with firm-fitting lid and cook in oven 45 minutes, or until rice is tender, without disturbing rice. When cooked, fluff with 2 forks. Reset oven temperature to 375°F.

GRAPE LEAVES: To stuff a grape leaf, place leaf vein side up on cutting board. Cut off stem. Put 1 tablespoon rice mixture on leaf. Fold stem end over rice, then the two sides toward the center, and roll up.

Line bottom of heavy 2-quart pot with remaining unstuffed grape leaves. Arrange stuffed leaves in pot in layers. Pour water, olive oil, and lemon juice over them. Put small plate as weight on top of stuffed leaves. Cover and cook in oven 1 hour or until tender. Let cool in cooking liquid in refrigerator.

PRESENTATION: Arrange on serving platter or individual plates. Garnish with lemon wedges.

24 to 30 stuffed grape leaves

More Grape Recipes

See Index for the following recipes:

MAIN DISH: Poached Chicken Hawaiian; DESSERTS: French Fruit Tart and Tartlets, *Le Clafouti*, *Macedoine de Fruits*.

GUAVAS

Somehow in this technological world Mexican farmer markets persist – those bustling ebullient centers for all of the good homegrown foods raised by the *campesinos* of the surrounding countryside. The stalls are packed with artistically arranged fruits and vegetables – in baskets and bins and hanging from rafters overhead, even fresh green herbs in huge bunches and boggling variety. In other sections of the aisles, live chickens and turkeys flap and squawk in protest while being examined by prospective cooks.

The scene may seem like pandemonium, but it is really a symphony of the senses, all of them – sight, sound, smell, feel, and taste. I love it. Sometimes, piercing through the melange of fragrances, I recognize one fine, favorite aroma that gives a tingling topnote to the whole bouquet. As my nostrils twitch, I know that somewhere nearby, amidst all this Gauguinesque profusion, there is nestled a small basket of unpretentious little yellow fruits sending forth their glorious vapors – *guayabas*, or guavas, as we call them in English.

There they are! Little round or oval-shaped yellow fruits, usually two to three inches in length, sometimes on the green side, sometimes with a pink blush. When you buy guavas, choose ones that are firm, on the verge of softening but not spotted. (If they're not quite ripe, let them stand at room temperature for a day or so.)

The way to eat a guava is to cut it in quarters and then cut out the hard little seeds in the center. The skin is thin and can be eaten or removed, depending on use. After its romantic assault on the nose, the flavor of guava is no disappointment. In the mouth, taste buds are treated to a luscious, juicy, zesty, cream-colored pulp which might resemble the taste of pineapple or strawberry, depending on the type of guava.

The shrublike guava trees are plentiful in Hawaii and Mexico and are now being cultivated in California and Florida, too. They have a rather short fruiting season – about six weeks in the summer. Hopefully this exquisite fruit – sweet with sparkling zing and generously endowed with vitamins A and C – will become available in more American fruit markets as the number of growers here increases.

When living in the tropics, one soon learns that most of the area's exotic fruits are best if eaten simply. Mexicans love guava compote, or in ice cream or sherbet. Occasionally an enterprising hostess will slather roast pork with guava sauce and garnish it with poached guava sections, or stuff chilies with chopped fresh guava (*chiles rellenos*, Mexico's fabulous stuffed peppers). This naturally sweet and vibrant fruit can be pureed for use in mousses, whips, or juice drinks, or cut up and mixed with yogurt, or used in chutney or relish. Guavas are full of pectin and with their extraordinary flavor, make excellent jelly and jam. Chef Dione Lucas liked to add a teaspoon of guava jelly to fine French brown sauces for that inexplicable touch of sweet zest.

ROAST PORK WITH GUAVA

DO-AHEAD TIP: *Guava puree and guava compote can be prepared a day ahead. Roast pork at serving time.*

1 3-pound loin of pork with bone, chined (cracked between rib joints), or 2-pound boned loin of pork

freshly ground white pepper

2 tablespoons unsalted butter, melted, or light vegetable oil (e.g., safflower)

½ cup light cream

⅔ cup chicken stock

½ cup sweetened Guava Puree (see recipe in this section)

½ recipe for Guava Compote (see recipe in this section); the custard sauce or whipped cream topping is not used

Preheat oven to 300°F. Trim excess fat off meat. Rub meat with pepper and tie snugly with string. Place on rack in roasting pan. Brush all over with butter or oil. Insert meat thermometer and cook in oven until temperature is 165° to 170°F. (35 to 40 minutes per pound). Mix cream and stock. While pork is cooking, baste several times with cream and stock mixture. About 15 minutes before meat is cooked, spread pork with guava puree. Reset oven temperature to 400°F. and cook until done.

PRESENTATION: Strain sauce that is in bottom of roasting pan and skim off fat. Slice pork thinly and arrange on hot serving platter. (Roast pork should always be sliced wafer thin; then it is never tough.) Warm guava compote in syrup in which guavas were cooked, drain, and arrange in mounds around meat. Serve sauce in separate dish.

4 to 6 servings

GUAVA COMPOTE

Poached Guavas

DO-AHEAD TIP: *Compote can be made 1 or 2 days ahead and refrigerated.*

- 12 to 15 ripe guavas
- ¾ cup light honey
- ¾ cup water
- 2 teaspoons fresh lemon juice
- 1 stick cinnamon bark

English Custard Sauce (see Index), or whipped cream (optional)

Cut black ends off guavas. Cut guavas in quarter wedges and remove seeds. Do not peel. (If guavas are peeled, they may fall apart when poached.) Combine honey, water, and lemon juice in deep, heavy pot and bring to a boil over low heat. Add cinnamon bark and guava sections. Simmer gently about 10 minutes. Do not cook any longer or guavas will become too soft. Let cool in syrup.

PRESENTATION: Serve in compote dishes with a little syrup. If desired, serving can be topped with whipped cream or custard sauce. Guava compote can also be used as topping on ice cream or cake.

6 servings

GUAVA PUREE

Use for ice cream, sherbet, mousse, or sauce.

- ripe, fresh guavas

Cut guavas into chunks. Without removing seeds or peel, rub through fine vegetable strainer. Or, remove seeds and peel and puree in food processor.

Depending on recipe or use, sweeten puree with light honey to taste. Add a few drops of lemon juice.

GUAVAS

WHIPPED GUAVA AND SWEET POTATO DESSERT

DO-AHEAD TIP: *This dessert can be prepared a day ahead and refrigerated.*

- 1 pound ripe guavas, seeded and peeled
- 2 pounds sweet potatoes or yams, baked and peeled
- ½ cup light honey
- ¾ cup heavy cream, whipped
- ground cinnamon (optional)

Puree guavas and sweet potatoes in food processor or rub through strainer. Leave in processor or transfer to mixer. Heat honey over low heat until it comes to a boil. Pour honey slowly into guava and sweet potato mixture, beating constantly. Continue beating until mixture is cool. Combine with whipped cream in mixing bowl and fold together lightly and evenly. Chill thoroughly. Serve in dessert glasses. If desired, sprinkle with cinnamon.

6 to 8 servings

More Guava Recipes

See Index for the following recipes:

MAIN DISH: *Chiles Rellenos*; SALAD: Tossed Greens Salad with Fruit; DESSERTS: French Fruit Tart and Tartlets, Fresh Fruit Ice Cream, Frozen Fruit Yogurt, Fruit Sherbet, *Macedoine de Fruits*.

KIWI FRUIT

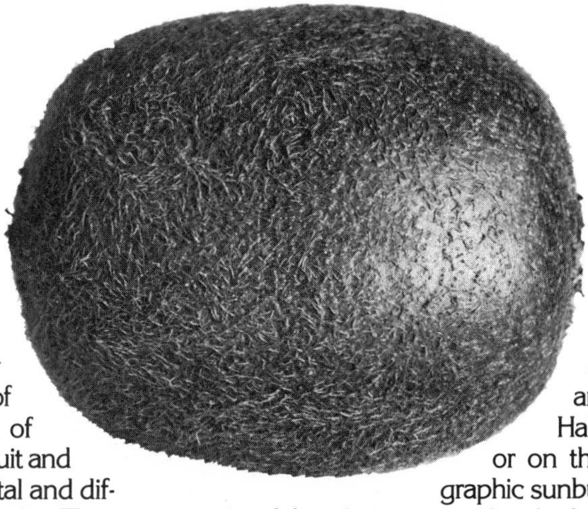

At Christmas time I like to set out a shiny silver bowl of dried slices of green kiwi fruit and red tomato, just an incidental and different touch of holiday hospitality. Thin cross-sectional slices of both fruits are beautiful patterns – the kiwi sunburst and the lacy spokes of tomato. Both fruits retain their brilliant colors when dried. Also, when dehydrated, both offer a tasty surprise: The characteristically gentle, and refreshing flavor of kiwi becomes a concentrated zest and the tomato seems sweeter, like real sun-ripened tomato. Sometimes I add dried banana or pear slices for Christmas white.

Kiwi fruit. This funny, furry-skinned fruit has its roots in China, where it was called *yang tao*. It found its way to New Zealand, where it was referred to as the Chinese gooseberry and where it was commercially cultivated for the first time early in this century. (Kiwi fruit grows on treelike vines, rather like grapevines, and a field of kiwi plants is called a vineyard.) When New Zealand growers decided to export this fascinating fruit to America, they rechristened it kiwi, after the tiny kiwi bird that is native to New Zealand. Within a few years (only since the mid-1970s) kiwis became the darling of fashionable *nouvelle cuisine* chefs and captured the gourmand market by storm. It has been a remarkably successful strategy to get Americans to welcome a very nondescript, almost ugly-looking fruit to our tables.

Like many exotic fruits, the kiwi's mousy exterior hides a feast that is sheer artistry in pattern and color, and subtle elegance in flavor. Halved – lengthwise, crosswise, or on the bias – the kiwi reveals a graphic sunburst – a yellow center, ringed with tiny jet seeds, which are soft and are eaten, set in bright green, syrupy flesh. A properly ripe kiwi gives to a little pressure with the thumb, like a ripe pear. Fruit that is a bit too firm can be ripened at room temperature. Kiwi has one of the most delectably sweet meats of any fruit, with a distinctive quality that is neither cloying nor acid. A few drops of lemon juice accent its flavor nicely. And, an average portion of 3½ ounces provides more than twice the recommended daily requirement of vitamin C for adults.

Kiwi fruit is now available in American markets year-round (thanks to harvests from new vineyards in California in seasons opposite to those of New Zealand). For eating out of hand, simply cut the fruit in half and eat it with a spoon. Slices of kiwi are a glamorous addition to salads, fruit bowls, and ice cream, or as topping for a cheesecake.

For breakfast, try a kiwi omelet. Simply enclose some small chunks of raw kiwi with a few shreds of muenster or jack cheese, and garnish the top with three or four very thin slices of kiwi, slightly overlapping.

For lunch, consider preparing kiwi open-face

sandwiches – rounds of whole grain bread the size of sliced kiwi, spread with cream cheese and covered with kiwi slices. Or mix chunks of kiwi with yogurt.

For dinner, sliced kiwi, perhaps sprinkled with a little ground ginger, can be the jewel adornment to plain-cooked chicken or seafood. Or, prepare a fashionable new dessert idea, fruit au gratin, with kiwi.

For use in these preparations, thinly peel off the fuzzy brownish skin.

KIWI FOOL

DO-AHEAD TIP: *Ingredients can be readied a day ahead. Combine at serving time.*

- **2½ cups pureed, strained kiwi fruit**
- **2 teaspoons lemon juice**
- **2 cups English Custard Sauce (see Index), or 1½ cups heavy cream, whipped**
- **2 kiwi fruit, peeled**

Combine kiwi fruit puree and custard sauce or whipped cream and fold together briefly. (Mixture should look "swirled" rather than thoroughly mixed.) Spoon into dessert bowl or individual dessert glasses and chill. Decorate with slices or wedges of kiwi fruit.

6 servings

FILLETS OF SOLE WITH KIWI FRUIT AND WHITE BUTTER SAUCE

Filets de Soles Kiwi, Beurre Blanc

Sole fillets can be sauteed or steamed (as described below).

DO-AHEAD TIP: *Ingredients can be readied several hours ahead. Sauce can be made about 30 minutes before serving and left to stand at room temperature. Fish should be cooked at serving time.*

FILLETS
- 6 medium to large fillets of sole
- 2 tablespoons fresh lemon juice

to saute fillets:
- freshly ground white pepper
- 3 tablespoons light vegetable oil (e.g., safflower)

to steam fillets:
- 1 bay leaf
- 6 peppercorns
- 1 small onion, sliced

WHITE BUTTER SAUCE
- 1 tablespoon finely chopped shallots
- 1½ tablespoons fresh lemon juice or white vinegar
- ¼ teaspoon freshly ground white pepper
- 8 tablespoons frozen unsalted butter, cut into ½-inch cubes

GARNISH
- 16 ⅛-inch-thick slices peeled kiwi fruit
- 12 small lemon wedges
- clusters of fresh parsley

FILLETS: Wash fillets in lemon juice and cold water and pat dry between paper towels. Fold each in half lengthwise.

To saute fillets, sprinkle fillets with pepper and pat lightly with flour. Heat oil in large saute pan. Saute fillets until golden brown on both sides. Remove to warm serving platter.

To steam fillets, combine bay leaf, peppercorns, and onion with 1 or 2 cups water in steamer and bring to a boil. Wrap fillets in greased aluminum foil or cheesecloth and place on steamer platform. Cover. Cook over low heat until fish is just firm.

WHITE BUTTER SAUCE: Combine shallots, lemon juice, and pepper in small saucepan and boil until liquid is reduced by half. Strain into small bowl. Stand bowl in saute pan half filled with hot water over low heat. Add butter, 2 or 3 pieces at a time, beating constantly with small wire whisk. Add more bits of butter as prior pieces become melted and creamy. Continue beating until all butter has been added and sauce has color and consistency of hollandaise. As soon as butter has been dissolved, immediately remove bowl from hot water and continue beating until sauce and bowl cool a little.

PRESENTATION: Arrange fish fillets on warm serving platter or individual plates. On top of each fillet, arrange 4 overlapping slices of kiwi fruit. Spoon about 2 tablespoons sauce over each fillet. Garnish with lemon and parsley. Serve at once.

6 servings

KIWI FRUIT

KIWI SABAYON AU GRATIN

Individual servings of sliced kiwi fruit, covered with lemon or orange sabayon sauce and lightly browned under the broiler.

DO-AHEAD TIP: *Kiwi fruit and apricot* coulis *can be prepared and assembled several hours ahead and refrigerated. Sabayon sauce should be prepared within half an hour of serving. Sauce should not be added to fruit and browned until serving time.*

KIWI FRUIT
8 kiwi fruit

APRICOT *COULIS* (puree sauce)
6 tablespoons apricot preserve

3 tablespoons unsalted butter

1 tablespoon water

ORANGE OR LEMON SABAYON SAUCE
6 egg yolks

3 tablespoons light honey

3 tablespoons fresh lemon juice or orange juice

1 tablespoon grated lemon rind or orange rind

KIWI FRUIT: Peel kiwi fruit and cut each into 4 lengthwise wedges. Cut 6 wedges in half lengthwise (to give 12 thin wedges) and set aside. Cut the remaining quarter wedges across into chunks.

APRICOT *COULIS:* In small saucepan, combine apricot preserve, butter, and water, and stir over low heat until preserve is dissolved. Rub mixture through strainer.

ORANGE OR LEMON SABAYON SAUCE: In medium-size bowl with rounded bottom, combine egg yolks, honey, lemon or orange juice, and grated lemon or orange rind. Beat with electric hand beater or manual rotary beater. Half fill large saute pan with water and bring just to the boiling point. Reduce heat to simmer. Stand bowl containing egg yolk mixture in simmering water and beat constantly until mixture is thick and smooth (the consistency and appearance of hollandaise sauce). Remove bowl from water and continue beating until sauce is *completely* cool.

PRESENTATION: Have ready 6 small ramekins or individual-size gratin dishes (¾- to 1-cup capacity) or heatproof glass custard cups. Place 1 tablespoon apricot *coulis* on bottom of each dish. Top with chunks of kiwi (reserving the narrow wedges for decoration). Cover with sauce. Place 2 thin wedges of kiwi on top of sauce on each dessert. Place desserts on broiler tray under broiler to lightly brown tops. (This takes only a few seconds, so watch carefully.) To serve, place hot desserts on dessert plates lined with paper doilies.

6 servings

More Kiwi Fruit Recipes

See Index for the following recipes:

DESSERTS: French Fruit Tart and Tartlets, Frozen Fruit Yogurt, Fruit Sherbet, *Macedoine de Fruits*, Refrigerator Cheesecake with Fresh Fruit Topping.

LEMONS

Natural lemon is such a universal, taken-for-granted ingredient and seasoning that I put to myself the question, "What lemon uses have impressed you most?" Surprisingly, in rapid-fire order, three:

First, Dione Lucas's lemon curd, a recipe she always credited to a sixteenth-century cookbook – except there seemed to be no published cookbooks of that period – so I, as has her family, have always suspected that this extremely shy and self-effacing artist in food created this heavenly lemony dessert cream herself.

The next foremost impression about lemon was actually a gradual realization, while living and working in Mexico, that a few drops of lemon is a much more all-purpose seasoning than we Americans normally use. On most Mexican tables is a ubiquitous dish of little wedges of *limon* (a citrus that has a most refined flavor, between the sharpness of lemon and the lustiness of our green lime). Mexicans unconsciously squeeze it over almost everything that is served to them, an indication that a few drops of lemon juice can replace a sprinkle of salt.

My most recent memorable lemon impression was the discovery of the ultimate topping for lemon pie – paper-thin slices of real lemon instead of bulbous puffs of sweet, flavorless meringue – as on the Golden Lemon Tart specialty at the fabulous Windows on the World restaurant in New York. I converted it from a commercial formula for 100 tarts to a family recipe for 1 tart as a presentation in our *Cooking with the Chef* show.

While lemons might be an everyday fruit, nature does not produce lemons as though they came off a production line. Lemons can be some of the most freakish of plants. The lemon tree produces blossoms, buds, and mature fruit simultaneously. Some lemons, if not picked, may grow to 12 to 17 inches in circumference. Sometimes these fruits develop in freakish colors, with stripes or streaks or with ridges like cockscombs or other odd shapes. Even the leaves can be strange and variable, with different patterns of white and green. Although lemons have the highest acid content of any fruit, there is also a sweet lemon, which can be eaten out of hand; but it is grown only as a novelty since it could not compete commercially with other sweet citrus fruits.

The fact that most of our supply comes from California is also due to a freak situation that occurred during the Gold Rush. Because fresh fruits and vegetables were scarce and expensive in the barren mining camps, scurvy was rampant. The men knew that lemon juice was a sure cure, so they planted lemon trees. Today California and Italy are the world's leading producers of lemons, although this fruit of the subtropics and tropics seems to have originated in Asia and Malaysia.

LEMONS

Columbus brought the first seeds to Haiti, which eventually found their way to Florida, where they flourished until disease and a heavy frost in 1894 wiped out most of the orchards, never to be replanted.

(Lemon is not the same fruit as "citron," the rind of which is candied and preserved for use in fruitcake and sweets. Citron is a pale yellow fruit that resembles the lemon but is larger, with thicker rind, lots of seeds, and less juice. It is grown mainly around the Mediterranean coast.)

Lemon is the sourest natural food. Since sourness is an important taste element, lemon juice, rind, and oil (cold-pressed from the rind) are all ideal for adding that touch of piquancy or zest which gives an appetizing accent to our cooking. Lemons are used in drinks, salad dressing, seasoning on meat and seafood, in pies, cakes, and cookies; they accent soups, juices, and sauces; they add zest to cooked vegetables. Lemon rubbed on meat, fish, and poultry adds a note of freshness and flavor. Lemon combined with spices is an excellent marinade for meat. Lemon juice sprinkled over cut apples, pears, bananas, avocados, and artichokes retards characteristic discoloration on these raw foods. Lemon juice can also be a mild bleaching agent for keeping white vegetables white (add a little to the water when cooking potatoes) or keeping bright color in vegetables by adding a few drops to the cooking water.

Useful Facts about Lemons

- Best-quality lemons have fine pebble-textured rind and are heavy for their size. Those with coarse skin or which seem lightweight probably have less juice. Lemons with slightly greenish skin are likely to have more acid than those that are deep yellow.
- Properly refrigerated, lemons will keep for as long as three months. Ideal storage temperature is 58° to 60°F.
- Lemons tend to shrivel after being kept for a long time. Immersing them in hot water for about half an hour helps to restore their freshness and will appreciably increase the amount of juice that can be extracted.
- A medium-size lemon, 2¾ inches by 2 inches, weighs about ¼ pound.
- One pound of lemons (about four medium-size) yields 8 to 12 tablespoons (½ to ¾ cup) of juice.
- The juice of one medium-size lemon contains 87 percent of the daily requirement of vitamin C for adults.
- A sprinkle of lemon juice over vegetables, soups, and salads is an ideal substitute for other seasonings.
- Grated lemon rind is an appetizing topnote to cakes and desserts, meat, poultry, and sauces.
- Lemon juice and lemon rind added to fruit and vegetables opens up the bouquet of natural flavors.
- Lemon juice can replace vinegar in almost all uses, especially in salad dressings. (Connoisseurs prefer lemon juice and oil to vinegar and oil in the classic dressing.)
- If lemon juice and lemon rind are to be used, grate the rind first, then squeeze the juice.
- Lemon juice can be used to sour milk. Add two tablespoons to one cup milk.

See the Guide for Grating, Shredding, Juicing, Cutting Citrus: Oranges, Lemons, Limes, Grapefruit, in the section on oranges.

BASIC LEMONADE

DO-AHEAD TIP: *Syrup can be made ahead and refrigerated for several weeks.*

- shredded rind of 3 lemons
- 1 cup fresh lemon juice
- 3/4 cup light honey
- 8 cups cold water
- thin lemon or orange slices, or mint sprig

To make syrup, combine lemon rind, lemon juice, and honey in saucepan. Bring slowly to a boil and simmer until rind is translucent. Strain and chill syrup.

At serving time, combine syrup with water in pitcher. Pour lemonade over ice in 14-ounce glasses, and garnish with lemon or orange slice or mint.

Yields 2 quarts

EGG LEMONADE

- 2 cups Basic Lemonade (1/2 cup chilled syrup with 1 1/2 cups water)
- 1 egg
- mint sprigs or thin lemon slices

Combine lemonade and egg in blender and beat thoroughly. Pour into frosted glasses. Garnish with mint or lemon slices.

Yields 2 cups

GRAPE JUICE LEMONADE

- 1/3 cup fresh lemon juice
- 1/4 cup light honey
- 1 cup grape juice
- 2 cups club soda
- thin lemon slices

Combine lemon juice, honey, and grape juice in blender and mix. Chill thoroughly. To serve, mix with club soda. Pour into chilled glasses filled with ice cubes. Hang lemon slice on rim of each glass.

4 servings

COLD LEMON SOUFFLE

DO-AHEAD TIP: *This dish should be prepared a day ahead in order to set.*

SOUFFLE
- 4 whole eggs
- 6 egg yolks
- 3/4 cup light honey
- grated rind of 3 medium-size lemons
- juice of 3 medium-size lemons (about 6 tablespoons)
- 3 tablespoons unflavored gelatin
- 1 1/4 cup heavy cream, whipped

DECORATION
- 1/4 cup light honey
- 2 tablespoons water
- shredded rind of 2 medium-size lemons

SOUFFLE: Prepare 1-quart (#6) souffle dish as follows: Tear off a length of aluminum foil or waxed paper 1½ times the outer girth of dish. Fold in half lengthwise and brush with oil. Wrap paper around outside of souffle dish and fasten with masking tape or string.

In mixer, combine eggs, egg yolks, and honey. Beat until mixture is light and very thick. Add lemon rind. Combine lemon juice and gelatin in small saucepan and stir over low heat until gelatin is dissolved. Using rubber scraper, quickly and evenly fold dissolved gelatin into egg mixture. Then fold in whipped cream. Put mixture into prepared souffle dish and let stand in refrigerator until set.

DECORATION: Combine honey and water in small saucepan and stir over low heat until blended. Add lemon rind and simmer gently until rind is translucent (5 to 10 minutes). Drain through strainer and blot rind on paper towels.

PRESENTATION: When souffle is set and ready to serve, remove collar. Arrange lemon rind as border around top of souffle, and place souffle on serving tray.

6 to 8 servings

THE GOLDEN LEMON TART

A specialty of the Windows on the World restaurant on top of the World Trade Center in New York.

DO-AHEAD TIP: *Tart can be prepared a day ahead and refrigerated.*

TART SHELL

1 baked 10- or 11-inch pastry shell of Plain Whole Wheat Short Pastry 1 or 2 (see Index)

FILLING

grated rind of 3 lemons

3/4 cup fresh lemon juice

3/4 cup light honey

1/4 cup water

2 tablespoons cornstarch

1 tablespoon unflavored gelatin

6 egg yolks

1 cup heavy cream, whipped

TOPPING

2 or 3 whole lemons

1/2 cup apricot jam

2 teaspoons fresh lemon juice

FILLING: In top of double boiler, combine lemon rind, lemon juice, honey, water, cornstarch, gelatin, and egg yolks. Stir mixture over simmering water until smooth and thick. Let cool to room temperature. Using rubber scraper, fold whipped cream into lemon mixture. Beat mixture with whisk to make it smooth. Fill pastry shell with lemon cream and chill in refrigerator (or briefly in freezer) until filling sets.

TOPPING: Slice lemons uniformly tissue-paper thin. (This can be done successfully with a very sharp chef's knife and a steady hand, an electric slicer, or a slicing rack called a mandoline.) Combine jam and lemon juice in small saucepan and stir over low heat until dissolved. Rub jam mixture through fine wire strainer.

Arrange lemon slices, overlapping, in concentric circles on top of tart, completely covering top. Using soft pastry brush, gently coat top of lemon slices with dissolved apricot jam to give tart a glistening glaze. Refrigerate finished tart until serving time.

PRESENTATION: Place tart (in or out of pastry baking dish) on paper doily on large round serving tray. Cut wedges about 2 to 3 inches wide for individual servings. Instead of trying to make sharp, neat cut through rind of lemon slices, lift edge of slices a little with your finger where cut is to be made, and cut through tart. Each serving should be covered with 2 or 3 slices of lemon.

8 to 10 servings

LEMON CHICKEN

Carved whole chicken or boned half breasts can be cooked in this savory lemon sauce. It is a fine company dish accompanied by crisp Cheese Fritters.

DO-AHEAD TIP: *Complete chicken recipe can be prepared a day ahead. At serving time, cover with aluminum foil and rewarm in 300°F. oven. Deep-fry fritters at serving time.*

- 1 3½- to 4-pound whole dressed chicken, or 6 half breasts of chicken, skinned and boned
- 2 tablespoons light vegetable oil (e.g., safflower)
- 2 tablespoons unsalted butter
- finely grated rind of 2 lemons
- 2 teaspoons finely chopped fresh garlic
- freshly ground white pepper
- 1 teaspoon tomato paste
- 1 teaspoon meat flavoring, (e.g., Marmite brewer's yeast extract, vegetable paste, or meat glaze)
- 2 tablespoons whole wheat pastry flour
- 1¼ cups chicken stock
- 1 cup sour cream
- 1 cup heavy cream, whipped
- 3 tablespoons fresh lemon juice
- 1 teaspoon light honey
- 1 teaspoon guava jelly
- 3 tablespoons freshly grated Parmesan cheese

Preheat oven to 350°F. Tie whole chicken. Heat 2 tablespoons oil in deep, heavy pot. Put whole chicken (breast side down) or chicken breasts in pot and brown on all sides. Remove chicken from pot and add 2 tablespoons butter. Add lemon rind, garlic, and pepper. Cook over low heat 2 minutes. Remove from heat and add tomato paste, meat flavoring, and flour, and blend to smooth paste. Add stock and stir over moderate heat until sauce comes to a boil. Reduce heat to a slight simmer.

In separate bowl, fold sour cream and whipped cream together. Add mixed cream, spoonful by spoonful, to simmering sauce, stirring vigorously with wire whisk after each addition. Then add lemon juice, honey, and jelly.

Carve whole chicken into serving pieces. Put carved chicken or chicken breasts in sauce in pot. Cook, uncovered, in oven about 30 minutes, or until tender. Occasionally spoon sauce over top of chicken. If sauce separates, it can be rebound by stirring in a little cold sour cream.

PRESENTATION: Arrange chicken on warm heatproof serving platter or gratin dish. Coat with sauce, sprinkle with Parmesan cheese, and brown under broiler. Serve accompanied by a separate plate of Cheese Fritters.

4 to 6 servings

CHEESE FRITTERS

Beignets de Fromage

These "cheese puffs" also make a delightful hors d'oeuvre.

DO-AHEAD TIP: *Dough can be made a day ahead and refrigerated. Deep-fry at serving time.*

- ½ cup water
- 4 tablespoons unsalted butter
- ½ cup whole wheat pastry flour
- 2 eggs
- ¾ teaspoon dry mustard
- ¼ teaspoon baking powder (without aluminum salts)
- 1 egg white
- ½ cup freshly grated Parmesan cheese
- about 2 cups light vegetable oil (e.g., safflower)

Place water and butter in 1-quart saucepan and bring to a rolling boil. Add flour, all at once. Stir over low heat 2 or 3 minutes, until mixture comes away from sides of pan. Place dough in mixer or processor and add eggs, one at a time, beating after each addition. When eggs have been added, continue beating dough until it is shiny. Add mustard and baking powder and mix well. Beat egg white to soft peaks and fold into dough with Parmesan cheese, using a rubber spatula.

Heat oil in deep fryer to 375°F. Drop teaspoonfuls of dough into hot oil and cook until fritters are golden brown all over. Remove with slotted spoon. Place on warm napkin on serving plate and serve at once.

4 to 6 servings

LEMON CURD TARTLETS

DO-AHEAD TIP: *Pastry shells and filling can be prepared up to 2 to 3 weeks ahead and stored in freezer. Add filling and topping at serving time.*

TARTLET SHELLS

12 baked 3½- or 4-inch tartlet shells of Plain Whole Wheat Short Pastry 1 or 2 (see Index)

LEMON CURD

finely grated rind of 2 large or 3 medium-size lemons

juice of 2 large or 3 medium-size lemons

⅔ cup light honey

3 eggs, well beaten

16 tablespoons cold unsalted butter, cut into ½-inch cubes

CHOICE OF DECORATION (optional)

1 cup heavy cream, whipped

fresh raspberries

coarsely grated carob bar, frozen

LEMON CURD: In top of double boiler over simmering water, combine lemon rind and lemon juice, honey, eggs, and butter. Stir with wooden spoon until mixture has consistency of thick cream sauce. Pour into shallow layer cake pan and place in freezer until very thick or set.

PRESENTATION: When ready to serve, place a couple of tablespoons of lemon curd in each pastry shell. (Filling need not be smoothed out.) Serve plain, or, if desired, top with border of whipped cream, piped through pastry bag fitted with medium star tube (#6 or #7), border of fresh raspberries, or sprinkling of coarsely grated carob.

Makes 12 tartlets

LEMON PILAFF

DO-AHEAD TIP: *Cooked rice without cheese freezes well. At serving time, rewarm in steamer and add cheese.*

- 1 tablespoon light vegetable oil (e.g., safflower)
- 1 large yellow onion, finely chopped
- 1 teaspoon finely chopped fresh garlic
- 1½ cups long grain brown rice
- 1 egg, beaten
- 3½ cups stock (e.g., chicken, vegetable, or soy—3½ cups water with 3½ teaspoons tamari soy sauce)
- 1 tablespoon grated lemon rind
- 2 tablespoons fresh lemon juice
- ¼ cup freshly grated Parmesan cheese

Preheat oven to 350°F. Combine oil, onion, and garlic in small saute pan and cook over moderate heat until onion is soft. Set aside.

In deep, heavy pot (about 1½-quart capacity), mix rice with beaten egg. Stir over moderate heat until rice kernels are dry and separate. Add onion and garlic mixture, stock, and lemon rind and juice. Stir over moderate heat until liquid comes to a boil. Cover pot with firm-fitting lid and cook in oven 1 hour, or until rice is tender, without disturbing it.

PRESENTATION: When rice is cooked, add 2 tablespoons grated cheese and toss with 2 forks. Rice can be pressed into lightly oiled mold and turned out onto serving plate, or simply piled into warm serving dish. Sprinkle remaining grated cheese over top.

4 to 6 servings

LEMON-WALNUT FROZEN YOGURT

This yogurt is a light and fine dessert.

DO-AHEAD TIP: *Frozen yogurt keeps well in freezer at 0°F. for 2 or 3 days. After that it will start to crystallize.*

- 2 cups plain yogurt (regular or low-fat)
- 8 tablespoons nonfat dry milk
- 1/3 cup light honey
- grated rind of 2 lemons
- 4 tablespoons fresh lemon juice
- 2 teaspoons unflavored gelatin dissolved in 2 tablespoons boiling water
- 1/4 cup chopped English or black walnuts
- 1 egg white

In mixing bowl, combine yogurt, dry milk, honey, lemon rind, and lemon juice, and dissolved gelatin, and mix well with whisk. Chill for 45 minutes. Transfer to drum of ice cream maker and process until half firm. Beat egg white to soft peaks, fold into half-frozen yogurt mixture with walnuts, and continue processing until mixture is firm. Transfer to freezer container and store at 0°F. in freezer. At serving time, allow frozen yogurt to soften a little.

4 servings

More Lemon Recipes

See Index for the following recipes:

APPETIZER: Seviche, Acapulco Style; SOUP: Avocado-Lemon Soup; DESSERTS: Cold Lemon-Carob Layered Souffle, Lemon Sherbet; BEVERAGE: Citrus Ade Concentrate with Buttermilk or Yogurt; SAUCES: Basic Vinaigrette Dressing, Citrus Sauce for Desserts, Honey Dressing, Lemon-Yogurt Dressing.

LIMES

There are two distinctly different types of limes, and, unfortunately, the type that I consider superior and as versatile as the lemon is not generally distributed beyond the areas where it is grown – southern Florida and Mexico. This lime is called Key lime or Mexican lime, or in Mexico, *limon*. It is a small, round citrus, 1 to 1½ inches in diameter, with a thin rind of greenish-yellow at maturity. Its flesh is faint yellow with just a tinge of green, and the flavor of its juice is delicately acid, not as sharply bitter as lemon nor as bold and pungent as the larger green lime. As related in the section on lemons, this *limon* is a remarkable all-purpose seasoning in Mexico, where a dish of little wedges is always on the table. A few drops on food, and its gentle piquance perks up palatability without masking or overwhelming.

Our familiar green lime is called the Tahiti or Persian lime by Florida producers and Bearss lime by California producers. It has the familiar elliptical shape of the lemon but is usually a little smaller, with a green rind and flesh greener than the Key or Mexican lime. It, too, is grown in Mexico, where it is called *lima* to differentiate it from the *limon*.

I think the robust Tahiti lime is a delicious fruit for its distinct flavor. I prefer a frosty glass of limeade over lemonade and lime sherbet over lemon. It is an interesting change from lemon with fish or meat, in iced tea, or in salad dressing. It is a must in the marinade for seviche. Its juice and rind make a fine lime pie, but it does not have the same taste nor is it as versatile as Key lime or *limon*.

CRANBERRY-LIME SUBLIME

This is an attractive red and green holiday dessert.

DO-AHEAD TIP: *Lime sherbet and cranberry jelly or sauce can be prepared 2 or 3 days ahead.*

- 1 **quart Lime Sherbet (see Index)**
- ½ **cup Cranberry Jelly or Cranberry Sauce (see Index)**
- 4 to 6 **thin lime slices**

Divide lime sherbet in chilled dessert glasses. Top each serving with spoonful of cranberry jelly or sauce. Slit each lime slice to center. Hang lime slice on side of each glass.

4 to 6 servings

LIME SOUFFLE WITH SABAYON SAUCE

DO-AHEAD TIP: *Souffle mixture, up to the point of adding egg whites, can be prepared several hours ahead, covered with plastic wrap, and left to stand at room temperature. At serving time, add egg whites and bake. Sauce should be prepared while souffle is baking.*

SOUFFLE
- 2 tablespoons unsalted butter
- 3 tablespoons whole wheat pastry flour
- ⅔ cup milk
- grated rind of 2 large limes
- juice of 2 large limes (¼ cup)
- 2 tablespoons light honey
- 4 egg yolks
- 6 egg whites

SABAYON SAUCE (optional)
- 3 egg yolks
- 2 tablespoons light honey
- 1 tablespoon lime juice

SOUFFLE: Preheat oven to 375°F. Brush 1-quart souffle dish with oil. Tear off length of aluminum foil or waxed paper 1½ times the outer girth of dish. Fold in half lengthwise and brush one side with oil. Wrap around souffle dish and fasten with string or masking tape.

Melt butter in 1-quart saucepan. Add flour and stir over low heat 1 minute. Remove from heat and add milk. Stir over moderate heat until mixture thickens. Add lime rind and juice, honey, and egg yolks, and mix well.

Beat egg whites to soft peaks. Fold egg yolk mixture into egg whites gently and evenly. Spoon souffle mixture into prepared dish. Bake 30 minutes, or until souffle rises and browns.

SABAYON SAUCE: Prepare sauce, if desired, about 10 minutes before souffle is finished baking. Place egg yolks, honey, and lime juice in small bowl. Beat with electric hand beater or manual rotary beater. Stand bowl in small saute pan half filled with hot water over low heat and beat constantly until mixture is thick and smooth (the consistency and appearance of hollandaise sauce). Remove bowl from water and continue beating until sauce is cool.

PRESENTATION: When souffle is done, gently place it on serving tray and remove collar. Serve sauce in separate bowl.

4 to 6 servings

LIME AND CAROB TART IN COCONUT-CRUMB CRUST

DO-AHEAD TIP: *Coconut crumb crust can be made in advance and frozen. Filled tart can be prepared a day ahead and refrigerated. Topping of lime slices and shaved carob should be added no more than 3 or 4 hours before serving.*

TART SHELL

1 baked 11-inch Coconut-Crumb Shell (see Index)

CAROB FILLING

¾ cup carob powder

1 teaspoon ground cinnamon

½ cup boiling water

3 tablespoons cold unsalted butter, cut into bits

2 egg yolks

LIME CHIFFON FILLING

3 eggs

8 tablespoons unsalted butter, at room temperature

⅓ cup light honey

4 tablespoons grated lime rind

6 tablespoons fresh lime juice

1½ tablespoons cornstarch

1 cup heavy cream, whipped

DECORATION

tissue-thin slices of fresh lime, enough to cover top of tart (use sharp chef's knife, electric slicer, or mandoline)

½ cup coarsely shredded carob bar

CAROB FILLING: Place carob powder and cinnamon in small saucepan. Add boiling water slowly while stirring with small whisk. Stir over low heat until mixture is completely blended. Add butter, bit by bit, stirring constantly. Remove from heat at once. Add egg yolks, one at a time, stirring until blended into mixture. Spread filling on bottom of tart shell.

LIME CHIFFON FILLING: Combine eggs, butter, honey, lime rind, lime juice, and cornstarch in top of double boiler. Stir over simmering water until mixture thickens. Spread mixture in layer cake pan or on small platter and chill. When cool, fold into whipped cream. Spread filling on top of carob. Chill filled tart in refrigerator.

PRESENTATION: Cover top with slices of lime. Scatter shredded carob on top of lime slices. Refrigerate finished tart until serving time.

8 to 10 servings

SESAME RICE

A sprinkling of fresh lime juice adds the topnote to this interesting rice mixture. Only lime, not lemon, gives it the right touch.

DO-AHEAD TIP: *Plain-cooked rice can be frozen. At serving time, rewarm rice and toss with sesame seed and pecan garnish.*

- **1 tablespoon light vegetable oil (e.g., safflower)**
- **4 tablespoons pecan halves**
- **¼ cup sesame seeds**
- **cayenne pepper**
- **1 bay leaf, crushed**
- **4 cups hot Plain-Cooked Brown Rice (see Index)**
- **3 tablespoons fresh lime juice**

Heat oil in small saute pan. Add pecans, and stir over moderate heat until nuts begin to brown a little. Remove from pan immediately. Add sesame seeds to pan with a dash of cayenne pepper and crushed bay leaf. Stir sesame seeds over moderate heat 1 minute. Remove pan from heat and add pecans to sesame seeds. Add sesame seed and pecan mixture to hot cooked rice and toss lightly with 2 forks. Transfer to hot serving dish or mold. Sprinkle lime juice on top.

4 to 6 servings

SEVICHE, ACAPULCO STYLE

This mixture of cubed raw fish and/or shellfish marinated to cold-cooked perfection in citrus juices is a piquant and refreshing appetizer. There are several seviche versions. In Acapulco, chopped tomato is added.

DO-AHEAD TIP: *Seviche should be prepared a day ahead in order to marinate.*

- **1 pound raw fish (e.g., sole, bass, pompano, haddock, trout, or catfish), skinned and boned; or raw shrimp, cleaned; or a combination**
- **¼ cup plus 2 tablespoons fresh lemon juice**
- **¼ cup fresh lime juice**
- **½ pound (1 large or 2 medium-size) ripe tomatoes, peeled, seeded, and diced**
- **½ cup finely chopped pearl onions**
- **2 tablespoons light vegetable oil (e.g., safflower)**
- **1 teaspoon fresh oregano, or ½ teaspoon dried oregano**

Wash fish and/or shrimp in cold water with 2 tablespoons lemon juice and dry between paper towels. Cut seafood into bite-size pieces (½- to ¾-inch cubes). Place seafood in porcelain bowl, pour lime and lemon juices over all, and let mixture stand in refrigerator overnight. Stir mixture occasionally.

PRESENTATION: When ready to serve, add tomato, onions, oil, and oregano. As first course at table, serve on individual plates or in large shells. For cocktail party, serve in large bowl or shell with plate of whole wheat or sesame crackers.

6 servings as first course or 18 as small hors d'oeuvres

FROSTY LIMEADE

- 2 teaspoons grated lime rind
- ¼ cup fresh lime juice
- 2 to 3 tablespoons light honey, to taste
- 1 cup ice cubes
- 1 lime slice

Blend all ingredients except garnish in blender until mixture is smooth slush. Pour into chilled glass. Hang lime slice on rim of glass. Serve with straw.

Yields 1 cup

More Lime Recipes

See Index for the following recipes:

DESSERTS: Frozen Avocado-Lime Souffle, Lime Sherbet, Mango-Lime Frozen Yogurt; BEVERAGES: Citrus Combo, Coco-Limon, Citrus Ade Concentrate with Buttermilk or Yogurt, Pineapple-Lime Frost; SAUCE: Citrus Sauce for Desserts.

MANDARINS

The tangerine, king of the mandarins, is a remarkable product of fruit "engineering," partly by nature and partly by man, to achieve the ultimate convenience food. I think this tribute to the tangerine published in *Gourmet* magazine over 20 years ago still says it: "A tangerine is an orange with a sense of fair play. Loose-skinned and easy peeling, segmented for bite-size convenience, it neither oozes, squashes, nor squirts at us. Even in the politest society, he who reaches for a tangerine, reaches for a sure thing. And the tangerine's sense of timing is faultless. With a November to April season, reaching a peak supply at Christmas, tangerine has been the reward in every good American child's Yuletide stocking for generations. Obliging in all ways, it is a most accommodating citrus."

Its main attractions, of course, are its zipper- or slip-skin, easy separation of its segments, and cool, refreshing, sweet juice, full of fragrance and zest—strong selling features that have encouraged a variety of hybrids. Some producers predict that by the early part of the next century mandarin-type oranges will exceed production of regular oranges. There are already so many hybrids being marketed by varietal or trade names that I found it helpful to identify the features of some of the more prominent ones:

Mandarin, the general name for all slip-skins, refers to three types of orange: satsuma, tangerine, and hybrids—which include tangelo, tangor (of which the popular Temple is one type), and a variety of others, including complex hybrids.

Satsuma is grown mainly in Japan; also in Florida. It is essentially seedless and small to medium in size.

Tangerine characteristically is medium to large in size, contains a few to many seeds, and is deep orange to red in color. There are many varieties, including the well-known Dancy, named for the "founder" of the tangerine industry in Florida and one of the foremost growers.

Clementine, or Algerian tangerine, can be seedless or have many seeds. It is small to medium, and orange in color.

Tangelo is a cross of tangerine and grapefruit (the name is a combination of tangerine and *pomelo*, or grapefruit). It looks like a tangerine, but it is more snugly attached. The tangelo is very juicy, with flavor like mixed orange and grapefruit but much sweeter than grapefruit.

Temple is perhaps the best known of the tangor. Its origin is a mystery, but it is believed to be a cross between tangerine and orange. It is juicy, with a spicy-sweet character. The Temple is larger than a tangerine, with a slightly rough red-orange rind. It is often called Temple orange in the market, although it is categorically a slip-skin mandarin.

Florida is by far the largest producing state. A lot of our mandarins also come from Mexico. The season runs from October to May, peaking from November through January. Like all citrus fruits, mandarins do not ripen after they have been picked. Choose those that are heavy for their size, which is a clue to lots of juice. A puffy appearance is normal for many varieties, but the fruit should still have weight and there should be no soft areas or mold.

Tangerine or any mandarin seems to be about the neatest way to have a snack or "drink" on the run, and pack in the vitamins (C and A). They're bright spots in salads and marvelous garnishes with poultry and fish, for color and flavor, and half-skins are attractive cups in which to serve a salad with tangerines, a fruit cocktail, ice cream, sherbet, or frozen souffle.

For juice, cut the fruit in half and press through a citrus juicer, the same as with an orange or lemon.

For whole segments, remove the sections carefully without breaking them. Pick off all strings. With the point of kitchen shears or the tip of a sharp paring knife, cut out the center core of each segment and surrounding seeds.

For half shells to use as cups, cut through the rind only, all around the middle of the mandarin, being careful not to cut into the flesh. Pull away the top half of the rind. Remove segments from the bottom half. Remove as much loose fiber as possible from both halves. (This method gives whole segments to use as desired. To juice flesh removed from shells, rub it through a vegetable strainer.) If the mandarin skin is snug, cut it completely in half and remove the flesh and fiber as described in the section on oranges.

For whole shells to use as cups with tops, cut off the top third of the mandarin. With a spoon, carefully remove the flesh from the top and scoop it out of the bottom. Remove as many fibers from the inside shell as possible. Fill the bottom shell with desired filling. Cover with the top shell, tilting it at an angle.

SPINACH, ENDIVE, MUSHROOM, AND TANGERINE SALAD

DO-AHEAD TIP: *When salad is assembled as described below and is not tossed, it will stay crisp and cold overnight in refrigerator.*

- **1 tablespoon finely grated tangerine rind**
- **¾ cup Basic Vinaigrette Dressing (see Index)**
- **1 pound spinach, well washed and dried**
- **3 heads Belgian endive**
- **6 medium-size firm white mushrooms, thinly sliced**
- **1 cup mandarin sections, any type, strings and seeds removed**
- **2 tablespoons finely chopped fresh chives, tarragon, or dill**

Add tangerine rind to dressing in screwtop jar and shake well. Pour dressing on bottom of salad serving bowl. Tear spinach in bite-size pieces and put in separate dry bowl. Thinly slice endive *on bias,* separate slices, and toss with spinach. Drop spinach and endive on top of dressing. Drop mushrooms on top of greens. Scatter mandarin sections on top of salad and sprinkle with chopped herb. Cover with plastic wrap and refrigerate until ready to serve. Then toss salad, coating all ingredients with dressing.

6 servings

COLD TANGERINE SOUFFLE

DO-AHEAD TIP: *This dessert should be prepared a day ahead in order to set.*

SOUFFLE

- 4 egg yolks
- 1/3 cup light honey
- 2 tablespoons unflavored gelatin
- 1 cup milk, scalded
- juice of 1 tangerine (about 1/4 cup)
- finely grated rind of 4 medium-size tangerines
- 1 cup heavy cream, whipped
- 3 egg whites

DECORATION

- sections of 2 tangerines, strings and seeds carefully removed
- 1/2 cup red currant jelly
- 1/2 cup finely chopped walnuts

SOUFFLE: Prepare 3- or 4-cup souffle dish by tearing off a length of aluminum foil or waxed paper 1 1/2 times the outer girth of dish. Fold in half lengthwise. Brush one side with oil. Wrap paper around dish and fasten with masking tape or string. Set aside.

Combine egg yolks and honey in mixer and beat until light and thick. Add gelatin. Continue beating while slowly adding scalded milk. Pour this custard mixture into saucepan and stir over low heat until it coats the back of a spoon. Add tangerine juice.

Transfer custard mixture to bowl over ice. Stir with whisk until cool. Add tangerine rind. Fold in whipped cream. Beat egg whites to soft peaks and fold into mixture. Spoon mixture into prepared souffle dish and refrigerate until set.

PRESENTATION: When souffle is set, remove paper collar. Dissolve jelly over low heat and let cool to room temperature. Gently spread jelly over top of souffle. Arrange border of tangerine sections around top. Stick walnuts around side of souffle that is above the dish. Refrigerate until ready to serve.

4 to 6 servings

TANGERINE SHERBET IN TANGERINE SHELLS

DO-AHEAD TIP: *This dessert should be prepared a day ahead in order to freeze well.*

SHERBET

1½ cups light honey

½ cup water

thinly pared rind of 4 tangerines and 2 oranges

2 cups juice, using juice of 2 oranges and remainder from tangerines

2 egg whites

TANGERINE SHELLS

6 whole small tangerine shells and tops, well chilled

6 fresh laurel or small lemon leaves (optional)

SHERBET: Combine honey and water in deep, heavy pot and bring slowly to boil. Add rind and simmer gently 5 minutes. Add fruit juice and strain. Let cool. Freeze juice mixture in churn-type ice cream maker. When sherbet is partially set, beat egg whites to soft peaks and add to sherbet in freezer drum. Continue freezing until sherbet is set.

PRESENTATION: Fill tangerine shells with frozen sherbet. If desired, stick laurel or lemon leaves in stem point of tops, and place tops on top of sherbet, slightly tilted. Store in freezer until serving time. (They will get frosty all over.) Serve on paper doilies on individual dessert plates.

6 servings

More Mandarin Recipes

See Index for the following recipes:

SALAD: Tossed Greens Salad with Fruit; DESSERT: *Macedoine de Fruits.*

MANGOES

"Un momentito, señora, por favor?" begged the Acapulco taxi driver as he drew the car to the curb of a Las Brisas drive. Along the tree-lined street where I was living, he had spied some mangoes that had fallen to the ground, which he went to gather. Carefully he placed them on the front seat, like treasures, his whole action respectful of the anticipated treat of this luscious fruit. (I have always been struck by the way people in the tropics, who have more variety and abundance of fresh fruit than anywhere else, regard fruit with such delight, absolute glee, from the common mango to the uncommon apple.)

Today mangoes are increasingly available in northern fruit markets, but they are yet to become a familiar or popular fruit in restaurants and homes. Perhaps the mango needs to be romanced by fashionable chefs to get others to take notice. It certainly has preeminent cooking credentials. This five- or six-inch-long oval-shaped fruit, covered with a smooth, sturdy greenish skin, has a nice, firm flesh similar to the peach. In comparison, the qualities of a properly ripe peach would be considered more delicate to the mango's richer orange color, more juice, and spicier, zestier flavor.

Thanks to my good friend Pepe Santiago, who is proprietor of the best Mexican-food restaurant and a meat market with Harrod-like displays in Acapulco, and owner of a fruit ranch to the south, I have learned a lot about mangoes. One Monday, when the restaurant is closed, Pepe invited me to accompany him on his weekly visit to the ranch. We traveled in Pepe's Jeep truck along the Costa Chica for about 100 miles to the south, to Las Lechugas. There, hectares upon hectares of mango trees (2,000 of them), tamarind trees, and, sprawling all over the ground, watermelon vines. I asked Pepe to which market he sends such a large mango crop. None. There are two families living and working on the ranch. Each day they pick and sell at least 200 boxes of mangoes (each box containing about 70 pounds – 30 to 35 fruits) at a stand on the federal highway. I was amazed. Who buys so many from a roadside stand? "The people from all around the countryside come and buy one or two boxes every three or four days during mango season. Mexican families have a lot of children, so one box doesn't last very long. Some of the crop is sold to a cannery for marmalade."

I asked Pepe to show me the best way to slice and peel a mango. He took a ripe fruit and a sharp knife and, with the grace and dexterity that is inherent in Mexicans, performed this demonstration: Holding the mango on its side, he cut off a lengthwise slice, as close to the stone as possible. He continued to cut lengthwise slices from around the mango until the stone was quite bare. (It is not a freestone.) Then, taking one slice at a time, he anchored it with a fork at one end and cut the flesh away from the skin. (Some people stand the mango on its end and follow the same cutting procedure.)

Later that week, back at his Tlaquepaque Restaurant, Pepe taught me how to prepare *chiles rellenos en nogada* (Mexican-style stuffed peppers with walnut sauce – often referred to as Mexico's national dish), with mango and a variety of other stuffings – pineapple, guava, cheese, meat and potato.

(If I rhapsodize about Mexican food, I am not alone. Famous novelist Richard Condon took time out to write a marvelous Mexican cookbook with his daughter Wendy, titled *The Mexican Stove.* "Mexican food," declared Condon, "is not only sensationally triumphant, but it has a wealth of health and more bounce to the ounce.")

Perhaps one reason that we northerners have yet to become truly mango-conscious is that too often we get green ones. Mangoes should be tree ripened (like citrus). They do not ripen satisfactorily after they are picked. A properly ripe mango will show tinges of yellow and red on its deep green skin and it will give a little to pressure from the thumb. There should be no brown spots. Almost all of our mangoes come from southern Florida. They are a super package of nutrients, a medium-size one (only 88 calories) containing more than 100 percent of an adult's daily requirement of vitamin A and 75 percent of his vitamin C needs.

Mangoes are around from January to late August, and are an exciting change in any recipe that calls for peaches – for example, salad, compote, pie, ice cream, sherbet, jam – and a beautiful addition to fruit platters with other tropical fruits. The spicy tang of fresh mango slices goes well with poultry and meat, or as chunks added to your favorite bread and stuffing for poultry. Cateress Susana Palazuelos garnishes barbecued pork with mango slices.

If you get some green or semiripe fruit, cook up some mango chutney. Delicious.

MANGO CHANTILLY

DO-AHEAD TIP: *This dish can be made a day ahead and refrigerated.*

- **4 ripe mangoes, sliced and peeled**
- **½ cup light honey**
- **2 cups heavy cream**
- **skinned sections of 2 oranges, cut into small bits and drained**
- **1 cup coarsely chopped pecans**

Puree mangoes in food processor until smooth. Add honey and process again. Beat heavy cream in large bowl over ice. Fold in mango puree. Then fold in oranges and pecans. Chill thoroughly. Serve in dessert glasses.

6 to 8 servings

MANGO OR PAPAYA CHUTNEY

Green seckel pears can be substituted for the mangoes or papayas in this recipe.

DO-AHEAD TIP: *Chutney should be prepared at least a week before use in order to allow it to ripen in the jar.*

- 1 pint cider vinegar
- 1 whole head garlic, each clove peeled
- ⅓ pound fresh ginger, cut into chunks
- ½ cup coriander seeds
- 2 teaspoons dried Italian red pepper
- 1 pound raisins, or more, if desired
- ½ bushel green or half-ripe mangoes or green papayas, sliced and peeled
- 4½ cups light honey

Place vinegar, garlic, ginger, coriander, and pepper in blender or processor and blend until smooth. Combine mixture with raisins, mangoes or papayas, and honey in large pot and cook until mangoes are transparent. Spoon into jars and seal according to manufacturer's instructions.

Yields about 4 quarts

POACHED MANGOES OR PEARS WITH CUSTARD SAUCE

DO-AHEAD TIP: *Poached fruit and custard sauce can be prepared a day ahead and refrigerated.*

- ½ cup light honey
- ½ cup water
- 2 strips lemon or orange rind
- 4 medium-size ripe mangoes, or 6 ripe pears (not too soft)
- 2 cups custard sauce (Creme Anglaise; see Index)
- ½ cup coarsely shredded carob bar, frozen

If mangoes are used, slice and peel them. If pears are used, core, peel, and cut them in halves or quarters.

Combine honey, water, and rind in deep, heavy pot and bring to a boil over low heat. Add mangoes or pears, bring syrup back to slight simmer, and cook fruit 5 minutes, turning it occasionally. Remove fruit with slotted spoon to serving dish. Continue to cook syrup until it is very thick. Pour reduced syrup over fruit.

PRESENTATION: At serving time, top fruit with custard sauce and sprinkle with carob.

6 servings

MANGO-LIME FROZEN YOGURT

DO-AHEAD TIP: *Frozen fruit yogurt keeps well in freezer at 0° F. for 2 or 3 days. After that it will start to crystallize.*

YOGURT

- 1 cup pureed ripe mango
- 1 tablespoon grated lime rind
- 2 tablespoons fresh lime juice
- 2 cups plain yogurt (regular or low-fat)
- ¾ cup nonfat dry milk
- ¼ cup light honey, or more to taste
- 2 teaspoons unflavored gelatin dissolved in 2 tablespoons boiling water
- 1 egg white

CHOICE OF GARNISH (optional)

- 4 thin lime slices
- 4 teaspoons chopped cashews
- few mint sprigs

In mixing bowl, combine pureed mango, lime rind, lime juice, yogurt, dry milk, honey, and dissolved gelatin, and mix well with whisk. Transfer to drum of ice cream maker and process until half firm. Beat egg white to soft peaks, fold into half-frozen yogurt mixture, and continue processing until firm. Transfer to freezer container and store at 0°F. At serving time, allow frozen yogurt to soften a little. Garnish as desired.

4 servings

More Mango Recipes

See Index for the following recipes:

SOUP: Iced Fruit Soup; MAIN DISHES: Chicken in the Snow, *Chiles Rellenos,* Fruit Omelet; SALADS: Cabbage and Fruit Salad with Honey Dressing, Tossed Greens Salad with Fruit; DESSERTS: French Fruit Tart and Tartlets, Fresh Fruit Ice Cream, Frozen Fruit Souffle, Frozen Fruit Yogurt, *Macedoine de Fruits,* Peaches of the Blushing Poppea, Swiss Plum Tart.

MELONS

If you are confused as I sometimes am about all of the different kinds of melon we encounter in our markets, what could be more useful to all of us than a mini-manual on melons? Different types do provide different clues for determining ripeness. And, if you're mad about melons, as many of us are, what is more maddening than getting stuck with a bad melon?

Mini-Manual on Melons
Botanically speaking, there are two separate melon families: *muskmelons*, which originated in Asia, and *watermelons*, which originated in Africa.

Muskmelons The general class of muskmelons was so named because of the pungent aroma of the ripe fruit. "Musk" is from the Persian, meaning a kind of perfume, and melon derived from the Latin *melopepo*, meaning "apple-shaped melon." My neighbor, international food critic/writer James Villas, is frankly obsessed with melons. During one of his trips to France, he purchased four of the French Cavaillon melons (cantaloupe type) and took them on the QE-2 for his return voyage. After a few hours in his stateroom, the sultry perfume of these melons had so permeated the air that Jim had to put them out in the hall in order to sleep. The next morning the whole corridor smelled of melon!

Cantaloupe: The name is taken from Cantaluppi, a former residence of the Popes near Rome where this melon was brought from Armenia and cultivated. The cantaloupe can be round or football shaped, but to be properly mature, it should be at least five inches in diameter. The formation of gray netting which covers the outside should be thick and raised. The background color of the skin should be slightly yellow, not green. There should be a delicate melon fragrance. An important clue as to whether or not the melon was picked at proper maturity is to look at the spot where it was removed from the vine. It should be a round, depressed hollow, indicating that the fruit detached from the stem easily. If the hollow is rough or has a bit of stem still attached, the melon is immature. And remember, sweetness ceases to develop once the cantaloupe is picked.

When cantaloupes are picked at the "full slip" moment, as the smooth hollow is called, the fruit can be held in commercial refrigeration for several days to suspend any further development. The consumer who acquires the melon can let it stand at room temperature for two to four days, during which time its flesh will soften and become juicier, but not sweeter. A good-quality cantaloupe has firm but not rubbery flesh with a small, dry seed cavity. Cantaloupes are available year-round with homegrowns peaking during June, July, and August.

Casaba: A large round melon, with yellow furrowed rind and pointed at the stem end. The casaba has creamy white flesh that is sweet and juicy but has little aroma.

Crenshaw: Considered to have superior eating quality – sweet, juicy, and fragrant, with a touch of spice. The crenshaw is a large melon, round or oblong, weighing seven to nine pounds, with a slightly furrowed, streaky green and gold exterior. The succulent flesh is salmon colored.

Persian: It looks like a large cantaloupe with the characteristic gray netting, except that the background of the Persian, when properly mature, is a light green color. The rind should give with a little pressure. Persians average 7½ inches in diameter and weigh about seven pounds. The peach/orange-colored flesh is sweet and fragrant.

Honeydew: The muskmelon with the light green, syrupy sweet flesh. It may be round or oval, and the rind should definitely be white, perhaps with just a trace of green. (There are some new hybrids of honeydew that have a dark green or very light creamy-colored rind and are slightly smaller than the average honeydew.) The blossom end can be hard to slightly springy. An important difference from the cantaloupe types is that the honeydew has no aroma. But, the honeydew will continue to ripen and sweeten *after* it is picked. It is the only melon that develops more sugar after picking. The flesh should be firm, very juicy, and very sweet with a rather mild flavor. Honeydews are available year-round but are most abundant from May to November.

Honeyball: A small honeydew that has a rind covered with netting. When properly ripe, the honeyball is soft and fragrant. The flesh can be white-green or pink. Its season is from June to November.

Watermelon African hieroglyphs indicate that men have been raising this hot-weather tonic for over 4,000 years. One of the more recent growers was myself. For one season I was the co-investor in a watermelon patch near Tres Palos, Mexico. It was a result of searching for a way to improve the income of my friends Miguel and Fujencia to support their eight children. After exploring various ideas with Miguel, we decided to rent some land and raise "*sandias, tomates, y cebollas*" (watermelons, tomatoes, and onions) that would surely be sold in the market in Acapulco. Miguel worked very hard and harvested excellent crops that were praised by all of my friends. The problem: no transportation of our own; it cost us more to get our crops transported to the market than we made. This caused us to reconsider this venture and ponder the feasibility of buying a truck. That would have been very expensive and bureaucratically involved. In the end we abandoned the farming business and, instead, purchased a gypsy taxi for Miguel to use for transporting workers to and from Acapulco, and he still operates it.

Today watermelons come in all sizes and colors, from large oblongs weighing up to 35 pounds to midgets, but always the taste treat inside should be red, crisp, sweet, wet flesh with a network of seeds. The flesh should not be mealy. The seeds, which can be white or black in different varieties, should be fully mature and hard.

Watermelon must be picked when fully ripe. The surest way to find out how ripe it is is to take a plug from it. Another clue is to examine the lower side, where it rested on the ground; if it is somewhat yellow instead of white or pale green, it is probably ripe. The size of watermelon is a quality factor insofar as the larger the melon, the more edible flesh per cubic inch. Taking Mexican and United States sources together, watermelons are on the market from March through October, but fortunately supply peaks when our desire is greatest – in June, July, and August.
Sugar Baby melons: These are midget watermelons, weighing eight to ten pounds, which have become quite popular.

All melons are low-calorie, healthful, convenience foods. Half a small cantaloupe contains more than 100 percent of the adult daily requirement of vitamin A and 100 percent of the required vitamin C. The honeydew contains a moderate amount of vitamin C and some A. The watermelon has an impressive density of nutrients: A four- by eight-inch wedge contains only 115 calories but provides half of the adult daily requirement of vitamin A, two-thirds of the vitamin C, plus 2.1 milligrams of iron.

Modern cooks are taking a more creative attitude toward melons. Melon aficionado Jim Villas is constantly experimenting with different ways to add melon to his meals, such as the recipe for cantaloupe with shrimp, included here. Cold melon soup and frosty melon drinks with yogurt or buttermilk are divine! The Gingered Cantaloupe Tart is the answer to a bumper crop of luscious local melons, and minted honeydew mousse is an airy delight to end a meal any time of the year. The wave of new cooking ideas surfaced watermelon ice (which has long been popular in Mexico). Any kind of melon also provides an elegant natural serving bowl. Little honey balls are delightful for this purpose: Cut off the top third, remove seeds, fill with fresh fruit mixture or sherbet, and replace top, tilted half open with a toothpick. Fill half cantaloupes for individual servings of all manner of cold soups, salads, and desserts. For a large serving dish, use a larger melon shell – filled with mousse, scoops of ice cream or sherbet, mixed fruit, and so on. Does any food presentation excite a lazy appetite better than a watermelon basket filled with a melange of cold, crisp, colorful fresh fruits? (When using a melon shell for a serving container, always cut a thin slice off the bottom so that the shell stands steady.)

Of course, melons have always been favorite party pleasers for hors d' oeuvres, with cheese or seafood, or to add color and spice to salads, fruit bowls, and drinks, or a refreshing sherbet, an interesting chutney. Watermelon rind pickles are a must on many holiday tables. A first course of honeydew with a sprinkle of ginger pleasantly titillates taste buds for the meal to come. And half of a ripe cantaloupe with a scoop of ice cream has no peer. Since melons have wide stretches of firm flesh, they can be cut into all sorts of shapes – balls, cubes, or slices – that can garnish appetizer trays, salads, or desserts. How about a dish of cantaloupe cubes covered with cold custard sauce?

CANTALOUPE WITH SHRIMP

DO-AHEAD TIP: *Filling can be prepared a day ahead. Assemble at serving time.*

- 2 to 3 pounds raw shrimp
- 1 tablespoon caraway seeds
- 4 to 6 small cantaloupes
- 2 tablespoons chili sauce
- 1 tablespoon tamari soy sauce
- juice of 1 orange
- 2 tablespoons finely chopped fresh dill, or 2 teaspoons dried dillweed
- 4 tablespoons extra virgin olive oil
- freshly ground white pepper
- 2 to 3 small, ripe tomatoes, peeled, halved, and seeds removed
- 4 to 6 pitted black olives, sliced
- 1/4 cup Basic Mayonnaise (see Index)
- 1/4 cup heavy cream, whipped

Place shrimp in pot, just cover with water, add caraway seeds, and bring slowly to a boil. Boil only until shrimp turn pink. Drain at once. Chill shrimp, then shell and devein all but 4 to 6 for garnish.

Cut top third off each cantaloupe. Remove seeds. Cut all melon flesh into balls. Set aside 4 to 6 balls for garnish. Mix chili sauce and tamari. Set aside. In large bowl, combine cleaned shrimp, all but reserved melon balls, orange juice, dill, chili sauce and tamari mixture, olive oil, and pepper. Mix well.

PRESENTATION: Fill each melon with mixture and *replace lids upside down*, fixing each at an angle with a cocktail pick to tilt it. Place tomato half on each lid. Artistically arrange a reserved unpeeled shrimp and a melon ball inside each tomato and garnish with a few slices of olive. Place melon on bed of crushed ice. Fold mayonnaise and whipped cream together and serve in separate bowl.

4 to 6 servings

GINGERED CANTALOUPE TART

DO-AHEAD TIP: *Tart should be prepared a day ahead in order to set.*

- **1** **10- or 11-inch pastry shell of Spicy Sweet Short Pastry (see Index); lattice topping is not used**
- **2** **large cantaloupes (7- to 8-inch diameter)**
- **4** **tablespoons orange juice**
- **3** **tablespoons fresh lemon juice**
- **2** **tablespoons grated orange rind**
- **2** **tablespoons light honey**
- **2** **teaspoons ground ginger**
- **1½** **tablespoons unflavored gelatin**
- **¾** **cup heavy cream, whipped**
- **¾** **cup apricot preserve**
- **1** **cup toasted Coconut Curls (see Index), or ½ cup toasted slivered almonds (optional)**

Prepare pastry shell and bake as directed.

Cut cantaloupes in halves and remove seeds. Scoop out 2 to 3 cups melon balls, (about ¾-inch size), enough to cover top of tart, and refrigerate. Cut rest of pulp from rind and cut large pieces into 1-inch cubes. Cut-up pulp should measure 3 cups.

Combine cut-up pulp (not balls), 2 tablespoons orange juice, 1 tablespoon lemon juice, orange rind, honey, and 1 teaspoon ginger in medium saucepan, and stir over moderate heat until mixture boils. Reduce heat to simmer and cook until cantaloupe is soft. Puree mixture in food processor and set aside.

Combine gelatin with 2 tablespoons orange juice and 1 tablespoon lemon juice in small saucepan and stir over low heat until gelatin is dissolved. Let cool to lukewarm and add to pureed cantaloupe mixture, stirring vigorously with whisk. Stand mixture over ice and stir with whisk to point of setting. Fold in whipped cream. Pour mixture into pastry shell. Refrigerate until set.

PRESENTATION: Dry cantaloupe balls between paper towels and arrange on top of cream mixture in tart shell (melon balls should cover top). Combine apricot preserve, 1 tablespoon lemon juice, and 1 teaspoon ginger in small saucepan and stir over low heat until mixture boils. Rub mixture through wire strainer and let cool to room temperature. Brush apricot syrup over cantaloupe balls. Refrigerate prepared tart until ready to serve. If desired, at serving time, sprinkle coconut curls or almond slivers on top of tart.

8 to 10 servings

MELON BASKET WITH MACEDOINE OF FRUIT

Small cantaloupes can be cut into small baskets, in the same manner as a large melon, and used for individual servings.

1 large muskmelon (any type) or watermelon (size depending on quantity of serving desired)

***Macedoine de Fruits* with Citrus Sauce (see Index) to fill melon basket**

Select bowl or tumbler that comes to two-thirds the height of the melon. Lay paring knife on dish and move it completely around melon, marking a line of even height all around with point of knife. Mark parallel lines over top – from side to side – for handle. (If you have a talent for design, you can take an ice pick and draw graffiti borders and patterns on the handle and exterior of the smooth green skin of a watermelon basket.)

With paring knife, make star or scallop-shaped cuts, cutting well through rind and flesh, following horizontal line all around melon, but *skipping area where handle is to be attached.* Then cut handle in straight lines. Carefully pull off top sections on each side of handle.

With melon baller, scoop out as many round balls as possible. Scrape inside of melon so that it is smooth. Pour out excess water. Chill empty.

PRESENTATION: At serving time, fill melon basket with fruit macedoine. Spoon citrus sauce over all.

Makes 1 large melon basket

MINTED HONEYDEW MOUSSE

DO-AHEAD TIP: *Mousse should be prepared a day ahead in order to set.*

- ½ cup light honey
- ½ cup water
- 1 cup finely chopped mint leaves
- 2 medium-size ripe honeydew melons (7 to 8 inch diameter)
- 3 tablespoons unflavored gelatin
- 1 tablespoon fresh lemon juice
- 3 egg whites
- ¾ cup heavy cream, whipped
- 6 to 8 mint sprigs

Combine honey and ¼ cup water in small saucepan and stir over low heat until mixture boils. Remove from heat, add mint, and let steep at room temperature 1 hour.

Cut melons in halves and remove seeds. First scoop out 2 to 3 cups melon balls (about ¾-inch size) for decoration and refrigerate. Cut remaining pulp from rind, cut large pieces in 1-inch cubes, and puree enough in blender or food processor to yield 2 cups. Set puree aside.

When syrup with mint has steeped, strain it. Combine gelatin, ¼ cup water, and lemon juice in small saucepan and stir over low heat until gelatin is dissolved. Stir dissolved gelatin into mint syrup with small whisk. Add syrup mixture to melon puree, stirring vigorously with whisk. Stand mixture in refrigerator until just at point of setting.

Beat egg whites to soft peaks. Add melon puree mixture to egg whites and stir with whisk until smooth. Fold in whipped cream lightly and evenly. Transfer mousse to serving bowl and refrigerate until set.

PRESENTATION: Arrange border of melon balls on top of mousse. Garnish with mint sprigs.

6 to 8 servings

MELONS

MUSKMELON OR WATERMELON SHERBET

For a colorful dessert, you can prepare 2 or 3 flavors of sherbet of different colors, such as watermelon, cantaloupe or mango, and lime, and compose each serving of 2 or 3 scoops of varicolored sherbet.

DO-AHEAD TIP: *Sherbet keeps well in freezer at 0° F. for 2 to 3 days. After that it will begin to crystallize.*

1½ quarts pureed muskmelon or watermelon

1 tablespoon fresh lemon juice

½ cup light honey

2 egg whites

Mix lemon juice and honey with pureed melon. Process mixture in ice cream maker until it is almost firm. Beat egg whites to soft peaks, add to sherbet mixture, and continue processing until sherbet is firm. Remove sherbet from drum and serve, or store in 0°F. freezer.

Yields 1½ quarts, 1 flavor

More Melon Recipes

See Index for the following recipes:

SOUP: Iced Fruit Soup; DESSERTS: Fruit Sherbet, *Macedoine de Fruits*; BEVERAGE: Melon with Buttermilk or Yogurt.

ORANGES

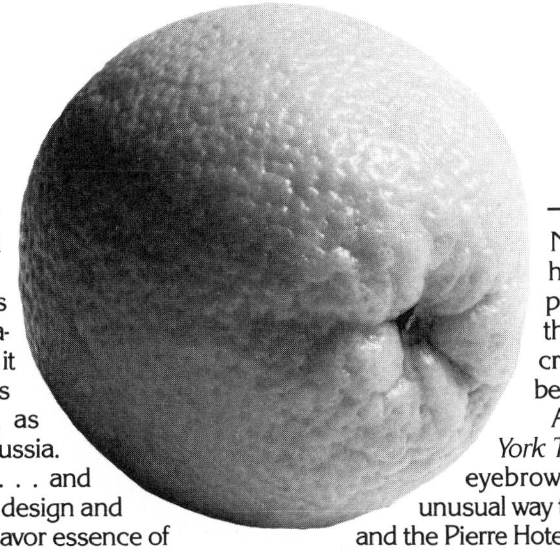

All the world loves an orange. It is as much treasured where it is plentiful, as in America, as where it is scarce, as in Russia. I love its color ("oranges . . . and lemons," the sun colors) in design and dress as well as food. The flavor essence of orange is an elixir that adds magic to any dish. Always I seem to sport a nicked knuckle sustained from grating an orange to add a bit of its spicy, oily rind to this or that.

In search of the world's most famous orange tart, one dark, drizzly night during the fall of 1968, my husband and I drove all around the Burgundian countryside, even getting lost on a private road in the middle of the Pommard vineyards. Our destination was the three-star restaurant Hotel de la Cote d'Or in Saulieu where Alexandre Dumaine, one of the great chefs of this century, reigned until his retirement. Gastronomes came from far and wide to partake of Dumaine's art; and when they went away, their praise was unanimous for a simple orange tart. Finally we found the dark, high-walled little village, typical old Burgundy, and were graciously greeted by chef Minot, Dumaine's protege, and his wife, who were about to close the restaurant for the night. They insisted on feeding us – Morvan ham, truffled Bresse chicken with aurora sauce, garnished with a timbale of fresh morels, local cheese, and . . . the *Tarte a l'Orange*. Never had we tasted such heady orange cream. We pleaded for the recipe, but that was the master's secret with which Minot had been entrusted.

A few years later in the *New York Times*, a reporter raised his eyebrows and then praised the unusual way the Wine and Food Society and the Pierre Hotel chose to serve the classic duck with orange combination. This occasion was a dinner honoring Count Alexandre de Lur-Saluces, owner of Chateau d'Yquem, at which a different vintage of his great sauterne wines was to be served with each course. For a main dish with this sweet wine, we of the society decided to serve plain, crispy-skinned roast duck garnished with half a fresh orange wrapped in cheesecloth. The only sauce with this duck was a squeeze of fresh orange juice. Perfect!

During a dreary New York winter, a gift box of golden, fragrant oranges from Florida is next best to being there. Just the sight of all those shiny oranges is like a burst of sunshine and it signals our own "orange bowl" festival with a star lineup of such favorites as tomato soup with orange, asparagus with orange sauce, orange and fennel salad with vinaigrette laced with orange, braised celery with orange, orange and honey bread, and such classics of which I'll never tire – crepes suzette, a *daube* (veal stew with orange), roast duck with orange. Ways to add orange sunshine to all types of dishes would probably fill a volume.

Columbus planted the first oranges in America. Today, except for when a dreaded killer frost hits the groves, oranges abound year-round. Harvest seasons of different varieties grown in California, Florida, Arizona, Texas, and Mexico – our main sources – overlap. Most of our oranges are sweet. Sour oranges are raised in Spain (the Seville, used for marmalade and liqueur) and in Mexico (the *naranja agria*, which has fragrant, lightly tart juice). The Spanish word for orange, *naranja*, reflects its original Persian name, *narang*, from which, somehow, our term "orange" also evolved.

Only good-quality oranges are likely to reach consumers. Oranges must be picked when they are ripe (they will not continue to ripen off the tree), and their ripeness is determined primarily by chemical analysis of the balance of sweetness and acidity in the juice. When the ideal blend has been reached, the oranges are generally orange in color, although that is not an absolute criterion. Florida and Texas oranges are occasionally dyed to improve their appearance and are stamped "color added."

The decision of picking the orange for the purpose is left to the consumer. Some of the main varieties are described below. The store's produce manager can usually explain the characteristics of other types on sale:

Blood or ruby: Small in size but excellent sweet quality.

Hamlin: Thin skin; 28 seeds; juicy; good sweet-acid blend.

Indian River: Thin skin; 17 to 20 seeds; juicy and rich.

Jaffa: Medium to large; nine seeds, sweet, juicy, and rich.

Navel: Good for eating out of hand, slices, or sections. Large; thick coarse skin which pulls easily away from flesh; segments separate easily; seedless; juicy; rich balanced flavor.

Valencia: Medium to large; six seeds; fairly easy to peel and segment; juicy.

(Note also varieties of mandarin or tangerine-type oranges described in the section on mandarins.)

A medium-size orange provides about ⅔ cup of fruit and juice. One pound of oranges (two medium-size or three small) yields 1 cup juice. One-half cup juice contains 56 calories and 62 milligrams vitamin C. A medium-size orange contains 39 calories and 43 milligrams vitamin C.

Guide for Grating, Shredding, Juicing, Cutting Citrus: Oranges, Lemons, Limes, Grapefruit

Grating: (When you wish to use rind and juice or flesh of citrus fruit, the rind is removed first, of course, whether it is grated or shredded.) For grated rind, the standard four-sided stainless steel grater/shredder is still the best tool. The finest grating side is best for grating citrus rind. Proceed carefully to avoid grated knuckles.

Shredding: Using a peeler, cut long strips of rind, working around the fruit. (The peeler is the best tool to avoid too thick a peeling with white part.) For short shreds (about ¾ inch in length), stack about four strips of rind on a cutting board, and with a sharp chef's knife, cut across in very thin shreds. For longer shreds, stack about four strips of peel and cut diagonally according to length desired. For any length, the shreds should always be extremely fine, literally hair-thin.

Juicing: Cut whole fruit in half horizontally. Press through a manual or electric citrus juicer. If the juicer does not have a strainer, pass juice through a wire strainer. An electric juice extractor is not suitable for citrus (except with special citrus attachment) because too much of the white pith will be extracted with the juice.

To juice small wedges of lemon or lime, when you want just a few drops of citrus juice and some of the zesty oil from the rind, use a special hand-clamp lemon squeezer.

Cutting peeled citrus: For nice slices or sections of orange, grapefruit, sometimes lemon or lime – for decorative use, with no flecks of pith – the fruit must be neatly peeled. A sharp chef's knife (straight edge) is imperative (ideally, about a 7-inch blade). Hold fruit on its side on a cutting board and cut a slice off the top, down to the flesh, leaving no pith showing. Take the fruit in your hand, and, beginning at the top, cut away peel (down to the flesh) in one continuous strip (like peeling an apple), all the way to the bottom of the fruit. If any bits of pith remain, cut them off.

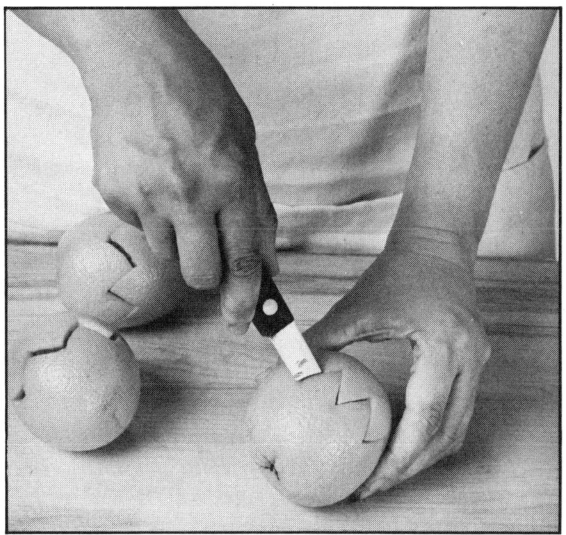

Star cut: This is a saw-tooth edge design around citrus halves. Take the whole fruit in your hand. Insert the tip of a sharp paring knife, cutting in and out in a zig-zag pattern all around the middle of the fruit. Be sure to insert the knife to the center of the fruit. When fruit has been cut all around, lift halves away from each other. To remove flesh and membrane, follow the instructions for cups or shells.

ORANGES

Skinned slices: Place peeled fruit on its side and cut slices with a sharp knife.

Skinned sections: Take the peeled fruit in your hand. With a sharp knife, cut out sections neatly from between dividing membranes. Remove seeds. When all sections have been cut out, squeeze remaining juice from membrane structure. (Properly cut sections will have no bits of pith attached. Be careful not to break the skinned sections.)

Halves with sections loosened: Usually done with grapefruit and oranges. The best tool is a serrated grapefruit knife. Cut whole fruit in half horizontally. Cut all around the fruit half between the flesh and the white part. Cut out the white center core. Cut around each section to loosen it from dividing membrane. Remove seeds.

Cups or shells: To use as containers for sherbet, ice cream, salad, or other fillings. Cut the whole fruit in half horizontally. Cut all around the fruit half between the flesh and the white part. Cut sections from dividing membranes. Remove sections. Pull out the core gently but firmly, bringing with it the membrane structure, leaving a neat shell.

ORANGE AND FENNEL SALAD

In this tossed salad, the bouquet of orange and fennel is a refreshing essence.

DO-AHEAD TIP: *Assembled salad can be prepared a day ahead. Do not toss with dressing until ready to serve.*

2 bunches escarole

¼ pound tender spinach leaves

4 ribs fennel (with leaf ends)

¾ cup Basic Vinaigrette Dressing (see Index)

2 tablespoons sour cream or yogurt

grated rind of 1 orange

skinned sections of 4 oranges

2 tablespoons chopped fresh parsley

1 tablespoon chopped fresh dill

Thoroughly wash and dry escarole, spinach, and fennel. Combine vinaigrette dressing with sour cream or yogurt and orange rind in screwtop jar and shake well.

Pour dressing into salad bowl. Cut or tear bite-size pieces of escarole and spinach and drop on top of dressing. Chop fennel stems and leaves and scatter them on top of greens. Arrange orange sections on top of fennel. Sprinkle chopped parsley and dill on top of salad. Cover with plastic wrap and refrigerate until serving time. Then toss and serve.

6 to 8 servings

CREME PORTUGUAISE
Tomato and Orange Soup

Tomatoes and oranges are a natural taste team, perhaps because both are storehouses of vitamin C. When we are at our farm in Cortona during tomato time, Felipe insists on a plate of sliced tomatoes and orange sections for breakfast every day. This soup, served cold, is a favorite at Acapulco luncheon parties. We also like it hot.

DO-AHEAD TIP: *Tomato and orange soup freezes well. To serve, thaw a little, then transfer to heavy pot, cover, and rewarm over low heat.*

SOUP

5 tablespoons light vegetable oil (e.g., safflower)

1 medium-size yellow onion, finely chopped

½ teaspoon finely chopped fresh garlic

6 medium-size ripe tomatoes, peeled, seeded, and chopped

2 tablespoons tomato paste

1 tablespoon cornstarch or arrowroot

2 cups stock (e.g., chicken, vegetable, or soy—2 cups water with 2 teaspoons tamari soy sauce)

½ cup light cream

grated rind of 2 oranges

¾ cup orange juice

GARNISH

4 to 6 thin orange slices

¼ cup heavy cream, whipped

if available, 4 to 6 fresh orange blossoms

SOUP: Heat 3 tablespoons oil in deep, heavy pot. Add onion and garlic, and cook over low heat 1 minute. Add tomatoes and cook over high heat 5 minutes. Remove from heat. Mix tomato paste with cornstarch or arrowroot and 2 tablespoons oil. Blend this mixture into tomatoes. Add stock and stir over moderate heat until mixture boils. Reduce heat to low and barely simmer 15 minutes.

Remove from heat. Add cream, orange rind, and orange juice. Process in blender or food processor. Adjust seasoning. Chill for cold serving.

PRESENTATION: Pour soup into individual serving bowls. Garnish each serving with orange slice, topped with spoonful of whipped cream, topped with orange blossom.

4 to 6 servings

ORANGES

DIONE LUCAS'S ROAST DUCK WITH ORANGE SAUCE AND ORANGE POTATOES

DO-AHEAD TIP: *Duck can be roasted ahead and rewarmed in 300° F. oven at serving time. Orange Potato Croquettes can be frozen, then deep-fried at serving time.*

DUCK

- 1 4-pound whole dressed duck
- 1 orange, quartered
- 1 garlic clove, bruised
- 2 peppercorns
- ¼ cup bitter orange marmalade

ORANGE SAUCE

- 2 teaspoons plus 1 tablespoon unsalted butter
- 1 duck liver
- finely shredded rind of 2 oranges (shredded lengthwise, 2 to 3 inches long)
- 2 teaspoons finely chopped fresh garlic
- 1 teaspoon tomato paste
- 1 teaspoon meat flavoring (e.g., Marmite brewer's yeast extract, vegetable paste, or meat glaze)
- 2 teaspoons cornstarch or potato flour
- ¾ cup stock (e.g., chicken, vegetable, or soy—¾ cup water with 1 teaspoon tamari soy sauce)
- ½ cup fresh orange juice
- ⅓ cup sweet orange marmalade

DUCK: Preheat oven to 375°F. Dry duck inside and out with paper towels. In cavity, insert orange, garlic, and peppercorns. Tie or truss duck. Place on rack in roasting pan and prick skin all over to release fat. Insert meat thermometer into thickest part of thigh, without touching bone. Roast to desired doneness (for medium-well, 180°F. internal temperature; about 1 hour and 30 minutes). After duck has cooked 40 minutes, turn back side up. After 20 minutes, turn breast side up. Occasionally reprick skin to release fat. Ten minutes before duck is done, spread bitter marmalade all over breast.

ORANGE SAUCE: Heat 2 teaspoons butter in small saucepan, brown liver, remove, and set aside. Add 1 tablespoon butter to pan. When melted, add orange rind and garlic, and cook over low heat 2 minutes without browning. Remove from heat and add tomato paste, meat flavoring, and cornstarch or potato flour, and blend. Add stock, orange juice, and sweet and bitter marmalades, and stir over moderate heat until mixture boils. Add pepper and jelly. Slice liver and add to sauce. Simmer sauce over low heat about 30 minutes. Then add orange sections (do not cook them; they should be kept whole).

PRESENTATION: Carve duck into serving pieces and arrange on warm serving platter. Spoon sauce over duck and arrange a pile of orange potato croquettes at each end of dish. Serve at once.

4 servings

DIONE LUCAS'S ROAST DUCK—continued

¼ cup bitter orange marmalade

freshly ground white pepper

1 teaspoon guava or red currant jelly

skinned sections of 2 oranges

ORANGE POTATO CROQUETTES

DO-AHEAD TIP: *Croquettes can be shaped and frozen. Put frozen croquettes directly in hot deep fat to cook.*

2 to 3 baking potatoes (1½ pounds), unpeeled, quartered

3 tablespoons unsalted butter

grated rind of 1 orange

2 eggs

cayenne pepper

¾ cup dry whole wheat bread crumbs

about 2 cups light vegetable oil (e.g., safflower)

Boil or steam potatoes until tender. Drain, remove skins, and puree in mixer just until smooth. Add butter, orange rind, 1 egg, and a dash of cayenne pepper, and mix briefly. On lightly floured surface, form mixture into cork shapes. Beat remaining egg. Brush croquettes all over with egg, then roll them in bread crumbs. Heat oil in deep fryer to 375°F. Deep-fry croquettes until golden brown. Drain on paper towels.

4 servings as garnish or accompaniment

ORANGE-BRAISED CELERY

DO-AHEAD TIP: *This dish can be prepared a day ahead and rewarmed in 300° F. oven at serving time.*

3 celery hearts
2 small onions, thinly sliced
2 small carrots, thinly sliced
freshly ground black pepper
5 tablespoons unsalted butter
1 teaspoon meat flavoring (e.g., Marmite brewer's yeast extract, vegetable paste, or meat glaze)
grated rind of 2 large oranges
juice of 2 large oranges
2 teaspoons tarragon vinegar
1 cup stock (e.g., chicken, vegetable, or soy—1 cup water with 1 teaspoon tamari soy sauce)
½ teaspoon cornstarch or potato flour
1 tablespoon finely chopped fresh parsley

Preheat oven to 375°F. Clean celery hearts and cut off tops, leaving stalks about 4 to 5 inches long. Place celery hearts in large pot, cover with water, and bring slowly to a boil. Drain at once and cut each in half lengthwise.

Arrange bed of half the onion and carrot slices on bottom of medium-size deep baking dish and sprinkle with pepper. Place the 6 celery heart halves on bed, in 2 layers, if necessary. Scatter remaining onions and carrots on top of celery. Melt 3 tablespoons butter in small saucepan over low heat. Add meat flavoring and stir until dissolved. Add orange rind, orange juice, vinegar, and stock, and bring to a boil. Pour this mixture over celery. Cover baking dish with buttered piece of waxed paper and the lid. Place in oven and braise celery 45 to 55 minutes, or until tender.

PRESENTATION: When celery is cooked, transfer to warm platter. Strain cooking liquid. Melt 2 tablespoons butter in small saucepan. Remove from heat, add cornstarch or potato flour, and blend. Add strained stock and stir over moderate heat until mixture boils. Reduce heat to very low and simmer 3 to 5 minutes. Pour over celery. Sprinkle with parsley. Serve at once.

6 servings as accompaniment

ASPARAGUS MALTAISE

Asparagus tips with orange hollandaise make a colorful appetizer, first course, or brunch or luncheon main course.

DO-AHEAD TIP: *Maltaise sauce can be prepared 4 to 5 hours ahead. Let stand at room temperature or leave in lukewarm water bath.*

- 2 egg yolks
- 2 tablespoons plain yogurt (regular or low-fat)
- 1 tablespoon fresh lemon juice
- 1 tablespoon orange juice
- ½ cup light vegetable oil (e.g., safflower)
- 1 tablespoon finely grated orange rind
- cayenne pepper
- 24 to 36 medium-size asparagus spears, well trimmed and cooked crisp-tender

Combine egg yolks, yogurt, lemon juice, and orange juice in small bowl and beat with small whisk. Stand bowl in medium-size saute pan half filled with hot water. Beat mixture with small whisk over low heat until thick. Whisking constantly, gradually add oil in slow, steady stream. Beat in orange rind and a dash of cayenne pepper.

PRESENTATION: To serve as dip appetizer, transfer sauce to small bowl, place in center of serving platter, and surround with asparagus spears. (For plate service at table, divide asparagus on individual plates and spoon ribbon of sauce over spears.)

4 to 6 servings as appetizer

ORANGES

ORANGE AND HONEY BREAD

DO-AHEAD TIP: *This bread freezes well.*

- 3 tablespoons unsalted butter
- ⅔ cup light honey
- 1 egg, well beaten
- 3 tablespoons grated orange rind
- 2½ cups sifted whole wheat pastry flour
- 3 teaspoons baking powder (without aluminum salts)
- ½ teaspoon baking soda
- ¼ cup chopped blanched almonds
- ½ cup finely chopped Brazil nuts or additional blanched almonds
- ¾ cup orange juice
- 1 or 2 tablespoons unsalted butter, melted

Preheat oven to 350°F. Combine butter and honey in mixer and beat thoroughly. Add egg and orange rind. In separate bowl, combine flour, baking powder, and soda, and sift together twice. Gradually add flour mixture to honey mixture. Then add nuts and orange juice and beat only until well mixed.

Butter 1½-quart loaf pan and add batter. Brush top with melted butter. Bake until bread is brown on top and has shrunk a little from sides of pan, about 40 to 50 minutes. Cool bread before removing from pan.

Makes 1 loaf

ORANGE SAFFRON RICE

DO-AHEAD TIP: *This rice can be cooked and frozen. Rewarm in steamer at serving time.*

- 1 cup long grain brown rice
- ½ beaten egg
- 1 tablespoon extra virgin olive oil
- 2 teaspoons saffron stigmas, crushed
- grated rind of 2 oranges
- 2½ cups stock (e.g., chicken, vegetable, or soy—2½ cups water with 2½ teaspoons tamari soy sauce)

Preheat oven to 350°F. Put rice in deep, heavy 1-quart pot. Add egg. Mix and stir over moderate heat until rice kernels are dry and separate. Add oil, saffron, and orange rind, and stir over low heat 2 minutes. Add stock and stir over moderate heat until mixture boils. Cover pot with firm-fitting lid and cook in oven 45 minutes without disturbing rice.

PRESENTATION: When rice is cooked, fluff with 2 forks. Serve in warm bowl, or rice can be pressed into oiled 2-cup mold or 4 individual ½-cup custard cups and turned out.

Yields 2½ cups

ORANGE SOUP *FELICITA*

This soup can be served hot or cold, either as first course or dessert.

DO-AHEAD TIP: *Soup can be refrigerated for a day or two.*

- ½ cup light honey, or more to taste
- 2 tablespoons very finely shredded orange rind
- ½ cup water
- 2 teaspoons arrowroot or cornstarch
- 4 tablespoons fresh lemon juice
- 2 tablespoons fresh lime juice
- 2 cups fresh orange juice
- 2 cups weak tea (orange, mint, or China)
- skinned sections of 1 large orange

Combine honey, orange rind, and water in small saucepan. Stir over low heat until blended; then barely simmer until rind is translucent. Combine arrowroot or cornstarch with lemon and lime juices in medium saucepan and stir until blended. Add orange juice, tea, and honey mixture and stir over moderate heat until mixture boils. Reduce heat to low and gently simmer 5 minutes. Taste and add more honey, if desired.

PRESENTATION: Serve soup hot or very cold, garnished with orange sections.

4 servings

SANGRITA
Piquant Orange Drink

Sangrita *is a popular drink mixture in Mexico, where it is prepared in the home and also bottled and sold in supermarkets. Traditionally,* sangrita *is served in a separate glass, accompanying tequila. The two are rarely, if ever, mixed together. The* sangrita *mixture by itself is a lively and tasty drink. This recipe is an adaptation of the original created by the Viuda (widow) Sanchez of Chapala, near Guadalajara, who is credited with having invented the* sangrita *and whose name is carried on one of the bottled brands. Contrary to some modern* sangrita *recipes, the original does not contain tomato juice.*

DO-AHEAD TIP: Sangrita *mixture will keep in refrigerator for about a month.*

- 1 cup orange juice
- ½ teaspoon tamari soy sauce
- 1 teaspoon red currant jelly
- 1 teaspoon fresh lemon juice
- ⅛ teaspoon Mexican hot sauce (e.g., Tabasco, Bufalo, or Dona Maria)
- orange slice

Combine all ingredients in blender and blend well. Chill thoroughly. Serve in chilled glass or earthenware mug, with ice, if desired. Garnish with slice of orange.

Yields 1 cup

SAUTEED FILLETS OF SOLE WITH ORANGE AND TOMATO

DO-AHEAD TIP: *Ingredients can be readied several hours ahead. Cook at serving time.*

8 tablespoons unsalted butter

skinned sections of 2 large oranges

3 medium-size ripe tomatoes, peeled, seeded, and quartered

4 fillets of sole

2 tablespoons fresh lemon juice

freshly ground white pepper

1 teaspoon finely chopped shallot

1 teaspoon finely chopped fresh parsley

½ teaspoon chopped fresh thyme, or ⅛ teaspoon dried thyme

¼ teaspoon finely chopped fresh garlic

thin lemon slices

Heat 1 tablespoon butter in large saute pan. Add orange and tomato sections and shake over high heat 1 minute. Remove with slotted spoon and keep warm. Wash fish fillets in lemon juice and cold water and dry between paper towels. Fold lengthwise, dust lightly with flour, and sprinkle with pepper. Melt 3 tablespoons butter in saute pan over moderate heat. When foaming, fry fillets until golden brown on both sides, turning only once.

Arrange fish fillets on warm serving platter. Arrange orange and tomato sections on side or at ends of serving dish. Strain butter in saute pan and return to pan with 4 more tablespoons butter. Stir butter with whisk over moderate heat. When foaming, add lemon juice, shallot, parsley, thyme, garlic, and a dash of pepper. Whisk vigorously 2 minutes, until flavors are blended. Spoon sauce over fish. Garnish with lemon slices. Serve at once.

4 servings

ORANGES

SAUTEED CALVES' LIVER WITH ORANGE

DO-AHEAD TIP: *Liver can be dusted with flour mixture several hours ahead of serving and refrigerated. Saute meat and prepare orange garnish at serving time.*

- 6 thick slices calves' liver
- 5 tablespoons unsalted butter
- 1 tablespoon chopped onions
- 2 teaspoons finely chopped fresh garlic
- 2 tablespoons chopped fresh parsley
- 4 tablespoons chicken stock
- 2 tablespoons light vegetable oil (e.g., safflower)
- 1 tablespoon light honey
- 1 large navel orange, unpeeled, cut horizontally into 6 slices, each about 3/16 inch thick
- 3 to 4 cups hot Plain-Cooked Brown Rice (see Index), preferably cooked in chicken stock instead of water
- 1/4 cup freshly grated Parmesan cheese

Dry liver between paper towels and dust lightly with whole wheat flour seasoned with a little ground white pepper, dry mustard, and chili powder. Pat to remove excess. Heat 3 tablespoons butter in large saute pan and brown liver on both sides (for rare serving; cook meat longer for medium or well done). Arrange meat on serving platter and keep warm.

Add 2 tablespoons butter to saute pan and melt over medium heat. Add onions and cook 1 minute. Add garlic and cook 1 minute. Add parsley and stock and stir briskly with whisk to pick up glaze on bottom of pan. Spoon pan sauce over liver.

In same saute pan, heat oil until very hot. Add honey and stir until mixture is blended. Add orange slices and brown lightly on both sides. Place orange slices between slices of liver. Toss rice with Parmesan cheese and serve separately.

6 servings

More Orange Recipes

See Index for the following recipes:

APPETIZER: *Pico de Gallo*; SOUPS: Iced Fruit Soup, Iced Raspberry Soup; SIDE DISH: Turkish Rice; SALADS: Cabbage and Fruit Salad with Honey Dressing, Tossed Greens Salad with Fruit; DESSERTS: French Fruit Tart and Tartlets, Fruit Fritters, Orange Sherbet, *Macedoine de Fruits*; BEVERAGES: Citrus Combo, Citrus Ade Concentrate with Buttermilk or Yogurt; SAUCES: Citrus Sauce for Desserts, Fresh Fruit Sauce.

PAPAYAS

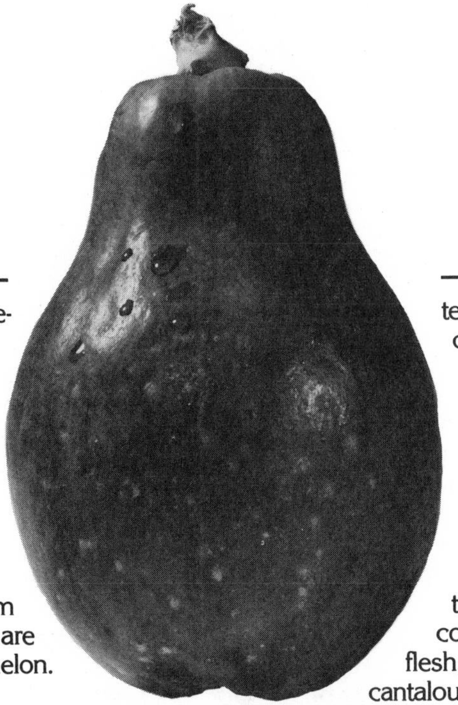

"Tree melon" best describes papaya. Although it is native to tropic America, most of the papayas we get in the temperate states come from Hawaii. These are shaped like large pears, 6 inches long and 3 to 4 inches in diameter. The Floridian and Mexican papayas usually range from 10 to 18 inches in length and are slightly narrower than a watermelon. All have a rather bumpy surface.

The papaya is generally sold when it is *almost* ripe, when its thin skin is still green but beginning to yellow, even in the markets in the tropics, because, when perfectly ripe, the papaya becomes very delicate to handle and should be eaten immediately. I became quite experienced with papaya while living in Acapulco during early 1976. My associate, Felipe de Alba, and I were finishing the manuscript for our natural foods French cookbook. I also did the marketing and cooking – attuned to Felipe's particular regimen, which he rigorously follows wherever he is – in Mexico, New York, Europe. With Felipe, breakfast, lunch, and dinner are each a ceremony in praise of natural foods. Each meal must include fresh fruit. When in Mexico, papaya (one of his favorites) was mandatory daily and must be perfectly ripe. The latter proved to be a learning experience.

At Felipe's instruction, the big green papaya was placed on top of the refrigerator to stand at room temperature for one, two, three, or four days, until it had turned completely yellow. Even then I dared not cut it until Felipe had touched it gently all over. If it yielded to a little pressure, he pronounced the fruit ready to eat. Sometimes brown spots began to appear on the skin and still it didn't pass the touch test. When finally it could be cut, the peach-colored flesh, which is about as thick as cantaloupe but more satiny, was like nectar custard. It was so tender that I could hardly remove the seeds and arrange cubes or slices on a plate without breaking them. When ripe, the fruit will keep well in the refrigerator for a week or so. One Hawaiian papaya yields about 3/4 cup puree.

The large center cavity of the papaya contains hundreds of round, blackish seeds, each enclosed in a gelatinous membrane, which are removed. The seeds are edible and have a spicy, pungent flavor. (Nutritionally, papaya seeds have a protein content comparable to that of soybeans – a highly touted vegetable protein source – and a high amount of crude fiber.) in Mexico, papaya seeds are used in a matter-of-course fashion. A few seeds can be added to vinaigrette or cream-type salad dressings. Beat dressing with seeds in blender or processor, and they will become like flecks of black pepper and add a slightly spicy note. Puree a few with a savory brown sauce to serve with poultry, game, or stew. Or strew some whole papaya seeds over fruit yogurt.

Health enthusiasts, such as Felipe, know that the papaya provides excellent nutrition. A cup of ½-inch cubes contains almost twice the daily requirement of vitamin C and about 75 percent of the necessary vitamin A, as well as useful amounts of other nutrients. It is low enough in sodium to be acceptable in low-sodium diets and contains only 39 calories in a 3½-ounce serving.

Papaya is famous for another health aspect, the enzyme "papain." Contained in the milky latex or juice of the fruit, leaves, and other parts of the plant, papain digests proteins and curdles milk. Thus, papaya can aid in the digestion of other foods. Tough meat is made tender by wrapping it in papaya leaves for a few hours, by washing it in water containing the juice, or by rubbing it with the juice. The tenderizing property of papaya leaves has long been common knowledge among tropical cooks, but only in recent years have meat tenderizers prepared from this plant become available commercially. However, there is very little papain in the ripe fruit.

Papaya is delicious. The tasty, juicy, smooth pulp can be served in many ways. Meatballs in papaya sauce are exotic. Or bake a flavorful chopped meat mixture in the hollow of a half papaya, using Hawaiian papaya halves for individual servings, or a large papaya half as a serving bowl. In Acapulco, Leonora's papaya souffle with coconut milk is famous. It is not really a souffle, just baked papaya puree, topped with the rich, thick, creamy liquid squeezed from fresh coconut pulp. Somehow this simple combination of two neighborly tropical fruits sends taste buds into orbit. Papaya goes well with citrus fruits – orange, grapefruit, lemon, and lime. It can be baked in pies (like pumpkin pie) and cakes, chunked in salads and fruit bowls, frozen as ice cream and sherbet, or preserved as marmalade, pickles, catsup, and chutney. Green papayas can be cooked as squash. Because papaya fruits throughout the year, it is available in all seasons.

Susana Palazuelos, whose mother and grandmother were renowned for their cooking talent, which Susana seems to have inherited, reminds me that Mexicans normally eat papaya plain, an everyday food that they enjoy very much. Sometimes they mix chunks with yogurt and sprinkle it with papaya seeds (as you would sunflower seeds or granola), or sprinkle with a few drops of lemon or lime juice. They also love *papaya agua fresca*. "We always prefer a fresh fruit drink for lunch," she says. (as can be witnessed by the many *agua fresca* vendors along city streets and village roads). "We especially love a fresh papaya drink, which many people also make at home. Just take chunks of ripe papaya. Blend. Mix to taste with a little water, some orange juice, honey, and a few drops of lemon juice; pour into a jar; and chill. Some people also blend a few papaya seeds with the pulp. Just a few. They give a good flavor."

PAPAYA CITRUS SALAD WITH PAPAYA SEED VINAIGRETTE

DO-AHEAD TIP: *Salad mixture can be made a few hours ahead. Arrange on lettuce leaves at serving time.*

2 to 3 cups ripe papaya cubes

1 cup skinned grapefruit sections, drained

1 cup skinned orange sections, drained

½ cup thinly sliced fresh kumquats (optional)

½ green bell pepper, shredded

2 pearl onions, cut into thin rings

2 large celery ribs, thinly sliced

½ cup shredded carrot

crisp Boston or romaine lettuce leaves

2 tablespoons finely chopped parsley

1 cup Papaya Seed Vinaigrette Dressing (see Index)

Combine papaya, grapefruit, orange, kumquat, if desired, pepper, onion, celery, and carrot in bowl and toss. Arrange individual servings on lettuce leaves and sprinkle with parsley. Serve with separate bowl of dressing.

4 servings

PAPAYAS

BAKED PAPAYA HALVES

DO-AHEAD TIP: *This dessert can be prepared ready to bake a day ahead. Bake at serving time.*

- 3 ripe Hawaiian papayas
- 6 teaspoons unsalted butter
- 1 teaspoon vanilla extract
- 6 tablespoons light honey
- ½ cup Coconut Milk (see Index), or heavy cream, whipped (optional)

Preheat oven to 350°F. Peel papayas, cut in halves, and remove seeds. Arrange halves, cut side up, in baking dish with about ½ inch water over the bottom. In the hollow of each half, place 1 teaspoon butter, a few drops vanilla, and 1 tablespoon honey. Bake until tender, about 30 to 45 minutes. If desired, a dollop of coconut milk or whipped cream can be dropped in each hollow when serving.

6 servings

NOTE: To prepare this dessert with the larger Florida or Mexican papayas, cut each into individual serving sections about 5 inches long and 3 or 4 inches wide. Combine butter, vanilla, and honey with ½ cup water in small saucepan and stir over low heat until mixture is blended. Omit pouring water on bottom of baking dish. Place papaya sections in baking dish, bathe with syrup, and baste occasionally while baking.

MEATBALLS IN PAPAYA SAUCE

Serve as hot hors d'oeuvre, or as main dish accompanied by brown rice.

DO-AHEAD TIP: *Meatballs and sauce can be prepared a day ahead. At serving time, rewarm meatballs in sauce and garnish with pieces of raw papaya.*

MEATBALLS

- 1½ pounds ground lean beef
- 2 tablespoons finely chopped onions
- 1 tablespoon finely chopped shallot or scallions
- 2 tablespoons finely chopped green pepper
- ½ cup coarse, fresh whole wheat bread crumbs

MEATBALLS: In large bowl or mixer, combine beef, onions, shallot or scallions, green pepper, bread crumbs, and egg, and mix lightly but well. Form into 1-inch balls and refrigerate about 30 minutes.

In deep, heavy pot, heat oil and add 1 tablespoon butter. When fat is hot, set heat at moderate, add a few meatballs, brown quickly on all sides, and remove from pot with slotted spoon. Continue browning all meatballs in this manner. (Do not put too many in pot at one time or too much juice will drain from meatballs and they will become dry and will not brown.) Set meatballs aside while preparing sauce.

MEATBALLS IN PAPAYA SAUCE—continued

1 large egg, beaten

1 tablespoon light vegetable oil (e.g., safflower)

1 tablespoon unsalted butter

SAUCE

1 tablespoon unsalted butter

1 teaspoon finely chopped fresh garlic

3 tablespoons grated orange rind

1 teaspoon tomato paste

1 teaspoon meat flavoring (e.g., Marmite brewer's yeast extract, vegetable paste, or meat glaze)

1½ cups strong chicken stock

½ cup orange juice

2 tablespoons light honey

1 cup pureed papaya

1 teaspoon guava or red currant jelly

2 tablespoons sour or heavy cream

about 2 cups cut papaya (1-inch cubes or 2-inch strips)

SAUCE: Add butter to pot in which meatballs were browned. When butter is melted, add garlic and orange rind and stir over low heat 1 minute. Remove from heat and add tomato paste and meat flavoring, and blend mixture. Add stock, orange juice, and honey, and stir over moderate heat until mixture boils. Add papaya puree and jelly, and bring to a boil. Add sour cream or heavy cream. Reduce heat to low and let sauce barely simmer 15 minutes, stirring occasionally with wire whisk.

PRESENTATION: At serving time, rewarm sauce. Add meatballs and warm them briefly in sauce. Transfer to warm serving dish. Garnish with pieces of raw papaya.

6 servings as main dish, more as hors d'oeuvre

PAPAYAS

LEONORA'S PAPAYA "SOUFFLE"

The "souffle" is more like a pudding; it does not puff because it contains no beaten egg white. The hot, baked fresh papaya is topped with cold coconut milk.

DO-AHEAD TIP: *Papaya mixture can be made a few hours ahead. Bake at serving time. Coconut milk can be made up to a week before and should be well chilled.*

about 3 cups pureed ripe papaya

light honey to taste (optional)

2 tablespoons cornstarch

4 tablespoons orange juice

½ cup Coconut Milk (see Index)

Preheat oven to 375°F. Sweeten papaya puree with honey, if desired. Mix cornstarch with orange juice and add to papaya. Spread mixture in shallow oiled baking dish. Bake about 45 minutes, or until set.

PRESENTATION: Spoon serving of hot papaya in dessert dish. Top with 1 or 2 tablespoons cold coconut milk.

4 servings

More Papaya Recipes

See Index for the following recipes:

MAIN DISH: Fruit Omelet; SALAD: Tossed Greens Salad with Fruit; DESSERTS: Frozen Fruit Yogurt, Fruit Sherbet, *Macedoine de Fruits*; BEVERAGE: Papayas, Peaches, Nectarines, or Apricots with Buttermilk or Yogurt.

PEACHES

The pearl of my little fruit-filled farm in Italy is a peach tree growing at the corner of the swimming pool. It bears *white* peaches, a fact I discovered only a few years ago, while there during September. (Our modest, homestyle pool has a most unusual landscape, being bordered on all four sides by rows of lettuces and spinach, yard-long beans, four-foot-high dill plants, a profusion of basil and other herbs, Italian peppers – because old Guido believes in taking agricultural advantage of such a nice, flat, fertile area.) On previous visits to *Il Mulinaccio*, I had dreamed of the peaches this tree must bear in season, but never did I suspect that its bounty would be the white variety, which is truly the peach of a peach.

I first became aware of the white peach during the late 1950s. A frequent perquisite of my job was to lunch at New York's Four Seasons Restaurant with my client, the president of Chanel perfumes and a most extraordinary gourmand, H. Gregory Thomas; Joe Baum, the modern impresario of fine restaurant dining; and James Beard, who needs no introduction. Often there might be another palate or two partaking of this culinary ceremony conducted in the middle banquette of the Grill Room.

On this occasion, after the usual procession of exotic degustations, which might include grouse from the Queen's shoot or the first snow peas grown in New Jersey, chef Albert Stockli presented each of us with a plain whole peach. Upon cutting it, cries of delight arose around the table. Albert had acquired some white peaches – from Virginia, he said. Being the neophyte of this august assembly, I was excited to eat the white peach and discover its own exquisite flavor. I thought I knew peaches. I had been raised on them, in Michigan, a peach state. Each August, there was always a holiday weekend or two on the shores of Lake Michigan. On our return to Saginaw, we stopped in Benton Harbor or St. Joseph for several bushels of local tree-ripened peaches, which we ate all the way home (no need to stop for hamburgers), and canned into jars of beautiful compote of halves, spiced (whole), and thick jam during the following week. I could not believe those peaches could be surpassed. Yet the white peach has an extra berrylike fragrance and flavor which makes it an epicurian legend.

Today it seems that good old-fashioned yellow peaches are almost as legendary as the white. I have felt as desperate as millions of others who have been victims of purchasing lovely-looking peaches at the greengrocer, *during the peach season*, only to cut them open and discover dry, porous flesh, like Styrofoam.

While commerce has produced many good innovations to bring variety and abundance of produce to urban America year-round, it may be doing a disservice to our appreciation of the peach. The peach is only at its best when tree ripened, which does present a challenge for commercial distribution. Nevertheless, if you, like I, cannot bear the affront of anything less than a peach in its prime state, then, before you reach for a peach, consider these facts and suggestions:

- An ideally ripe peach – one that is firm, yielding a little to pressure from the thumb, and is rich in sweetness and juice – must ripen on the tree.
- The peach stops developing sweetness once it is picked from the tree. The reason is that peaches do not have the reserve of starch which, in fruits such as pears, continues to convert to sugar after the fruit's removal from the plant.
- Peaches for commercial sale are generally picked at a stage called "proper maturity." At this point the velvety skin is yellow all over with no tinge of green, but may or may not have a blush. The peach flesh will continue to soften and develop some additional juice and flavor. It will *not* develop any more sweetness.
- Peaches are one of the most perishable fruits. Peaches which are tree ripened are so tender that in the process of commercial handling they bruise easily and soon break down.
- If you have your own peach trees, by all means, allow them to ripen on the tree. They should attain a full yellow color with some blush. Taste-test one. If it is firm with lots of sweet juice, it is ready to eat. Pick others with the same criteria. During the season, a peach tree might require three or four pickings.
- If you must purchase your peaches, the only certain way to tell if a peach is suitably edible is to invest in a test on the spot. Buy only one and bite or cut it. If it has firm wet flesh and is sweet enough for your standard, it probably will become a little more juicy when allowed to stand at room temperature a few hours to a day (either in a fruit ripener or exposed, but out of direct sunlight). If the flesh is not runny-wet, save your money. (When I was married, I eventually adopted this system of buying one peach to test, after seeing my husband flatly reject so many that were not absolutely sweet and flavorful.)

In its botanical description, the peach has a rather romantic-sounding name – *Prunus persica* – and is traced from China to northern India, southeast Russia, Persia, Greece, Italy, and eventually to America by our pioneers. Today California, South Carolina, Michigan, and Georgia are our largest producing states. In Chinese folklore, the peach was considered so perfect that it was symbolic of immortality, and its blossoms so beguiling that the lord of the manor never permitted peach trees to be planted near the windows of the lady's boudoir. In the first known cookbook, Apicius of ancient Rome recorded recipes for pickling peaches.

The large single pit in the center of the peach may be a clingstone, semifreestone or freestone. Those of the early harvest (beginning in May) are generally clingstone or semifreestone, while most of the later varieties (arriving in late July or August) are freestones. Clingstones tend to have firmer flesh – good for canning. Freestones are characteristically more flavorful.

When you find good peaches, yes, buy or gather them by the bushel. For a short spell, enjoy them fresh as a snack out of hand; in shortcake (fabulous); in salad; with cream, of course; with yogurt; in pies or tarts; pureed in a frosty, creamy buttermilk or yogurt drink, cold soup, or mousse; or in ice cream or sherbet. They're great in all kinds of desserts, from crisp-coated fritters to the elegant Melba bathed in red raspberry syrup. Peaches have a natural spice in their flavor that flatters chicken, duck, veal, pork, and beef.

To eat a fresh peach, just rub it with your hands to remove some of the fuzz. The skin can be removed in the same manner as for apricots. Sprinkle freshly peeled peaches with lemon juice to avoid discoloration. Sliced peaches can be dried in a home dehydrator to be eaten as a snack or reconstituted in a little hot water for use over cereal, or in yogurt. They can be frozen or preserved. Peaches are very nutritious: A medium-size fruit, with only 38 calories, is a rich source of vitamin A plus vitamin C and minerals.

Nectarines

Increasingly, nectarines are sharing the spotlight with peaches. Today's nectarine is exactly like a peach except that it has a smooth instead of a fuzzy skin. But this has not always been so, and the marriage has been a fickle process.

Originally nectarines were small and white fleshed. They, too, are an ancient fruit. The name comes from the Greek word, *nekter*, meaning "drink of the gods." Noting their similarity to the peach, man was quick to try to cross the two fruits in an attempt to produce a fuzzless peach. What happens is that when the nectarine plant is first crossed with a peach, the first generation comes in as peaches. It is then necessary to back-cross the breeding to get one out of four nectarines. Some horticulturists predict that by the end of this century the nectarine may replace the peach.

Nectarines are interchangeable with peaches in any recipe, and they are a perfect portable food.

PEACH COMPOTE WITH ORANGES AND ALMONDS

DO-AHEAD TIP: *Peaches can be poached a day ahead. At serving time, assemble dish and brown under broiler.*

- 8 peaches (not too ripe)
- juice of 1 lemon
- 4 tablespoons unsalted butter
- thinly shredded rind of 1 orange
- ½ cup light honey
- ½ cup water
- 4 whole cloves
- skinned sections of 2 oranges
- ¼ cup almond slivers

Peel peaches, cut neatly in halves, remove stones, and sprinkle with lemon juice. In saute pan large enough to hold peaches, melt butter. Add orange rind, honey, water, and cloves, and stir over moderate heat until mixture is blended. Reduce heat to low and simmer 3 minutes. Then add peach halves and simmer 10 minutes.

PRESENTATION: Arrange peaches in shallow, heatproof serving dish. Decorate with orange sections. Pour syrup from saute pan over arrangement. Scatter almonds over top and brown lightly under broiler.

8 servings

PEACH MELBA

DO-AHEAD TIP: *Peaches should marinate in raspberry syrup for at least 1 hour, or longer. Assemble dish with ice cream at serving time.*

- **1 cup seedless red raspberry preserve**
- **1 tablespoon lemon juice**
- **6 large, perfect ripe peaches**
- **1 cup heavy cream**
- **1 tablespoon light honey**
- **1 teaspoon vanilla extract**
- **¼ cup toasted almond slivers**
- **1 quart Basic Vanilla Ice Cream (see Index), frozen firm**

Combine raspberry preserve and lemon juice in small saucepan. Stir over moderate heat until preserve is dissolved. Rub through fine strainer and set aside. Peel peaches, cut neatly in halves, put in bowl, and coat with raspberry syrup. Let fruit marinate in refrigerator for at least 1 hour. At the same time, chill serving platter (preferably silver or other metal).

Beat heavy cream over ice until almost stiff. Add honey and vanilla and beat until cream holds its shape.

PRESENTATION: Arrange scoops of vanilla ice cream on center of serving platter. Arrange peach halves along each side and coat with raspberry syrup. Put whipped cream in pastry bag fitted with star tube and decorate platter. Scatter almonds over top. Serve at once.

6 servings (2 peach halves per serving)

BRAISED BREAST OF DUCK OR CHICKEN WITH PEACHES

Boned half breasts of duck are not as readily available as chicken breasts, but they are a duck lover's delight. If it is necessary to buy 2 ducks to prepare this dish, the leg pieces can be skinned and steamed, to be eaten for lunch or snack, hot or cold.

DO-AHEAD TIP: *Poultry breasts can be cooked a day ahead, up to the point of adding hollandaise or whipped cream to sauce. At serving time, rewarm meat in 300° F. oven and continue preparation.*

- 1 tablespoon light vegetable oil (e.g., safflower)
- 2 tablespoons unsalted butter
- 3 medium-size firm mushrooms, sliced
- 2 duck or chicken livers
- 4 to 6 half breasts of duck or chicken, skinned and boned
- ½ teaspoon finely chopped fresh garlic
- 2 tablespoons grated orange rind
- 1 teaspoon tomato paste
- 1 teaspoon meat flavoring (e.g., Marmite brewer's yeast extract, vegetable paste, or meat glaze)
- 1 cup strong chicken stock
- ¼ cup orange juice
- 1 tablespoon light honey
- ¾ cup pureed fresh peaches
- 1 teaspoon guava or red currant jelly
- ½ cup Hollandaise Sauce (see Index), or ⅓ cup heavy cream, whipped
- 4 to 6 fresh peaches, peeled and quartered

In deep, heavy pot, heat oil. Add 1 tablespoon butter and let it melt and foam. Add mushrooms and stir over high heat 2 minutes. Remove mushrooms with slotted spoon and set aside. Brown livers; remove and set aside. Lightly brown duck or chicken breasts on both sides and remove from pan. Reduce heat to low, add 1 tablespoon butter and melt it. Add garlic and orange rind, and stir over low heat 2 minutes. Add tomato paste and meat flavoring and blend. Add stock, orange juice, and honey, and stir over moderate heat until mixture boils. Add peach puree and jelly and bring to a boil. Place breasts in pot and coat with sauce. Cook over low heat about 20 minutes, or until done.

PRESENTATION: Arrange breasts on heatproof serving platter or gratin dish. Whisk hollandaise sauce or whipped cream into sauce. Add mushrooms and peaches. Spoon sauce mixture over breasts and brown top lightly under broiler. Slice livers neatly and arrange as garnish on top of dish.

4 to 6 servings

PEACHES OF THE BLUSHING POPPEA

Peaches and Mango with Currant Syrup and Almonds

Poppea was the mistress and eventually the wife of Emperor Nero. This dessert was created by my client, H. Gregory Thomas, when he was the president of Chanel, for the times we lunched in the formidable Forum of the 12 Caesars in New York. The dish was prepared tableside on the gueridon *by the captain, under the searing gaze of all of the Caesars in the surrounding portraits. It is a dish made to order for the host who likes to dash off an impromptu* piece de resistance *with a flourish.*

DO-AHEAD TIP: *Have all ingredients ready on a preparation tray.*

2 tablespoons unsalted butter

2 tablespoons light honey

4 tablespoons red currant or raspberry jelly

4 whole peaches or 8 halves (fresh or canned)

1½ cups sliced mangoes (fresh or canned)

1½ cup heavy cream, whipped, or thick Creme Fraiche (see Index)

4 tablespoons slivered almonds

Place saute pan or chafing dish over moderate heat. Add butter and melt it. Add honey and jelly and stir until blended with butter. Add peaches and bathe with syrup to glaze. Add mango slices. Reduce heat and warm fruits for a moment.

PRESENTATION: Place whole peach (or 2 halves) and some slices of mango on each dessert plate and coat with syrup. Top with whipped cream or creme fraiche. Sprinkle with almonds.

4 servings

More Peach and Nectarine Recipes

See Index for the following recipes:

MAIN DISHES: *Chiles Rellenos*, Chinese Barbecued Spareribs with Peaches or Pineapple; DESSERTS: Bessie's *Apfel Kuchen* (with peaches), Cobbler, *Coeurs a la Creme*, Crepes Stuffed with Fresh Fruit, Custard Sauce (with peaches), French Fruit Tarts and Tartlets, Fresh Fruit Ice Cream, Frozen Fresh Fruit Souffle, Frozen Fruit Yogurt, Fruit Fritters, Fruit Shortcake, *Le Clafouti*, *Macedoine de Fruits*, Refrigerator Cheesecake with Fresh Fruit Topping; BEVERAGE: Papayas, Peaches, Nectarines, or Apricots with Buttermilk or Yogurt; SAUCE: Fresh Fruit Sauce.

PEARS

Pears are the quintessence of autumn, but really good ones are exceedingly rare. When I was married, a very special (and unscheduled) meal was our "pear brunch." Living in Westchester County, New York, my husband and I made weekend forays for homegrown fruits and vegetables all around the countryside, including neighboring Connecticut and New Jersey. Lionel's favorite fruit was the pear, and for his exacting palate, the perfect pear must be so syrupy and sweet that he could eat it with a spoon, literally lifting out the flesh like a piece of melon. Whenever we found such likely candidates, we also headed to the cheese shop – for the pear's perfect companion.

Both of us still recall those snappy Sunday mornings in the fall, brunching in front of a crackling fire, on a bowl of pears, some mild cheese – perhaps taleggio and Swiss – and sturdy Italian bread, accompanied by the Sunday paper, background stereo music, and Grapfen, our gourmet dachshund, who insisted on his share of the feast.

I think of these pear brunches when traveling in Italy, where a piece of fruit comes as a matter of course at the end of the meal, like pasta at the beginning of the meal. Invariably I select a choice pear in season, and with it a local cheese.

Just the appearance of a pear is so appetizing. What would a Della Robbia wreath be without pears? There is the incredible sight of a whole garden of espaliered pear trees at Chateau Mission Haut-Brion in Bordeaux. For centuries, the French have glorified the pear in seeing who could produce the finest species, displayed on the primly patterned trees, as can be seen when you peer into walled-in gardens along the train route from Paris through the Loire Valley. In Touraine, jars of pear jam and jelly are specialties, and in the city of Angers we have eaten an utterly fabulous dessert of hollowed-out pear filled with pear ice cream and covered with syrup, called *poire belle angevine glacee.*

Yes, pears have inspired poets and gastronomes for a long time. They were eaten in the Stone Age. Homer referred to them as the gift of the gods. The catch is that, obviously, all of these praises to the pear referred to good-quality pears. The trick is to pick the pear at the right moment of maturity so that it can complete its best ripening off the tree.

Timing for pear picking is a sensitive decision. Ideally, pears should be picked when they are still green but mature enough to yield to a little thumb pressure. At this point a pear ripens much better off the tree than on. When the pear is picked at this moment of maturity, it will develop a juicier, sweeter flavor and smooth texture, as the starch content converts to sugar. If the

PEARS

pear is left to ripen on the tree, the flesh is likely to become coarse, woody, or gritty. If the pear is picked before it yields to a little pressure, its potential juices and sweetness will never flow to desired ripeness.

Therefore, apart from having your own pear tree, buying a pear can be a blind item. If the pear in the fruit market is still hard (does not give to a little pressure), reject it. If it does depress with a gentle push of the thumb, then hope that this is a condition of correct picking judgment and not that it is wilting and shriveling from age.

When you buy pears from a commercial source, it is wise to give the pear another one, two, or three days to complete its ripening process. Put it in a paper bag, a plastic bag with a few holes, or a covered fruit ripener bowl, with a damp sponge or wad of cotton to supply humidity. Pears picked at proper maturity will continue to develop juice, sweetness, and tenderness.

If you wish to poach pears or use them for other cooking or baking purposes, take them when they are still firm and just before they are fully ripe. For eating, like our pear brunch, wait until they are fully ripe and can be eaten like a wedge of melon. (Once a pear is fully ripe, it will keep well in the refrigerator for perhaps a week.)

Most of the pears supplied to city markets come from California, Oregon, Washington, and Michigan. Their peak season is from August through November. Although there are over 3,000 varieties of pears, the names you are most likely to encounter are the following:

Anjou: Bell-shaped, with green-yellow skin, sometimes with a slight blush. White sweet flesh with spicy, sweet flavor; all-purpose.

Bartlett: Bell-shaped, yellow with red blush. Most popular commercial pear; medium quality and flavor; all-purpose.

Bosc: Wide bottom with long tapering neck, cinnamon-russet skin. Yellowish-white flesh; very juicy; rich aroma; fine flavor; all-purpose.

Clapp Favorite: Resembles the Bartlett. Sweet; all-purpose.

Comice: Large roundish shape, greenish-yellow to yellow with red blush. Superior pear in quality and flavor. Flesh is very fine.

Seckel: Small, yellow-brown. Excellent spicy flavor; all-purpose, but especially good for cooking and preserving.

Pears always suggest a special treat. In addition to the "pear brunch," consider a pear soup, or garnish the Thanksgiving turkey with spiced poached pear halves filled with cranberry sauce. Perhaps pear fritters strike your fancy, or a pear and potato salad, gingered pear sherbet, or dressed-up poached pears – with carob sauce and whipped cream or stuffed with dates and nuts. If there's an ample supply, put up some pear butter (always a welcome gift) or seckel pear chutney.

Once peeled, fresh pears discolor quickly. Discoloration can be retarded by rinsing in lemon juice. For fruit bowls and salads, it is best to peel pears, rinse in lemon juice, and add to preparation just before serving. After being cooked, pears do not discolor.

DATE-NUT STUFFED PEARS IN APRICOT SAUCE

DO-AHEAD TIP: *This dish can be made a day ahead.*

PEARS
6 large, firm, ripe pears

4 tablespoons fresh lemon juice

SYRUP
½ cup apricot preserve

grated rind of 1 orange

½ cup light honey

1 cup water

STUFFING
½ cup finely chopped dates

¼ cup chopped walnuts or pecans

2 tablespoons dry whole wheat bread crumbs

⅓ cup toasted slivered almonds

PEARS: Preheat oven to 325°F. Peel pears carefully with peeler, leaving stem attached. Remove core from bottom with point of peeler, without piercing through top of pear. Rinse pears in lemon juice.

SYRUP: In heavy pot large enough to stand all pears upright, combine preserve, orange rind, honey, and water. Stir over low heat until mixture boils. Stand pears in pot and bathe them with syrup. Cover and cook in oven until pears are tender but still firm (about 30 to 45 minutes, depending on ripeness). Let cool in syrup.

STUFFING: Mix dates, nuts, and bread crumbs together. When pears are cool, remove from syrup, drain on paper towels, and carefully fill centers with date-nut mixture.

PRESENTATION: Stand pears upright on shallow serving dish. Coat with apricot syrup. Scatter almonds over top.

6 servings

PEAR FONDUE

Pear halves poached in apricot syrup, filled with pastry cream, and garnished with almonds.

DO-AHEAD TIP: *This dish can be made a day ahead. Assemble presentation at serving time.*

- 6 large, firm, ripe pears
- 4 tablespoons fresh lemon juice
- ½ cup apricot preserve
- grated rind of 1 orange
- ½ cup light honey
- 1 cup water
- 2 cups Vanilla Pastry Cream (see Index)
- ½ cup toasted slivered almonds

Remove blossom ends and stems from pears. Peel with peeler. Cut in halves lengthwise and remove center cores with melon baller. Rinse with lemon juice.

In heavy pot large enough to hold pears, combine apricot preserve, orange rind, honey, and water. Stir over low heat until mixture boils. Reduce heat to very low, add pears, and barely simmer until pears are just tender (10 to 15 minutes). Remove from heat and let pears cool in syrup.

PRESENTATION: Arrange pear halves, cut side up, on serving plate. Put pastry cream in pastry bag fitted with medium star tube (#6 or #7) and pipe dome of pastry cream on center of each pear half. Spoon syrup over all. Sprinkle with almonds.

6 servings

PEAR GARNISHES WITH ROAST TURKEY

Turkey time also happens to be pear time. The big bird can be most handsomely and tastily accessorized with a garnish of seasonal fresh pears in several ways: poached pear halves filled with cranberry sauce or jelly; poached pear halves filled with mincemeat or chutney; or whole poached spiced seckel pears.

BASIC POACHED SPICED PEARS

These pears can be used as dessert, garnish, or accompaniment.

DO-AHEAD TIP: *Poached pears can be stored in refrigerator for about a week.*

PEARS

6 to 8 large, firm, ripe pears, or 24 seckel pears

2 tablespoons fresh lemon juice

SYRUP

24 whole cloves

3/4 cup light honey

grated rind of 2 limes

juice of 2 limes

1 1/2 cups cider, white grape juice, or water

PEARS: If large pears are used, remove blossom ends and stems from pears. Peel with peeler. Cut in halves lengthwise and remove center cores with melon baller. Rinse with lemon juice.

If seckel pears are used, leave them whole with stems on. Do not peel or core. Wash in lemon juice and water. Prick in a few places with wooden food pick.

Stick 1 clove into each pear half or whole seckel pear.

SYRUP: In deep, heavy pot, combine honey, lime rind, lime juice, and cider, grape juice, or water. Stir over low heat until mixture boils. Reduce heat to very low, add pears, and cook fruit in barely simmering syrup until just soft (about 10 to 15 minutes). Let cool in syrup until ready to use.

Makes 12 to 16 large pear halves or 24 whole seckel pears

PEAR UPSIDE-DOWN TART

DO-AHEAD TIP: *This dish can be prepared a day ahead.*

- 2 tablespoons unsalted butter, softened
- ½ cup light honey
- 1 teaspoon grated lemon rind
- ½ teaspoon ground cinnamon
- 3 pounds firm, ripe pears (5 to 6 pears), peeled, cored, quartered, and sprinkled with lemon juice
- ½ quantity of dough for Plain Whole Wheat Short Pastry 1 (see Index), chilled
- 1 cup Creme Fraiche (see Index) or heavy cream, whipped

Preheat oven to 400°F. Select baking dish, such as Pyrex, 7½ to 8½ inches in diameter and 2 to 2½ inches deep. Grease inside with 1 tablespoon butter. In small saucepan, combine 1 tablespoon butter, honey, lemon rind, and cinnamon. Stir over low heat until mixture is blended. Set aside.

Cut pear quarters in halves lengthwise. Arrange bottom layer of pears in baking dish in pinwheel design, filling in spaces with a few pieces on top. Sprinkle with one-third of honey mixture. Fill with rest of pears. Sprinkle with remaining honey mixture. Roll out pastry dough ⅛ inch thick. Cut it in a circle about ¼ inch larger than top of baking dish. Place over pears and tuck edges inside dish. Cut a ⅜-inch-diameter hole in the center and about 4 or 5 small slashes around top to allow steam to escape. Bake in lower third of oven 60 minutes. (If top begins to brown too much, cover with piece of aluminum foil.) Then chill tart thoroughly.

PRESENTATION: When ready to serve, slide knife around edge of chilled tart. Place heatproof serving plate on top of baking dish, invert, and remove dish. Preparation now looks like a pear dome. Place pear tart under broiler until lightly browned. Serve with separate bowl of creme fraiche or whipped cream.

4 to 6 servings

PEAR VICHYSSOISE

DO-AHEAD TIP: *The vegetable and pear mixture should be prepared a few hours to a day ahead in order to chill thoroughly. Add cream at serving time.*

- 2 large baking potatoes (about 1 pound), peeled and sliced
- 4 large leeks, well washed and sliced
- 2 celery ribs, sliced
- 1 Bermuda onion, sliced
- 1 cup water
- freshly ground white pepper
- 4 cups strong chicken stock
- 1 pound firm, ripe pears, peeled, cored, and chopped
- 1½ cups light cream
- ¼ cup heavy cream
- ½ cup chopped fresh chives

Put potatoes, leeks, celery, onion, and water in deep, heavy pot. Bring water to a boil, cover, and cook over moderate heat until vegetables are tender. Season with pepper. Add stock and pears. Puree in blender or food processor, or rub through fine vegetable strainer. Chill thoroughly.

PRESENTATION: Add light cream and heavy cream to chilled soup. Serve in chilled bowls, ideally embedded in plates of chipped ice. Serve chives in separate bowl.

6 to 8 servings

POIRES BELLE HELENE A LA CAROUBE

Poached pears with vanilla ice cream, carob sauce, and almonds

DO-AHEAD TIP: *Pears can be poached and sauce prepared a day ahead. Assemble with ice cream and almonds at serving time.*

- 6 large, firm, ripe pears
- 4 tablespoons fresh lemon juice
- 3/4 cup light honey
- 1 1/2 cups water
- 1/2 vanilla bean (scraping and pod), or 1 teaspoon vanilla extract
- 1/4 teaspoon ground cardamom
- 6 scoops Basic Vanilla Ice Cream (see Index)
- 1 1/2 cups Carob Sauce (see Index)
- 1/3 cup toasted slivered almonds

Preheat oven to 325°F. Remove blossom ends and stems from pears. Peel with peeler. Cut in halves lengthwise and remove cores with melon baller. Rinse with lemon juice.

In heavy pot large enough to hold pears, combine honey, water, vanilla, and cardamom, and stir over low heat until mixture boils. Remove from heat, add pears, and cook in oven until just soft. Remove from oven and let cool in syrup.

PRESENTATION: For individual serving, arrange 2 pear halves on dessert plate, place scoop of ice cream in center, cover with carob sauce, and sprinkle with almonds.

6 servings

POACHED WHOLE PEARS WITH SOUR CREAM SAUCE OR YOGURT SAUCE

DO-AHEAD TIP: *Pears and sauce can be made a day ahead.*

PEARS
- 6 to 8 large, firm, ripe pears
- 4 tablespoons fresh lemon juice

SYRUP
- 6 to 8 whole cloves
- ¾ cup light honey
- grated rind of 2 limes
- juice of 2 limes
- 1½ cup cider, white grape juice, or water
- 2 cups Sour Cream Dessert Sauce or Yogurt Dessert Sauce (see Index)

PEARS: Preheat oven to 325°F. Peel pears with peeler, leaving stem attached. Remove core from bottom with point of peeler, without piercing through top. Rinse pears in lemon juice. Stick 1 clove next to stem of each pear.

SYRUP: In heavy pot large enough to stand all pears upright, combine honey, lime rind and lime juice, and cider, grape juice, or water. Stir over low heat until mixture boils. Stand pears in pot and bathe with syrup. Cover and cook in oven until pears are just soft (about 30 to 45 minutes, depending on ripeness). Let cool in syrup.

PRESENTATION: Stand pears in crystal dessert bowl. Pour syrup over all. Serve dessert sauce in separate bowl.

6 to 8 servings

SPICED PEAR SHERBET

DO-AHEAD TIP: *Sherbet keeps well in freezer at 0° F. for 2 or 3 days. After that it will start to crystallize.*

- 2 cups pureed firm, ripe pears
- 2 tablespoons fresh lemon juice
- 1 teaspoon grated lemon rind
- ½ teaspoon ground ginger
- ¼ teaspoon ground cardamom
- 1 cup grapefruit juice
- 2 tablespoons light honey, or more to taste
- 2 egg whites

As soon as pears are pureed, add lemon juice and lemon rind and mix. In mixing bowl, combine pear puree, ginger, cardamom, grapefruit juice, and honey. Process mixture in electric churn-type ice cream maker until it is almost firm. Beat egg whites to soft peaks, add to sherbet mixture, and continue processing until sherbet is firm. Remove sherbet and serve, or store in 0°F. freezer. After sherbet has been stored in freezer, allow it to soften a little before serving.

Yields about 1 quart or 4 to 6 servings

PEARS

SPICED PEAR FROZEN YOGURT

A pleasing light dessert. If desired, serve with a dab of Strawberry Sauce or Carob Sauce (see Index).

DO-AHEAD TIP: *Frozen yogurt keeps well in freezer at 0°F. for 2 or 3 days. After that it will start to crystallize.*

- 2 cups pureed firm, ripe pears
- 2 tablespoons fresh lemon juice
- 1 teaspoon grated lemon rind
- 2 cups plain yogurt (regular or low-fat)
- 3/4 cup nonfat dry milk
- 1/2 teaspoon ground ginger
- 1/4 teaspoon ground cardamom
- 2 tablespoons unflavored gelatin dissolved in 2 tablespoons boiling water
- 2 egg whites

As soon as pears are pureed, add lemon juice and lemon rind and mix. In mixing bowl, combine pear puree, yogurt, dry milk, ginger, cardamom, honey, and dissolved gelatin, and mix well with whisk. Transfer to drum of ice cream maker and process until half firm. Beat egg whites to soft peaks, fold into mixture, and continue processing until mixture is firm. Transfer to a freezer container and store at 0°F. in freezer. Before serving, allow frozen yogurt to soften a little.

Yields 1 quart or 6 servings

More Pear Recipes

See Index for the following recipes:

CONDIMENT: Mango or Papaya Chutney (with seckel pears); SALAD: Cabbage and Fruit Salad with Honey Dressing, *Salade Provencale*; DESSERTS: *Dulce de Camote*, French Fruit Tart and Tartlets; Fruit Fritters, *Le Clafouti*, *Macedoine de Fruits*, Poached Mangoes or Pears with Custard Sauce and Carob.

PINEAPPLES

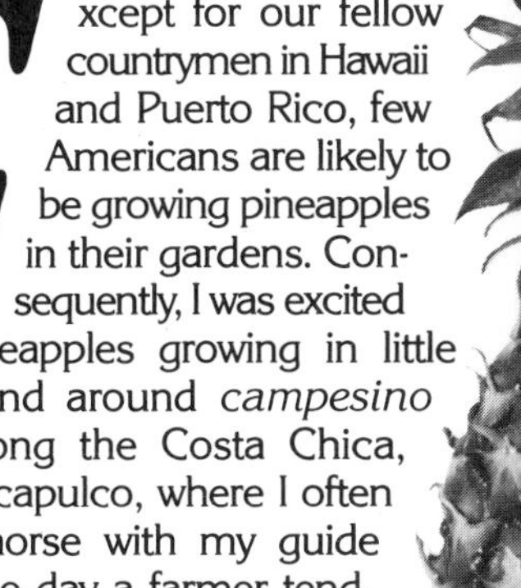

Except for our fellow countrymen in Hawaii and Puerto Rico, few Americans are likely to be growing pineapples in their gardens. Consequently, I was excited to see pineapples growing in little plots of land around *campesino* houses along the Costa Chica, south of Acapulco, where I often rode my horse with my guide Miguel. One day a farmer tending his crop invited us to eat one. There in that hot, shadeless field, sucking the nectar of sun-ripened pineapple which Miguel had cut into wedges with his machete, was a moment in gourmet paradise. I purchased a couple of the ripe-and-ready fruits, tied them to the saddle, and carried them home. That evening at dinner the subject was pineapple, and chef Pepe offered to teach me his pork stew with pineapple specialty.

Pineapples achieve perfect ripeness only on the plant. Thus, it is not possible for most of us to enjoy the pineapple's maximum goodness, but a timely picked pineapple still projects a tropical splendor perhaps more than any other fruit. Fresh pineapples are available in all months of the year, with a peak supply from March through June; and they can be quite ripe if you know how to choose them from the bin in the fruit market. Accept the fact that the pineapple will not become any sweeter than it was at the moment it was picked (because it has no starch reserve to convert into additional sugar, like the banana or pear can). Then follow these guidelines:

- Select a pineapple that is plump, fresh looking, and as large as possible. The larger the fruit, the greater the proportion of edible flesh. (A two- to three-pound pineapple has less than 30 per cent edible flesh, while half of a five-pound pineapple has more flesh than a whole three-pound fruit.)
- Fresh, deep-green crown leaves are a good sign. A fruit that is old looking, dry, with brown leaves, should be avoided.
- Fragrance is a good sign, but usually the fruit is kept too cold to be fragrant.
- A good indicator of ripeness is when nearly all of the eyes at the base have turned yellow. Fruit at this state should be rushed to market, at which point it can last up to four weeks in refrigeration.
- The ease with which leaves can be pulled out is *not* a good sign of quality.
- The thump test is of no value.

• Avoid pineapples with bruised areas, shown by discolored spots or soft spots, which are susceptible to decay.
• Other signs of decay are mold, an unpleasant odor, and eyes that have turned watery and darker in color.

The pineapple is believed to be native to tropical America and was discovered by Columbus on the island of Guadaloupe. Eventually the pineapple was planted in most of the tropical areas around the world. Europeans were delighted not only with its flavor and fragrance but also with the noble appearance of its conical shape, its texture like a cloak of rich brocade, and crown of spiring leaves. The pineapple became a popular feature in the Careme-type architectural dessert creations of the eighteenth century as well as a favorite motif in the period's decorative arts. In furniture, tapestries and objets d'art, the pineapple was ubiquitous as the symbol of hospitality. Today Hawaii, Puerto Rico, and Mexico are the sources of pineapples marketed in the United States.

Pineapples are a versatile food: sliced, cubed, crushed, or juiced. If pineapple is harvested sufficiently ripe, no sweetening is needed. With pineapple present, a luxurious ambience prevails in salads, appetizers and kebabs; fruit bowls; in garnishes for all manner of main dishes; in cakes, cookies, ice cream and custard cream; jams, pickled condiments, and special productions – such as the hollowed half-shell used as the container for a fruit macedoine or mousse, or the luau presentation. Any favorite poultry or seafood salad is given a festive touch when mixed with chunks of pineapple and served in the pineapple shells. If available, arrange salad-filled pineapple shell(s) on banana or lemon leaves and surround with hibiscus flowers.

Pineapples are relatively low in calories, only 74 to a cup, with a substantial contribution of vitamin C, magnesium, and fiber, as well as other vitamins and minerals. With so many ways to add its luscious touch to everyday eating, it is a standing invitation to indulge and be healthy. Thread cubes of pineapple on any combination of kebabs. Add chunks and juice to sauces for seafood, poultry, and meat dishes, or accompany steaming rice with sauteed pineapple rings and a sprinkling of crisp, toasted, slivered almonds. Good eating seems to be guaranteed by adding pineapple. Perhaps the pleasure of pineapple starts with the mastery of peeling it:

How to Peel and Cut Pineapple

For slicing or dicing: Slice pineapple crosswise with a large, sharp knife into one-inch-thick slices. With a paring knife, peel each slice. Make the peeling thick enough to remove the eyes, or thinner, removing the eyes with the tip of a vegetable peeler or apple corer. Then cut into desired shapes.

For serving in the quarter shell: Wash the pineapple. With a large, sharp knife, start at the center of the leafy crown and saw gently down the spikes, cutting it in half lengthwise. Cut each half into two lengthwise pieces. With a paring knife, cut about 1/4 inch from the skin, loosening the wedge completely. Remove the wedge of pulp, cut off the core, and slice or cut the pulp into chunks. The pulp can be replaced in the quarter shell, or the shell can be filled with one of the many salad possibilities involving pineapple.

For serving in the complete shell: There is a special knife which cuts a pineapple into six sections while coring it. For serving luau style, there is a special barrel-type knife which sections the fruit into spears and leaves the shell intact. The shell can be used for drinks or, in the case of small pineapples, as salad or appetizer cups.

For serving in the half shell: Slice the pineapple in half lengthwise through the crown. Using a curved knife, scoop out the core and flesh. Refill with chunks for snacks, fruit salad topped with sherbet or cottage cheese, or pineapple mousse.

For serving luau style: Cut a thick slice from the top and the bottom of a fresh, ripe pineapple, saving the bottom slice. Run a sharp, thin, long knife blade around the pineapple between the rind and the meat, leaving an intact shell 3/8 inch thick. To do this, cut the pineapple from either end to the halfway point, keeping the knife blade pointed toward the rind. Push the cylinder of pineapple out the big end by pressing from the small end. Cut the cylinder in half lengthwise, then cut each half into quarters. Cut away and discard the core adhering to the quarters. Cut the quarters into lengthwise strips, place the bottom on a plate, over which rests the pineapple shell. Fill with the pineapple strips.

PINEAPPLES

FROZEN PINEAPPLE SOUFFLE IN PINEAPPLE SHELL

DO-AHEAD TIP: *This dish should be made a day ahead in order to freeze.*

- 1 medium-size ripe pineapple
- 3 egg yolks
- 1 whole egg
- ⅓ cup light honey
- 2 cups heavy cream, whipped
- 1 tablespoon fresh lemon juice
- ¼ cup blanched pistachios

To prepare pineapple, cut it in half lengthwise, a little off-center. Using small, sharp knife, cut out pulp from both halves, being careful not to injure shell or skin of the larger half. Remove center cores and puree pulp. Drain a little of the juice through wire strainer. Cut leaf end from larger pineapple shell and reserve for decoration. Chill large shell in freezer.

In mixer, beat egg yolks, whole egg, and honey until mixture is thick and stiff. Fold in half of the whipped cream lightly and evenly. Add 2 cups pureed pineapple pulp and lemon juice and fold into mixture. Pile into larger pineapple shell and freeze.

PRESENTATION: Replace leaf end on shell, securing it with toothpicks. Put remaining whipped cream in pastry bag fitted with medium star tube (#6 or #7) and pipe rosettes all around edge of shell. Sprinkle pistachios over top. Store in freezer until serving time.

4 to 6 servings

LOBSTER AND PINEAPPLE SALAD WITH PINK DRESSING

One lobster serves 4 people in an elegant presentation.

DO-AHEAD TIP: *This dish can be made a day ahead and refrigerated. Coat with dressing and arrange lobster shell decoration at serving time.*

SALAD

- 3 cups Plain-Cooked Brown Rice (see Index)
- 2 medium-size ripe tomatoes, peeled, seeded, and shredded
- ⅓ cup Basic Vinaigrette Dressing (see Index)
- 4 to 6 ½-inch-thick fresh pineapple slices
- 1 2- to 2½-pound lobster, steamed or plain-boiled

PINK DRESSING

- 2 eggs, separated
- 1 tablespoon fresh lemon juice
- 1½ teaspoons dry mustard
- 1 tablespoon sweet paprika
- 1 tablespoon tomato paste
- 1 cup light vegetable oil (e.g. safflower)
- 2 tablespoons heavy cream
- light cream for thinning (if necessary)

SALAD: Combine rice, tomato, and dressing in bowl and toss lightly. Spread mixture on bottom of shallow serving dish. Arrange pineapple slices on top of rice.

Carefully remove lobster meat from shell, keeping the head and tail shells and little claws intact and reserving them. Cut lobster meat into bite-size pieces and place on top of pineapple slices. Rinse shells, rub with a little oil, and set aside.

PINK DRESSING: Combine egg yolks, lemon juice, dry mustard, paprika, and tomato paste in mixer or food processor and beat well. Continue beating while very slowly adding oil. Mixture should be consistency of mayonnaise. Fold in heavy cream. Beat egg whites to soft peaks and fold evenly into dressing. Thin with a little light cream, if necessary, for coating consistency.

PRESENTATION: At serving time, coat entire assembly with pink dressing. Place lobster shells and little claws in shape of lobster on top of presentation. Serve at once.

4 servings

PINEAPPLE ROAST DUCK

This recipe requires a total of 2 small fresh pineapples.

DO-AHEAD TIP: *Duck can be roasted and sauce prepared a day ahead. Duchess Potato Rosettes can be made several days ahead and frozen. At serving time, rewarm duck in 300° F. oven, rewarm sauce, prepare pineapple garnish, thaw and brown potatoes, and assemble dish.*

DUCK

- 2 4-pound whole dressed ducks
- 2 small onions, each stuck with 1 whole clove
- 4 pineapple slices
- 2 garlic cloves
- 6 peppercorns
- ½ cup apricot preserve

SAUCE

- 3 tablespoons unsalted butter
- 2 duck livers
- 1 teaspoon finely chopped fresh garlic
- 1 cup finely chopped pineapple
- 1 teaspoon tomato paste
- 1 teaspoon meat flavoring (e.g., Marmite brewer's yeast extract, vegetable paste, or meat glaze)
- 2 teaspoons cornstarch or potato flour
- 2 cups stock (e.g., chicken, vegetable, or soy—2 cups water with 3 teaspoons tamari soy sauce)
- ½ cup apricot preserve
- freshly ground white pepper

To prepare fresh pineapples, peel, core, and cut into ½-inch-thick slices. Reserve 12 slices. Finely chop enough of the remaining to equal 1 cup.

DUCK: Preheat oven to 350°F. Dry ducks inside and out with paper towels. In cavity of each duck, insert 1 onion, 2 pineapple slices, 1 garlic clove, and 3 peppercorns. Tie or truss ducks. Prick skin all over to release fat while cooking.

Place ducks on rack in shallow roasting pan. Insert meat thermometer in thickest part of thigh of 1 duck. Roast until thermometer registers doneness desired (for medium-well, about 180°F. internal temperature). It is not necessary to baste ducks, but occasionally reprick skin to release fat. After ducks have been in oven 45 minutes, turn over, breast side down; after 30 minutes, turn them breast side up again and roast until done. About 10 minutes before ducks are done, spread preserve on breasts.

SAUCE: Heat 2 tablespoons butter in medium saucepan. When very hot, brown duck livers and then remove from pan. Add another tablespoon butter to pan with garlic and pineapple. Cook over moderate heat 2 or 3 minutes, until pineapple is warmed. Remove from heat and add tomato paste, meat flavoring, and cornstarch or potato flour, and blend mixture. Add stock, preserve, and pepper. Stir sauce over moderate heat until it boils. Reduce heat to very low, return livers to sauce, and let sauce barely simmer 30 minutes.

PINEAPPLE ROAST DUCK—continued

GARNISH

- 8 ½-inch-thick pineapple slices
- 2 tablespoons unsalted butter
- 1 tablespoon light honey

GARNISH: Dry pineapple slices between paper towels. Heat butter in saute pan. Add honey and blend. When hot, add pineapple slices and glaze to golden brown on both sides.

PRESENTATION: Carve cooked ducks into serving pieces. Arrange on warm serving platter or gratin dish. Spoon sauce over them. Cover with glazed pineapple slices, slightly overlapping them. Arrange potato rosettes around sides or at each end of platter.

6 to 8 servings

DUCHESS POTATO ROSETTES

DO-AHEAD TIP: *Potato rosettes can be made several days ahead and frozen. Thaw at room temperature or rewarm in 300° F. oven and brown under broiler.*

- 3 baking potatoes (about 1½ pounds)
- 1 egg
- 1 egg yolk (optional)
- 3 tablespoons unsalted butter or light vegetable oil (e.g., safflower)
- cayenne pepper
- 2 tablespoons unsalted butter, melted

Cut potatoes in quarters. Steam or boil until tender. Remove skins. Puree in mixer. Add whole egg and yolk, if desired, and mix. Add butter or oil and a few grains of cayenne pepper and mix again. Do not beat potatoes too much, or mixture will become thick and gummy.

Put potato mixture in pastry bag fitted with large star tube (#8 or #9). Pipe rosettes on oiled baking sheet. Brush with melted butter and brown lightly under broiler.

6 to 8 servings

PINEAPPLES

PINEAPPLE CHEESE BALLS

DO-AHEAD TIP: *Cheese balls should be made several hours ahead in order to chill and become firm.*

- **8 ounces cream cheese**
- **½ teaspoon dry mustard**
- **¼ teaspoon curry powder**
- **¼ teaspoon tamari soy sauce**
- **Tabasco sauce or cayenne pepper, to taste**
- **⅓ cup crushed pineapple, well drained**
- **½ cup finely chopped cashews, almonds, or walnuts**

In mixer, beat cream cheese until softened. Add mustard, curry powder, and tamari, and mix well. Add Tabasco or cayenne pepper to taste. With rubber scraper, fold in crushed pineapple. Chill mixture in refrigerator or freezer until firm enough to shape into 1-inch-diameter balls. Roll balls in chopped nuts. Store in freezer or refrigerator until serving time.

PRESENTATION: If desired, insert cocktail pick into each ball. Arrange on serving plate or stick into grapefruit or small head of cabbage.

Makes 24 to 30 balls

PORK WITH PINEAPPLE

Puerco con Piña

This is a Mexican casserole-style dish. Traditionally, it is made with chunks of meaty pork from the back ribs, called cotillas de puerco. *If back ribs (meatier than spareribs) are not available, shoulder pieces (stew meat) are just as good.*

DO-AHEAD TIP: *This dish can be prepared a day ahead, up to the point of adding celery and peppers. At serving time, add these ingredients and rewarm.*

- **3 pounds pork back ribs or shoulder, trimmed of fat and cut into 2-inch pieces (as for stew)**
- **about 2 cups water**
- **4 tablespoons light vegetable oil (e.g., safflower)**
- **4 tablespoons unsalted butter**
- **1 teaspoon finely chopped fresh garlic**

Put pork in heavy pot or large saute pan with water and cook, uncovered, until almost done without letting meat get too brown. (Water will be gradually absorbed; add a little more if necessary.) Turn meat occasionally to brown on all sides.

Heat oil in large, heavy pot. Add butter and heat until melted. Add garlic, onion, and jalapeno pepper, if desired, and cook over low heat until onion is soft but not browned. Remove from heat, add flour, and stir to blend mixture. Add stock and stir over moderate heat until sauce comes to a boil and thickens. Add tamari, jam or jelly, and cream and stir over moderate heat until well mixed. Add pork and pineapple, turn

PORK WITH PINEAPPLE—continued

1 medium-size Bermuda or yellow onion, finely chopped

1 jalapeno pepper (hot), fresh or canned, finely chopped (optional)

3 tablespoons whole wheat pastry flour

3 cups strong chicken stock

1 tablespoon tamari soy sauce

½ cup pineapple jam or jelly

2 tablespoons heavy cream

1½ cups fresh or canned plain pineapple cubes, cut into about ½-inch dice

3 large celery ribs, cut into 1-inch pieces

1 green bell pepper, seeded and cut into 1-inch pieces

1 cup 1-inch pineapple cubes

4 to 6 cups hot Plain-Cooked Brown Rice (see Index)

heat to low, and cook until meat is tender. Then add celery and green pepper and cook briefly (these vegetables should be crisp and retain color). Add pineapple cubes but do not cook.

PRESENTATION: Transfer pork and sauce mixture to warm serving casserole or platter. Accompany with rice in separate bowl or molded.

6 servings

PINEAPPLES

TEPACHE
Pineapple Cider

Tepache *(pronounced teh-patch-eh) is an old Mexican household fruit drink favored by children and adults alike. It is surprising that* tepache *has not made its way north along with the taco and tostada. It is a simple mixture that uses 1 pineapple and, amazingly, can be replenished with more water as used and will dispense zesty drinks for several weeks or all summer.*

DO-AHEAD TIP: Tepache *must be started at least 5 days before serving, to permit fermentation.*

TEPACHE

1 very ripe pineapple (if necessary, allow pineapple to stand 2 or 3 days in fruit ripener or brown bag to develop maximum juice; it should be quite soft, almost to the point of being too ripe for normal use)

6 quarts water

4 cups light honey

CHOICE OF GARNISH
pineapple stick

mint sprig

twist of lemon or lime rind

TEPACHE: Cut off pineapple leaves. Chop entire pineapple, including peel, into about 1-inch chunks. Put pineapple in crock or large pot (about 10-quart capacity) and add water. Let stand at room temperature 2 full days.

Add honey and let stand at room temperature 3 days, during which time most of the fermentation takes place. Transfer liquid and pineapple chunks to large covered container and refrigerate. *Tepache* is ready to drink, but will continue slow fermentation. It can be kept indefinitely in refrigeration. If desired, supply can be extended by adding half as much water as amount of liquid removed when a drink is drawn.

PRESENTATION: Strain *tepache* liquid into very cold glass or earthenware mug. Garnish as desired.

Yields about 6 quarts (more, if water is added to basic mixture as drinks are poured)

More Pineapple Recipes

See Index for the following recipes:

APPETIZER: *Pico de Gallo*; MAIN DISHES: Chicken in the Snow, *Chiles Rellenos*, Chinese Barbecued Spareribs with Peaches or Pineapple, Poached Chicken Hawaiian; SALADS: Cabbage and Fruit Salad with Honey Dressing, Tossed Greens Salad with Fruit; DESSERTS: Banana Ice Cream in Pineapple Boats, Fresh Fruit Ice Cream, Frozen Fruit Yogurt, Fruit Fritters, Fruit Sherbet, *Macedoine de Fruits*, Refrigerator Cheesecake with Fresh Fruit Topping; BEVERAGES: Coco Piña, Pineapple and Carrot Juice, Pineapple and Lime Frost.

PLUMS

"Plum good!" cheered the young head-of-household as he planted a mere shoot of a greengage plum tree in the backyard of his new homestead on the occasion of his first-born, duly christened Marion Louise Ottilia in honor of all of the godmothers. (My stern Teutonic father was not without humor. When my next and youngest sisters were born, symbolic peach and apple trees were planted, respectively.)

My greengage plum tree is a beautiful tree, commanding the corner of our property facing Shattuck Road; a rather prim-looking tree with branches growing upward instead of spreading or drooping – a real optimistic spirit in this tree. In the spring it was thick with fluffy white flowers. During the summer it was laden with luscious, sweet, greenish-yellow plums.

Because it stood in the backyard where we played in the sandbox and on our swings, much of its fruit was devoured on the spot. Occasionally Mother was able to salvage enough from its branches to can delicious sauce and jam for the winter. (Plum jam with its big sweet skins was one of my favorites – on homemade bread. I usually tried to pick most of the skins out of the jar, leaving the pulp for the others.) Only two years ago I drove past the big white house and felt a rush of memories, seeing my tree and its sisters still growing as Father had planted them.

Greengage is only one of a large variety of smallish fruits which fit between the apricot and the cherry, all of the genus *Prunus*. All are tree-borne and have a single flat-sided seed in the center. There are two main branches of the plum family, the European species and the Japanese species, both of which are cultivated in America. Foremost of the European types are the Italian prune plum (freestone; blue-purple in color; with sweet, firm flesh), the green and yellow gages (freestone; sweet with a slight tang), Damson (clingstone; purple-black; too tart to eat raw; excellent for cooking). The Japanese varieties are usually larger than the European types, about two inches in diameter, and have a yellow background color overlaid with varied shades of red. Most are clingstone and, when ripe, are juicy and sweet for eating out of hand. In America, seasonal produce from various states is on the market from May through September. The fresh plums we find during the winter months usually come from South America and South Africa.

Plums contain a variety of nutrients in modest amounts, mainly vitamin A. Depending on the tart level, fresh plums can be eaten raw or added to fruit salad or compote. They are an excellent garnish with poultry and meat, especially duck and pork. Little Jack Horner indeed knew a good pie when he put in his thumb and pulled out a plum, whether it was deep dish or open face. Use pureed plums in whip, plum butter, or preserve. Add a little mustard and ginger to strained plum preserve (preferably Damson) for the classic Chinese plum sauce (or "duck sauce," as it is called in Chinese restaurants). And easiest of all, cook up some pitted plums, with the skins, for good plum jam.

Prunes

The dried plums Americans call prunes can be any plum that contains enough sugar to preserve it without fermentation while drying when its pit is not removed. (When pits are removed and plums subsequently dried, they are called dried plums, not prunes.) Prunes should be stored in a cool, dry place or in the refrigerator. To properly interpret French menus and recipes, the French *prune* (pronounced pryn) means "fresh plum," and the word *pruneau* means "dried plum" (our prune) and . . . "bullet."

Prunes, naturally, have a nutritional composition similar to plums but about three times as great because much of the water has been removed and the solids have been concentrated. This brings the vitamin A and iron up substantially, while vitamin C is virtually lost.

Prunes are handy and tasty as appetizer stuffables, and as garnishes with meat, poultry, and rice or other cooked grain dishes. Soak and puree prunes for a rich whip, quick bread, souffle, mousse, or baked pudding. The old-fashioned combination of stewed prunes and apricots is still an all-American favorite for breakfast or dessert anytime.

Prune Appetizers Packaged pitted prunes are best for stuffing as appetizers. Soaking prunes to remove pits leaves the flesh too soft for serving. Here are some ideas for prune appetizers:

- Fill pitted prunes with cream cheese mixed with a little finely grated orange rind. Bring the edges together so that no cheese shows. Insert cocktail picks.
- Fill pitted prunes with a dab of crunchy peanut butter mixed with horseradish. Close and insert cocktail picks.
- Fill pitted prunes with fine liver pate. Close and insert a toasted almond sliver in the opening of each. Insert cocktail picks.
- Cut water chestnuts in halves and toss in a mixture of one tablespoon tamari soy sauce and two teaspoons dry mustard. Insert half a water chestnut in each pitted prune and close. Arrange stuffed prunes on a baking sheet, brush with melted butter, and place in preheated 375°F. oven until heated through. Insert cocktail picks.
- Have ready sauteed chicken livers, allowing one-half to one-fourth liver per prune, depending on size. Season the inside of pitted prunes with ground pepper and a bit of prepared mustard. Insert a small piece of chicken liver and one toasted almond sliver, and close. Arrange stuffed prunes on a baking sheet and place in preheated 375°F. oven until heated through. Insert cocktail picks.

SWISS PLUM TART

Spicy sweet pastry filled with fresh plums and chopped nuts and encrusted with more chopped nuts. When plums are out of season, mango is a tasty substitute.

DO-AHEAD TIP: *Baked, filled tart can be prepared a day ahead and refrigerated.*

TART SHELL

- 1 baked 8- or 9-inch pastry shell of Spicy Sweet Short Pastry (see Index), with reserved unbaked dough for lattice topping
- 2 tablespoons dry whole wheat bread crumbs

FILLING

- 1 to 1½ pounds fresh sweet plums (e.g., Italian prune or greengage), pitted and quartered, or 3½ cups peeled, sliced ripe mangoes
- ½ cup finely chopped walnuts or pecans
- ¼ cup light honey
- ¼ cup red currant jelly (if dark plums are used), or apricot preserve (if green or yellow plums or mangoes are used)
- 1 egg, beaten

TART SHELL: Preheat oven to 350°F. Sprinkle bread crumbs on bottom of baked pastry shell.

FILLING: In mixing bowl, combine plums or mangoes, ¼ cup chopped nuts, honey, and currant jelly or apricot preserve, and mix carefully with wooden spoon. Fill pastry shell with fruit mixture. Roll out reserved dough between two sheets of floured waxed paper. Cut dough into ½-inch-wide strips long enough to span top of tart, and arrange in lattice (criss-cross) fashion. Press strips down at rim and pinch off excess. Brush top of pastry with beaten egg and sprinkle with ¼ cup chopped nuts. Bake 30 to 35 minutes.

8 servings

PORK CHOPS WITH PRUNES

DO-AHEAD TIP: *Prunes should be soaked overnight. Cook pork chops and sauce at serving time.*

- 16 prunes
- 1 cup chicken stock
- 4 pork loin chops, about 1 inch thick
- 1 tablespoon light vegetable oil (e.g., safflower)
- 1 tablespoon unsalted butter
- freshly ground white pepper
- 1 tablespoon red currant jelly
- 2 tablespoons heavy cream

Soak prunes overnight in stock. Heat oil in saute pan and add butter. When butter foams, add chops and brown on both sides. Reduce heat to low and cook meat, uncovered, about 30 minutes.

Meanwhile, simmer prunes in stock in which they soaked, about 5 minutes. Drain and reserve liquid.

When chops are cooked, arrange on hot serving platter, encircle with prunes, and keep warm. Pour stock from prunes into saute pan, add pepper, and boil until reduced by half, constantly stirring and scraping pan. Add jelly and stir until dissolved. Add cream and bring just to boiling point. Spoon sauce over chops and serve at once.

4 servings

PRUNES SARAH BERNHARDT

DO-AHEAD TIP: *This dish should be started 3 days before serving.*

- 1 pint white grape juice or orange juice
- 1½ tablespoons light honey
- 4 strips orange or lemon rind
- 24 prunes
- 2 cups Creme Chantilly (see Index)
- ½ cup coarsely chopped toasted almonds
- bunch of fresh violets

Combine grape or orange juice, honey, and orange or lemon rind in medium heavy pot and bring to a boil over low heat. Add prunes and barely simmer 30 minutes. Refrigerate prunes in syrup 3 days.

PRESENTATION: Place prunes in crystal serving dish. Strain syrup and pour it over prunes. Put creme chantilly in pastry bag fitted with medium star tube (#6 or #7) and cover prunes with rosettes of whipped cream. Sprinkle with almonds. Decorate with fresh violet blossoms (edible).

4 servings

ROAST DUCK WITH PRUNES OR FRESH ITALIAN PLUMS

DO-AHEAD TIP: *Duck and sauce can be cooked a day ahead, but do not carve duck. At serving time, cover duck with aluminum foil and rewarm in 300° F. oven, rewarm sauce over low heat, carve duck and assemble presentation.*

DUCK

- ¾ pound prunes or 1½ pounds fresh Italian plums
- 1 4-pound whole dressed duck
- 1 garlic clove

SAUCE

- 1 tablespoon unsalted butter or light vegetable oil (e.g., safflower)
- duck giblets (heart, liver, gizzard)
- 1 teaspoon finely chopped fresh garlic
- 6 medium-size firm mushrooms, sliced
- 1 teaspoon fresh lemon juice
- freshly ground white pepper
- 1 teaspoon tomato paste
- 2 teaspoons meat flavoring (e.g., Marmite brewer's yeast extract, vegetable paste, or meat glaze)
- 2 teaspoons cornstarch or potato flour
- 1 cup stock (e.g., chicken, vegetable, or soy—1 cup water with 1½ teaspoons tamari soy sauce)
- 1 teaspoon red currant jelly
- 1 bay leaf
- 2 tablespoons finely chopped fresh chives, or dried chives

DUCK: If prunes are used, place in pot, cover with water, bring to a boil, and simmer about 20 minutes. If fresh Italian plums are used, combine ¼ cup light honey with 1 cup water in pot, bring to a boil over low heat, add plums, and simmer about 10 minutes. Drain prunes or plums and reserve cooking liquid.

Preheat oven to 300°F. Dry duck inside and out with paper towels. In cavity, insert garlic clove and about 6 prunes or plums. Tie or truss duck. Prick skin all over to release fat while cooking. Insert meat thermometer in thickest part of thigh. Place duck on rack in roasting pan and cook in oven until desired degree of doneness (about 180°F. for medium-well, or about 1 hour and 30 minutes).

SAUCE: Heat butter or oil in medium saucepan and brown giblets. Remove giblets from pan and add garlic. Stir over low heat 1 minute. Add mushrooms, lemon juice, and pepper, and shake over high heat 2 minutes. Remove from heat, add tomato paste, meat flavoring, and cornstarch or potato flour, and blend mixture. Add stock and ¾ cup reserved cooking liquid from prunes or plums. Stir over moderate heat until mixture boils. Add jelly, bay leaf, and giblets. Adjust seasoning, reduce heat to very low, and simmer 15 minutes. Then remove bay leaf and add prunes or plums. Rewarm sauce when ready to serve.

PRESENTATION: When duck is cooked, carve into serving pieces and arrange on warm serving platter or gratin dish. With slotted spoon, arrange prunes or plums around duck. (Remove giblets for other use.) Spoon sauce over duck. Sprinkle chives over top.

4 servings

SARAH BERNHARDTS

Prune and almond drop cookies.

DO-AHEAD TIP: *Cookies can be stored in sealed container in freezer.*

- 3 tablespoons unsalted butter
- 2 tablespoons light honey
- 2 tablespoons molasses
- 1 egg, beaten
- 3/4 cup plus 2 tablespoons sifted whole wheat pastry flour
- 1/8 teaspoon baking soda
- 1/8 teaspoon ground cinnamon
- 1/4 cup coarsely chopped toasted almonds
- 3/4 cup chopped pitted prunes
- 1 teaspoon vanilla extract
- 3 dozen untoasted almond slivers (optional)

Preheat oven to 375°F. Beat butter in mixer until light and creamy. Add honey and molasses and beat. Add egg and beat. In separate bowl, sift together flour, baking soda, and cinnamon. Add to wet ingredients and mix thoroughly. Add chopped almonds, prunes, and vanilla. Operate mixer only until well mixed.

Line baking sheet with waxed paper and oil top of waxed paper. Take tiny bits of dough (about 1/2 to 3/4 inch in diameter) with tip of teaspoon and drop onto baking sheet. If desired, stick almond sliver into top of each drop. Bake 10 to 15 minutes, depending on size of drops.

Makes about 3 dozen 1-inch cookies

More Plum and Prune Recipes

See Index for the following recipes:

MAIN DISH: *Chiles Rellenos*; SALAD: Cabbage and Fruit Salad with Honey Dressing; DESSERTS: Bessie's *Apfel Kuchen* (with plums), Cobbler, Frozen Fruit Yogurt, *Le Clafouti*, *Macedoine de Fruits*.

POMEGRANATES

Ever since I met my first pomegranate in Chinatown 30-odd years ago, I have studied this fascinating fruit, knowing there had to be a better way to capture the rich red juice encapsuled around hundreds of seeds. The answer, of course, is the juice extractor. Scoop chunks of pulp out of the shells, push them through the machine, and in seconds you have almost a cupful of the familiar, zesty-sweet, grenadine-color juice from one pomegranate. (Grenadine syrup, of course, is made with pomegranate juice.)

I use fresh pomegranate juice for all kinds of cooking surprises – in pomegranate sherbet, mixed with other fruit juices, mixed with buttermilk or yogurt for a frosty creamy drink, in mousse, in cold souffle, as fruit sauce over rice, custard, or ice cream. Recently we served carafes of pomegranate juice mixed with fresh grape juice as an aperitif at a natural foods brunch in New York. The combination is a cool pink color, and the fresh pomegranate juice adds zip to sweet fruit juices.

It is curious how we Americans can be so exploratory about foods and cuisines and at the same time shy away from certain foods that have been around for years, like the pomegranate. Perhaps the ease of juicing it through the extractor will encourage people to enjoy it more often. Pomegranates are quite a common food in other countries. When we traveled through Tunisia, it seemed as though scoops of pomegranate with a squeeze of fresh orange juice were served with every meal.

In Mexico the pomegranate is a favorite food decoration, on almost anything and everything. There they open the pomegranate (called *granada* in Spanish), separate the seed capsules, and sprinkle them over all kinds of savory and dessert dishes. A scattering of red pomegranate seeds is mandatory on top of *Chiles Rellenos en Nogada*, considered Mexico's national dish because it displays the colors of the country's flag – the *green* stuffed pepper, covered with *white* nut sauce, and decorated with *red* pomegranate seeds.

Pomegranate literally means "seedy apple," a true description. The fruit has a hard, brownish-yellow to red rind, like an orange rind that has become dry and brittle. It is a decorative and protective ball packed with many capsules, each filled with juicy crimson red pulp and a seed. The edible portion is the membrane-enclosed wet pulp around each seed.

It is a most exotic fruit, believed to be native to Persia and adjacent countries and mentioned in the Old Testament several times under the name of *rimmon.* Its flowers and fruits had a place in religious rites and mythology. On account of its profusion of seeds, the ancients connected it with procreation, increase, and abundance, and

POMEGRANATES

believed that Aphrodite, goddess of love, planted it on the island of Cyprus. In North America, it was discovered growing in Georgia and California in the 1700s with no explanation of its origins. Today the pomegranate prospers in almost all subtropical areas. Most of our pomegranates come from California during the fall.

Because we seem so reluctant to buy pomegranates, sometimes they stay in the store too long and spoil. So, it is important to recognize a good-quality fruit, one that has an unbroken rind, with no sign of decay, is heavy for its size, and has a fresh, not dried-out, appearance. Do examine pomegranates carefully. I once bought a dozen at $1 each and found four to be decayed inside. Large sizes are better because the seed capsules are fatter and juicier. (Regardless of size, all pomegranates have approximately the same number of seeds.)

To eat pomegranates, as we did in North Africa for breakfast or dessert, simply quarter the fruit and scoop the insides into a serving bowl. It is not necessary to separate the seeds, just leave them in chunks. Portions are served on individual plates or in cups. To make a Tunisian pomegranate compote, cut large oranges in half horizontally. Remove the segments and snip out all membrane from the shells. Cut pomegranates in half and scoop out bite-size chunks of pulp. Fill the orange cups with pomegranate chunks and orange segments. Sprinkle with a little orange juice. The recipes for Breast of Chicken with Peppers and Pomegranate and *Chiles Rellenos en Nogada* demonstrate how Mexican cooks use the separated pomegranate seeds for garnish.

Pomegranates are a good source of natural sugar, with only 63 calories in a 3½-ounce portion, and a good supplement of nutrients. They have long been credited with mysterious medicinal value. Mohammed once instructed his followers, "Eat the pomegranate, for it purges the system of envy and hatred."

BREAST OF CHICKEN (OR PORK CHOPS) WITH PEPPERS AND POMEGRANATE

Pechugas (o Chuletas de Cerdo) con Rajas y Granada

This dish is the specialty of chef Pedro Ortega Martinez of Estoril Restaurant in Mexico City. In Mexican cookery, rajas *(pronounced ra-has) means* sliced *peppers as opposed to whole or chopped peppers.*

DO-AHEAD TIP: *This dish can be prepared a few hours in advance and arranged on heatproof serving platter. At serving time, cover with aluminum foil, rewarm in 300° F. oven, and decorate with parsley and pomegranate seeds.*

- 4 half breasts of chicken, skinned and boned, or 4 pork loin chops, each 1 inch thick
- 2 tablespoons light vegetable oil (e.g., safflower)
- 4 green bell peppers, seeded and cut into ½-inch-wide strips
- ¼ cup finely chopped yellow onions
- 1 teaspoon finely chopped fresh garlic
- 1 bay leaf
- ¼ cup chicken stock
- ½ cup finely chopped raw potato
- 1 cup light cream
- freshly ground white pepper
- 1 cup diced Swiss or jack cheese
- 2 tablespoons finely chopped fresh parsley
- separated seeds of 1 pomegranate

Saute breasts of chicken or pork chops in oil until cooked. Arrange on serving platter and keep warm.

If saute pan is dry, add more oil, and heat. Add peppers, onions, garlic, and bay leaf, stir, and cook over moderate heat 2 minutes. Add stock and potato. Bring to a boil, cover, and cook over moderate heat until vegetables are soft (only about 5 minutes). Remove bay leaf. Add cream (just enough to make a sauce), season with pepper, and bring to a boil. Gradually add cheese, stirring until all cheese is melted.

PRESENTATION: Spoon sauce over meat. Sprinkle top with parsley and pomegranate seeds.

4 servings

More Pomegranate Recipes

See Index for the following recipes:

MAIN DISHES: *Chiles Rellenos*, Poached Chicken Hawaiian; BEVERAGES: Pink Pearl.

RAISINS

Raisins, of course, are dried grapes. Golden or sultana raisins are Thompson seedless grapes, and dark raisins are usually muscat grapes with the seeds removed.

Most cooks regard raisins as a staple on the pantry shelf. They're just there – to throw a handful into a batch of muffins, to dress up some rice, to dramatize some hors d'oeuvres, to scatter over coffee cake, to add to chutney or applesauce. They're indispensable! Raisins punctuate ordinary foods with dots of excitement. I shall never forget Felipe's delight when I added raisins to his favorite carrot cake for the first time. Of course, the addition of a few chopped nuts and a thick, gooey maple frosting helped to enhance his dessert experience.

Raisins are also a favorite energy food for eating out of hand. They are especially useful for satisfying restless tots during travel or other long periods between meals (certainly healthier and less sticky than candy). Like fresh grapes, they are mainly sugar with modest amounts of vitamins and minerals. Being dried grapes, with most of the water removed, the sugar and nutrients are more concentrated.

Remember raisins (and dried currants) for contrasty and tasty accents on canapes. Use them to decorate fillings and spreads of cream cheese, Roquefort cheese, pate, peanut butter, or chipped beef.

MIXED GREENS AND RAISIN SALAD

DO-AHEAD TIP: *All ingredients, including dressing, can be assembled in salad bowl a day ahead, covered with plastic wrap, and refrigerated.*

- 1 small head escarole
- 1 small head Boston lettuce
- ½ bunch watercress
- 1 small head chicory (curly endive)
- ¼ pound spinach leaves
- ½ cup dark or golden raisins, or combination
- 2 hard-cooked eggs
- 1 cup Basic Vinaigrette Dressing (see Index)

Wash and dry salad greens thoroughly. Pour ½ cup vinaigrette dressing on bottom of large salad bowl. Tear collection of greens into bite-size pieces, dropping them into salad bowl on top of dressing. Save some of the lighter-colored leaves from the lettuce heart for the top. Scatter raisins on top of greens. Cut each egg into quarter wedges and arrange like points of a star in center of salad. (At this point, salad can be covered with plastic wrap and refrigerated until it is to be served. As long as salad is not tossed with dressing, leaves will stay crisp.)

6 servings

RAISINS

SPINACH (OR BROCCOLI) WITH RAISINS AND PINE NUTS

This unlikely combination is a memorably marvelous first course or vegetable accompaniment.

DO-AHEAD TIP: *This dish can be assembled in the serving dish a few hours ahead. At serving time, rewarm in 300°F. oven. Top with grated cheese and butter, and brown under broiler.*

- 2 pounds fresh spinach, well washed, or 2 pounds broccoli, trimmed and coarsely chopped
- 2 tablespoons unsalted butter
- 3 tablespoons extra virgin olive oil
- 1 teaspoon finely chopped fresh garlic
- freshly ground white pepper
- 4 tablespoons golden or dark seedless raisins
- 4 tablespoons pine nuts (pignolis)
- 3 tablespoons freshly grated Parmesan cheese
- 1 tablespoon unsalted butter, melted

If spinach is used, place it in a large pot, sprinkle with a little water, cover, and cook over high heat until wilted, turning leaves occasionally. Drain through a colander, pressing down with back of saucer to remove excess moisture. Chop spinach coarsely.

If broccoli is used, plain-cook it in a steamer or covered pot with a little water until just tender. Drain well.

Heat butter and oil in deep, heavy pot. Add garlic and pepper, and cook over low heat 1 minute. Add raisins and pine nuts and cook over low heat 1 minute. Add spinach or broccoli and mix well.

PRESENTATION: Arrange vegetable mixture on gratin dish or shallow heatproof serving dish. Sprinkle grated cheese and melted butter on top. Brown under hot broiler.

4 to 6 servings

CHRISTMAS CARROT CAKE

Rich with raisins and nuts and titillating spice, this cake adds a festive touch anytime, anywhere, and will certainly brighten a carry-along meal. Best of all, it can be stored in the freezer for several months, handy to cut off a portion when you want it. (Because it contains oil and honey, this cake does not freeze hard.) For a special treat, it can be frosted with thick, fluffy Maple Icing. For Christmas, decorate cake plate with a couple of holly sprigs.

DO-AHEAD TIP: *To freeze, wrap cake (unfrosted) securely in heavy aluminum foil and enclose in sealed plastic bag.*

- 3 cups whole wheat pastry flour
- 2½ teaspoons baking powder (without aluminum salts)

Preheat oven to 325°F. Sift together flour, baking powder, soda, cinnamon, ginger, nutmeg, and allspice and set aside. Combine oil and honey in mixer and beat until blended. Add 1 cup sifted dry ingredients and mix. Add remaining dry

CHRISTMAS CARROT CAKE—continued

1 teaspoon baking soda

1 teaspoon ground cinnamon

1 teaspoon ground ginger

½ teaspoon freshly grated nutmeg

½ teaspoon ground allspice

⅔ cup light vegetable oil (e.g., safflower)

¾ cup light honey

4 eggs

2 cups finely grated raw carrots (or, use carrot fiber from juice extractor)

½ cup dark or golden raisins

1 cup chopped walnuts or pecans

ingredients alternately with eggs (1 at a time), mixing well after each addition. Add carrots. Last, mix in raisins and nuts. Pour into oiled tube pan.

Bake about 1 hour and 30 minutes, or until cake rebounds to touch. After removing cake from oven, allow to cool to room temperature in pan. Loosen sides and carefully invert onto cake plate.

18 to 24 servings

MAPLE OR HONEY ICING

DO-AHEAD TIP: *This icing will hold up well for 1 or 2 days in freezer.*

2 cups light honey or maple syrup

¾ cup egg whites (6 to 8 egg whites)

Heat honey or maple syrup in small saucepan over very low heat just to boiling point. In mixer, beat egg whites to soft peaks. Continue beating while slowly adding honey or maple syrup in very thin stream. Beat until frosting holds its shape and is cool. Using spatula, spread frosting all over cake.

Yields enough icing to thickly cover 10-inch-diameter layer cake or tube cake

RAISINS

COOKIES WITH RAISINS

It seems as though raisins and cookies just naturally go together. Here is a collection of four kinds of cookies with raisins that can be made in tiny sizes for fancy dinner party petits fours or larger for the family cookie jar.

DO-AHEAD TIP: *All of these cookies can be stored in sealed container in freezer.*

WALNUT ROCKS

These are tiny drop cookies.

- 8 tablespoons unsalted butter
- 2 tablespoons molasses
- 6 tablespoons light honey
- 1 egg, beaten
- 1¼ cups sifted whole wheat flour
- ¼ teaspoon baking soda
- 1 teaspoon baking powder (without aluminum salts)
- ½ teaspoon ground cinnamon
- ½ teaspoon ground cloves
- ¾ cup rolled oats
- ¼ cup plain yogurt (regular or low-fat)
- ½ cup coarsely chopped English or black walnuts
- ½ cup chopped dark raisins
- about 4 dozen walnut halves, halved (optional)

Preheat oven to 375°F. Beat butter in mixer until light and creamy. Add molasses and honey and beat. Add egg and beat. Sift together flour, soda, baking powder, cinnamon, and cloves. Add rolled oats to flour mixture. Add dry ingredients and yogurt to wet ingredients, mixing after each addition. Add nuts and raisins and operate mixer only until dough is mixed.

Line baking sheet with waxed paper and oil top of waxed paper. Take tiny bits of dough (about ½ to ¾ inch in diameter) with tip of teaspoon and drop on baking sheet. If desired, stick piece of walnut on top of each drop, pressing it into dough a little. Bake about 12 minutes, depending on size of drops.

Makes about 8 dozen 1-inch cookies

SPICE BALLS

4 tablespoons unsalted butter

1/4 cup light honey

1/2 beaten egg

1/4 cup miller's bran

3 tablespoons dark raisins

1 cup sifted whole wheat pastry flour

1/2 teaspoon baking powder (without aluminum salts)

1/2 teaspoon ground cinnamon

1/8 teaspoon mace

1/4 teaspoon ground cloves

1/4 teaspoon freshly grated nutmeg

1 teaspoon vanilla extract

Beat butter in mixer until light and creamy. Add honey and beat. Add egg and beat. Mix in bran and raisins. Sift together flour, baking powder, cinnamon, mace, cloves, and nutmeg. Add to wet ingredients with vanilla. Operate mixer only until dough is well mixed. Chill dough in refrigerator until it can be shaped into balls between your hands.

Preheat oven to 400°F. Line baking sheet with waxed paper and oil top of waxed paper. Take about 1/2 teaspoon dough and shape into a ball between your hands, and place on baking sheet. (Ball should be about 3/4 inch in diameter.) Form all dough into balls and place on baking sheet. Bake about 10 minutes, depending on size of balls.

Makes about 4 dozen 3/4-inch cookies

HONEY BEES

These are tiny drop cookies.

6 tablespoons light honey

2 tablespoons unsalted butter

1/2 beaten egg

3/4 cup plus 2 tablespoons sifted whole wheat pastry flour

1/4 teaspoon baking soda

1/8 teaspoon ground cloves

1/2 teaspoon ground cinnamon

1/2 cup chopped dark or golden raisins

Preheat oven to 400°F. In small saucepan, warm honey and butter until butter is melted. Let mixture cool a little. Transfer honey and butter mixture to mixer, add egg, and beat. Sift together flour, baking soda, cloves, and cinnamon. Add flour mixture to wet ingredients and mix well. Add raisins.

Line baking sheet with waxed paper and oil top of waxed paper. Take tiny bits of dough (about 1/2 inch in diameter) with tip of teaspoon and slip onto baking sheet. (Wet finger to slip dough off teaspoon.) Bake about 15 minutes, depending on size of drops.

Makes about 3 dozen 1- to 1 1/2-inch cookies

(continued)

COOKIES WITH RAISINS – continued

RAISIN TRIOS

These are little lemon cookies, each topped with 3 raisins. For variation, jam can be sandwiched between pairs of these cookies, if desired.

COOKIES
- 4 eggs
- 6 tablespoons light honey
- grated rind of 1 lemon
- ½ teaspoon vanilla extract
- 2 cups sifted whole wheat pastry flour
- ⅔ cup unsalted butter, melted
- about 12 dozen dark raisins

RASPBERRY SYRUP (optional)
- ¼ cup seedless red or black raspberry preserve
- 1 teaspoon fresh lemon juice

COOKIES: Preheat oven to 300°F. In top of double boiler combine eggs, honey, lemon rind, and vanilla, and beat with rotary beater over simmering water until mixture is hot. Remove from heat and beat until cold and frothy. Using rubber scraper, fold in flour lightly and evenly. Then lightly fold in melted butter.

Line baking sheet with waxed paper and oil top of waxed paper. Put dough in pastry bag fitted with ½-inch plain tube. Pipe tiny mounds (about ½ inch in diameter) on baking sheet. Decorate each mound with triangle of 3 raisins, pushing them into the dough – which will flatten the mound to about 1 inch in diameter. Bake 20 to 25 minutes, depending on size of mounds.

RASPBERRY SYRUP: Combine preserve and lemon juice in small saucepan and stir over moderate heat until preserve is dissolved. Let cool to room temperature. When cookies are cool, raspberry syrup can be sandwiched between pairs of cookies. (Any unused mixture can be returned to original jar.)

Makes about 4 dozen 1-inch single cookies or 2 dozen sandwiched cookies

More Raisin Recipes

See Index for the following recipes:

MAIN DISH: *Chiles Rellenos*; SIDE DISH: Turkish Rice; DESSERT: *Dulce de Camote.*

RASPBERRIES

With fresh raspberries today going at $3 or more for a half pint, it seems a fairy tale that once I wallowed in the freshest of this lovely fruit. Only recently I sat with Aunt Selma Dunn in Saginaw, and we recalled the days when many of the cousins during our school years came to her farm on the hill, tied lard cans around our waists, and picked raspberries, usually during the month of July. I think we were paid a nickel a bucket.

Picking raspberries at Aunt Selma's farm had all of the elements of a chapter out of the *Bobbesey Twins.* Mother, sister Kathryn, and I went to Mother's sister's farm early in the morning, where she and Aunt Florence would spend the day quilting or perhaps canning a batch of the previous day's picking of raspberries. Together with cousins Bob and Carol, my sister and I set out for the Dunn farm on the other side of the woods. First we chased each other through the lane that cut through the fenced pastures and fields where cows and horses were grazing and Uncle Ernie and his helpers were working the crops. The little woods that separated the Schoenheit and Dunn farms was a dark, cool, mossy glen with violets, jack-in-the-pulpits, and other pretty little flowers growing under the tall trees, intersected with several tiny brooks of clear, bubbly water, and a considerable traffic of squirrels, chipmunks, and rabbits. All of us loved that woods, and we often played hide-and-seek there.

Raspberry picking is not a backbreaking job. Raspberry bushes (actually brambles) grow upright, so the fruit is picked at waist level; and when the berries are properly red and ripe, they slide off their stamens with the greatest of ease. Since the picking crew comprised mostly cousins of school age, the acres of raspberry rows resounded with chatter, shouts, and songs; and we probably ate as many berries as we picked. Come to think about it, for all of the lavish picnics and holiday feasts we had at Aunt Selma's during raspberry picking time, we never stayed to eat, because nobody was hungry. (It was just as well; after picking, the Dunns still had to crate the berries and take them to the city market at the crack of dawn.)

My parents purchased a good quantity of Aunt Selma's raspberries. They were one of our favorite fruits. During the season, we ate fresh ones over cereal, with cream, and in pies and shortcake. As we picked, Mother canned raspberry jam and sauce. Mother was a talented cook and always treated food with the greatest respect and care. Delicate as raspberries are, those in her canned sauce always remained firm and whole, never disintegrating or becoming mushy, and were so perfectly spaced in the jar; they were perennial blue-ribbon winners at the county fair. This sauce was so good during the winter months, either plain, or with a dollop of cream, or over hot cereal. (Despite the Depression, our mid-Michigan cuisine was quite gourmet, thanks to my father's farming and his farmer friends, Mother's cooking and baking prowess, and three daughters to help with the garden and kitchen work.)

Raspberries, both wild and cultivated, grow in the temperate zone all over the world. We even have wild raspberries on our farm in Tuscany. I serve them absolutely plain, nestled in a fresh grape leaf. There are black, red, and white raspberries. Some years ago, my husband and I came across white raspberries being sold at roadside stands near Salem and Rockport, Massachusetts. They are exquisite but do not have the spirited flavor of the red.

If you must purchase your pleasure of raspberries from the market, you certainly want to be sure of getting good ones – at today's prices! Choose raspberries that appear fresh, bright, plump, and well shaped. Avoid wet or leaky berries. A stained container alerts you to overripe or damaged berries. Refrigerate them until ready to use or serve. Like most fruits, raspberries contain a range of nutrients; especially notable – their level of iron, the B vitamins, and vitamin C.

Besides the homespun ways of eating raspberries in my childhood, raspberries find their way into a host of sophisticated desserts, such as open-face raspberry tart and tartlets; mousse; hot, cold, and frozen souffles; co-starred with currants in the English summer pudding; ice cream and sherbet; cold soup; and the royal red robe for the peach Melba. Raspberry puree as sauce adds the fruit's elegance to an even longer list of uses, such as pouring or spreading over cake, ice cream, *coeur a la creme*, Bavarian cream, custard, and flummery. Even raspberry jam isn't just for spreading on toast. It's the filling for spicy-crusted linzer tart and linzer cookies, and is a favorite in jelly roll, layer cake, and coffee cake. When fresh raspberries are out of season, raspberry jam can be dissolved over low heat, strained, and used as sauce. I personally do not think raspberries freeze well; it is such a disappointment to see how mushy and broken down they become.

To clean raspberries: Rinse berries gently and briefly in cold water. Drain them on paper towels. *Do not let berries soak in water.*

ICED RASPBERRY SOUP

DO-AHEAD TIP: *Soup keeps well in refrigerator for 1 or 2 days.*

- **2 cups fresh raspberries, or 2 boxes frozen raspberries**
- **1 cup orange juice**
- **3/4 cup white grape juice or weak China tea**
- **2 tablespoons red currant jelly**
- **2 teaspoons arrowroot or cornstarch**
- **light honey to taste**
- **1/2 cup heavy cream, whipped**
- **1 tablespoon grated orange rind**

Combine raspberries and orange juice in blender or food processor and puree. Rub through fine strainer and transfer to medium saucepan. Add grape juice or tea. Mix currant jelly with arrowroot or cornstarch and add to soup mixture. Stir over low heat until mixture boils. Add honey to taste. Reduce heat to very low and simmer 10 minutes. Chill thoroughly.

PRESENTATION: Serve in individual bowls embedded in crushed ice. Garnish with float of whipped cream sprinkled with orange rind.

4 servings

FLUMMERY

This is a shimmery gelatin mold of fine whole wheat cereal made cloudlike with beaten egg white and whipped cream. Fresh raspberry sauce is poured over the mold. Flummery is also very colorful and tasty when served with fresh blueberry or blackberry sauce (see Index for Fresh Fruit Sauces).

DO-AHEAD TIP: *Mold and sauce can be made a day ahead.*

MOLD

- **1 cup white grape juice or strained orange juice**
- **1 cup water**
- **½ cup fine whole wheat cereal (not cracked texture)**
- **½ cup light honey**
- **2 teaspoons vanilla extract**
- **2 tablespoons unflavored gelatin**
- **1 tablespoon fresh lemon juice**
- **4 egg whites**
- **¾ cup heavy cream, whipped**

SAUCE

- **1 cup seedless red raspberry preserve or red currant jelly**
- **1 tablespoon fresh lemon juice**
- **2 cups fresh ripe raspberries**

MOLD: Combine grape or orange juice and water in heavy pot and bring to a brisk boil. Stir in cereal. Reduce heat to low and continue to cook, stirring frequently, until mixture becomes very thick. Remove from heat and stir in honey and vanilla. In small saucepan, combine gelatin, lemon juice, and 2 tablespoons water and stir over low heat until gelatin is dissolved. Stir into whole wheat mixture.

Beat egg whites to soft peaks. Place whole wheat mixture over ice and stir until it begins to cool. Fold in egg whites. Next, fold in whipped cream. Oil 1½-quart mold or 7-inch springform pan. Spoon whole wheat mixture into mold and chill in refrigerator until set.

SAUCE: Combine preserve or jelly and lemon juice in small pan and stir over low heat until dissolved. Pour syrup over fresh raspberries and chill thoroughly.

PRESENTATION: Turn whole wheat gelatin mold out onto serving plate. (To loosen mold other than springform, slide small, thin knife around edge of mold, then hold mold in bowl of hot water for a moment.) Spoon raspberry sauce over top and let drip down sides. Serve.

6 servings

RASPBERRY MOUSSE 1

Mousse aux Framboises

Mousse with egg yolks.

DO-AHEAD TIP: *Mousse can be made a day ahead and refrigerated.*

MOUSSE

- 6 whole eggs
- 4 egg yolks
- ½ cup light honey
- grated rind of 1 lemon
- 2¼ tablespoons unflavored gelatin
- 2 tablespoons fresh lemon juice
- ¼ cup water
- ¾ cup heavy cream, whipped
- 1½ cups strained fresh raspberry pulp

DECORATION

- 1 cup heavy cream, whipped
- ½ cup cleaned whole fresh raspberries
- ½ cup finely chopped walnuts

MOUSSE: Combine eggs, egg yolks, and honey in mixer and beat until mixture is light and stiff. Remove bowl from machine and fold in lemon rind. In small saucepan, mix gelatin, lemon juice, and water, and stir over low heat until gelatin is dissolved. Let cool a little and fold gelatin into egg mixture. Next, fold in whipped cream. Then fold in strained raspberry pulp. Pour mousse into serving bowl and chill in refrigerator.

DECORATION: Put whipped cream in pastry bag fitted with star tube (any size). Pipe rosettes all over top of mousse and top each with whole raspberry. Sprinkle border of walnuts around edge of bowl. Refrigerate until ready to serve.

8 servings

RASPBERRY MOUSSE 2

Mousse without egg yolks.

DO-AHEAD TIP: *Mousse should be made a day ahead in order to set.*

- **½ cup light honey**
- **1 cup cold water**
- **2½ cups cleaned fresh whole raspberries**
- **1 tablespoon unflavored gelatin (if mousse is to be served in bowl), or 2½ tablespoons gelatin (if mousse is to be molded)**
- **3 egg whites**
- **1½ cups heavy cream, whipped**

Have ready 1½-quart mold. Combine honey and ½ cup water in medium saucepan and stir over low heat until mixture is blended. Reserve ½ cup raspberries for decoration and add rest to honey syrup. Cover and cook over low heat until raspberries are soft. Rub mixture through fine strainer to remove seeds. Soften gelatin in ½ cup water, add to hot raspberry sauce, and stir until mixture is blended. Cool in refrigerator.

Beat egg whites to soft peaks and fold into raspberry puree. Also fold in *half* of the whipped cream. Fill serving bowl or mold with mousse and chill until set.

PRESENTATION: When mousse is firm, turn out onto serving plate. (To loosen mousse from mold, slide small, thin knife around edge of mold and hold mold in bowl of hot water for a moment. Place serving plate bottom side up on top of mold and invert.)

To decorate either bowl or mold of mousse, put rest of whipped cream in pastry bag fitted with star tube and pipe border around top or side. Decorate with reserved raspberries.

4 to 6 servings

LINZER COOKIES

Linzer dough is spicy sweet short pastry. Raspberry filling is sandwiched between linzer cookies to resemble the classic linzer tart in miniature.

DO-AHEAD TIP: *Cookies can be stored in airtight container in freezer.*

COOKIES

- 1¼ cups whole wheat pastry flour
- 2 teaspoons ground cinnamom
- ¼ teaspoon ground cardamom
- ½ teaspoon freshly grated nutmeg
- 4 tablespoons unsalted butter
- 1½ egg yolks
- 2 tablespoons light honey
- 1 teaspoon vanilla extract

RASPBERRY SYRUP

- ¼ cup seedless red or black raspberry preserve
- 1 teaspoon fresh lemon juice

COOKIES: Preheat oven to 350°F. In food processor, combine flour, cinnamon, cardamom, and nutmeg, and process until mixed. Add butter and process until mixture resembles coarse meal. In small bowl, mix egg yolks, honey, and vanilla. Add to flour mixture and process until blended but still crumbly. Stop processor, gather mixture with your hands, and transfer to work surface. Form a ball.

Between floured sheets of waxed paper, roll dough out to 3/16 inch thickness. Cut in rounds with 1½-inch cutter. Then, using plain pastry tube with ½-inch opening, cut centers out of *half* of the rounds to form rings. Reroll remaining dough and cut in rounds, then cut half of these rounds into rings. Place on baking sheet and bake about 15 minutes. Let cool.

RASPBERRY SYRUP: Combine preserve and lemon juice in small saucepan and stir over moderate heat until preserve is dissolved. Let cool to room temperature.

When cookies are cool, spread raspberry syrup all over tops of whole rounds. Cover with rings. Chill in refrigerator or freezer until filling is set.

Makes about 2 dozen 1½-inch cookies.

More Raspberry Recipes

See Index for the following recipes:

DESSERTS: Beignets Souffles with Fruit Syrup or Fruit Sauce; *Coeurs a la Creme*, Crepes Stuffed with Fresh Fruit, English Custard Sauce (with raspberries), English Summer Pudding, French Fruit Tart and Tartlets, Fresh Fruit Ice Cream, Frozen Fresh Fruit Souffle, Frozen Fruit Yogurt, Fruit Sherbet, Fruit Shortcake; Peach Melba, Refrigerator Cheesecake with Fresh Fruit Topping; BEVERAGE: Cran-Raspberry Froth; SAUCES: Fresh Fruit Sauce; Fruit Syrup.

RHUBARB

Between the three-sisters fruit trees in my parents' backyard (planted at the birth of each daughter) were four indomitably hardy and prolific rhubarb plants – to Father's delight and my youthful dislike. Until only a few years ago, rhubarb just didn't make my list of favorable foods. That changed when I decided to try tart rhubarb puree in mousse, ice cream, and frozen yogurt. Now it's "rah rah" for rhubarb!

Then, the deeper I got into rhubarb's lore, the more I grew to like it. I had no idea that this strange-looking plant, which shoots long, thick, red spears from the ground with heads of large, crinkly leaves like spinach, dates back to antiquity, 2,700 B.C. at least. In China, the rhubarb root is still used as medicine. Although rhubarb is botanically a vegetable (a member of the buckwheat family), the U.S. Customs Court of Buffalo, New York, of all places, officially declared on July 17, 1947, that it is a fruit and not a vegetable since its principal use in the home is like that of other types of fruit. Although the issue had to do with the level of import duty – lower on fruit than vegetables – the only woman judge on the court made the ruling, a reminder that our austere black-robed jurists share the dimension of domestic life. Today Americans consume 24 to 30 million tons of rhubarb, supplied by the states of Washington, Michigan, and California, testament that somebody out there likes plenty of rhubarb, or pie plant, as it is sometimes called.

Only the stalk is used for eating. (The beautiful rhubarb leaf contains a high content of oxalic acid characterized by soluble salts and can be quite poisonous.) The stalks usually are allowed to grow to a length of 18 to 24 inches, about 1 inch in diameter, and a color of rosy pink to cherry red before they are cut. Fresh rhubarb should be firm, crisp, and tender. It should quickly snap if bent. Stale rhubarb is wilted and flabby.

Rhubarb sauce and puree: Rhubarb is wonderfully easy to prepare. Just wash the stalks well, cut them into one-inch chunks, and put them in a deep, heavy pot. With two pounds of rhubarb, add $^3/_4$ cup light honey and the grated rind of 1 lemon. Cover and cook over low heat until rhubarb is soft. This is good basic stewed rhubarb to eat plain or with a spoonful of creme fraiche or sour cream, to use as a base for pie, or to puree in the processor or blender for use in mousse, ice cream, cold soup, and fantastic frozen yogurt. And, as my father constantly reminded me, rhubarb is good for you – it does contain modest levels of iron and vitamins A and C.

RHUBARB MOUSSE

DO-AHEAD TIP: *Mousse can be made a day ahead and refrigerated.*

- 6 whole eggs
- 4 egg yolks
- ¼ cup light honey
- 2 tablespoons unflavored gelatin
- 2 tablespoons fresh lemon juice
- 4 tablespoons water
- 2 cups Rhubarb Puree (see recipe in this section)
- 1 cup heavy cream, whipped
- ¼ cup toasted sliced or slivered almonds

Combine eggs, egg yolks, and honey in mixer and beat until mixture is light and stiff. In small saucepan, mix gelatin, lemon juice, and water, and stir over low heat until gelatin is dissolved. Let cool a little and fold gelatin into egg mixture. Lightly and evenly fold in rhubarb puree. Pour mousse into serving bowl and chill in refrigerator.

PRESENTATION: Put whipped cream in pastry bag fitted with star tube (any size). Pipe rosettes on top of mousse. Stick almonds in whipped cream. Refrigerate until serving time.

8 servings

RHUBARB PUREE

This mixture can be used for mousse, sherbet, ice cream.

DO-AHEAD TIP: *Rhubarb puree keeps well in the freezer.*

- 1 pound rhubarb, cleaned and cut into 1-inch pieces
- ⅓ cup plus 1 tablespoon light honey
- grated rind of ½ lemon

In deep, heavy pot, combine rhubarb, honey, and lemon rind. Cover and cook over low heat until rhubarb is soft. Stir occasionally to prevent scorching. Puree mixture in food processor or blender.

Yields 2 cups

RHUBARB SHERBET

DO-AHEAD TIP: *Sherbet keeps well in freezer at 0° F. for 2 or 3 days. After that it will start to crystallize.*

- 2 cups Rhubarb Puree (see recipe in this section)
- 1 cup orange juice
- 2 egg whites

Combine rhubarb puree and orange juice. Process mixture in ice cream maker until almost firm. Beat egg whites to soft peaks and add to sherbet mixture. Continue processing until firm. Remove sherbet from drum and serve, or store in 0°F. freezer.

Yields about 1 quart

Another Rhubarb Recipe

See Index for the following recipe:

DESSERT: Rhubarb Ice Cream.

STRAWBERRIES

Two ways of earning summer money as a youngster were picking strawberries in June and raspberries in July.

To pick strawberries, we walked two miles out the "new road" to the Davis farm, picked through the cool of the morning (the ideal time to pick this fruit), and walked back. Strawberry picking was a backbreaking job, as we crawled along the rows, reaching under the leaves of the meandering runners to select only properly ripe, firm fruit. Even commercial strawberries must still be picked by hand because no machine has yet been invented that can remove the berries at the right ripeness without injuring them.

Those homegrown strawberries emitted a pungent strawberry fragrance and were rich tasting and red all the way through. A slice of hot, freshly baked bread slathered with just-made strawberry jam is a feast that is still high on my list of outstanding gastronomic impressions. At family reunion picnics, the *piece de resistance* of the predictable fare was always strawberry shortcake. The aunts' potluck menu became quite standard and was still going strong when I was honored at a homecoming party years later: baked beans, baked ham, roast chicken, German potato salad, cole slaw with cooked dressing, sliced peeled tomatoes, corn on the cob, head cheese, pot cheese, brick cheese, Frankenmuth sausages, crock pickles, homemade wheat and pumpernickel breads, crock butter, and – the strawberry shortcake. Everything was homegrown and homemade, naturally.

Ours was the old-fashioned kind of strawberry shortcake – biscuit dough baked in a sheet pan, then cut in squares and halved horizontally. For an individual serving, melted butter was poured on the bottom layer, then a ladle of slightly crushed sweetened berries, then the top of the biscuit, covered with another generous ladle of strawberries and just a dab of thick cream from the morning's milking.

American Indians were actually cultivating strawberries when Massachusetts settlers arrived. The Indians called strawberries *wuttahimneash*, which they mixed with meal to make bread. The strawberry is at home in many climates and appears as a native fruit on every continent except Africa and Australia, and New Zealand. In Europe, the dainty wild strawberry, called *fraise de bois* (wood strawberry) is an unbelievable burst of flavor for its size. I was amused recently as I came across a journal that my husband Lionel Braun and I had kept of a gastronomic tour of France we made in the early 60s. In it we recorded the menus of all of our meals. In every restaurant in which we ate – in Paris, Champagne, Burgundy, Bordeaux – and Switzerland, Lionel ordered *fraises de bois*! My role was to order another dessert so that he could taste a variety and still have his strawberries. I was ecstatic to discover the little berries growing beneath the underbrush on my farm in Italy and remembered the Roman Ovid's tender epithet to the wild strawberry "which disappears beneath its modest foliage, but whose presence the scented air reveals." I understand that now *fraises de bois* are also cultivated in Europe.

Modern Americans' insatiable appetite for strawberries has spurred strawberry growing as an industry in Arkansas, California, Florida, Louisiana, Maryland, Michigan, New Jersey, and Mexico, to provide us with a year-round supply. Strawberries must be picked when ripe, with caps left on. They do not continue to ripen after they are removed from the vine. Berries that are partly white or green are immature and have poor flavor that will never develop. Unfortunately these are too often the berries on the bottom of the baskets in the markets, with the ripe ones neatly covering the top. Time was when you could shake the basket to see what was underneath. If a customer did that in a city market today, the manager would probably have apoplexy. Watch for stained containers, which indicate the presence of bruised or overripe berries. Strawberries are highly perishable. They should be kept in a cold and humid place in the retail store as well as in the home and used as soon as possible.

Strawberries are also a rich nutritional package, with good levels of vitamin C and iron, and a range of other vitamins and minerals. It is particularly important to remember that removal of the cap greatly increases the loss of vitamins and minerals. Therefore, strawberries should be stored in the refrigerator as long as possible, to be washed and stemmed just before serving or adding to a preparation.

The strawberry has one of the most beguiling perfumes of all fruits, which, together with its sensuous shape and glowing red color, has inspired a volume of irresistible ways to tempt us. One of the most dazzling is the tart topped with dozens of shiny red domes. Another is the pristine white heart of cream (*coeur a la creme*) bathed with ruby-red strawberry sauce. Other visions of strawberry desserts which dance through the heads of gastronomes – homemade vanilla custard ice cream swirled with crushed fresh strawberries, hot strawberry souffle with cold strawberry sauce, or cold or frozen strawberry souffle decorated with more of the provocative fruit, a majestic mold of strawberry Bavarian cream, strawberry mousse, strawberry Napoleon, strawberry sherbet, glazed strawberries with stems on clouds of whipped cream topping rice *a l'imperatrice*, strawberry and rhubarb pie, and – simply a dish of garden-fresh strawberries covered with creme fraiche, creme chantilly or English custard. The French have a special day, June 5, to celebrate their love of the strawberry, usually with crepes stuffed with strawberries. Dione Lucas interpreted the crepes Suzette idea with strawberries. Nouvelle cuisine followers have gone agog over dressings and sauces with strawberry vinegar. Quite an imperial fruit. I think I shall make some strawberry jam and bake some bread.

STRAWBERRY MOUSSE

Mousse aux Fraises

DO-AHEAD TIP: *This dish should be prepared a day ahead in order to set.*

MOUSSE

- 6 whole eggs
- 4 egg yolks
- ½ cup light honey
- grated rind of 1 orange
- grated rind of 1 lemon
- 2½ tablespoons unflavored gelatin
- ½ cup orange juice
- 1 teaspoon fresh lemon juice
- 3 tablespoons water
- ¾ cup heavy cream, whipped
- 1½ cups pureed strawberries

DECORATION

- 1 cup red currant jelly
- 1 tablespoon orange juice, or 1 teaspoon lemon juice
- 30 or more perfect ripe strawberries, cleaned and stemmed

MOUSSE: Combine eggs, egg yolks, and honey in mixer and beat until mixture is light and stiff. Remove bowl from mixer and fold in orange rind and lemon rind. In small saucepan, combine gelatin, orange juice, lemon juice, and water, and stir over low heat until gelatin is dissolved. Cool gelatin mixture a little. Then, using rubber spatula, lightly and evenly fold it into egg mixture. Fold in whipped cream. Then fold in crushed strawberries. Pour mousse into serving bowl and place in refrigerator to set.

DECORATION: Combine currant jelly and orange or lemon juice in small saucepan and stir over low heat until jelly is dissolved. Rub through wire strainer and let cool to room temperature. Cover top of mousse with whole strawberries, stem end down. Gently brush strawberries with dissolved currant jelly to give them a nice glaze. Return mousse to refrigerator until serving time.

6 to 8 servings

STRAWBERRIES

CREPES AUX FRAISES A LA SUZETTE

Crepes with Strawberries, Suzette Style

DO-AHEAD TIP: *Crepes can be prepared several days ahead and frozen. Butter and sauce can be prepared a few hours ahead. Assemble dish at serving time.*

CREPES

8 to 12 6-inch Basic Crepes (see Index)

CURRANT BUTTER

6 tablespoons unsalted butter

1 teaspoon grated lemon rind

3 tablespoons cassis syrup (currant syrup), or red currant jelly

SAUCE

8 tablespoons unsalted butter

4 tablespoons cassis syrup or red currant jelly

⅓ cup red currant jelly

1 tablespoon grated lemon rind

2 cups cleaned strawberries (if berries are small, leave whole; if large, halve or quarter them)

CURRANT BUTTER: Beat butter in mixer or food processor until light and creamy. Add lemon rind and cassis syrup or currant jelly, and beat again. Spread a little of this butter on the underside (the side cooked last) of each crepe. Fold crepe into quarters and set aside.

SAUCE: Combine all ingredients in saute pan, bring to a boil over low heat, and simmer 3 minutes. Leave in pan.

PRESENTATION: When ready to serve, place folded crepes in sauce in pan. Scatter strawberries on top of crepes. Warm over low heat. Serve at once.

4 servings

NOTE: Cassis syrup is available in food specialty shops. It is more concentrated than currant jelly.

STRAWBERRY SOUFFLE OMELET

Dents de Lion (Lion's Teeth Omelet)

This is a delightful impromptu dessert, as easy to make as an omelet, that is unusual, elegant, and delicious. These are puffy little omelets, folded in half, showing big grins of whole red strawberries and white whipped cream. By adding arrowroot or cornstarch, the omelets can be made an hour ahead and will hold up in a warm oven.

DO-AHEAD TIP: *Omelets can be prepared an hour before serving time and kept warm in a 225° F. oven. Assemble with whipped cream and strawberries when ready to serve.*

FILLING

- 3/4 cup heavy cream
- 1 teaspoon vanilla extract
- 1 tablespoon light honey
- 20 whole ripe cleaned strawberries
- 1/2 cup red currant jelly, rubbed through fine strainer

OMELETS

- 3 eggs, separated
- 1 tablespoon light honey
- 1 teaspoon arrowroot or cornstarch

FILLING: Have filling ingredients ready before omelets are prepared. Beat heavy cream over bowl of ice until almost stiff. Add vanilla and honey and continue beating until cream holds its shape. Refrigerate.

OMELETS: Beat egg yolks, honey, and arrowroot or cornstarch with rotary or hand beater until mixture is light and creamy. Beat egg whites to soft peaks. Using rubber spatula, fold egg yolk mixture gently and smoothly into egg whites.

Preheat oven to 225°F. and have baking sheet ready. Heat medium omelet or saute pan. Wipe pan with butter or oil. Put one-fourth of egg mixture in pan and spread to a round shape, about 4 inches in diameter. Brown omelet on one side. Turn with spatula and brown other side. Transfer omelet to baking sheet and hold in warm oven. Prepare 3 more omelets in this manner.

PRESENTATION: Have warmed individual serving plates ready. Place one-fourth of whipped cream in center of each omelet and fold in half. Arrange folded omelets on plates. Dip whole strawberries in currant jelly and stand them in the open edge of the omelets (about 5 strawberries in each omelet). Serve at once.

4 servings

STRAWBERRIES

SUN TAN STRAWBERRIES

DO-AHEAD TIP: *Carob sauce can be made a day ahead and reheated to coat berries. Dip strawberries in sauce within an hour before serving.*

- **1 quart perfect, firm ripe strawberries, with stems attached**
- **½ cup carob powder**
- **½ teaspoon ground cinnamon**
- **4 to 5 tablespoons boiling water**
- **½ teaspoon vanilla extract**
- **1½ tablespoons cold unsalted butter, cut into bits**
- **⅓ to ½ cup heavy cream**

Briefly rinse berries under running water and dry gently in towel. Refrigerate berries until ready to coat.

Combine carob powder and cinnamon in small saucepan and add 4 tablespoons boiling water and vanilla. Stir with small whisk until well blended. (Mixture will be stiff and tend to cling to whisk, but if it is still dry, add another tablespoon hot water.) Place mixture over low heat and add butter, bit by bit, stirring constantly with whisk. Add ⅓ cup heavy cream and blend. Stir over low heat 8 minutes.

Dip chilled strawberries into sauce to form coating up to shoulders of berry. Place coated berries on dessert tray. (If sauce is too thick, add a tablespoon or more of cream. If sauce curdles, add a tablespoon or two of cold cream.)

Quick-chill carob-coated strawberries in freezer for 10 to 15 minutes; then transfer to refrigerator. To serve, arrange on tray or on individual dessert plates.

6 to 8 servings

More Strawberry Recipes

See Index for the following recipes:

MAIN DISH: Potato Pancakes with Fruit Sauce; DESSERTS: *Coeurs a la Creme*, Crepes Stuffed with Fresh Fruit, English Custard Sauce (with strawberries), French Fruit Tart and Tartlets, Fresh Fruit Ice Cream, Frozen Fresh Fruit Souffle, Frozen Fruit Yogurt, Fruit Sherbet, Fruit Shortcake, Refrigerator Cheesecake with Fresh Fruit Topping, *Riz a l'Imperatrice*; BEVERAGE: Strawberries with Buttermilk or Yougurt; SAUCE: Fresh Fruit Sauce.

Special Treats

APPLE-PEARS

The exploring connoisseur will occasionally encounter a small, green, russeted, pear-shaped fruit identified as an apple-pear. When ripe, it has the crispness and flavor of an apple and is usually eaten out of hand. However, if you are endowed with a windfall, the fruit may be prepared in the various ways of apple. Apple-pear is a distinct variety, not a cross between apple and pear. Its origin is rooted in China, and today most are still grown in China and Japan, although some are produced in California. The original Chinese name was *Sha-li*, which means "sand pear."

BREADFRUIT

It is indeed the "bread" in many tropical and subtropical regions of the world, such as Guatemala, Polynesia, the Philippines, and parts of Africa, Indonesia, and Hawaii. In America, breadfruit trees grow in Florida and the Caribbean, and the fruit is marketed in large cities throughout the United States where there are colonies of people from tropical zones.

Our friend Copeland Marks, an authority on Guatemalan and Far Eastern cuisines, describes breadfruit trees as magnificent with the huge fruits hanging from them, fruits the size of large cantaloupes. They look like big, wrinkly, green melons. The locals eat green and ripe breadfruit. The green are much like white potatoes, the ripe are similar to sweet potatoes, and they can be prepared in the many ways the potato is cooked.

According to Copeland, among the natives of those lands where breadfruit is the staff of life, there aren't really any "recipes" for it. Just peel the fruit, cut into ¼- to ½-inch-thick slices, arrange on a baking sheet, and bake in a moderate oven for 15 to 20 minutes. It becomes "bread," like toast, not as dry but chewy and tasty. In the Florida-Caribbean area, however, the breadfruit repertoire is a little more prolific, where it is sauteed or plain-cooked for use in salads, fritters, and casseroles – literally treated like potato. It can even be made into vichysoisse.

BREADFRUIT

CANDIED BREADFRUIT

DO-AHEAD TIP: *This dish can be prepared a day ahead. Bake at serving time.*

- **2 ripe breadfruit**
- **4 tablespoons unsalted butter**
- **⅔ cup light honey**

Boil or steam whole breadfruit 2½ to 3 hours. Preheat oven to 400°F. Cut breadfruit in halves and scoop out pulp. Heat butter and honey in small saucepan until mixture is blended. Arrange layers of breadfruit in buttered casserole or baking dish. Drizzle a little butter and honey mixture over each layer. Bake 30 minutes.

6 to 8 servings

CASHEW APPLES

When riding my horse through the villages and hills of Guerrero, Mexico, I like to exercise Pajarito at a fast trot! But under the tropical sun, my guide, Miguel, prefers to lope along, shaded by his sombrero and lulled by *mariachi* from the transistor radio in his pocket, and the distance between us lengthens. One day, east of Tuncingo, I was struck by the vision of the most perfect red apple hanging from a tree growing in the middle of nowhere. I waited for Miguel to catch up. He picked it and handed it to me with that charming smile that always came when he could introduce me to something lovely in his world. On closer examination, the fruit was even more incredible. Out of its bottom protruded one big cashew nut!

Cashew may be the only fruit of which we eat both fruit and nut. But, beware, before you eat the nut, as I was about to do when Miguel said, *"No, no, Maria, no bueno."* He explained that the shell around the nut can cause considerable irritation – a rash. The cashew plant, I learned later, is related to poison ivy. When the shell is removed, the nut, of course, is edible, although it is usually dried (which is the way I prefer cashews, called "raw" when packaged) and more often, roasted (when some of the cashew's characteristic sweetness seems to dissipate).

Since the seed grows outside the fruit, the cashew apple is completely a soft, peachlike, juicy fruit. Some cashew apples are sweet and tasty. Others can be acid and puckery. The trees grow throughout the Caribbean area and southern Florida.

CHERIMOYAS

Fruits such as cherimoya, custard apple, ilama, soursop, and sugar apple are related and are common from southern Florida on through the Caribbean and Mexico. One of the charms of the subtropics, the kind that isn't advertised in neon by the big resort hotels on the *avenida de tourista*, is the endless array of exotic fruits which are strange to most visitors. Only recently have some of them been exported to northern markets as specialties – fruits like the cherimoya, sapodilla, sapote, granadilla, star apple. Even in Mexico, you come upon them only if you browse in the local markets, venture where the locals live and eat, observe, inquire, and try the unfamiliar foods.

I met the cherimoya after a morning of waterskiing with Mexican sculptor Victor Salmones, in an episode which exposed the artist's deep compassion and his love for the good things of nature. (Salmones's bronzes are mounted in museums and public locations around the world, and his *Narcissus* is a national monument on a high rock promontory that surveys all of Acapulco Bay. Yet, in "his Acapulco," Victor's preference for simple pleasures perhaps explains why his art speaks to all.) Every morning, early, while most of Acapulco sleeps, Victor heads for the lagoon about ten miles north of town, a lakelike body of water rimmed with thick tropical jungle on the inland side and a narrow sandbar on the other, separating it from the Pacific. For about two hours, Victor skis; I applaud from the boat. Afterward we head for the palapa on the sandy shore to eat brunch of fried fresh-caught *mojarra* (like sand dabs), *tortillas al mano* and *platanos* (plantains).

One day a little boy came to our table with a couple of strange-looking fruits. They were about the size of apples, with rough greenish-brown skin that looked and felt as though it were covered with fleshy, prickly scales. Victor beamed at the child. "Ah, cherimoya!" The muchacho beamed, too, as Victor paid him precious pesos for bringing such treasure. "These," Victor informed me, "are delicious fruit. They will be our dessert today."

After we finished the fish, Victor took the cherimovas, peeled the thin skin, and sliced the white pulp. It is soft like custard, with seeds that are easily removed when eaten. The juicy flesh is very refreshing (sweet but not cloying), but, as Victor explained, the cherimoya must be perfectly ripe, or it can be tart. Cherimoyas and their cousins range in size from three to six inches long. The fruit is usually eaten raw. The pulp can be pureed and used to make tasty ice cream, sherbet, or a cooling drink.

CRABAPPLES

The flowering crabapple tree is perhaps one of the most aesthetic of fruit trees as the pink buds on its low, sweeping branches burst into cascades of snow-white blossoms. Two picture-perfect crabapple trees graced the sloping lawn of lawyer Christian Winter's home in our town, presenting seasonal spectaculars which we could view from our front window. During the summer the decorative trees were thick with green leaves and had begun developing dainty fruits that by autumn would become coral to rosy red and fall to the ground. The Winters had no children, so my sisters and I were invited to gather and take the fruit each year – and we did it eagerly. Mother made those crabapples into tart, amber-colored jelly, a favorite for spreading on the hot, homemade bread that she baked every Saturday. (We drew lots for the end piece of the loaf, which was a wall of crisp crust.)

Crabapples are not for eating out of hand or raw in any way, unless you fancy a sour, puckery taste. These apples are only about 1½ inches in diameter. Wild and cultivated crabapples are found throughout North America, as far north as Alaska, and in China and Siberia.

If you are blessed with a supply of this natural delicacy, cook them up as jelly, crabapple butter, or spiced whole crabapples. Spiced crabapples are an attractive and piquant garnish with roast pork or cold meats and are the traditional garland of honor encircling the platter bearing roast suckling pig. Crabapple butter can be used as puree for an interesting sherbet or other dessert preparations. Because of their rarity and goodness, glasses of clear, glittering crabapple jelly make treasured gifts for hosts and at Christmas.

CRABAPPLES

SPICED CRABAPPLES

- 4 pounds firm, ripe crabapples
- 4 sticks cinnamon bark
- 2 tablespoons whole cloves
- 2 cups light honey
- 1½ cups white or cider vinegar

Wash crabapples. Do not pare or remove stems. Remove blossom ends. Prick skins to prevent fruit from bursting. Tie cinnamon bark and cloves in cheesecloth bag. Combine honey, vinegar, and spices in bag in deep, heavy pot and boil 10 minutes. Add crabapples, a few at a time, and cook slowly until tender. Carefully remove from syrup and pack whole crabapples in sterilized jars. When all crabapples have been cooked, fill jars with boiling syrup, leaving ¼ inch headspace. Seal jars as directed by manufacturer. Process 15 minutes in boiling water bath. Let cool.

Yields 4 to 5 pints

DRIED CURRANTS

The tiny berries that are dried and marketed as "dried currants" are actually a variety of grape and no relation to fresh currants. Dried currants are small seedless Vinifera grapes called Zantes, named after one of the Greek islands where they have grown for centuries. It is said that they took on the name "currant" as a corruption of "Corinth," the Greek city which claims them as its main export.

Despite the dichotomy of the name, a canister of dried currants in the pantry is indispensable. Although they are tinier than raisins, they are tastier and have more zest. Add a handful to coffee cakes and rolls, fruit breads, cakes, cookies, and puddings – alone or in the company of raisins. Use them to decorate hors d'oeuvres and cookies. And, declares Mrs. Beeton in her venerable English cookbook, "...we could not make a plum pudding without currants."

GOOSEBERRIES

When I was a child, the school-free days of summer were occupied with bike riding on the "new road" (a freshly paved two-lane strip reaching far into the country, with a traffic count of about two cars per hour), lots of reading, and, with Mother's permission, creating and cooking special family dinners (sometimes a bit too exotic for Father). We did plenty of hoeing, weeding, and picking ripening fruits and vegetables, and "picking over" endless baskets of fruits for canning. In our provincial society at that time, there was no such notion as sending children off to summer camp. The entire family went to a cottage on the bay for a few weeks, and took other short trips around the natural vacation land that Michigan is, with sometimes a longer journey to visit relatives. Above all, summertime was canning season, and my sisters and I were integral members of the operation. Each arrival of the different colorful, tasty fruits meant fragrant cobblers, pies, and shortcakes on the table that week, and luscious sauces, jams, jellies, and more pies to brighten bored palates during the long gray winter.

Certain fruits were canned in large volume, such as strawberries, cherries, peaches, blueberries, raspberries, plums, grapes and apples; and then there were lesser supplies of "novelties," such as gooseberries. In Michigan, we canned green gooseberries. Neither Kathryn, Helen, nor I nibbled very many of these as we methodically nipped off the stem and the frill of brown foliage on the bottom of each berry. Except for a pie or two, our gooseberries went mainly into jam, which was really one of the best. Sometimes Mother combined gooseberries with red currants, an excellent mixture since both are of the same plant family.

The English take a proprietary interest in gooseberries. They consider them to be indigenous to the British Isles and growing them is basic to the skill of English gardeners. They claim to have cultivated the gooseberry to its present high state of perfection, in size and flavor. Besides their beloved gooseberry fool (a mixture of gooseberry puree with heavy cream or custard) English specialties include jam and jelly, of course, gooseberry pudding – baked or boiled – gooseberry trifle, gooseberry vinegar and wine, and a favorite fish dish – mackerel with gooseberry sauce. Their recipes usually specify "green" gooseberries and "red" gooseberries, which are soft and have a light amber color. The latter are sweet and can be eaten out of hand. The green are usually cooked, with some sweetening added. There are also pink gooseberries.

In America, gooseberries are a localized specialty, their shipment restricted by federal and state laws in order to control a fungus called "white pine blister" which grows on the gooseberry plant and attacks the white pine. The thorny bushes generally thrive in the cooler flat areas of New England, the Great Lakes, and the northern Pacific Coast. Fresh gooseberries are in season from May through August. They can grow as large as one inch in diameter, and in England they claim that some grow as large as hen's eggs.

Like their currant cousins, gooseberries have a refreshingly tart flavor. They are always cooked with the skins, which can be strained later for a smooth puree. Nutritionally, gooseberries are low in calories (only 59 in one cup) with high levels of vitamin A and potassium, a good dose of vitamin C, phosphorus and calcium, and a range of other minerals. Firm green or ripe gooseberries freeze well, plain or with syrup.

GOOSEBERRY FOOL

DO-AHEAD TIP: *Ingredients can be prepared a day ahead. Combine at serving time.*

- **2½ cups well-chilled Gooseberry Puree (see recipe in this section)**
- **2 cups Custard Sauce (see Index), or 1½ cups heavy cream, whipped**
- **2 kiwi fruit, peeled (optional)**

Combine gooseberry puree and custard sauce or whipped cream and fold together until lightly swirled (not mixed). Spoon into dessert bowl or individual dessert glasses and chill. If desired, decorate with slices or wedges of kiwi fruit.

6 servings

GOOSEBERRIES

GOOSEBERRY PUREE

This mixture can be used for Gooseberry Fool, sauce, sherbet, or ice cream.

DO-AHEAD TIP: *Gooseberry puree will keep in refrigerator for about a week, or longer in freezer.*

- 1 pound (about 2 cups) green gooseberries
- 3 tablespoons water
- 1/4 cup light honey
- 1 teaspoon grated lemon rind

Top and tail gooseberries. Combine all ingredients in saucepan and bring to a boil. Reduce heat to simmer and cook until berries are tender. Rub through fine food strainer.

Yields about 1 1/4 cups

GOOSEBERRY SAUCE FOR FISH

Spoon a ribbon of this creamy, tart sauce over poached, broiled, or sauteed fillets of mackerel or sole.

DO-AHEAD TIP: *Gooseberry sauce can be made a day ahead and refrigerated. Rewarm at serving time.*

- 4 tablespoons unsalted butter
- 1 1/2 tablespoons whole wheat pastry flour
- cayenne pepper
- 3/4 cup light cream or half-and-half
- 1 sprig celery leaf
- 1/2 bay leaf
- 2 tablespoons heavy cream
- 1 cup Gooseberry Puree (see recipe in this section)

Melt butter in 3-cup saucepan. Remove from heat, add flour and a few grains of cayenne pepper and blend. Add light cream or half-and-half, celery leaf, and bay leaf. Stir over low heat until sauce thickens and just comes to a boil. Remove celery and bay leaf. Add heavy cream and stir over low heat 1 minute.

Add gooseberry puree to sauce and stir over low heat until sauce is warm.

Yields about 2 cups

KUMQUATS

For the real-life story about those intriguing kumquat fruits one associates with Oriental cuisines, I went to Rosa de Carvalho Ross, my teacher in Chinese cooking and my friend. Despite her name, Rosa is mainland Chinese, having been born and raised in Macao (across the bay from Hong Kong), of an old Portuguese settler family. Hers must have been a wonderful home environment, nourished by a very versatile family cook who served up Chinese, English, and Continental dishes as well as Macao (a blend of Portuguese cooking methods with Oriental foods and seasonings).

Today Rosa shares this glorious gastronomic heritage with Americans by operating her "Wok On Wheels," a mobile cooking school and catering business in New York. We have cooked together many times. Our sessions are always prolonged because I am fascinated with the stories and back-home explanations that accompany her visit. One Christmas season, when I had purchased a basket of fresh kumquats (which appear here only during the winter months), I quizzed Rosa about how the Chinese in China really eat them.

"We didn't eat them very often," she recalled. "In China, too, they are a winter fruit. We bought them fresh, on miniature plants in little pots around the time of Chinese New Year [February] and placed them around the house, much as you do with poinsettias at Christmastime. In some homes the kumquat plants were arranged around the household shrine. We also bought fresh ones not on the plant but which always had some stems and leaves attached, and sometimes we would buy crystallized kumquats which came in a box, like candy.

"In China kumquats are only a festive food. During Chinese New Year time, people visit each other's homes a lot. Each home had ready a large lacquered tray with partitions containing all kinds of snack foods – some savory, some sweet – deep-fried tidbits, nuts, crystallized fruits – always kumquats (the Chinese name, *chin kan*, means 'golden seed') – and always a pile of 'lucky money' in red paper envelopes. All of these things signified prosperity."

These tiny fruits, shaped like miniature footballs one to two inches long with rind and flesh like an orange, are unusual in that the taste sensations are the direct opposite of the orange. For a perfectly ripe kumquat, the skin is completely orange, tender and sweet; and the flesh, of which there is very little, is tart. Although it contains a couple of seeds, they are rather soft, so that the whole raw fruit can be popped into the mouth, skin and all, and what a treat! They will keep for quite a while without refrigeration and are high-density capsules of vitamins A and C.

Although the fruit is still available only during the winter months, kumquat trees (normally 10 to 12 feet high) are being grown in the southeastern United States, providing us with a greater abundance of fresh ones, which are by far the best. Fresh kumquats poached in honey syrup remain rich with zest and texture. They require only ten minutes of cooking and can be stored indefinitely in the refrigerator, handy to serve as compote or to use as a garnish for poultry or meat. I've discovered that fresh kumquats are also a festive idea when used as colorful little boat containers for hors d'oeuvre fillings and for petits fours with sweet fillings. As a fine touch, add a few to salads and fruit bowls, cut in halves, wedges, or slices.

KUMQUATS

KUMQUAT BOATS

These fresh kumquat boats can be filled with a savory mixture for hors d'oeuvres or a sweet mixture for petits fours.

BOATS
fresh kumquats, halved lengthwise, flesh and seeds carefully removed

HORS D'OEUVRE FILLINGS
creamed sharp cheese such as Roquefort. Top with piece of walnut.

salmon roe (red caviar).

piquant seasoned cream cheese. Top with chopped nuts or bits of pimiento.

cream cheese mixed with sturgeon roe (black caviar).

PETITS FOURS FILLINGS
chopped dates. Roll in chopped nuts.

chopped dried figs. Roll in grated coconut.

POACHED FRESH KUMQUATS IN SPICY SYRUP

These poached kumquats in spicy syrup can be a perfect surprise ending to a dinner party, perhaps accompanied by a plate of homemade little cookies. Since poached kumquats will keep for a long time in the refrigerator, they offer other opportunities for interesting touches to cooking, such as a sprightly garnish for chicken, turkey, duck, pheasant, veal, or pork (which might be roasted, sauteed, or cold). The cooking syrup becomes very zesty from the kumquat rind; pour any extra over fresh fruit.

- 1 pint basket whole kumquats, stems and leaves removed
- ½ cup light honey
- ½ cup water
- 1 stick cinnamon bark

Combine honey and water in deep, heavy pot and bring slowly to a boil. Reduce heat to very low. Add cinnamon bark and whole kumquats. Cook over very low heat only until fruits have lost their rawness but are still firm (about 10 minutes), turning fruit occasionally. Let cool and store in cooking syrup.

LOQUATS

Fresh loquats are rare in the United States; canned ones are available in Oriental and specialty food stores. The loquat is a small, round fruit, 1½ to 3 inches in diameter, with a yellow-orange skin with a downy finish. The juicy flesh might be white to deep orange, with large black seeds. It has a delicious sweet flavor with just a gentle touch of acidity, similar, perhaps, to a cherry taste.

The loquat is best eaten fresh but can also be poached, used in pie, and preserved as compote or jelly. This lovely fruit has long been popular in China, Japan, northern India, and around the Mediterranean. In the United States, some loquat trees, which are evergreen, are planted for ornamental as well as fruit purposes.

LOQUAT AMBROSIA

DO-AHEAD TIP: *Fruit mixture should be prepared a few hours before serving in order to chill.*

- **1 cup peeled loquat chunks**
- **3 bananas, sliced**
- **1 cup orange sections**
- **1 cup pineapple cubes**
- **2 to 3 tablespoons light honey (optional)**
- **½ cup shredded coconut**

Combine loquats, pineapple, orange, and banana, and chill. At serving time, drain off juice and fold with mayonnaise. Arrange on lettuce leaves. Garnish with pecans.

4 servings

LOQUAT FRUIT SALAD

DO-AHEAD TIP: *Fruit mixture should be prepared a few hours ahead in order to chill.*

- **2 cups peeled, thinly sliced fresh loquats**
- **1 cup diced pineapple**
- **1 cup orange sections**
- **1 cup sliced banana**
- **⅓ cup Basic Mayonnaise (see Index)**
- **crisp lettuce leaves**
- **¼ cup pecans**

Combine loquat, banana, orange, and pineapple. Mix gently with honey, if desired. Transfer to serving bowl and chill thoroughly. At serving time, sprinkle with coconut.

4 servings

Another Loquat Recipe

See Index for the following recipe:

DESSERT: *Macedoine de Fruits.*

LYCHEES

Lychees are special. They have been the treat supreme for the Chinese for many centuries. In the eighth century, history records, a T'ang Dynasty emperor in Peking, Hsuan Tsang, organized relays of horsemen to bring daily supplies of fresh lychees all the way from Kwantung in the south for Yang Kuei-fei, his favorite concubine, who had a passion for them. Apparently this display of self-indulgence pushed the patient citizenry, who had to content themselves with dried lychees, to the point of rebellion and the downfall of the dynasty.

The Chinese love of lychees has never waned. My Chinese cooking teacher, Rosa Ross, tells me that the season for fresh lychees was always eagerly awaited by young and old. (They never had them canned, as they are sold in America.) In the cool of the evening, Chinese families in Macao would sit on their verandas with big bowls of fresh lychees, shelling, seeding, and popping them into their mouths as they visited. There was always comment about the size of the seed, which can range from the size of a pignoli to that of an almond. (The bigger the seed, the poorer the quality of the fruit, according to the Chinese.) Rosa says they devoured fresh lychees by the pounds.

She told me an amusing tale about her aunt, who, like the eighth-century lady, also had an immoderate passion for lychees. Auntie lived in Hong Kong, but in the last weeks of her pregnancy was staying at Rosa's family's home on the mainland to be near the hospital where she planned to have her delivery. The time was fresh lychee season. To please auntie and take her mind off her discomfort, Rosa's father brought home a huge bag of the fresh fruits, perhaps ten pounds, and they feasted on the veranda until midnight, especially auntie. During the night she developed terrible stomach cramps and was rushed to the hospital, believing her baby was about to arrive. Alas, the pains were not of child labor but of lychee labor.

Lychees (pronounced lye-chees; also spelled litchee and lichee) are native to southern China. The fresh fruit is truly a titillating tidbit of nature. It is about the size and color of a strawberry. Peel away the red, nubby, leathery skin, and you have a succulent mouthful of sweet translucent white flesh (about the consistency of a grape), which surrounds a single seed. Lychees grow in loose clusters on evergreen trees which can grow 40 feet tall. Today some lychee trees are also cultivated in Hawaii, California, and Florida.

For lychees, we would do well to follow the experienced Chinese and enjoy these fruits fresh in their season, short though it may be, and then go on to the next delights of nature's cycle. Yes, they can be used in a salad, fruit bowl, gelatin dessert, or on ice cream, but to enjoy them most, sit on your veranda, or under a tree, or on the beach in the warmth of a summer's eve, peeling and popping luscious lychees into your mouth.

Some Chinese also like to snack on dried lychees, called "lychee nuts." When dried, the red shell becomes brown and brittle and the shrunken flesh tastes rather like a prune.

CHINESE CHICKEN BALLS WITH LYCHEES

This dish was interpreted by Rosa Ross and can be prepared in either a wok or a saute pan.

DO-AHEAD TIP: *Chicken mixture can be made ahead. Cook at serving time.*

CHICKEN

2 half breasts of chicken, skinned and boned

2 thin slices fresh ginger

2 teaspoons tamari soy sauce

1 tablespoon cornstarch

CHICKEN: Cut chicken into strips and process in food processor with ginger until smooth. Add tamari and cornstarch and process again. Set aside.

CHINESE CHICKEN BALLS WITH LYCHEES – continued

SAUCE

- **1 cup peeled and seeded lychees or drained canned lychees**
- **3/4 cup chicken stock**
- **2 scallions, cut into 1-inch pieces**
- **2 teaspoons cornstarch mixed with 1 tablespoon cold water**

Plain-Cooked Brown Rice (see Index)

SAUCE: Combine all sauce ingredients in bowl and set aside.

Heat about 1/2 inch oil in wok or small saute pan. Form chicken mixture into lychee-size (1-inch) balls. Drop them in hot oil and fry until golden brown all over. Remove with slotted spoon and drain on paper towels.

Remove oil from pan, leaving about 1/2 teaspoon. Remove lychees and scallions from sauce, add to hot pan and give them one or two quick turns. Add sauce mixture and stir until it thickens to gravy consistency. Add chicken balls and stir gently until heated through. Transfer to hot serving dish. Serve rice in separate dish.

2 servings

More Lychee Recipes

See Index for the following recipes:

MAIN DISH: Chicken in the Snow; DESSERT: *Macedoine de Fruits.*

MAMEYS

The first time I ate mamey (pronounced mah-may) was many years ago while breakfasting on the terrace of a high-rise condominium overlooking Acapulco Bay. I was staying with Carmen Lopez Figueroa, a grand lady, and long one of my favorite people. I have never been much of a breakfast eater, and Carmen was urging me to at least have some fresh fruit from the tray that was always lavishly stocked on the serving bar. (A fresh fruit tray is omnipresent in most Mexican homes, each a fascinating display of seemingly endless variety in type, color, and shape.)

"What is that?" I asked, pointing to an oval-shaped fruit about six inches long with a dull brownish skin like rough leather. Carmen beamed. "That is one of the most beautiful fruits in all creation, called 'mamey'," she said. "Cut it open and you will see the color of the Acapulco sunset." We sliced it in strips like melon. As usual, Carmen's description was on the mark. The flesh glowed with the richest hues of orange and red, and it had a texture like butter. (In the center there are one to four seeds, which are easily removed.) The flavor was equally rich – a blend of apricot and peach and perfectly sweet.

The mere mention of *dulce de mamey* starts most Mexicans salivating. It is a kind of pudding, and often each family has its own recipe, handed down through generations. Different versions from two fine chefs are given here. Acapulco locals also love mamey ice cream and sherbet. Other ways to use mamey are in mousse, tart, or salad. Or simply serve chilled chunks with cold custard sauce, yogurt, or sour cream. This lovely fruit grows on rather large trees, some as tall as 50 to 60 feet, which are native to the Caribbean and southern Florida. Occasionally the fruit is shipped as a specialty. Look for it and try it.

MAMEYS

DULCE DE MAMEY 1

This is the recipe of Jose Santiago Arreola of Guadalajara and Acapulco, which is always a rave at my dinner parties in Acapulco for visiting Americans.

DO-AHEAD TIP: *This dish can be prepared 2 or 3 days ahead and refrigerated.*

- 2 mameys (6 to 8 inches long)
- ½ cup heavy cream
- 2 tablespoons vanilla extract
- ⅔ cup light honey
- 2 cups milk
- 3 egg yolks
- ¼ cup dark raisins or chopped, pitted prunes

Cut mameys in halves and remove seeds. Scoop pulp from skins. Place pulp in processor or blender with cream, vanilla, and honey, and process until smooth. Set aside.

Scald milk. Beat egg yolks in mixer until light. Continue beating egg yolks while slowly adding hot milk. Add mamey mixture. Transfer to saucepan and stir over low heat until mixture just comes to a boil. Remove from heat and let cool to room temperature. Then pour into shallow crystal serving dish. Scatter raisins or prunes on top. Chill thoroughly.

6 servings

DULCE DE MAMEY 2

This is the recipe of Susana Palazuelos's grandmother, of Mexico City.

DO-AHEAD TIP: *This dish can be prepared 2 or 3 days ahead and refrigerated.*

- 3 mameys (6 to 8 inches long)
- ¾ cup light honey
- 1 tablespoon fresh lemon juice
- ½ cup finely ground almonds or pignolis
- ½ teaspoon ground cinnamon

Cut mameys in halves and remove seeds. Scoop pulp from skins. Puree pulp in food processor or rub through fine strainer. Set aside.

In deep, heavy pot, combine honey and lemon juice and bring to a boil over low heat. Add puree and nuts. Stir over moderate heat until thick. Let cool to room temperature, transfer to serving bowl, and chill. Dust top with cinnamon.

6 to 8 servings

More Mamey Recipes

See Index for the following recipes:

DESSERTS: Fresh Fruit Ice Cream, Frozen Fruit Yogurt, Custard Sauce (with mameys).

PAPAWS

Contrary to the venerable Oxford dictionary and the understanding of many people, papaw is not the same fruit as papaya. Papaw is native to central and southern regions of the United States, particularly the bottomlands of the Missouri River. An experienced authority on papaws is fellow food explorer and raconteur Frank Baker. At age 84, Frank vividly recalled for me his Huck Finn forays near his home in Atcheson, Kansas:

"As youngsters, we used to hike in the river bottoms near Bean and Sugar Lakes on the Missouri side and around Doniphan Lake on the Kansas side. Along the way we would find papaws, a luscious fruit growing on scrubby swamp trees, usually in the early summer. We ate them raw. They had a creamy yellow inside with lots of little seeds. They might be three to six inches in length and shaped like a short, fat banana, medium green in color. The flesh was sweet, rich, custardlike, and slightly aromatic. Papaws were never in any great abundance, nor were they ever served at home." Papaws are rarely cultivated.

PASSION FRUIT

In the tropics, fresh fruits are usually the best thirst quenchers, and from Florida throughout the Caribbean, South America, and Hawaii, the passion fruit is one of the best. The name comes from the flowers, whose parts were thought by imaginative Spanish missionaries to symbolize the nails, wounds, and crown of thorns of the crucifixion, or passion of Christ. Passion fruit is also called *granadilla*, which is not to be confused with *granada*, the Spanish name for pomegranate.

There are many kinds of passion fruit, in sizes giant and small. The small, about the size of an egg or a little larger, with a thin brittle rind that might be purple, red, or yellow, are filled with juicy yellow pulp and edible seeds. Natives often break open a fruit and suck out its juice on the spot. The larger passion fruit looks like a melon with green skin. Its shell contains flesh about 1½ inches thick, and the cavity is filled with yellow seeds. Passion fruit is usually available in United States markets in the fall. It is highly perishable.

Passion fruit has a sweet, mildly acid flavor, which is marvelously refreshing and an excellent source of vitamins A and C. The giant passion fruit can be peeled and cut into slices like melon, sprinkled with a bit of powdered coriander or lime juice before serving. Most passion fruit cookery calls for the strained juice or syrup rather than the pulp. Extract the juice with a sieve instead of a food mill, which tends to break bits of the seeds. Use passion fruit juice or syrup in iced drinks, punch, frozen desserts, pie, jelly, barbecue sauce, and gelatin.

PASSION FRUIT SYRUP

Use for fruit drink or punch base, sherbet, or ice cream. Syrup keeps well in refrigerator for about 2 weeks. If you have a large supply of passion fruit, the recipe quantity can be increased proportionately and preserved. Pour hot syrup mixture into hot sterile bottles and seal. It will keep this way for about 6 months.

2 cups water

2 cups light honey

1½ cups strained passion fruit pulp or juice

Combine water and honey and bring to a boil over low heat. Add passion fruit pulp or juice and bring slowly to a boil again. Simmer 2 minutes. Chill and use as desired.

Yields 5 cups

PASSION FRUIT

PASSION FRUIT BARBECUE SAUCE

DO-AHEAD TIP: *Sauce can be mixed a day ahead and refrigerated.*

- 1/4 cup catsup
- 2 tablespoons passion fruit juice
- 1/2 teaspoon finely chopped garlic
- 2 tablespoons tamari soy sauce
- 1 tablespoon light honey
- 1 tablespoon orange juice
- 1 teaspoon grated orange rind
- few drops Tabasco sauce

Mix all ingredients. Brush on chicken or meat to be broiled or baked.

Yields about 1/2 cup

PASSION FRUIT SAUCE FOR FRUIT FRITTERS AND PANCAKES

Good with banana or pineapple fritters or with pancakes.

DO-AHEAD TIP: *Sauce can be made a day ahead and rewarmed for serving.*

- 1/3 cup light honey
- 1 1/2 tablespoons cornstarch
- 1/8 teaspoon ground ginger
- 1/2 cup boiling water
- 2 tablespoons unsalted butter
- 2/3 cup passion fruit juice

In small bowl, mix together honey, cornstarch, and ginger. Add water gradually. Transfer to small saucepan and bring slowly to a boil. Add butter and passion fruit juice. Stir until butter is dissolved and mixture is blended. Serve hot.

Yields about 1 cup

PERSIMMONS

If you are not quite at ease about buying, preparing, and eating the intriguing persimmon, let me try to dispel any of its mystery in a few short sentences.

The Oriental persimmon, which is the type sold in most American fruit markets in the fall and early winter, when properly ripe (that is, slightly soft to the touch), is indeed sweet and delicious with just a *slight* puckery action in the mouth. It can be and is eaten raw by connoisseurs, or it can be cooked as in the classic persimmon pudding. Personally, I prefer to eat persimmons raw, including a cold pudding recipe. Persimmon flavor is quite delicate and when cooked can easily be overwhelmed by other flavors such as spices.

In America there are two kinds of persimmons. Those sold in the markets are the Oriental or Japanese variety that today are grown in California. They are larger than a plum, more toward the size of a medium tomato, but oblong/conical in shape with a green-collared stem. The skin color ranges from yellow to dark orange-red. Inside, the flesh is orange and may be seedless or have as many as eight seeds, with a custardlike texture. The first Japanese persimmons were sent here by Commodore Perry and planted near Washington, D.C., only to be killed by an early frost. Later, grafted trees were cultivated in California and Georgia.

There is also an American, or wild, persimmon, which is native from Connecticut and southern Iowa to Florida and Texas. This species produces a small pulpy fruit which may vary from ½ to 2 inches in diameter. It is yellow or orange with a reddish cheek and has large seeds embedded in its soft flesh. It is not generally sold in commercial markets.

Persimmons can be eaten out of hand or used in salads, puddings, gelatin, mousses, pies, sherbet, or pureed sauces. Be sure that the fruit is ripe! Green persimmon makes a sortie on the mouth that is not soon forgotten. Unripe, it is laden with tannic acid, and the notorious pucker action that it causes is unpleasant to even the most avid persimmon fanciers.

To enjoy this delicacy of the Orient, select firm, fully colored fruits and hold them at room temperature until they are soft. Or, ripen them by placing them in a plastic bag with ripe apples to remove the astringency. The taste will be deliciously sweet with only the faintest acid tinge. When they are ready, refrigerate and eat as soon as possible.

When served plain at the table, they are cut in halves, served with a wedge of lemon or lime, and eaten with a spoon. To prepare persimmon for pudding, choose soft, ripe fruit with transparent skin. Peel and strain, or remove center fiber and seeds, and puree in a blender or food processor. (One large Oriental persimmon, about three inches long, gives about one cup of puree.) If the pulp is not to be used immediately, stir one tablespoon lemon juice into each two cups of pulp to prevent discoloration.

COLD PERSIMMON PUDDING

DO-AHEAD TIP: *Pudding can be made a day ahead and refrigerated.*

2 cups pureed soft, ripe persimmons

½ cup light honey

1 tablespoon grated orange rind

2 tablespoons orange juice

1 teaspoon fresh lemon juice

⅔ cup heavy cream, whipped

ground ginger

In food processor or mixer, beat together persimmon pulp, honey, orange rind, orange juice, and lemon juice. Fold in whipped cream. Spoon into serving bowl and chill. Just before serving, sprinkle with ground ginger.

4 servings

PERSIMMONS

BAKED PERSIMMON PUDDING

DO-AHEAD TIP: *Ingredients can be readied several hours ahead. Mix and bake at serving time.*

- 1 cup sifted whole wheat pastry flour
- 2 teaspoons baking soda
- 1/4 teaspoon ground cinnamon
- 1/4 teaspoon freshly grated nutmeg
- 2 cups pureed soft, ripe persimmons
- 2 eggs, well beaten
- 1 cup milk
- 1/2 cup light honey
- 1 1/2 tablespoons unsalted butter, melted, or light vegetable oil (e.g., safflower)
- 1/2 cup raisins or chopped nuts (optional)
- whipped cream, as desired

Preheat oven to 350°F. Mix and sift together flour, soda, cinnamon and nutmeg. In mixer, combine persimmon pulp, eggs, milk, honey, and butter or oil. Beat thoroughly. Add flour mixture. Beat only until ingredients are well mixed. Add raisins or nuts, if desired. Pour into oiled 2-quart baking dish. Bake 45 minutes, or until inserted knife comes out clean. Serve hot or warm. Top each serving with whipped cream.

8 servings

PLANTAINS

The plantain is usually thought of as a large, gummy type of banana, starchy – not sweet – used for cooking. This is partially a misconception. Some bananas are not sweet and some plantains are. The plantain is an important food in tropical areas, where it is regarded as essential as the potato is for northern countries. They can be bought year-round in United States markets catering to people of Spanish, West Indian, and Latin American cultures, and with increasing frequency elsewhere.

Generally speaking, the plantains imported into this country are never eaten raw. They are longer and thicker skinned than regular bananas, and have natural brown spots and rough areas on their skin. The plantain contains 86 calories in a 3 1/2-ounce portion and is a good source of complex carbohydrate, vitamin C, thiamine, riboflavin, niacin, potassium.

Usually starchy rather than sweet, plantains make wonderful vegetable accompaniments – mashed, broiled, baked, or sauteed. They should be used before reaching full ripeness. The most common way of using them is to skin them, cut them lengthwise into slices about 1/2 inch thick, and saute them until they are a deep golden brown. Try them this way with eggs for brunch. Or bake plantains in a moderate oven until they are tender, bathing them with a little honey and melted sweet butter, or just serve with lots of butter. Pureed plantain offers an unusual, delectable main dish accompaniment. Boil briefly in water, puree, and season to taste.

PLANTAIN CASSEROLE

A different starch accompaniment to poultry or meat.

DO-AHEAD TIP: *Ingredients can be readied a few hours ahead. Mix, assemble, and bake at serving time.*

- **2 ripe plantains, thinly sliced**
- **6 tablespoons unsalted butter, or 4 tablespoons light vegetable oil (e.g., safflower)**
- **2 cups grated muenster cheese**
- **1 teaspoon ground cinnamon**
- **3 eggs, separated**
- **2 tablespoons light honey**
- **2 tablespoons dry whole wheat bread crumbs**

Preheat oven to 350°F. Fry plantain slices in 2 tablespoons butter or oil until golden brown. Drain on paper towels.

Mix cheese and cinnamon together. Beat egg yolks until frothy and thick, then add honey and beat again. Beat egg whites to soft peaks. Fold egg yolk mixture into whites.

Butter 1½-quart baking dish and dust with bread crumbs. Spread one-fourth of egg mixture on bottom of dish, then one-third of plantains, ⅔ cup cheese, and dot with butter or oil. Repeat layers, ending with egg mixture. Bake until set, about 15 minutes.

4 servings

FRIED GREEN PLANTAINS

Serve as accompaniment to chicken, beef, pork, or seafood.

DO-AHEAD TIP: *Plantains can be sauteed a few hours ahead. At serving time, flatten sauteed slices and fry again.*

- **2 green plantains**
- **4 tablespoons light vegetable oil (e.g., safflower)**

Cut both ends off plantains. Cut each plantain in half horizontally and let stand in hot water 5 minutes. Peel and dry with paper towels. Cut into 1-inch-thick slices. Heat 2 tablespoons oil in saute pan and fry plantain slices over high heat until just soft. Drain on paper towels. Press pieces with the ball of your hand to flatten them, like little pancakes. Add 2 tablespoons oil to saute pan and heat very hot. Fry pieces in hot oil until golden. Remove and drain on paper towels. Serve.

4 servings

PLANTAINS

BAKED PLANTAIN

Platano al Horno

Serve as an accompaniment—similar to a baked potato.

4 plantains (plantains must be ripe—spotted black all over; if green, let stand until black)

unsalted butter, as desired

Preheat oven to 400°F. Rub plantains with oil. Cut slit down middle of each. Place in oven and bake the same as a potato. When cooked, slit will open and pulp will puff. Serve with chunks of butter.

4 servings

PRICKLY PEARS

In Mexican markets are piles of small oval-shaped green cacti, perhaps three inches long and one inch in diameter, covered with spines or single thorns. I have rarely encountered them in "continental" homes in Mexico, but my village friend Miguel introduced me to *tunas.* There are two varieties—the larger ones with sweet white flesh and the small ones with red flesh and more concentrated sweetness. *Tunas* are the fruit of the same plant from which comes the cactus leaf called *nopale,* which is delicious eaten as a cooked vegetable with vinaigrette sauce.

To eat the prickly pear, the spines are pared off or singed. The fruit (thinly peeled, if desired) is sliced or cut in chunks, chilled, and served raw as dessert. Prickly pears are filled with little seeds that can be eaten or not. In Mexico, the red *tuna* is also commercially produced into *queso de tuna* (tuna cheese), a very sweet concentrate of the fruit, which is eaten with cheese for dessert.

Prickly pears are also referred to by horticulturists as Indian figs or barberry figs. Curiously, some are also grown in the states of Washington and Oregon.

QUINCES

One of my annual Christmas stocking gifts for my mentor Dione Lucas was a jar of quince jelly. Quinces have long been a favorite fruit of the English and the French, and Dione remained solidly English in her heart while her artistic soul was *haute Francaise.* Invariably she used her quince jelly with apple, either mixing it with apple filling for pie, or using it as glaze on trimly sliced toppings on apple tartlets. (When fresh quinces are available, the English also add a few slices to apple pie for improved flavor.)

Until so many of our fruits were so greatly improved within the last 100 years, quinces were widely grown as a garden delicacy. However, quinces can only be used cooked. So, their popularity declined as other fruits developed more desirable table qualities.

The quince is a most aromatic fruit with a strong, sweet odor and a distinctive and delicate flavor. It looks like a lumpy, woolly pear with a greenish-yellow color until it ripens in the late fall, when it becomes entirely yellow. The flesh may be creamy white to apricot color. The texture is very woody until it is ripe and cooked, when it resembles firm pears. Even when ripe, the quince is very hard, tart, and astringent.

With their persistent tart flavor and large content of pectin, quinces make excellent marmalade, jelly, jam, butter, preserves, syrup, and fruit paste.

SAPODILLAS

The sapodilla is a favorite fruit in the subtropics. I like to eat it when I'm in Mexico. It is also available in Puerto Rico and southern Florida. Locals usually eat this deliciously sweet fruit out of hand.

The sapodilla fruit is round, about 3½ inches in diameter, with a thin, tannish, scruffy skin. The flesh is yellowish-brown, tender, sometimes smooth, sometimes granular, but like honey when ripe. The pulp can be pureed and used for an exotic mousse, sherbet, or ice cream.

The sapodilla tree itself has special interest. When the bark is tapped, a milky latex exudes, called chicle, which is the base for chewing gum.

SAPOTES

Whenever I have the opportunity to prepare a dinner party for visiting Americans in Acapulco, I try to serve a *dulce de sapote negro* for dessert. Guests are presented with a dessert cup filled with a shiny black puree, looking for all the world like freshly poured tar but cold as cold. It is a moment of dessert drama. As guests bravely taste this curious food, taste buds begin to dance with surprised delight. The taste is like chocolate with a fresh fruit flavor, heightened with a bit of orange zest and juice.

Black sapotes, white sapotes, yellow sapotes, and sapodillas all are members of the Sapotacea family which grow throughout the tropics and subtropics, including Florida and California, dispensing their exotic, rich, custardlike fruits, the most delectable being the black.

The black sapote resembles a large, round, green tomato on the outside. There is also a black sapote which is smaller and oval in shape. When ripe, the sapote skin is dull olive green, which tends to break in small grainy pieces; in the hand, properly ripe fruit feels like a soft marshmallow. After it is ripe, sapote may be refrigerated.

To peel the black sapote, cut it in four to six wedges. Use a small spoon to remove the seeds and underdeveloped seed capsules. Then carefully scoop out the pulp. Happily, sapote freezes well. Just put scooped-out pulp in a plastic container, and it will keep in the freezer for about six months without any appreciable loss of flavor.

For cooking, black sapote pulp is usually pureed with a little orange zest and juice, or vanilla, which becomes the basic ingredient to add to other preparations such as mousse or ice cream. Another popular Mexican way of using black sapote is as an *agua fresca*, a cold fruit drink.

DULCE DE SAPOTE NEGRO

Somehow the name of this dish sounds better in Spanish (pronounced dūl-seh deh sapōteh nay-gro) than in its English translation—sweet of black sapote. The puddinglike mixture can also be frozen as sherbet. To do so, add 2 beaten egg whites when sherbet is almost frozen.

3 to 4 ripe black sapotes (sapotes must be very soft; an unripe sapote is inedible.)

½ to ¾ cup light honey, to taste

1 teaspoon grated orange rind

2 cups orange juice

2 tablespoons finely shredded orange rind

Remove stems from sapotes. Pull off green skin with your fingers. You now have a dark brown, thick pulp. Inside are hidden almond-shaped seeds. Remove these with your fingers. In food processor, combine sapote pulp, honey, and orange rind and orange juice, and puree. Chill. Mixture is bright, shiny black-brown. Serve in crystal dessert cup or dish. Sprinkle a few fine shreds of orange rind on each serving.

4 to 6 servings

SAPOTES

AGUA FRESCA DE SAPOTE

This is a refreshing fruit drink.

DO-AHEAD TIP: *Beverage can be stored in refrigerator for a week or so.*

mixture for *Dulce de Sapote Negro* (see recipe in this section)

orange juice

water

orange slices

To the mixture for *dulce de sapote negro*, add enough orange juice and water (to taste) to bring to beverage consistency. Chill thoroughly. Serve in chilled tall glasses filled with ice cubes. Hang an orange slice on rim of each glass.

Yields 1½ to 2 quarts

STAR APPLES

Just when I think I'm about to qualify as an experienced "local," one of my friends in Mexico springs a new surprise on me. It happened again one evening in Acapulco when I was dining with Baron Jay de Laval, the food guru of Mexico. Jay has taught me much about the natural foods of the land and has himself created so many beautiful ways to serve them, which he has done for innumerable parties, for Presidents, and for Pope John Paul during his visit to Mexico.

Jay lives on one of the mountains east of Acapulco, with a view overlooking the whole town as well as the bay beyond. At nighttime the lights of the city glitter in the darkness around the water like a diamond tiara. On this evening, Jay suggested we have dessert on the balcony. He brought a bowl filled only with round, shiny, purple-colored fruits, about three inches in diameter. When he cut one in half, I saw a presentation no human chef could compose. The halves were filled with soft, juicy flesh in the most incredible design – the color next to the skin was a ring of deepest purple, like the skin, which graduated to a ring of magenta and a center of pale mauve, almost white. In this area the seeds were arranged in a flared starlike pattern around a pink dot of a core. As far as I know, the only way to eat a star apple (*cainito* in Spanish) is raw. Sometimes the fruits are sliced paper thin and used as adornments on desserts. To crush the flesh or treat it any other way would seem a travesty.

Star apple is strictly a tropical fruit. Its trees are cultivated as a specialty in southern Florida, the Caribbean, Mexico, and Hawaii. The fruit usually ripens in April and May, when its flesh is sweet, mild, and slightly gelatinous. (The star apple is not to be confused with the carambola, which is yellow with an elongated, ridged body, and which, when cut, does indeed produce slices in the shapes of stars.)

TAMARINDS

Tamarind is one of the most popular flavors in fruit drinks and desserts throughout Mexico and the Caribbean. It has a sprightly, spicy zest which gives one a great pick-up and refreshment. This spirited flavor comes from the most unglamorous brown pods which hang from large, spreading trees growing along roadsides, in yards, and on my friend Pepe's fruit ranch.

The tamarind fruit is a flat, cinnamon-colored pod, three to eight inches long, like a large brown bean. The outer skin is brittle. Inside are brown pulp and several plump seeds. In Mexico I rested under many *tamarindo* trees in the countryside where I rode my horse, and observed baskets of pods in the markets, bottled tamarind syrup in the *super mercados*, tamarind *ate* (jellylike candy), and the tamarind drink (*agua fresca*) everywhere. One day I just had to taste one of the raw fruit. As I had been warned, it was very acid.

Most uses call for a syrup of sweetened tamarind pulp. In addition to the delicious icy-cold *agua fresca*, the locals love tamarind sherbet and ice cream. The whole pods are soaked in cold water overnight. Then the seeds are removed, and the pulp is used according to various recipes. Tamarind also grows in the Far East, where it has been used for centuries in Chinese and Indian cooking.

AGUA DE TAMARINDO

Tamarind Water

DO-AHEAD TIP: *This recipe must be started a day in advance of serving in order for tamarinds to soak.*

½ pound tamarinds

3 quarts water

light honey to taste

Rinse tamarinds in water. Place in pot, cover with water and soak pods overnight. Reserve soaking water. Remove seeds from pulp, and strain pulp and skins through fine vegetable strainer. Mix with soaking water and sweeten with honey to taste. Chill and serve very cold, with ice cubes.

Yields about 3 quarts

UGLI FRUIT

Occasionally this Caribbean curiosity finds its way to northern fruit markets. It is an oddity because it is such a miserable-looking piece of fruit—about the size of a grapefruit, but grossly misshapen with very coarsely pebbled skin. It is a yellowish color with light green blotches that turn orange when the fruit is ripe. Inside, this ugly has lots of pink, juicy pulp that is nearly seedless and a rather delightful orangey flavor. When you find one, do try it. Eat it like an orange. (In that marvelous-sounding Jamaican dialect, it is pronounced hoogli.)

PART II

Fruit Medley

THE VERSATILE FRUITS

Fruits beguile our appetites in innumerable ways. They can change places with one another in many recipes. They may appear as a medley in others. The recipes in this section can be prepared with a choice of fruits, those that may be in season or a fruit that is a particular favorite, or incorporate several with equal billing in the same dish.

Since we were youngsters, we have pondered the many choices of fruit flavors in ice cream. Old-fashioned shortcake can be enjoyed the summer long – from strawberries in May and June, to raspberries in July, to blueberries and peaches in August and September. Cobblers, likewise. Or, you can serve the season's best over a delicate white heart of cream, a dessert supreme for the fruit of any season. If cheesecake is your *piece de resistance*, a colorful, shiny topping of almost any fruit makes it a gala, professional-looking presentation.

Even before the dessert, there are drinks, appetizers, soups, salads, and main dishes which can feature different fruits in their season. For hot weather time, a collection of fruit coolers made with buttermilk or yogurt can be either tall, frosty drinks or bowls of cold, pastel-colored soup embedded in ice. Any time of the year, a crisp greens salad seems more exotic when garnished with various fresh fruit. An ordinary cabbage salad, with the addition of fruits and honey dressing, can enliven winter menus.

Our fruit variety section offers more main dishes with fruit appeal: Under a cloud of meringue, Chicken in the Snow may disclose the presence of lychees, mangoes, or pineapple. Mexican *Chiles Rellenos*, the most beautiful and tasty stuffed peppers, decorated with a sprinkling of juicy red pomegranate capsules, might contain pineapple, mangoes, or raisins and prunes. What a medley! You don't need a barbecue grill to make Chinese spareribs. They can be cooked to perfection in a wok or oven and deliciously complemented with peaches or pineapple.

I have always been impressed with the French treatment of fruit. Nothing could be simpler than the open-face fruit tart or tartlets made either with short pastry or puff pastry, but the precise arrangement of whole or cut fresh fruit of the season in the pastry shell, covered with a clear red or golden glaze, is a picture almost too good to eat.

There are also dishes that are mixed bouquets of two or more fruits. The foremost, perhaps, is the classic fruit macedoine, or fruit bowl. A zesty citrus sauce (lemon, lime, and orange rinds in honey syrup) literally makes each fruit sparkle. Others include: an appetizer tray, *Pico de Gallo* (Spanish for "beak of the rooster"), offering beak-shaped bites of orange, pineapple, and apple with cucumber and jicama, rinsed in lemon juice and sprinkled with piquant chili powder; Poached Chicken Hawaiian, with grapes, apples, pineapple, and pomegranate seeds; the cold Lemon-Carob Layered Souffle, an appealing composition in presentation and flavor. And, a mixture of dried fruits is as festive as confetti in the favorite Mexican classic, *Dulce de Camote*.

PICO DE GALLO

FRUIT USE: apple, orange, pineapple.

Literally translated, pico de gallo *(pronounced peekoh-deh-guy-yo) means "beak of the rooster," which the wedge-shaped pieces of fresh raw fruits and vegetables resemble. The* pico de gallo *tray of fruits rinsed in lemon juice and dusted with a little chili powder is a classical Mexican appetizer.*

DO-AHEAD TIP: *Fruit and vegetable tidbits can be prepared, sprinkled with lemon juice, and arranged on serving tray several hours ahead, but do not sprinkle with chili powder until ready to serve.*

- **1 large orange**
- **1 large cucumber**
- **1 jicama (traditional; usually available in California and Southwest; now also in northern markets)**
- **1 large tart apple**
- **about ½ cup fresh lemon juice**
- **good-quality chili powder (with a little bite)**

All of the fruits and vegetables are cut into bite-size wedges as follows:

Cut orange into ½-inch-thick horizontal slices. Do not peel. Cut each slice into quarter, sixth, or eighth wedges, depending on size of orange.

Cut off top and bottom tips of cucumber. Do not peel. Cut in ½-inch-thick slices and cut slices into bite-size sections.

Peel and cut pineapple into ½-inch-thick slices. Cut slices into bite-size wedges.

Peel and cut jicama into ½-inch-thick slices. Cut slices into bite-size wedges.

Core apple, but do not peel. Cut into ½-inch-thick slices and cut slices into bite-size wedges.

Toss each *separate* group of fruit pieces with 1 or 2 tablespoons lemon juice.

PRESENTATION: Arrange groups of fruit and vegetable pieces on serving plate. (On round plate, they might be arranged like a cartwheel, separated by "hedgerows" of parsley). When ready to serve, sprinkle each fruit group with chili powder. (The peel on the orange, cucumber, and apple wedges is eaten.)

Makes about 30 servings of 4 pieces each

ICED FRUIT SOUPS

FRUIT CHOICE: apricot, boysenberry, cherry, mango, melon, nectarine, peach.

When hot weather kills the family's appetite and turns the kitchen into a sauna, it is time to get creative about meals. Whip up some delicious but quick cold soups, using seasonable fresh fruits, pureed or juiced—then blend with a complementary liquid. They become instant dishes that are refreshing and nourishing. Cold soups should be served very cold, ideally with the soup bowl embedded in a plate of chipped ice.

Fruit soups are exceedingly easy to prepare. They really require no recipe. Puree choice of fresh fruit, such as apricots, boysenberries, sweet cherries, mangoes, melons, nectarines, or peaches. To thin the puree and add flavor, use such liquids as buttermilk (superb!), yogurt, or light tea (such as mint, orange, or China). Add a few drops of lemon or lime juice or a sprinkling of grated rinds. Garnish soup serving with fresh mint leaves, a sprinkle of spice, or a few pieces of the subject fruit; or, float a spoonful of sour cream on a slice of lime, sprinkled with chopped mint.

For some simple but excellent fruit soup examples, use the beverage recipes Apricot Nectar with Buttermilk or Yogurt, Melon with Buttermilk or Yogurt, Peaches, Nectarines, or Apricots with Buttermilk or Yogurt (see Index).

When serving cold melon soup, present individual servings in melon shells.

CHICKEN IN THE SNOW

FRUIT CHOICE: lychee, mango, pineapple.

A fine and unusual company dish for buffet or sit-down service: under a blanket of fluffy white meringue, tender bits of poached chicken and seafood with fruit, water chestnuts, and snowpeas.

DO-AHEAD TIP: *This dish can be cooked a day ahead, up to the point of adding the meringue topping. At serving time, rewarm in 300°F. oven, then cover with meringue, and brown top lightly under broiler.*

CHICKEN

1 3- to 4-pound whole dressed chicken, or 2 smaller chickens

3 cups stock (e.g., chicken, vegetable, or soy—3 cups water mixed with 4 teaspoons tamari soy sauce)

2 pounds medium-size raw shrimp, shelled, deveined and halved

2 tablespoons light vegetable oil (e.g., safflower)

1 pound snowpeas, trimmed (top, tail, and string removed)

1½ cups sliced water chestnuts

2 cups cubed fresh pineapples or mangoes, or 1 cup pitted and quartered fresh lychees

SAUCE

1 teaspoon light honey

1 tablespoon cornstarch or potato flour

reserved stock from cooking chicken

freshly ground white pepper

3 egg yolks

MERINGUE

4 egg whites

CHICKEN: Tie or truss chicken and put in deep, heavy pot. Add stock and bring to a boil. Reduce heat to low, cover pot, and simmer chicken until tender, about 30 minutes. Remove chicken from pot and let cool. Strain stock and reserve.

While chicken is cooking, prepare shrimp. Dry well between paper towels. Heat oil in saute pan, add shrimp, and stir until they turn pink. Set shrimp aside. Plain-cook snowpeas until barely tender.

When chicken is cool, remove all skin and bone from meat. Cut meat into 1-inch pieces. Spread chicken and shrimp on bottom of large gratin dish or shallow heatproof serving dish. Scatter water chestnuts, snowpeas, and fruit on top of chicken and seafood.

SAUCE: In medium saucepan, combine honey, cornstarch or potato flour, and 4 tablespoons reserved stock, and blend mixture. Add 2 cups stock and stir sauce over moderate heat until boiling. Season with pepper. In small bowl, beat egg yolks and add 2 or 3 tablespoons hot sauce. Remove saucepan from heat and stir yolk mixture into sauce. Return pan to low heat and stir sauce until blended. Do not boil, or sauce will curdle. Spoon sauce over food preparation and keep warm.

MERINGUE: Beat egg whites to soft peaks. Cover chicken preparation with egg whites. Place dish under broiler until top of meringue is delicately tinged with brown. (Or it can be browned in preheated 375°F. oven.) Serve at once.

8 servings

CHILES RELLENOS

FRUIT CHOICE: apricot, guava, mango, nectarine, peach, pineapple, pomegranate, prune, raisin.

*This beautiful and delicious dish of plump stuffed peppers, which look as though they have never been cut open, can be prepared days in advance. The master recipe can be varied by stuffing the peppers with a variety of fruits and serving them with either walnut sauce (*Chiles Rellenos en Nogada*) or tomato and broth sauce (*Chiles Rellenos en Caldillo*). All of the stuffing and sauce recipes are for 4 servings of 2 peppers each.*

DO-AHEAD TIP: *Peppers can be stuffed and coated and sauce prepared 2 or 3 days ahead and refrigerated. At serving time, warm stuffed peppers in sauce.*

PEPPERS

8 medium-size green mild peppers (either traditional *chile poblano*, which looks like an elongated bell pepper and is neither hot nor sweet, or green or red bell pepper, which is more common in the U.S.)

STUFFINGS

choose from apricot, guava, nectarine peach, pineapple, or any combination; meat and potato with raisins and prunes; cheese; recipes follow

COATING

whole wheat pastry flour

2 eggs, separated

SAUCE

either *salsa nogada* (walnut sauce) or *caldillo* (Mexican tomato and broth sauce) can be used with any stuffing; recipes follow

GARNISH

½ cup heavy cream, whipped

for stuffed peppers with *salsa nogada*, separated seeds of 1 pomegranate (optional)

To prepare peppers: The Mexican technique for removing skin, veins, and seeds from peppers to be stuffed is as follows: Leave peppers whole (ideally with 1- to 2-inch piece of stem attached, with which to hold peppers when coating and frying). Place peppers directly on high gas burner flame or under *hot* broiler and quickly char skin all over (without cooking pepper). Wrap toasted peppers in damp cheesecloth or towel and let stand about 20 minutes to cool (during which time peppers will also partially steam-cook). Unwrap peppers and pick off charred skin with your fingers or small knife. Cut one vertical slit in side of each pepper and carefully remove seeds, veins, and core. Rinse peppers and blot dry. (Peppers skinned and seeded in this manner can be refrigerated for 2 or 3 days before stuffing.)

To stuff peppers: Cut slit in side, carefully insert stuffing, close and reshape.

To coat and fry stuffed peppers: Sprinkle stuffed peppers liberally with flour and pat off excess. Beat egg whites until stiff. Add egg yolks and continue to beat until well mixed but still frothy. Using your hands, cover peppers with egg froth. Pour ½ inch vegetable oil in saute pan and heat to 350°F. Fry coated stuffed peppers. Turn over to fry other side. With slotted spoon, transfer peppers to plate lined with double thickness of paper towels. (This procedure, also, can be done a day or two ahead.)

To serve: Rewarm sauce. Place fried coated peppers in sauce, only long enough to briefly warm and soak with a little sauce. Arrange 1 or 2 peppers on individual serving plate. Spoon a little sauce over peppers. Top with spoonful of whipped cream. When serving stuffed peppers with walnut sauce, sprinkle with separated pomegranate seeds, if available.

STUFFINGS

FRESH FRUIT (any of the following):
- diced mango
- seeded and diced guava
- chopped pineapple
- peeled and diced peach, nectarine, or apricot
- combinations of any of the above fruits
- shredded coconut with any of the above fruits (optional)

Stuff peppers with desired fruit or a combination, allowing about ¼ cup stuffing per pepper.

PICADILLO (meat, potato, raisin, prune)

- ½ pound ground beef
- ½ pound ground pork
- 1 medium-size yellow onion, chopped
- 1 to 2 teaspoons chopped serrano chili (small, green hot chili, available fresh or canned), or freshly ground black pepper
- 1 cup diced cooked potatoes (about ½-inch cubes)
- ¼ cup dark or golden raisins
- ¼ cup pitted and diced prunes

Saute beef and pork in hot, dry pan until pink. Add onion and chili or pepper and cook until meat is done. Add potatoes, raisins, and prunes, and stir over moderate heat 2 or 3 minutes to blend flavors. Carefully fill each pepper with stuffing.

(continued)

CHILES RELLENOS – continued

CHEESE

- **½ medium-size Spanish onion, thinly sliced lengthwise**
- **1 teaspoon finely chopped fresh garlic**
- **1 tablespoon fresh oregano, or 1 teaspoon dried oregano**
- **16 finger-size strips *queso fresca* or *queso blanco* (Spanish-American type cheese available in U.S.) or 1½ cups ricotta cheese**

In a small bowl, toss onion, garlic and oregano. Insert a little of this mixture into each pepper. Add 2 strips *queso fresca* or *queso blanca* or 2 to 3 tablespoons ricotta to each pepper.

SAUCES

SALSA NOGADA

- **4 tablespoons unsalted butter**
- **½ medium-size yellow onion, chopped**
- **¼ cup walnuts, finely chopped – almost to paste consistency (if available, use green or fresh walnuts; soak green walnuts in hot water to loosen and remove skin; if green walnuts are not available, use regular dry walnuts; it is not necessary to remove skin of dry walnuts)**
- **1 medium-size ripe tomato, skinned, seeded, and chopped**
- **¼ teaspoon freshly grated nutmeg**
- **freshly ground black pepper**
- **4 dried juniper berries, crushed**

Saute onion in 2 tablespoons butter until translucent. Add walnuts, tomato, nutmeg, pepper and juniper berries. Stir over moderate heat 1 minute and transfer to small bowl.

In same saute pan, combine 2 tablespoons oil, 2 tablespoons butter, and garlic, and stir over moderate heat 2 minutes. Add flour and stir into mixture. Add onion, walnut, and tomato mixture, and stir over moderate heat 1 minute. Add tomato puree or paste, cream, stock, tamari, and pomegranate juice or currant jelly. Puree sauce in blender until smooth. Return sauce to saute pan and simmer 3 minutes.

2 tablespoons light vegetable oil (e.g., safflower)

1 teaspoon finely chopped fresh garlic

1 tablespoon whole wheat pastry flour

½ cup tomato puree, or 2 tablespoons tomato paste

½ cup heavy cream

1 cup strong chicken stock

½ teaspoon tamari soy sauce

2 tablespoons pomegranate juice, or 2 teaspoons red currant jelly

CALDILLO

2 tablespoons light vegetable oil

1 teaspoon finely chopped fresh garlic

1 medium-size yellow onion, sliced lengthwise

2 medium-size ripe tomatoes, peeled and coarsely chopped

1 tablespoon fresh oregano leaf, or 1 teaspoon dried oregano

1 tablespoon chopped serrano chili, fresh or canned (optional)

1½ cups strong chicken broth

Heat oil and garlic in saute pan. Add onion, tomatoes, oregano, and chili, and saute 2 or 3 minutes, or until onions are translucent. Add broth (enough to bring sauce to soup consistency). Simmer until flavors have blended.

CHINESE BARBECUED SPARERIBS WITH PEACHES OR PINEAPPLE

FRUIT CHOICE: peach, pineapple.

Hors d'oeuvre or main dish. Suggested vegetable accompaniment for main course: simple vegetable stir-fry such as green beans, asparagus, snowpeas or broccoli, or broiled tomato.

DO-AHEAD TIP: *Spareribs should be marinated at least 8 hours or overnight. They can be cooked a day ahead. At serving time, rewarm and add fruit garnish.*

- **4 pounds pork spareribs, cracked at 2- to 3-inch lengths and separated**
- **2 medium-size yellow onions, sliced**
- **¼ cup plus 1 tablespoon tamari soy sauce**
- **¼ cup plus 1 tablespoon water**
- **3 tablespoons hoisin sauce**
- **2 tablespoons light honey**
- **1 teaspoon 5-spice powder**
- **⅛ teaspoon ground ginger**
- **1 tablespoon unsalted butter**
- **1 tablespoon light honey**
- **4 to 6 peaches, peeled and halved or quartered, or 4 to 6 ½-inch-thick pineapple slices, halved or quartered**

Arrange ribs in shallow roasting pan. Combine remaining ingredients in medium bowl and mix well. Pour over ribs, turning to coat completely. Let ribs marinate in refrigerator at least 8 hours, or overnight.

Preheat oven to 325° F. Bake ribs in sauce, turning 3 or 4 times, for 1 hour and 30 minutes. (Sauce remaining in roasting pan can be reduced over high heat and used to glaze ribs.)

PRESENTATION: In saute pan, melt butter, add honey, and stir until blended. Add fruit, turn heat to high, and turn fruit once or twice until tinged with brown. Place meat on warm serving platter. Arrange fruit on side.

4 servings

NOTE: Hoisin sauce and 5-spice powder can be purchased at specialty food stores and Chinese markets.

FRUIT OMELETS

FRUIT CHOICE: avocado, banana, cantaloupe, mango, papaya.

Two fruit-filled omelets to serve as a light main dish—for brunch, lunch, or supper: avocado, and cheese and fruit. The cheese and fruit omelet is a luncheon specialty at Blackbeard's in Acapulco.

BASIC OMELET

- **2 or 3 eggs, as desired**
- **1 teaspoon water**
- **1 tablespoon unsalted butter or light vegetable oil (e.g., safflower)**

Preheat omelet pan or 10-inch saute pan over low heat 5 minutes. Combine eggs and water in mixing bowl and beat until well mixed. Add butter or oil to hot pan. Add egg mixture. Using dinner fork in one hand, stir eggs in circular motion. Simultaneously with the other hand, shake pan back and forth over the heat.

When eggs are nearly set, quickly spread egg mass evenly over bottom of pan using back of fork. Then place desired filling on top of eggs in the center. With back of fork, begin to fold omelet over on itself, starting at the edge nearest the handle of the pan. Tip pan, flip half of omelet over on itself, and slide it onto a hot serving plate.

1 serving

FRUIT FILLINGS

AVOCADO

- **¼ cup cubed ripe avocado (½-inch cubes)**
- **¼ cup cubed, skinned, and seeded ripe tomato**
- **1 teaspoon finely chopped pearl onion**
- **½ teaspoon fresh lemon juice**
- **½ cup Hollandaise Sauce (see Index)**

Combine avocado, tomato, onion, and lemon juice in small bowl and toss lightly. Add mixture to basic omelet, fold, and turn out onto heatproof serving plate. Cover omelet with Hollandaise sauce and brown top lightly under broiler.

CHEESE AND FRUIT

- **3 tablespoons diced banana**
- **3 tablespoons diced cantaloupe, mango, or papaya**
- **2 tablespoons shredded Swiss or jack cheese, or 1 tablespoon freshly grated Parmesan cheese**
- **1 teaspoon unsalted butter, melted**
- **1 sprig crisp watercress**

Lightly toss together fruit and cheese. Fold mixture into basic omelet and turn out onto warm serving plate. Brush with melted butter and garnish with watercress.

POACHED CHICKEN HAWAIIAN

FRUIT USE: apple, grape (white), pineapple, pomegranate.

A dramatic dish for buffet: tender breasts of chicken with rich chicken sauce containing white grapes and apple, garnished with pineapple, chutney, and pomegranate seeds.

DO-AHEAD TIP: *Cooking, up to presentation assembly, can be done a day ahead. At serving time, rewarm chicken and sauce, prepare pineapple garnish, and arrange dish.*

- **6 to 8 half breasts of chicken, skinned and boned**
- **3 cups chicken stock**
- **2 slices fresh ginger root**
- **6 tablespoons unsalted butter**
- **4 tablespoons whole wheat pastry flour**
- **½ teaspoon finely chopped fresh garlic**
- **2 tablespoons curry powder**
- **1 tablespoon light honey**
- **¾ cup skinned and seeded white grapes**
- **1 cup diced apples**
- **¼ cup heavy cream**
- **6 ½-inch-thick fresh pineapple slices, not cored**
- **6 tablespoons chutney**
- **½ cup pomegranate seeds (optional)**
- **4 to 6 cups hot Plain-Cooked Brown Rice (see Index)**

Place chicken breasts in deep, heavy pot, add stock and ginger, bring to a boil, and simmer over low heat until done. Remove breasts from pot and remove skin. Strain stock, set 2 cups aside for sauce, and pour rest over breasts to keep meat moist.

In medium-size saucepan, melt 3 tablespoons butter. Add flour and stir over moderate heat until bubbling but not browning. Add garlic and curry powder, and stir over low heat 1 minute. Remove from heat and add reserved strained stock. Stir sauce over moderate heat until it boils. (Sauce at this point will be quite thick. It will thin when fruits are added.)

In saute pan, melt 2 tablespoons butter. Add honey and stir until blended with butter. Add grapes and apples. Stir over moderate heat until apples are just beginning to soften (not too long; you don't want to lose fresh quality.) Add fruit mixture to chicken sauce. Fold in cream.

PRESENTATION: Melt 1 tablespoon butter in saute pan, raise heat to high, and quickly brown pineapple slices on both sides. Drain chicken breasts and arrange on warm serving platter. Cover with sauce. Decorate sides of platter with pineapple slices. Place spoonful of chutney in middle of each pineapple slice. If desired, scatter pomegranate seeds over chicken. Serve rice in separate bowl.

6 servings

POTATO PANCAKES WITH FRUIT SAUCE

FRUIT CHOICE: apple, strawberry.

My Jewish mother-in-law (Isobel Walters) was a glorious concert soprano whose rendition of the Lord's Prayer at New York City banquets never failed to reduce the late Cardinal Spellman to tears. Cooking, however, was not one of Isobel's talents, except for potato pancakes. After my husband learned how she made them, he often prepared them for Sunday night supper with applesauce or strawberries and chipolatas. *These little potato pancakes, with apple sauce spiked with freshly grated horseradish, are also a good accompaniment to brisket of beef or pork chops.*

DO-AHEAD TIP: *Mixture preferably should be made when ready to cook so potatoes do not discolor. The addition of cracker or matzoh meal will help to keep mixture white.*

4 baking potatoes (about 2 pounds)

1 small yellow onion, finely chopped

2 eggs

freshly ground white pepper

1/3 cup cracker meal or matzoh meal (optional)

about 2 cups light vegetable oil (e.g., safflower)

1 1/2 cups Apple Sauce (see Index), sliced peaches, or sliced or crushed strawberries sweetened with a little honey, or other fresh fruit

Peel potatoes and grate them finely. Put grated potatoes in white kitchen towel and squeeze out as much water as possible. Put drained grated potato in mixing bowl. Add onion, eggs, pepper, and cracker or matzoh meal, if desired. Mix thoroughly. Heat 2 tablespoons oil in saute pan. When oil is hot, drop spoonfuls of potato mixture in pan and fry until golden brown on both sides. Drain on paper towels. Serve with separate bowl of apple sauce or fresh fruit.

4 to 6 servings as accompaniment

TURKISH RICE

FRUIT USE: lemon, orange, raisin (golden and dark).

Saffron rice with almonds, orange and lemon rinds, and raisins.

DO-AHEAD TIP: *This rice can be prepared a few hours ahead and rewarmed in the steamer or slow oven.*

- 1 Spanish onion, finely chopped
- 1 tablespoon light vegetable oil (e.g., safflower)
- 1½ cups long grain brown rice
- 1 egg, beaten
- freshly ground white pepper
- 1 tablespoon saffron stigmas, crushed and mixed with 2 tablespoons hot water
- 3½ cups water or stock (e.g., chicken, vegetable, or soy—3½ cups water with 3½ teaspoons tamari soy sauce)
- ½ teaspoon ground cardamom
- 2 tablespoons blanched split almonds
- 2 tablespoons dark raisins
- 2 tablespoons golden raisins
- 1 tablespoon grated orange rind
- 1 teaspoon grated lemon rind

Preheat oven to 350°F. In small saute pan, cook onion in oil until soft but not browned. Set onion aside. In deep, heavy pot (about 1½-quart capacity), mix rice with egg. Stir over moderate heat until kernels are dry and separate. Season with pepper. Add onion, saffron, and stock. Stir over moderate heat until liquid comes to a brisk boil. Add cardamom, almonds, raisins, and orange and lemon rinds, and stir mixture. Cover with firm-fitting lid and cook in oven 1 hour, or until rice is tender. When cooked, fluff rice with 2 forks.

PRESENTATION: Cooked rice can be packed into lightly greased mold and turned out onto warm plate, or simply piled into warm serving bowl.

4 to 6 servings

SALADE PROVENCALE

FRUIT CHOICE: apple, pear.

This bright, sunny-looking salad contains potatoes, green beans, tomatoes, apples or pears, tuna fish, and lettuce. Serve as a main dish, or an interesting first course.

DO-AHEAD TIP: *Mixture can be prepared a day ahead, up to presentation assembly. Assemble within 2 to 3 hours of serving and refrigerate.*

- **2 cups diced cooked potatoes**
- **2 cups cooked green beans, cut into ½-inch pieces**
- **1 pound ripe tomatoes (about 3 medium-size) peeled, seeded, and diced**
- **1½ cups diced tart apples or firm, ripe pears, cored but not peeled, rinsed in lemon juice**
- **1½ cups water-packed tuna fish, separated into bite-size chunks**
- **¾ cup small p itted rip e d ives**
- **1 cup Basic Vinaigrette Dressing (see Index)**
- **1 large or 2 small heads Boston lettuce, washed, dried, and crisped**
- **4 hard-cooked eggs, quartered lengthwise**
- **¼ cup finely chopped fresh parsley**

Put potatoes, beans, tomatoes, apples or pears, tuna fish and ripe olives in mixing bowl and toss together lightly. Add ½ cup vinaigrette dressing, mix lightly, and allow to marinate a few minutes, or overnight.

PRESENTATION: Tear lettuce leaves into large pieces and line large salad bowl. Pile salad mixture on top of lettuce. Sprinkle remaining ½ cup dressing over mixture. Arrange egg sections around edge of dish. Scatter parsley over center.

4 servings as main dish or 8 as salad course

CABBAGE AND FRUIT SALAD WITH HONEY DRESSING

FRUIT USE: apricot, orange.

This recipe uses shredded cabbage salad with dried apricots and fresh orange sections. Many other fruits—apples, pears, peaches, mangoes, pineapple—could also be used.

DO-AHEAD TIP: *Ingredients can be prepared a day ahead. Combine at serving time.*

- **4 cups finely shredded green or savoy cabbage**
- **½ cup diced dried apricots**
- **1 cup orange sections, well drained**
- **½ cup Honey Dressing (see Index)**
- **crisp parsley or watercress sprigs**

Chill all ingredients. At serving time, combine all ingredients except parsley or watercress and pile into chilled salad bowl. Garnish with parsley or watercress.

4 to 6 servings

TOSSED GREENS SALAD WITH FRUIT

FRUIT CHOICE: apple, apricot, avocado, fig, grapefruit, guava, mandarin, mango, orange, papaya, pineapple.

A salad bowl of mixed greens garnished with fruit instead of vegetables provides a rather exotic and simple change of pace.

DO-AHEAD TIP: *Salad can be composed a day ahead. Toss at serving time.*

½ cup Basic Vinaigrette Dressing, Papaya Seed Vinaigrette Dressing, or Lemon-Yogurt Dressing (see Index)

any combination of 2, 3, or 4 types of the following greens, mixed in quantity desired:

lettuce: Boston, romaine, leaf types

spinach

chicory (curly endive)

Belgian endive

escarole

watercress

dandelion greens

any of the following, as garnish:

shredded tart apple and shredded Swiss cheese

avocado with any citrus fruit sections, mango, papaya, pineapple

fig sections with mandarin, orange, or grapefruit

apricots or guavas with walnuts

any citrus with sliced fresh mushrooms and chopped leaf herbs

Pour dressing on bottom of salad bowl. Tear or cut greens in bite-size pieces and drop on top of dressing. Arrange fruit on top of greens. Cover with plastic wrap and refrigerate. Do not toss salad until ready to serve.

4 servings

BEIGNETS SOUFFLES WITH FRUIT SYRUP OR FRUIT SAUCE

FRUIT CHOICE: apricot, raspberry.

Beignets souffles are puffy dessert dumplings, actually dabs of cream puff paste which are dropped into deep hot fat and puffed up like little clouds. They are delicious with fruit syrup, or with fresh fruit sauce. Beignets (pronounced bay-ynay) must be fried immediately before serving and will probably deflate in about half an hour.

DO-AHEAD TIP: *Beignet dough can be made a few hours ahead. Fruit syrup can be prepared several days ahead and refrigerated. Deep-fry beignets at serving time.*

- ½ cup cold water
- 4 tablespoons unsalted butter, cut into cubes
- ½ cup whole wheat pastry flour
- 2 small eggs
- ½ teaspoon light honey
- 2 egg whites
- ½ teaspoon baking powder (without aluminum salts)
- about 2 cups light vegetable oil (e.g., safflower)
- 1 cup Apricot Syrup or Raspberry Syrup (see Index), with 1 teaspoon grated lemon rind added to mixture before heating, or any seasonal Fresh Fruit Sauce (see Index)

Combine water and butter in medium saucepan and warm over low heat until butter melts and mixture comes to a boil. Remove from heat and add flour to liquid all at once. Return pan to low heat and stir with small whisk until mixture is smooth and comes away from sides of pan. Transfer dough to mixer or food processor. Add eggs, 1 at a time, beating after each addition. Add honey and continue beating until mixture is shiny. Beat egg whites to soft peaks. Add dough to egg whites, sprinkle with baking powder, and fold ingredients together smoothly and evenly, using rubber scraper. Chill batter in refrigerator at least 30 minutes, or up to 8 hours.

PRESENTATION: Heat oil in deep fryer to 375°F. When ready to serve, fry beignets by dropping teaspoonfuls of dough into deep hot fat and cooking until puffed and golden brown all over. (When 1 side is cooked, beignet will automatically flop over.) Drain on paper towels. Pile in mound on serving plate. Serve with separate bowl of fruit syrup or sauce.

4 servings

COBBLER

FRUIT CHOICE: apple, blackberry, blueberry, cherry, peach, plum.

A cobbler is really a baked shortcake—sweetened fruit in a baking dish, covered with fluffy biscuit dough, and baked. Serve hot, topped with whipped cream or ice cream.

DO-AHEAD TIP: *Fruit can be prepared a few hours ahead. Shortcake dough can be made ahead up to the point of adding honey and milk. Assemble and bake at serving time.*

Shortcake Dough (see Index)

3 tablespoons unsalted butter, softened

½ to ¾ cup light honey, depending on sweetness of fruit

¼ teaspoon ground cinnamon

¼ teaspoon freshly grated nutmeg

2 teaspoons arrowroot or cornstarch

1 teaspoon grated lemon rind

4 cups firm, ripe fruit; any of the following:

- **peeled and sliced apples**
- **cleaned blackberries**
- **cleaned blueberries**
- **pitted ripe sour cherries**
- **pitted and halved sweet cherries**
- **peeled and sliced peaches**
- **pitted and halved or quartered plums**

1 cup heavy cream, whipped, or 1 cup Creme Fraiche, or 1 pint Basic Vanilla Ice Cream (see Index)

Preheat oven to 400°F. Have ready about 8-inch-diameter baking dish or pan, 2 to 2½ inches deep (such as Pyrex baking dish). Turn dough out onto lightly floured board. Gently and firmly fold over dough 2 or 3 times and form into a ball. Pat or roll dough to about ½ inch thickness or large enough to cover baking dish. Set aside.

In small saucepan, combine 2 tablespoons butter, honey, cinnamon, nutmeg, arrowroot or cornstarch, and lemon rind. Stir over low heat until blended. Add this sauce to fruit and mix.

Place fruit in baking dish. Lightly place dough on top to cover. Dot with 1 tablespoon butter. Bake about 30 minutes, or until dough is baked.

PRESENTATION: Place baking dish on serving tray. Serve hot. Spoon some biscuit and fruit on individual serving plates. Top with whipped cream, creme fraiche, or ice cream.

6 to 8 servings

COEURS A LA CREME

FRUIT CHOICE: peach, raspberry, strawberry.

These pristine little white cream hearts are like little white clouds over which fresh fruit sauce is poured.

DO-AHEAD TIP: *Cream hearts should be prepared a day ahead in order to set.*

- **8 ounces cream cheese**
- **¼ cup light honey**
- **scraping of ½ vanilla bean, or 1 teaspoon vanilla extract**
- **1 cup heavy cream, whipped**
- **6 large fresh grape leaves, or 12 galox leaves (optional)**
- **3 cups Fresh Fruit Sauce (see Index): strawberry, raspberry, or peach**

Prepare lining for 6 individual *coeur a la creme* china or wicker molds as follows:

From length of 4 thicknesses of cheesecloth, cut 6 squares, each large enough to line mold with a 2-inch margin or overhang all around. Mix 2 cups iced water with 1 tablespoon lemon juice and 1 teaspoon baking soda. Soak cheesecloth squares in this solution while preparing creme mixture.

Beat cream cheese in mixer until smooth and creamy. Add honey and vanilla and beat thoroughly. Add whipped cream and *fold* together lightly and evenly, using rubber scraper.

Wring cheesecloth squares damp-dry and line molds, leaving 2-inch overhang all around sides. Fill molds with cream cheese mixture and fold cheesecloth overhang over the tops. Place molds on rack on jelly roll pan and chill in refrigerator at least 8 hours, or overnight.

PRESENTATION: Unmold and unwrap each cream heart onto fresh grape leaf or pair of galox leaves on individual dessert plate. Serve with separate bowl of fresh fruit sauce.

6 servings

COLD LEMON-CAROB LAYERED SOUFFLE

FRUIT USE: lemon, carob.

The layers of lemon and carob cream rising above the souffle dish present an attractive yellow and brown free-form look.

DO-AHEAD TIP: *This dish should be prepared a day ahead in order to set.*

COLD LEMON-CAROB LAYERED SOUFFLE—continued

- 11 tablespoons carob powder
- ½ teaspoon ground cinnamon
- 6 tablespoons water
- 6 eggs, separated
- ½ cup light honey
- 3 tablespoons unflavored gelatin
- 1½ cups light cream
- grated rind of 2 lemons
- ½ cup fresh lemon juice
- 1½ cups heavy cream, whipped

Wrap collar around 4-cup souffle dish or straight-sided serving dish as follows: Take strip of aluminum foil or waxed paper 1½ times the outer girth of the dish and fold in half lengthwise. Brush 1 side with oil. Wrap foil or waxed paper around dish. Fasten with masking tape or string. The 6-inch-high paper collar will be about twice as high as the dish, to contain the mixture that will be above the top of the dish.

Combine 10 tablespoons carob, cinnamon, and water in small saucepan. Stir with small whisk over low heat until dissolved and smooth. Do not boil. Set mixture aside.

Beat eggs yolks and honey in mixer until thick and light in color. Reduce speed and add gelatin. Heat light cream in medium saucepan over low heat just to a boil. Slowly pour hot cream into egg yolk mixture, beating constantly. Pour mixture into large saucepan and stir over low heat until custard coats the back of a spoon. At this point there will be about 1½ quarts basic custard mixture.

Pour half of the custard mixture into a medium bowl. Stir dissolved carob into half of custard mixture. Stir lemon rind and juice into the other half. Cool both mixtures in refrigerator.

Beat egg whites to soft peaks. When carob and lemon mixtures are cool, fold half of egg whites into each mixture. Set aside one-third of whipped cream for topping. Fold half of remaining whipped cream into the carob mixture and half into the lemon mixture. Refrigerate until mixtures are just at point of setting.

Spoon half of carob mixture into souffle dish. Carefully spoon half of lemon mixture on top of carob mixture. Then spoon remaining half of carob mixture on top of lemon mixture. Cover with remaining half of lemon mixture. Chill souffle in refrigerator until thoroughly set. Spread reserved whipped cream on top of souffle. Sprinkle remaining carob powder (1 tablespoon) through wire strainer on top of whipped cream. Return to refrigerator until ready to serve.

PRESENTATION: Carefully remove collar. Place souffle on doily-lined serving plate. Offer some of the carob and lemon layers for each serving.

6 to 8 servings

CREPES STUFFED WITH FRESH FRUIT

FRUIT CHOICE: peach, raspberry, strawberry.

DO-AHEAD TIP: *Crepes can be prepared several days ahead and frozen. Stuff with fruit at serving time.*

- 6 6-inch Basic Crepes (see Index)
- 2 cups thinly sliced peaches, whole cleaned raspberries, or halved or quartered strawberries
- ½ cup apricot preserve (if peaches are used)
- ½ cup red currant jelly (if raspberries or strawberries are used)
- 1 teaspoon fresh lemon juice
- 2 tablespoons light honey
- 2 tablespoons unsalted butter
- 1 cup Yogurt Dessert Sauce (see Index) or 1 cup heavy cream, whipped

Dissolve apricot preserve or red currant jelly with lemon juice in small saucepan over low heat and let cool to room temperature. Combine sweetening with fruit and let stand in refrigerator 1 hour. In small saucepan, combine honey and butter, and stir over low heat until honey is dissolved. Set aside.

PRESENTATION: Spread about ⅓ cup fruit on underside (the side cooked last) of each crepe and roll or fold crepe. Using long, wide spatula, transfer crepes to heatproof serving plate. Brush tops with honey and butter mixture and place under broiler until tops are lightly browned. Again using spatula, serve onto individual plates. Top each serving with spoonful of yogurt dessert sauce or whipped cream.

6 servings

MACEDOINE DE FRUITS
Mixed Fruit Bowl

FRUIT CHOICE: apple, apricot, banana, blueberry, cherry, fig, grape, grapefruit, guava, kiwi fruit, loquat, lychee, mandarin, mango, melon, nectarine, orange, papaya, peach, pear, pineapple, plum, strawberry.

The French culinary term macedoine *(pronounced ma-seh-dwahn) is derived from Macedonia, a "mixture" of small countries in the Middle East conquered by Alexander the Great. The fruit macedoine can be of fresh or poached fruits. The fresh fruit macedoine popularly appears on French restaurant menus as* macedoine de fruits rafraichis. *In the classical preparation, a zesty syrup is poured over the fruit, such as the Citrus Sauce for Desserts (see Index). The essence of citrus rinds in this sauce seems to open up the fruit flavors, the same way in which citrus essences are used to accent the fragrance of fine perfume. The citrus acid also helps to keep the lovely color of the fruits. For an excellent fresh fruit macedoine, assemble any quantity of 3 or more kinds of fruit. Some suggestions and how to prepare them follow.*

DO-AHEAD TIP: *Ideally, fruit for macedoine is prepared a few hours to a day ahead in order to chill thoroughly.*

MACEDOINE DE FRUITS—continued

apples, (tart, firm), cored, peeled (optional), and cut into bite-size chunks

apricots, peeled and quartered or sliced

bananas, peeled and cut into 1/4-inch-thick slices

blueberries, cleaned, whole

cherries (sweet), halved and pitted

figs (fresh), quartered

grapes, (white, red, or black), halved and seeded

grapefruit (white or pink), skinned sections

guavas, seeded and quartered or sliced

kiwi fruit, peeled and quartered or sliced

loquats, peeled and cut into chunks

lychees, peeled and seeded

mandarins, segmented and seeds removed

mangoes, peeled and cut into chunks

melon (muskmelon types and watermelon), cut into balls with melon baller

oranges, skinned sections

papayas, seeded and cut into chunks

peaches and nectarines, peeled, pitted, and sliced

pears, peeled (optional), cored, and sliced or cut into chunks (use only firm pears and add at last minute to avoid discoloring)

pineapple, peeled, cored, and cut into cubes

plums, halved or quartered and pitted

strawberries, stemmed, whole or cut (depending on size)

Fruit and syrup should be well chilled. Just before serving, pile fruit in chilled serving bowl—or melon or pineapple shell—and spoon citrus sauce over all. If desired, accompany with plate of little cookies. An elegant dessert.

FRENCH FRUIT TARTS AND TARTLETS

FRUIT CHOICE: apricot, banana, blueberry, grape, grapefruit-orange, guava, kiwi fruit, mango, nectarine, peach, pear, raspberry, strawberry.

Open-face French fruit tarts are ravishing ways to serve seasonal fresh fruits, at their peak of color, texture, and flavor. There are several classic ways of preparing these tarts; fruit arranged in a rectangle of crisp, flaky puff pastry; fruit arranged in a large round short pastry shell; and fruit fillings in short pastry tartlet-size shells, all shiningly glazed with fruit syrup.

DO-AHEAD TIP: *All of these fruit tarts and tartlets can be made a day ahead and refrigerated.*

FRENCH FRUIT TART WITH PUFF PASTRY

- **1 pound unbaked Whole Wheat Puff Pastry (see Index)**
- **1 egg, beaten**
- **2 cups Vanilla Pastry Cream (see Index), or ¾ cup fruit preserve (same flavor as glaze), dissolved**
- **choice of fruit filling, glaze, and garnish; recipes follow**

Turn dough out onto lightly floured surface and roll to thickness of $\frac{3}{16}$ inch. Cut out 12 × 6-inch rectangle; transfer to dampened baking sheet. From remaining pastry, cut 2 strips 12 × 1½ inches and 2 strips 5 × 1½ inches. Lightly moisten 1 inch of outer edge of rectangle. Set dough strips atop outer edges to form double thickness, moistening with water so strips adhere. Freeze.

Preheat oven to 375°F. Thoroughly prick center of tart (not raised edges) with fork. Brush top edges with beaten egg. Bake until pastry has risen and is slightly browned, about 30 to 40 minutes. Check pastry after 5 minutes of baking; if bottom is puffed, remove from oven and prick again with fork until dough deflates. When pastry is done, remove from oven and let cool on rack for 20 minutes. Pull out any extra pastry in center so inside is flat.

Transfer tart shell to serving platter. Spread bottom with pastry cream or dissolved preserve. Cover with fruit, glaze, and garnish as described for respective fruit fillings. Chill in refrigerator until serving time.

8 servings

FRENCH FRUIT TART WITH SHORT PASTRY

1 baked 10- or 11-inch pastry shell of Plain Whole Wheat Short Pastry 1 or 2 (see Index)

3 tablespoons fine dry whole wheat bread crumbs or graham cracker crumbs

1 teaspoon ground cardamom

2 cups Vanilla Pastry Cream (see Index), or ¾ cup fruit preserve (same flavor as glaze), dissolved

choice of fruit filling, glaze, and garnish; recipes follow

Mix crumbs and cardamom and sprinkle over bottom of baked pastry shell. Spread with pastry cream or fruit preserve. Cover with fruit, glaze, and garnish as described for respective fruit fillings. Chill in refrigerator until serving time.

8 servings

FRENCH FRUIT TARTLETS WITH SHORT PASTRY

A charming serving idea is to offer a selection of different fruit fillings on a large tray.

12 baked 3½- to 4-inch tartlet shells of Plain Whole Wheat Short Pastry 1 or 2 (see Index)

3 tablespoons fine dry whole wheat bread crumbs or graham cracker crumbs

1 teaspoon ground cardamom seeds

2 cups Vanilla Pastry Cream (see Index)

choice of fruit filling, glaze, and garnish; recipes follow

Leave baked tartlet shells in tins. Mix crumbs and cardamom, and sprinkle over bottom of each shell. Spread with pastry cream. Cover with fruit, glaze, and decoration as described for respective fruit fillings. Chill in refrigerator until serving time.

Makes 12 tartlets

(continued)

FRENCH FRUIT TARTS AND TARTLETS—continued

FRUIT FILLINGS FOR FRENCH FRUIT TARTS

The following suggestions for fresh fruit, glaze, and garnish can be used on short pastry or puff pastry tart or tartlet shells. The quantities given will fill 1 10- or 11-inch short pastry tart shell, or 1 12 × 6-inch puff pastry tart shell, or 12 3½- or 4-inch short pastry tartlet shells. The strawberry and kiwi fruit topping can be used only with tart shell filled with vanilla pastry cream.

APRICOT, NECTARINE, PEACH, OR PEAR

- 4 cups peeled, pitted or cored, halved or quartered fruit
- 3 tablespoons fresh lemon juice
- 1 cup water
- 1 cup apricot preserve
- ½ cup toasted slivered almonds

So that fruit does not discolor, mix 2 tablespoons lemon juice with 1 cup water and pour over fruit as soon as it is peeled. Let stand in this rinse until ready to use.

For glaze, combine apricot preserve and 1 tablespoon lemon juice in small saucepan and stir over low heat until preserve is dissolved. Rub through fine wire strainer. Let stand at room temperature. Drain fruit and blot on paper towels. Arrange fruit in concentric circles or rows on top of pastry cream or preserve in tart shell, completely covering top. Brush fruit with dissolved preserve. Sprinkle with almonds.

GRAPE, GUAVA, KIWI FRUIT, MANGO, OR GRAPEFRUIT-ORANGE

- 1 cup apricot preserve
- 1 tablespoon fresh lemon juice
- any of the following:
  - 3 cups peeled and seeded white grapes
  - 4 cups peeled and seeded guava halves
  - 4 cups peeled and sliced or quartered kiwi fruit
  - 4 cups peeled and sliced mangoes
  - 4 cups skinned grapefruit and orange sections, mixed, well drained
- 1 cup heavy cream, whipped (optional)

For glaze, combine apricot preserve and lemon juice in small saucepan and stir over low heat until dissolved. Rub through fine wire strainer. Let stand at room temperature. Cover top of pastry cream or preserve in tart shell with selection of fruit. Brush dissolved preserve over top of fruit. If desired, put whipped cream in pastry bag fitted with medium star tube (#6 or #7) and pipe scallops or rosettes around edge of tart.

FRENCH FRUIT TARTS AND TARTLETS—continued

BANANA

- 4 cups sliced bananas (about 3/8 inch thick)
- 3 tablespoons fresh lemon juice
- 1 cup apricot preserve
- 1 cup heavy cream, whipped (optional)

Sprinkle banana slices with 2 tablespoons lemon juice. For glaze, combine apricot preserve and 1 tablespoon lemon juice in small saucepan and stir over low heat until dissolved. Rub through fine wire strainer. Let stand at room temperature. Drain fruit and blot on paper towels. Arrange banana slices in concentric circles or rows on top of pastry cream or preserve in tart shell, completely covering top. Brush fruit with dissolved preserve. If desired, put whipped cream in pastry bag fitted with medium star tube (#6 or #7) and pipe scallops or rosettes around edge of tart.

BLUEBERRY, RASPBERRY, OR STRAWBERRY

- 1 cup red currant jelly
- 1 tablespoon fresh lemon juice
- 3 cups whole, firm blueberries or raspberries, or 4 cups stemmed whole strawberries
- 1 cup heavy cream, whipped (optional)

For glaze, combine currant jelly and lemon juice in small saucepan and stir over low heat until jelly is dissolved. Let stand at room temperature.

If blueberries or raspberries are used, cover top of pastry cream or jelly in tart shell with blueberries or raspberries.

If strawberries are used, cover top of pastry cream or jelly in tart shell with whole strawberries, *standing each one stem end down.*

Brush top of fruit completely with dissolved currant jelly. If desired, put whipped cream in pastry bag fitted with medium star tube (#6 or #7) and pipe scallops or rosettes around edge of tart.

KIWI FRUIT AND STRAWBERRIES
(fruit topping without glaze)

- 2 cups cleaned and stemmed whole, firm strawberries
- 2 cups peeled, sliced, wedged, or chunked kiwi fruit
- 1 cup heavy cream, whipped (optional)

At serving time, cover top of pastry cream with strawberries, stem end down, leaving a little space between berries. Between strawberries, stick pieces of kiwi fruit. If desired, put whipped cream in pastry bag fitted with medium star tube (#6 or #7) and pipe scallops or rosettes around edge of tart.

FROZEN FRESH FRUIT SOUFFLE

FRUIT CHOICE: apricot, blueberry, mango, nectarine, peach, raspberry, strawberry.

This frosty, frothy souffle can be whipped up in about 15 minutes, using almost any fresh fruit puree.

DO-AHEAD TIP: *Frozen fresh fruit souffle should be prepared at least 8 hours ahead in order to freeze, and keeps well in the freezer at 0°F. for 2 or 3 days.*

FRUIT

- 2 cups pureed fresh ripe fruit; any of the following:
  - apricots
  - blueberries (strained)
  - mangoes
  - nectarines
  - peaches
  - raspberries (strained)
  - strawberries
- 1 tablespoon fresh lemon or lime juice
- 2 tablespoons red currant jelly (for blueberries)

SOUFFLE

- 3 egg yolks
- 1 whole egg
- ⅓ cup light honey
- 1 cup heavy cream
- ⅓ cup toasted grated coconut (optional)
- complementary Fresh Fruit Sauce or Fruit Syrup (optional; see Index)

FRUIT: Mix pureed fruit with lemon or lime juice and set aside. If blueberries are used, also add currant jelly.

SOUFFLE: Select 3-cup souffle dish or straight-sided glass bowl. Take length of aluminum foil or waxed paper 1½ times girth of dish, fold in half lengthwise, wrap around dish, and fasten with masking tape or string. The collar should extend about 2 inches above the dish.

In mixer, beat egg yolks, egg, and honey until mixture is thick and stiff. Beat heavy cream in large bowl over ice. Add egg mixture to whipped cream and fold together lightly and evenly, using rubber scraper. Then fold in pureed fruit. Pour mixture into prepared dish. Sprinkle coconut on top. Place in 0°F. freezer to freeze.

PRESENTATION: Carefully remove collar and place souffle in its dish on doily-lined serving plate. Spoon servings onto individual dessert plates.

4 servings

FROZEN FRUIT YOGURT

FRUIT CHOICE: apricot, banana, blackberry, guava, kiwi fruit, mamey, mango, nectarine, papaya, peach, pineapple, prune, raspberry, strawberry.

Homemade frozen fruit yogurts are delicious—a delightfully different and welcome light refreshment after a sumptuous meal. Some frozen yogurt dessert specialties are the Lemon-Walnut, Spiced Pear, and Mango-Lime (see Index). Here is a basic recipe in which other seasonal fruits can be used for tart frozen fruit yogurt. Also, frozen fruit yogurt can be served with fruit salads instead of sherbet.

DO-AHEAD TIP: *Frozen fruit yogurt keeps well in freezer at 0° F. for 2 or 3 days. After that it will begin to crystallize.*

- 1 cup pureed fresh fruit; any of the following:

apricots	mangoes
bananas	papayas
blackberries (strained)	peaches or nectarines
guavas	pineapples
kiwi fruits (strained)	raspberries (strained)
mameys	strawberries
	or soaked and pitted prunes

- 1 teaspoon grated lemon rind
- 1 tablespoon fresh lemon juice
- 2 cups plain yogurt (regular or low-fat)
- ¾ cup nonfat dry milk
- 2 tablespoons light honey, or more to taste
- 2 teaspoons unflavored gelatin dissolved in 2 tablespoons boiling water
- 1 egg white
- pieces of subject fruit, mixed fruits, or mint sprig (optional)

In mixing bowl, combine pureed fruit, lemon rind and juice, yogurt, dry milk, honey, and dissolved gelatin, and mix well with whisk. Transfer to drum of ice cream maker and process until half firm. Beat egg white to soft peaks, fold into half-frozen yogurt mixture, and continue processing until mixture is firm. Transfer to freezer container and store at 0°F. in freezer. At serving time, allow frozen fruit yogurt to soften a little. Garnish as desired with fruit or mint.

Yields about 1 quart

FRUIT FRITTERS

FRUIT CHOICE: apple, apricot, banana, cherry, orange, peach, pear, pineapple.

Pieces of fresh fruit coated with crisp, light batter are a quick and downright upright dessert for any occasion, including breakfast or brunch. Serve with complementary fruit, carob, or maple syrup, or Sour Cream Dessert Sauce or Yogurt Dessert Sauce (see Index).

DO-AHEAD TIP: *Batter and fruit can be prepared several hours ahead. Deep-fry at serving time.*

BATTER

1 whole egg

1 egg, separated

1 teaspoon light honey

½ cup whole wheat pastry flour

1 tablespoon light vegetable oil (e.g., safflower)

4 tablespoons milk

1 teaspoon baking powder (without aluminum salts)

CHOICE OF FRUIT

3 to 4 apples, peeled, cored and cut into ½-inch-thick slices

8 to 12 apricots, peeled, pitted, and halved

3 or 4 bananas, peeled, cut through lengthwise, and again in pieces 1½ to 2 inches long

2 cups pitted sweet cherries

2 cups separated orange segments

4 to 6 peaches or nectarines, peeled, pitted, and quartered

3 to 4 large, firm, ripe pears, peeled, cored, quartered, and rinsed in lemon juice

2 cups cubed pineapple (1-inch cubes)

BATTER: In small bowl, combine egg, egg yolk, and honey and beat well with small whisk. Add flour, oil, and milk and beat until batter is smooth. Sprinkle baking powder on top of batter and stir with whisk only until mixed. In separate bowl, beat egg white to soft peaks. Add to batter and fold in lightly and evenly. Let batter rest in refrigerator at least 30 minutes, or several hours, if more convenient.

FRUIT: Have choice of fruit prepared and well drained on paper towels. Heat oil in deep fryer to 375°F. Dip piece of fruit in batter and then fry in deep hot fat until golden brown all over. Drain on paper towels.

4 servings

FRUIT SHORTCAKE

FRUIT CHOICE: blackberry, blueberry, cherry (sweet), peach, raspberry, strawberry.

DO-AHEAD TIP: *Fruit can be prepared several hours ahead and chilled. Shortcake dough can be made up to the point of adding honey and milk. Bake at serving time.*

- quantity of 1 recipe for Shortcake Dough (see Index)
- 6 cups fresh, ripe fruit; any of the following:
  - cleaned and slightly crushed blackberries
  - cleaned and slightly crushed blueberries
  - pitted and halved sweet cherries
  - peeled and sliced peaches
  - cleaned raspberries
  - cleaned, stemmed, and slightly crushed strawberries
- light honey
- 3/4 cup red currant jelly (if blueberries or cherries are used)
- 8 tablespoons unsalted butter, melted
- 1 1/2 cup heavy cream, whipped

Preheat oven to 400°F. Turn dough out onto lightly floured board. Gently and firmly fold over dough 2 or 3 times and form into a ball. Pat dough to 1/2 inch thickness. Cut into rounds with 3- to 3 1/2-inch cutter and place on oiled baking sheet. Bake about 15 minutes, or until lightly browned. (Or pat dough as a sheet in baking pan.)

Sweeten blackberries, peaches, raspberries, or strawberries with honey to taste and chill. If blueberries or cherries are used, combine red currant jelly and honey in 2-quart saucepan and stir over low heat until dissolved. Add fruit, mix, and stir over low heat 2 minutes. Chill.

PRESENTATION: For individual serving, split hot biscuit or cut piece of biscuit sheet and split. Place bottom half on serving plate and brush with melted butter. Cover with ladleful of fruit. Cover with top of biscuit. Ladle more fruit over all and top with whipped cream. Prepare all servings in this manner. Serve at once.

8 servings

FRUIT SHERBETS

FRUIT CHOICE: apricot, blackberry, blueberry, grapefruit, guava, kiwi fruit, lemon, lime, mamey, mango, nectarine, orange, papaya, peach, pear, pineapple, pomegranate, raspberry, strawberry (see Index for other specialty fruit sherbets).

Fresh fruit ice, sherbet, or sorbet *(the French word for sherbet, which has come into popular usage in America) is a refreshing sweet, in hot weather, certainly, and as a light contrast with winter foods, too. Sherbets are colorful, festive desserts when garnished with other fresh fruits— whole or sliced pieces, puree, or syrup.*

The new kitchen machines have made fresh fruit sherbets, as well as ice cream and frozen yogurt, quick and easy to prepare. Just puree fruit in the blender or food processor, sweeten with a little honey syrup, and freeze. The new countertop electric churn ice cream makers are ideal. Sherbet can, of course, be made in an ice cube tray in the freezing unit of the refrigerator, but it must be stirred occasionally to break up larger ice crystals.

For a silken rather than flaky, icy texture, unflavored gelatin and/or beaten egg white are added to the sherbet mixture. If you wish a hard, icy sherbet, omit the gelatin and egg white. Freezing sherbet in an electric churn-type ice cream maker will produce a firm but not hard consistency. If you wish it harder, to serve as scoops, such as in a hollowed melon or pineapple shell, pack the sherbet in a freezer container and store in the freezer at 0° F.

DO-AHEAD TIP: *Sherbet keeps well in freezer for 2 or 3 days. After that it begins to crystallize.*

FRUIT SHERBET MADE WITH FRUIT PUREE

½ cup light honey, or more to taste

½ cup water

2 tablespoons fresh lemon juice

3 cups pureed fresh fruit; any of the following:

blackberries, blueberries, raspberries, cleaned, puree strained

strawberries, cleaned

apricots, guavas, mameys, mangoes, nectarines, papayas, peaches, pears, peeled and seeded

kiwi fruit, peeled, puree strained

pineapple, peeled and cored

2 egg whites

Combine honey, water, and lemon juice in small saucepan and stir over low heat until mixture is blended. Add to fruit puree. Process mixture in electric churn-type ice cream maker until it is almost firm. Beat egg whites to soft peaks, add to sherbet mixture, and continue processing until sherbet is firm. Remove sherbet from drum and serve, or store in 0°F. freezer.

Yields about 1¼ quarts

GRAPEFRUIT SHERBET

- 2½ cups grapefruit juice
- ½ cup orange juice
- 2 tablespoons finely grated grapefruit rind
- ½ cup light honey, or more to taste
- ¼ cup water
- 2 teaspoons unflavored gelatin
- 1 egg white

Combine grapefruit juice, orange juice, grapefruit rind, and honey in medium saucepan and stir over low heat until mixture boils. Simmer 3 minutes. Combine gelatin with water and add to hot syrup. Stand syrup in freezer until chilled.

Process chilled syrup in ice cream maker until mixture is almost firm. Beat egg white to soft peaks, add to sherbet mixture, and continue processing until sherbet is firm. Remove sherbet from drum and serve, or store in 0°F. freezer.

Yields about 1 quart

LEMON SHERBET

- ½ cup fresh lemon juice
- 4 tablespoons finely grated lemon rind
- ⅔ cup light honey
- 1⅓ cups plus 4 tablespoons water
- 2 teaspoons unflavored gelatin
- 1 egg white

Combine lemon juice and rind, honey, and 1⅓ cups water in medium saucepan, and stir over low heat until mixture boils. Simmer 3 minutes. Combine gelatin with 4 tablespoons water and add to hot syrup. Stand syrup in freezer until chilled.

Process chilled syrup in ice cream maker until mixture is almost firm. Beat egg white to soft peaks and add to sherbet mixture. Continue processing until sherbet is firm. Remove sherbet from drum and serve, or store in 0°F. freezer.

Yields about 1 quart

LIME SHERBET

- 1 cup fresh lime juice
- ½ cup finely grated lime rind
- 1 cup light honey
- 2 cups plus 4 tablespoons water
- 2 teaspoons unflavored gelatin
- 1 egg white

Combine lime juice, lime rind, honey, and 2 cups water in medium saucepan, and stir over low heat until mixture boils. Simmer 3 or 4 minutes, until rind is translucent. Combine gelatin with 4 tablespoons water and add to hot syrup. Stand syrup in freezer until chilled.

Process chilled syrup in ice cream maker until mixture is almost firm. Beat egg white to soft peaks and add to sherbet mixture. Continue processing until sherbet is firm. Remove sherbet from drum and serve, or store in 0°F. freezer.

Yields about 1½ quarts

(continued)

FRUIT SHERBETS—continued

ORANGE SHERBET

3 cups fresh orange juice

finely grated rind of 1 orange

½ cup light honey, or more to taste

2 tablespoons water

2 tablespoons fresh lemon juice

2 teaspoons unflavored gelatin

1 egg white

Combine orange juice, orange rind, and honey in medium saucepan, and stir over low heat until mixture boils. Simmer 3 minutes. Combine gelatin with water and lemon juice, and add to hot syrup. Stand syrup in freezer until chilled.

Process chilled syrup in ice cream maker until mixture is almost firm. Beat egg white to soft peaks and add to sherbet mixture. Continue processing until sherbet is firm. Remove sherbet from drum and serve, or store in 0°F. freezer.

Yields about 1 quart

POMEGRANATE SHERBET

1½ cups pomegranate juice (pulp of 2 pomegranates processed through juice extractor)

1 cup orange juice

2 tablespoons finely grated orange rind

½ cup light honey, or more to taste

½ cup plus 4 tablespoons water

2 teaspoons unflavored gelatin

1 egg white

Combine pomegranate juice, orange juice, orange rind, honey, and ½ cup water in medium saucepan and stir over low heat until mixture boils. Simmer 3 minutes. Combine gelatin with 4 tablespoons water, add to hot syrup, and stir until gelatin is dissolved. Stand syrup in freezer until chilled.

Process chilled syrup in ice cream maker until mixture is almost firm. Beat egg white to soft peaks, add to sherbet mixture, and continue processing until sherbet is firm. Remove sherbet from drum and serve, or store in 0°F. freezer.

Yields about 1 quart

ICE CREAM (PLAIN AND MIXED WITH FRESH FRUIT)

FRUIT CHOICE: apricot, banana, blackberry, blueberry, carob, coconut, date, guava, mamey, mango, nectarine, peach, pineapple, raspberry, rhubarb, strawberry.

If fresh fruit and cream is super, then fruit and ice cream must be superior. And, homemade *ice cream with fresh fruit must be dessert heaven. For some of my fancier dinner parties, which might feature such productions as a pheasant galantine or quail with white grapes in aspic, I love to surprise guests with a simple dish of homemade French vanilla custard ice cream bathed in fresh fruit sauce. Many svelte and diet-conscious guests succumb to a second helping of this gastronomic delight while muttering resolves to fast tomorrow. Isn't that what the joy of eating is all about—debits and credits? Double fruit ice cream may be the ultimate treat—like strawberry ice cream, with fresh strawberries over it.*

With the new lightweight countertop ice cream makers, ice cream, sherbet, and frozen yogurt are so easy to prepare. These new machines require only 3 or 4 trays of ice cubes. The mixtures are simple. Once frozen, your dessert can be stashed in the freezer (at 0° F) for 2 or 3 days. Just remember that the longer it is stored, the more it will form into larger, harder ice crystals.

DO-AHEAD TIP: *Ice cream keeps well in 0° F. freezer for 2 or 3 days. After that it will begin to crystallize.*

BASIC FRENCH VANILLA CUSTARD ICE CREAM

- **¾ cup light honey**
- **½ cup water**
- **6 egg yolks**
- **scraping of ½ vanilla bean, or 2 teaspoons vanilla extract**
- **2 cups heavy cream**
- **2 cups light cream or half-and-half**

Combine honey and water in small saucepan and stir over low heat until blended. Set aside. Beat egg yolks in mixer until light and frothy. Continue beating while slowly adding honey syrup. Beat until mixture is thick and cold. Add vanilla. Add heavy cream and light cream or half-and-half. Pour into drum of ice cream maker and process until firm. Remove paddle and pack down in drum or transfer to freezer container. Harden in freezer at 0°F.

Yields about 1½ quarts

BASIC VANILLA ICE CREAM

- **3 eggs**
- **½ cup light honey**
- **2 teaspoons vanilla extract**
- **2 cups heavy cream**
- **2 cups whole milk or double-strength reconstituted nonfat dry milk**

Beat eggs until light and frothy. Add honey and beat until thick. Add heavy cream and milk. Pour into drum of ice cream maker and process until firm. Remove paddle and pack down in drum or transfer to freezer container. Harden in freezer at 0°F.

Yields about 1½ quarts

(continued)

ICE CREAM—continued

FRESH FRUIT ICE CREAM (MIXED OR SWIRL)

fresh ripe fruit; any of the following:

- 1½ cups peeled and thinly sliced apricots, mangoes, nectarines, or peaches, pureed
- 3 cups sliced bananas, pureed
- 2 cups whole blackberries, blueberries, or raspberries, pureed and strained (to remove seeds)
- 3 cups sliced and seeded guavas, pureed
- 3 cups sliced mamey, pureed
- 3 cups cubed pineapple, pureed
- 3 cups whole strawberries, pureed

grated rind of 1 lemon

2 tablespoons light honey

mixture for Basic French Vanilla Custard Ice Cream or Basic Vanilla Ice Cream

Mix pureed fruit with lemon rind and honey, and chill.

For ice cream mixed with fruit, put basic ice cream mixture in ice cream maker and process until almost firm. Add fruit puree and continue processing until firm. Remove paddle and pack down in drum or transfer to freezer container. Harden in freezer at 0°F.

For fruit swirl ice cream, put basic ice cream mixture in ice cream maker and process until *firm*. Remove paddle. Add fruit puree and mix with long wooden spatula, leaving it in swirls (not well mixed). Pack down in drum or transfer to freezer container. Harden in freezer at 0°F.

Yields about 2½ quarts

DATE-NUT ICE CREAM

mixture for Basic French Vanilla Custard Ice Cream or Basic Vanilla Ice Cream

1 cup finely chopped pitted dates

½ cup finely chopped English or black walnuts

Process basic ice cream mixture in ice cream maker until almost firm. Add dates and nuts and process until firm. Remove paddle and pack down in drum or freezer container. Harden in freezer at 0°F.

Yields about 2 quarts

CAROB ICE CREAM

ingredients for Basic French Vanilla Custard Ice Cream or Basic Vanilla Ice Cream

1½ cups Coating Carob (see Index)

Proceed to prepare basic ice cream mixture. Just before adding cream, add carob mixture. Then add cream.

Put mixture in ice cream maker and process until firm. Remove paddle and pack down in drum or freezer container. Harden in freezer at 0°F.

For carob swirl ice cream, prepare basic ice cream mixture and freeze until firm. Remove paddle and add carob mixture. Fold carob mixture into ice cream with long wooden spatula, leaving it in swirls (not well mixed). Pack ice cream down in drum or freezer container and harden in freezer at 0°F.

Yields about 2 quarts

RHUBARB ICE CREAM

2 cups Rhubarb Puree (see Index)

mixture for Basic French Vanilla Custard Ice Cream or Basic Vanilla Ice Cream with vanilla flavoring omitted from either recipe

Put basic ice cream mixture in ice cream maker and process until almost firm. Add chilled rhubarb puree and continue processing until firm. Remove paddle, pack down in drum or freezer container, and harden in freezer at 0°F.

Yields about 2½ quarts

RICH COCONUT ICE CREAM

This ice cream is flavored with rich coconut milk rather than grated coconut. Serve it plain, with any fruit sauce (especially good with citrus sauces or purees), carob sauce, or crisp, toasted shredded coconut or Coconut Curls (see Index).

mixture for Basic French Vanilla Custard Ice Cream or Basic Vanilla Ice Cream, with vanilla flavoring omitted and 1 cup Coconut Milk (see Index) substituted for 1 cup heavy cream

Process coconut ice cream mixture in the ice cream maker until firm. Remove paddle and pack down in drum or freezer container. Harden in freezer at 0°F.

Yields about 1½ quarts

DULCE DE CAMOTE

FRUIT CHOICE: apple, apricot, currant, date, pear, raisin.

The mention of dulce de camote *makes Mexicans' eyes glaze and taste buds tingle— a cold puddinglike dessert of orange-zested sweet potato puree studded with a medley of dried fruits and nuts (fruity like a fruit cake), topped with thick cream. The name* dulce de camote *(dool-ceh deh cah-moh-teh) means simply a sweet or dessert made of sweet potato.*

DO-AHEAD TIP: *This dish should be prepared 2 to 3 days before serving to allow flavors to blend.*

- **2 pounds sweet potatoes or yams**
- **¼ cup light honey**
- **finely grated rind of 1 large orange**
- **1 teaspoon vanilla extract**
- **1 teaspoon ground cinnamon**
- **½ cup coarsely chopped walnuts or pecans**
- **¼ cup raisins, currants, or chopped pitted dates**
- **¼ cup chopped dried fruit (e.g., apples, apricots, pears), or a combination**
- **¾ cup heavy cream, whipped, Creme Fraiche (see Index), or thick sour cream**

Preheat oven to 450°F. Wrap sweet potatoes or yams in aluminum foil and bake until soft. Remove skins and process pulp in food processor until smooth. Transfer pureed pulp to mixing bowl.

Combine honey and orange rind in small saucepan. Warm mixture over low heat 3 minutes. Add to sweet potato pulp. Also add vanilla, cinnamon, nuts, and all fruits. Stir well. Cover mixture and let stand in refrigerator 2 to 3 days.

PRESENTATION: Serve in individual dessert glasses, topped with cream.

4 to 6 servings

REFRIGERATOR CHEESECAKE WITH FRESH FRUIT TOPPING

FRUIT CHOICE: apricot, blackberry, blueberry, kiwi fruit, peach, pineapple, raspberry, strawberry.

So many fruits are works of art in their natural appearance as well as flavor. This light refrigerator cheesecake is the perfect platform on which to star fresh fruit in its whole natural splendor.

DO-AHEAD TIP: *Cheesecake should be prepared a day ahead to set. Add fruit topping a few hours before serving.*

REFRIGERATOR CHEESCAKE – continued

CRUST
mixture for 1/2 quantity of Crumb Crust (see Index)

FILLING
3 tablespoons unflavored gelatin
1/4 cup cold water
3 egg yolks
1/3 cup light honey
1/4 cup hot water
20 ounces cream cheese, at room temperature
grated rind of 1 lemon
1 tablespoon fresh lemon juice
1 teaspoon freshly grated nutmeg
3 egg whites
1 cup heavy cream, whipped

CRUST: Preheat oven to 350°F. Generously grease 9-inch springform cake pan with softened butter. Cut round of paper to fit in bottom of pan. Press two-thirds of crumb mixture against sides of pan, but not on bottom. Bake crust 10 minutes and let cool. Reserve one-third of crumb mixture.

FILLING: Soak gelatin in cold water 5 minutes. In medium mixing bowl, combine egg yolks with honey and water and beat with whisk until mixture is blended. Place bowl in saute pan half filled with hot water, over low heat. Beat mixture until it thickens. Add softened gelatin and stir until it is blended into mixture. Set mixture aside to cool.

Beat cream cheese in mixer until smooth. Add egg yolk mixture and mix thoroughly. Add lemon rind, lemon juice, and nutmeg. Pour mixture through fine wire strainer. Beat egg whites to soft peaks. Using rubber scraper, fold whites lightly and evenly into egg yolk mixture. Then fold in whipped cream. Pour filling into prepared cake pan. Sprinkle reserved crumb mixture on top. Chill cheesecake until set (2 to 3 hours in freezer, or longer in refrigerator).

PRESENTATION: To transfer cheesecake to serving plate, place serving plate bottom side up on top of cheesecake in cake pan. Invert, release spring, and remove cake pan. Remove paper round from top of cake. Cover top of cake with fresh fruit. Refrigerate until serving time.

10 servings

CHOICE OF TOPPING
fresh fruit; enough of any of the following to cover top of 9-inch cake:

apricots, peeled and quartered. Arrange in concentric circles on top of cake. Brush lightly with 1/2 cup Apricot Syrup (see Index).

blueberries, cleaned, whole. Mix blueberries with 1/2 cup Red Currant Syrup (see Index). Spread on top of cheesecake.

kiwi fruit, peeled and thinly sliced or quartered. Spread cheesecake with 1/2 cup Apricot Syrup (see Index). Arrange kiwi fruit in concentric circles on top.

peaches, peeled and neatly sliced. Arrange in concentric circles on top of cheesecake. Brush lightly with 1/2 cup Apricot Syrup (see Index).

strawberries, cleaned and stemmed, whole. Arrange strawberries stem end down on top of cheesecake. Brush lightly with 1 cup Red Currant Syrup (see Index).

BUTTERMILK OR YOGURT COOLERS AND OTHER FRUIT DRINK COMBINATIONS

FRUIT CHOICE: apricot, banana, carob, coconut, cranberry, grapefruit, lemon, lime, muskmelon, nectarine, orange, peach, pineapple, raspberry, strawberry.

Here's a collection of fresh fruit drinks that are not only colorful, flavorful, and refreshing, but lower in calories than standard cola drinks and milk shakes. These recipes are generally for 1 serving but can easily be doubled or tripled. All you need is a blender and plenty of chilled glasses. (Remember that ice cubes dilute flavor.) A juice extractor is handy for certain fruits like pomegranate (delicious!), apple, or pear. The addition of ¼ proportion of extracted pomegranate juice adds a lovely roseate color and lively flavor pick-up to extracted juice of fresh grapes and grapefruit, orange, and pineapple juices. To transform fruit drinks into visions of temptation, serve them in stemmed glasses that have been frosted in the freezer, and with suggestive garnishes.

APRICOT NECTAR WITH BUTTERMILK OR YOGURT

½ cup apricot nectar, chilled

½ cup buttermilk or plain yogurt, chilled

¼ teaspoon fresh lemon juice

mint sprig

Blend and pour into chilled glass. Garnish with mint.

Yields 1 cup

COCO-CAROB

DO-AHEAD TIP: *For frothy consistency, prepare at serving time.*

4 tablespoons carob powder

¼ teaspoon ground cinnamon

¼ cup boiling water

1 teaspoon light honey

8 tablespoons nonfat dry milk

2 cups ice cubes

2 tablespoons Coconut Milk (see Index)

Dissolve carob and cinnamon in hot water. Combine all ingredients in blender and blend until thick and smooth. Pour into 1 or 2 chilled glasses.

Yields 2 cups when frothy

BANANA WITH BUTTERMILK OR YOGURT

½ large ripe banana

½ cup buttermilk or plain yogurt, chilled

½ teaspoon light honey

¼ teaspoon fresh lemon juice

lemon slice

Blend and pour into chilled glass. Hang lemon slice on rim of glass.

Yields 1 cup

CITRUS COMBO

½ cup grapefruit juice, chilled

½ cup orange juice, chilled

1 tablespoon lime juice

mint sprig

Blend three juice ingredients and pour over ice in 14- to 16-ounce glass. Garnish with mint.

Yields 1 cup

COCO LIMON: LIME AND COCONUT MILK WITH BUTTERMILK OR YOGURT

2 tablespoons fresh lime juice

2 tablespoons Coconut Milk (see Index)

1 tablespoon light honey

¾ cup buttermilk or plain yogurt, chilled

lime slice

Blend and pour into chilled glass. Hang lime slice on rim of glass.

Yields 1 cup

(continued)

BUTTERMILK OR YOGURT COOLERS—continued

COCO PIÑA: PINEAPPLE AND COCONUT MILK WITH BUTTERMILK OR YOGURT

- ½ cup unsweetened pineapple juice or pureed pineapple, chilled
- ½ cup buttermilk or plain yogurt, chilled
- 2 tablespoons Coconut Milk (see Index)
- pineapple spear

Blend and pour into chilled glass. Garnish with pineapple spear.

Yields 1 cup

CRAN-RASPBERRY FROTH

DO-AHEAD TIP: *For frothy consistency, prepare at serving time.*

- ¾ cup cranberry juice
- 2 tablespoons seedless red or black raspberry jam, or ¼ cup fresh raspberry puree, or ½ cup raspberry sherbet
- ½ teaspoon fresh lemon juice
- 3 large ice cubes (about ¼ cup)
- orange slice or pineapple spear (optional)

Blend until very frothy and smooth. Pour into large chilled glass. Garnish with orange slice or pineapple spear, if desired.

Yields 1½ cups when frothy

CITRUS ADE CONCENTRATE WITH BUTTERMILK OR YOGURT

- 1 cup buttermilk or plain yogurt, chilled
- 3 tablespoons frozen citrus concentrate—orange, lemonade, or limeade
- orange, lemon, or lime slice

Blend and pour into chilled glass. Hang fruit slice on rim of glass.

Yields 1 cup

FROSTED CAROB

DO-AHEAD TIP: *For frothy consistency, prepare at serving time.*

- 4 tablespoons carob powder
- 1/4 teaspoon ground cinnamon
- 1/4 cup boiling water
- 1 teaspoon light honey
- 8 tablespoons nonfat dry milk
- 2 cups ice cubes

Dissolve carob and cinnamon in hot water. Combine all ingredients in blender and blend until thick and smooth. Pour into 1 or 2 chilled glasses.

Yields about 2 cups when frothy

MELON WITH BUTTERMILK OR YOGURT

- 1 cup ripe muskmelon cubes (any type)
- 1/2 cup buttermilk or plain yogurt, chilled
- 1 teaspoon light honey
- 1/2 teaspoon fresh lemon juice
- 1/2 teaspoon grated lemon rind
- 2 or 3 melon balls

Blend and pour into chilled glass. Garnish with melon balls threaded on skewer.

Yields 1 cup

PAPAYA, PEACHES, NECTARINES, OR APRICOTS WITH BUTTERMILK OR YOGURT

- 1/2 cup cubes of peeled ripe papaya, peach, nectarine, or apricot
- 1/2 cup buttermilk or plain yogurt, chilled
- 1 teaspoon light honey
- 1 teaspoon fresh lemon juice
- fresh fruit slice or mint sprig

Blend and pour into chilled glass. Garnish with fresh fruit slice or mint.

Yields 1 cup

(continued)

BUTTERMILK OR YOGURT COOLERS – continued

PINEAPPLE AND CARROT JUICE

Surprised? It's great!

- **2/3 cup unsweetened pineapple juice, chilled**
- **1/3 cup fresh carrot juice (from juice extractor)**
- **pineapple spear or carrot stick**

Blend and pour into chilled glass. Garnish with pineapple spear or carrot stick.

Yields 1 cup

PINEAPPLE-LIME FROST

DO-AHEAD TIP: *Prepare pineapple ice cubes ahead. Blend drink at serving time.*

- **1 cup unsweetened pineapple juice ice cubes (1 average ice cube tray holds 2 cups liquid)**
- **1 egg white**
- **1 tablespoon fresh lime juice**
- **lime slice or pineapple spear**

Blend until mixture is frothy and smooth. Pour into chilled glass. Garnish with lime slice or pineapple spear.

Yields about 2 cups when frothy

BUTTERMILK OR YOGURT COOLERS—continued

PINK PEARL

DO-AHEAD TIP: *For frothy consistency, blend at serving time.*

- 1 cup grapefruit juice
- 1/4 cup fresh lemon juice
- 1/4 cup extracted pomegranate juice
- 1 tablespoon light honey
- 1 egg white
- 1 cup ice cubes
- mint sprigs

Blend and pour into chilled wine or old-fashioned glasses. Garnish with mint.

Yields about 3 cups when frothy

STRAWBERRIES WITH BUTTERMILK OR YOGURT

- 1/2 cup sliced ripe strawberries
- 1/2 cup buttermilk or plain yogurt, chilled
- 1 teaspoon light honey (or to taste, depending on ripeness of strawberries)
- 1/2 teaspoon fresh lemon juice
- sliced strawberry or mint sprig

Blend and pour into chilled glass. Garnish with strawberry or mint.

Yields 1 cup

PART III

Basics

BASIC RECIPES

Many of the fruit recipes in this book include basic preparations such as dressings, sauces, syrups, creams, doughs, pastry, or rice. These basics are grouped here for easy and frequent reference, and they are different from traditional counterparts. Here these standards have been interpreted in the use of all natural ingredients. Like the fresh fruit with which they are used, the natural conversions of basic preparations aim toward emphasis of wholesome food and unmasked flavor.

Grouping the recipes for these everyday preparations in a separate section offers the opportunity to examine the application of natural cooking guidelines in practice, which is gaining increasing interest among professional and amateur cooks, and to understand the principles. Readers can apply these guidelines in all of their cooking and use these basic recipes for many other purposes. For example, our recipes for whole wheat short pastry (pie dough) are standard and can be used for quiches or any other tart or pie shell.

No salt is present in these recipes, nor in any others in this book. *New York Times* food editor Craig Claiborne used his own experience to bring national attention to the fact that salt is not imperative to the joy of eating, as he demonstrated in the fine recipes in *Craig Claiborne's Gourmet Diet* (Times Books, 1980). Nature offers a variety of fine seasoning agents, such as lemon juice, which enhance or "open up" other flavors. Of course, those who desire salt can add it.

On the sweet side of the taste scale, *honey is used instead of sugar.* Honey is a natural sweetener, but because it, too, is mainly empty calories, it is used sparingly. Honey does contain one-third more sweetening power than a comparable amount of sugar; therefore, less honey is required. Converting a recipe to use liquid honey instead of dry sugar, especially in baking, requires careful restructuring and testing. And molded desserts (usually mousse or Bavarian creme mixtures for cold souffles) sweetened with honey instead of sugar require a little extra gelatin to set.

Chocolate is a favorite in dessert cooking, but here chocolate is avoided because of its high content of caffeine and the need to add sugar to make it sweet. Instead, *carob*, a natural fruit with a flavor similar to chocolate, is suggested. It is naturally sweet and is described in detail in the section on carob.

Whole grain flour can replace refined flour in almost every cooking and baking use, even in puff pastry. Whole wheat crepes can be thin and delicate but gain a rich nutty flavor crepes made with refined flour don't have. Short pastry and cream puff paste convert equally well. Whole wheat biscuit dough, including shortcake and cobbler topping, are also delicate and flavorful. (One of our short pastry recipes offers the alternative of using *vegetable oil instead of butter*, a natural food preference. With oil, the dough will not hold together in a sheet. It must be patted into the pan like a crumb crust and will have a taste and texture similar to crumb crust.)

Successful preparation of puff paste, that ultimate achievement of pastry-making art – tissue-thin layers of crisp buttery dough – still eludes many who attempt even the standard method with refined flour. The trick is to stretch the dough thinner and thinner over ever-thinning layers of butter through a series of rollings, but never allow the dough and butter to mix (achieved by keeping the dough and butter composition chilled and, thereby, separate). After many experiments with whole grain flours, I finally discovered that whole wheat puff pastry could be achieved by using whole wheat *bread* flour, which contains more gluten (the component in the wheat kernel that gives dough elasticity) than whole wheat pastry flour, and giving the initial flour and water mixture a thorough beating in the food processor to develop the elasticity. Voila!

The ingredient *baking powder without aluminum salts* is composed of calcium acid phosphate, bicarbonate of soda, and cornstarch, is double acting, can be used in the exact quantities called for in any recipe, and leaves no aftertaste. It is available in specialty and natural food stores as well as some supermarkets.

The recipes in this book also demonstrate how to use vegetable oil in fine cooking (as it is in the cuisines of southern France and Italy, for example). Unsalted butter is specified where the flavor or performance of butter is preferred for the quality of the dish. In using vegetable oil for general cooking purposes, and especially dessert use, we specify *light vegetable oil (e.g., safflower)*. A good cook is a connoisseur of the many wonderful kinds of vegetable oils available today and the dishes they complement, such as olive oil in Mediterranean cuisines, sesame oil in Chinese and Middle Eastern preparations, and a variety in different salads. For a light oil that imposes neither its flavor nor oil presence, we recommend safflower oil (which fortunately also happens to be the oil lowest in saturated fat).

Another basic natural ingredient which may be new to some readers is the use of *brown rice instead of white*. Brown rice doesn't have to be gray and gummy. If the kernels are first coated with egg, the way kasha has been cooked for ages, and then liquid added and cooked, the cooked kernels will be tender, fluffy and separate, with a nice golden cast. Brown rice is rich tasting. It freezes and thaws well so that it can be cooked in extra quantity to have on hand for various uses.

DRESSINGS

BASIC MAYONNAISE

DO-AHEAD TIP: *This mayonnaise keeps well in the refrigerator for at least a month, as long as no cream is added. Cream to thin it can be added at time of use.*

- 2 egg yolks
- cayenne pepper
- 1 teaspoon dry mustard
- 2 tablespoons fresh lemon juice
- 1½ cups light vegetable oil (e.g., safflower)
- light or heavy cream (optional)

Combine egg yolks, a few grains cayenne pepper, mustard, and lemon juice in food processor and process until well blended. Activate processor and very slowly pour vegetable oil through feed tube, literally in a fine stream. If thinner consistency is desired, add cream, 1 tablespoon at a time. Mayonnaise can also be made in mixer, following the same procedure.

Yields 1¾ cups

HONEY DRESSING

Good with fruit or cabbage salads.

DO-AHEAD TIP: *Dressing keeps well in refrigerator for a week or so.*

- ½ teaspoon dry mustard
- 2 teaspoons tamari soy sauce
- ⅛ teaspoon freshly ground white pepper
- 2 tablespoons fresh lemon juice
- ½ cup light vegetable oil (e.g., safflower)
- 2 teaspoons finely chopped onions
- 3 tablespoons light honey
- 1 teaspoon celery seeds

Combine all ingredients in screwtop jar and shake well.

Yields ¾ cup

BASIC VINAIGRETTE DRESSING

DO-AHEAD TIP: *Dressing can be refrigerated for several weeks.*

- 1 teaspoon tamari soy sauce
- ½ teaspoon light honey
- 1 teaspoon dry mustard
- ½ teaspoon freshly ground pepper
- 2 tablespoons fresh lemon juice
- 1 teaspoon finely chopped fresh garlic
- 2 tablespoons virgin olive oil
- ½ cup light vegetable oil (e.g., safflower)
- 1 egg, or 2 tablespoons heavy cream

Combine all ingredients in 1-pint screwtop jar and close tightly. Shake mixture vigorously, until it emulsifies a little. Refrigerate.

Yields about 1 cup

PAPAYA SEED VINAIGRETTE DRESSING

- ingredients for Basic Vinaigrette Dressing
- 2 tablespoons fresh papaya seeds

Combine all ingredients for basic vinaigrette dressing *except egg or heavy cream* in blender or food processor. Add papaya seeds. Process until seeds are ground like black pepper. Transfer mixture to screwtop jar. Add egg or cream and shake vigorously. (If egg is added to blender or food processor, dressing will be too thick, almost like mayonnaise.)

Yields about 1 cup

SAUCES

LEMON-YOGURT DRESSING

Use with any tossed greens salad.

DO-AHEAD TIP: *This dressing keeps well in refrigerator for about a week.*

- 1 tablespoon fresh lemon juice
- ⅛ teaspoon dry mustard
- ¼ teaspoon chopped fresh garlic
- 1 teaspoon chopped fresh tarragon or thyme, or ¼ teaspoon dried tarragon or thyme
- 6 tablespoons plain yogurt (regular or low-fat)
- 2 tablespoons freshly grated Parmesan cheese
- ¼ teaspoon grated lemon rind
- freshly ground white pepper

Combine all ingredients except pepper in screwtop jar and shake until well mixed. Grind pepper on top of tossed salad at the table – to get pepper fragrance.

Yields ½ cup

SWEET SAUCES, SYRUPS, CREAMS

CITRUS SAUCE FOR DESSERTS

This fragrant sauce composed of three citrus rinds—lemon, lime, and orange—will brighten the flavors of any mixture of fruits. It is delicious over ice cream. It will keep indefinitely in the refrigerator.

- pared rind of 2 lemons
- pared rind of 2 limes
- pared rind of 2 oranges
- 1½ cups light honey
- 2 cups water

Cut strips of rinds into fine, short shreds (very thin; about ¾ inch long). In deep, heavy 1½-quart pot, combine citrus rinds, honey, and water. Stir over low heat until mixture comes to a boil. Simmer gently until rinds are translucent. Chill sauce before using.

Yields 4 cups

CAROB SAUCE

Serve hot or cold.

DO-AHEAD TIP: *This sauce keeps well for a week or two in the refrigerator and longer in the freezer.*

- 1 cup powdered carob
- 1 teaspoon ground cinnamon, or 2 teaspoons vanilla extract
- 1¼ cups light cream or milk
- 1 tablespoon light honey (optional)
- 4 tablespoons frozen unsalted butter, cut into bits (optional)
- ½ cup heavy cream, whipped (optional)

Combine carob, cinnamon or vanilla, and light cream or milk in medium saucepan. Stir vigorously with small whisk over low heat until mixture is smoothly blended and shiny. Stir in honey, if desired.

For richer, thicker sauce, keep sauce over low heat and stir in butter, bit by bit.

For fluffier sauce, (with or without butter addition), fold whipped cream into hot sauce, if it is to be served hot, or cooled sauce, for cold serving.

Yields 1½ cups basic pouring sauce, or 1¾ cups with butter added, or 2½ cups with whipped cream added

COATING CAROB

DO-AHEAD TIP: *Coating carob will keep in refrigerator or freezer. Rewarm to use.*

- ¾ cup carob powder
- ¾ teaspoon ground cinnamon, or 1 teaspoon vanilla extract (optional)
- ½ cup boiling water
- 3 tablespoons unsalted butter, cut into bits

Place carob powder and cinnamon or vanilla, if desired, in small saucepan. Add boiling water slowly while stirring with small whisk. Stir vigorously over low heat until completely blended. Add butter, bit by bit, stirring constantly. Remove from heat at once.

Yields about 1 cup

CREME CHANTILLY

Sweetened Whipped Cream

DO-AHEAD TIP: *Creme chantilly can be prepared a day ahead and refrigerated.*

- 1 cup heavy cream
- 1 tablespoon light honey
- scraping from 4-inch piece vanilla bean, or 1 teaspoon vanilla extract

Place large round-bottom metal bowl over ice and pour in heavy cream. Beat with large piano wire whisk until it thickens but is not stiff. Add honey and vanilla and continue beating until cream holds its shape. Do not beat any longer, or cream will separate.

Yields 2 cups

CREME FRAICHE

Just about everyone who has visited France has been captivated by the subtle but distinctive flavor of creme fraiche, which is invariably served with fresh berries, added to other fruit desserts, and often used in savory sauces. Besides its fine flavor, it is particularly useful in cooking because, unlike sour cream, it will not curdle when heated to high temperatures. Also, it can be used like butter or oil to coat seafood, poultry, or meat to be roasted or broiled (to enclose the moisture) but it adds only half the calories.

Although creme fraiche literally means fresh cream, it is actually "matured cream." In France, naturally occurring lactic acids and ferments in raw cream work to thicken the cream, changing the flavor from sweet to nutty and slightly acidic. Sweet cream or unmatured French cream is called fleurette.

Creme fraiche need not be only a delicious memory of dining in France. You can have it here, too. It is as simple as adding 2 tablespoons of buttermilk to 1 cup of heavy whipping cream (as described below) or you can purchase a dried French lactic bacteria packaged by Solait.

DO-AHEAD TIP: *Creme fraiche made with buttermilk will keep in the refrigerator for about 10 days.*

- 1 cup heavy cream, at room temperature
- 2 tablespoons cultured buttermilk (low-fat or regular)

Combine cream and buttermilk and pour into clean, warm glass jar. Cover tightly and stand jar in warm place for 12 to 24 hours. When mixture has set or is almost firm, transfer it to the refrigerator, where it will become more solid.

Yields 1 cup

CREME PATISSIERE A LA CAROUBE

Carob Pastry Cream

DO-AHEAD TIP: *Pastry cream keeps well for 2 or 3 days in refrigerator.*

- 8 tablespoons carob powder
- 3 tablespoons light honey
- 1½ teaspoons vanilla extract
- ½ teaspoon ground cinnamon
- 6 tablespoons water
- 1 whole egg
- 1 egg yolk
- 3 tablespoons whole wheat pastry flour
- 1 tablespoon unflavored gelatin
- ¾ cup milk
- 2 egg whites
- 1 cup heavy cream, whipped

Combine carob, 1 tablespoon honey, ½ teaspoon vanilla, cinnamon, and water in small saucepan. Stir with small whisk over low heat until mixture is smooth and shiny. Set aside.

In mixer, combine egg, egg yolk, flour, and 2 tablespoons honey and beat thoroughly. Add gelatin and beat again. Put milk and 1 teaspoon vanilla in 1½-quart saucepan and bring slowly to a boil. Remove from heat at once and pour hot milk into egg mixture, stirring constantly.

Transfer egg and milk mixture to saucepan and stir over low heat until it just comes to a boil. Place saucepan over bowl of ice and stir mixture vigorously with whisk until it cools and thickens. Add carob mixture and beat well. Beat egg whites to soft peaks and fold into egg and carob mixture. Then add whipped cream, spoonful by spoonful, stirring it in vigorously with small whisk after each addition.

Yields about 2 cups

CREME PATISSIERE A LA VANILLE

Vanilla Pastry Cream

DO-AHEAD TIP: *Pastry cream can be prepared 2 or 3 days ahead and refrigerated.*

- 1 whole egg
- 1 egg yolk
- 3 tablespoons whole wheat pastry flour
- 2 tablespoons light honey
- 1 tablespoon unflavored gelatin
- ¾ cup milk or reconstituted nonfat dry milk
- ¼ vanilla bean (scraping and pod), or 1 teaspoon vanilla extract
- 2 egg whites
- 1 cup heavy cream, whipped

Combine egg, egg yolk, flour, and honey in mixer and beat thoroughly. Add gelatin and beat again. Put milk and vanilla in 1½-quart saucepan and slowly bring to a boil. Remove from heat at once and slowly pour hot milk into egg mixture, stirring constantly.

Transfer egg and milk mixture to saucepan and stir over low heat until it just comes to a boil. Remove saucepan from heat and place over bowl of ice. Continue to stir mixture with whisk until it cools and thickens. Beat egg whites to soft peaks and fold into egg and milk mixture. Then add whipped cream, spoonful by spoonful, beating vigorously with whisk after each addition. The mixture now should be medium-thick, smooth, and creamy.

Yields about 2 cups

FRESH FRUIT SAUCES

Apple, apricot, blackberry, blueberry, orange, peach, raspberry, strawberry

Serve these lively fresh fruit sauces over custard, coeur a la creme, *ice cream, sherbet, mousse, cake, yogurt, pancakes, pudding. The following recipes call for 1 to 2 cups fresh fruit (depending on whether a syrupy or thick fruit sauce is desired).*

DO-AHEAD TIP: *Fresh fruit sauces keep well in refrigerator 2 or 3 days.*

APRICOT SAUCE

- 2 to 3 cups peeled, sliced fruit
- 1 cup apricot preserve
- 2 teaspoons fresh lemon juice

Dissolve jelly or preserve with lemon juice in small saucepan over low heat. *For blueberry sauce only,* add fruit to hot syrup and let cool. *For all other fruit sauces,* let syrup cool and add fruit.

Yields 2 to 3 cups

FRESH FRUIT SAUCES—continued

BLACKBERRY SAUCE

2 cups cleaned whole fruit, slightly crushed

1 cup seedless black raspberry preserve

2 teaspoons fresh lemon juice

BLUEBERRY SAUCE

2 to 3 cups cleaned fruit

1 cup red currant jelly

2 teaspoons fresh lemon juice

ORANGE SAUCE

2 cups skinned orange sections, drained

1 cup orange marmalade

2 teaspoons fresh lemon juice

PEACH SAUCE

2 to 3 cups peeled, sliced fruit

1 cup apricot preserve

2 teaspoons fresh lemon juice

RASPBERRY SAUCE

2 cups cleaned whole fruit

1 cup red currant jelly

2 teaspoons fresh lemon juice

STRAWBERRY SAUCE

2 cups cleaned, halved or quartered fruit

1 cup seedless black raspberry preserve

2 teaspoons fresh lemon juice

(continued)

FRESH FRUIT SAUCES — continued

APPLE SAUCE

This sauce can be eaten as is with yogurt or cream, used as dessert filling, or as topping over whole wheat flour or potato pancakes. Apple sauce mixed with freshly grated horseradish and served with or without potato pancakes is a classic accompaniment to boiled or roast beef, or pork.

DO-AHEAD TIP: *This sauce keeps well in refrigerator for at least a week.*

- **4 large green cooking apples, peeled, cored, and cut into thick slices**
- **½ cup apricot preserve**
- **grated rind of 1 lemon**
- **2 tablespoons light honey, or more to taste**
- **2 tablespoons unsalted butter**

Combine all ingredients in deep, heavy pot. Cover and cook over moderate heat until apples are mushy and in bits. Sauce can be used this way, or it can be pureed in food processor or blender until smooth.

Yields 2 to 3 cups

CUSTARD SAUCE

Creme Anglaise

The cream supreme— the perfect sauce with seasonal fresh fruit, especially chunks of mamey or peaches, or raspberries or strawberries. It can be used hot or cold.

DO-AHEAD TIP: *Sauce keeps well in refrigerator 2 or 3 days.*

- **4 egg yolks**
- **⅓ cup light honey**
- **½ vanilla bean (scraping and pod), or 2 teaspoons vanilla extract**
- **1½ cups light cream or double-strength reconstituted nonfat dry milk**
- **½ cup heavy cream, whipped (optional)**

In mixer, beat egg yolks, honey, and vanilla bean scraping or extract until mixture is light and thick. Put light cream in medium saucepan with vanilla pod and bring to a boil slowly. Pour hot cream slowly into egg yolk mixture, beating constantly. Transfer mixture to saucepan and stir over low heat until it thickens and coats the back of a spoon.

For fluffy sauce, fold in whipped cream: For hot serving, fold whipped cream into hot sauce. For cold serving, chill sauce, then fold in whipped cream.

Yields 2 cups

FRUIT SYRUPS

Apricot, raspberry, red currant

Use to glaze dessert toppings, sandwich between cakes and cookies, pour over ice cream, sherbet, fresh or stewed fruit, pancakes, or waffles.

DO-AHEAD TIP: *All of these syrups keep well in the refrigerator for at least a month. Rewarm to dissolve.*

APRICOT SYRUP

½ cup apricot preserve

1 teaspoon fresh lemon juice

RASPBERRY SYRUP

½ cup seedless red or black raspberry jam

1 teaspoon fresh lemon juice

RED CURRANT SYRUP

½ cup red currant jelly

1 teaspoon fresh lemon juice

Combine jelly, preserve, or jam with lemon juice in small saucepan and stir over low heat until dissolved. Rub through fine wire strainer. Let cool to room temperature. Use as needed. (Any unused mixture can be returned to original jar.)

Yields ½ cup

SAUCES

HOLLANDAISE SAUCE

DO-AHEAD TIP: *Hollandaise sauce with butter can be held in a pan of lukewarm water. Hollandaise sauce with vegetable oil can be held at room temperature.*

- 2 egg yolks
- 2 tablespoons fresh lemon juice
- 2 tablespoons light cream, yogurt, or sour cream
- cayenne pepper
- 6 tablespoons frozen unsalted butter, cut into ½-inch cubes, or ½ cup light vegetable oil (e.g., safflower)

Combine egg yolks, lemon juice, light cream, yogurt, or sour cream, and a few grains of cayenne pepper in small round-bottom bowl, and beat with small whisk until blended. Stand bowl in saute pan half filled with simmering water. Beat sauce over low heat until it is thick. Continue beating while slowly adding butter (bit by bit) or oil (in a very thin stream).

Yields about 1 cup

SOUR CREAM DESSERT SAUCE

DO-AHEAD TIP: *Sauce can be refrigerated for 3 or 4 days.*

- ½ cup heavy cream, whipped
- 1 cup thick sour cream
- 1 tablespoon light honey
- grated rind of 1 lemon
- ½ teaspoon freshly grated nutmeg
- ¼ teaspoon ground ginger

Fold whipped cream and sour cream together. Then fold in honey, lemon rind, nutmeg, and ginger. Chill thoroughly before serving.

Yields 2 cups

YOGURT DESSERT SAUCE

DO-AHEAD TIP: *Sauce can be refrigerated for 3 or 4 days.*

- 1 ½ cups plain yogurt (regular or low-fat)
- ¾ cup nonfat dry milk
- 2 tablespoons light honey
- grated rind of 1 lemon
- ½ teaspoon freshly grated nutmeg
- ¼ teaspoon ground ginger

Beat yogurt and dry milk with whisk until thick and creamy. Beat in remaining ingredients. Chill thoroughly before serving.

Yields 2 cups

PLAIN WHOLE WHEAT SHORT PASTRY 1 (WITH BUTTER)

Pate Brisee or *Pate a Foncer*

DO-AHEAD TIP: *Unbaked or baked pastry shell(s) can be frozen. Leave in baking container and enclose in sealed plastic bag.*

- **2 cups whole wheat pastry flour, not sifted**
- **10 tablespoons cold unsalted butter, cut into ½-inch cubes**
- **2 teaspoons lemon juice**
- **¼ to ⅓ cup iced water**

To mix dough in food processor, put flour and butter in processor bowl with steel blade in place. Run machine on and off for about 5 seconds, just to break up butter *coarsely*. Through feed tube, add lemon juice and ¼ cup iced water. Again run machine on and off until dough roughly begins to mass together (only a few seconds). If dough can be gathered from bowl, remove. If it is still dry, cover bowl and add another 1 or 2 tablespoons iced water, 1 tablespoon at a time, through feed tube, running machine briefly after each addition. Turn dough out onto unfloured work surface and quickly form into a ball. (Do not knead.) Wrap in plastic wrap and chill about 30 minutes to 1 hour in refrigerator to become more workable. (Or, dough can be used at once.)

To mix dough by hand, put flour in mixing bowl. Add butter. Quickly rub flour and butter between your fingertips until mixture resembles *coarse* meal. Add lemon juice and ¼ cup iced water and quickly gather dough into mass. If mixture is still dry, add another 1 or 2 tablespoons iced water, 1 tablespoon at a time. Turn dough out onto unfloured work surface and quickly form into a ball. (Do not knead.) Wrap in plastic wrap and chill about 30 minutes to 1 hour in refrigerator to become more workable. (Or, dough can be used at once.)

To bake large pastry shell, preheat oven to 350°F. Have ready 10- to 12-inch flan ring on baking sheet or jelly roll pan, or pie pan or 1-inch-deep, round porcelain baking dish; wide rolling pin, roll of waxed paper, and dried beans or raw rice (to anchor paper lining).

Spread 24-inch strip of waxed paper on work surface and dust with flour. Place ball of dough in center and sprinkle with a little more flour. Flatten ball a little with rolling pin and cover with another sheet of waxed paper. Roll dough between sheets of waxed paper to a round large enough to line flan ring or baking container. Remove top sheet of waxed paper. Use bottom sheet to turn dough into baking container. With your fingers, shape dough firmly against inside. Run rolling pin over rim to trim off excess dough. Flute edge with your fingers. Prick bottom of dough with fork in several places. (If filling to be used is quite liquid, such as custard for quiche, do not prick all the way through.) Place sheet of waxed paper on top of dough and cover with dried beans or raw rice. (During baking, steam will form and cause dough to puff. Anchoring the paper lining will keep pastry shell flat.)

Bake pastry shell 25 minutes. Then remove weight and waxed paper and return pastry to oven for another 10 minutes or so to finish baking bottom. Pastry shell is now ready to use in recipes calling for baked pastry shell.

Tartlet and/or boat pastry shells are little pastry molds ranging in size from 1 to 4 inches that are used for hors d'oeuvres, dessert pastries, and small savory preparations. Lining them, regardless of how many, is a quick and trim process.

Preheat oven to 350°F. Arrange tartlet and/or boat tins in a cluster on jelly roll pan or baking sheet. (They should be touching each other.) Spread 24-inch length of waxed paper on surface and dust with flour. Place ball of dough in center and sprinkle with a little more flour. Flatten dough a little with a rolling pin and cover with another sheet of waxed paper. Roll dough between two sheets of waxed paper to a round large enough to cover assembled tins. Remove top sheet of waxed paper. Use bottom paper to turn dough on top of cluster of baking tins. Gently and firmly roll rolling pin over dough on tins, which automatically cuts dough to fit each tin. Shape dough firmly inside each tin. Prick bottoms with fork. Cut squares of waxed paper to a size a little larger than molds and pat one inside each mold, weighing paper down with dried beans or raw rice. Remove excess dough from baking sheet. (This may be re-rolled to line additional molds.)

Bake pastry shells 10 to 15 minutes, depending on size of molds. Remove weight and waxed paper. Return pastry to oven for a few minutes to finish baking bottoms. Shells are now ready to use in recipes calling for baked tartlet and/or boat pastry shells.

Makes 1 10- to 12-inch pastry shell or 12 tartlet shells, 3½ to 4 inches each, or 36 to 48 hors d'oeuvre-size tartlet shells. For 2-crust pie, use 1½ quantity of recipe

PLAIN WHOLE WHEAT SHORT PASTRY 2 (WITH VEGETABLE OIL)

Pate Brisee or *Pate a Foncer*

When vegetable oil is used instead of butter, short pastry dough is less cohesive. It must be patted into the baking container like a crumb crust, and the baked result is more like a crumb crust. It is not advisable to use a flan ring with vegetable oil short pastry since the baked pastry shell would be too crumbly to be removed from the baking mold without support. It does seem to adhere well enough for small tartlet shells to be removed from tins. Also because of its crumb nature, this dough is difficult to use for top crust or for pastries that are to be wrapped or folded, such as turnovers.

DO-AHEAD TIP: *Unbaked or baked pastry shell(s) can be frozen. Leave in baking container and enclose in sealed plastic bag.*

2 cups whole wheat pastry flour or stone ground whole wheat bread flour

4 tablespoons light vegetable oil (e.g., safflower)

2 teaspoons fresh lemon juice

¼ cup iced water

Combine flour and vegetable oil in mixing bowl and mix with your fingers. Add lemon juice and iced water. Gather mixture into mass and shape into a ball. If mixture is still too dry, add more iced water, 1 tablespoon at a time. (Do not use food processor; it will activate gluten too much, resulting in hard and tough baked pastry.)

To bake large pastry shell, preheat oven to 350°F. Have ready 10- to 12-inch pie pan or 1-inch-deep, round porcelain baking dish. Spread 24-inch strip of waxed paper on work surface and dust with a little flour. Place ball of dough in center and sprinkle with a little more flour. Flatten dough a little with rolling pin and cover with another sheet of waxed paper. Roll dough between sheets of waxed paper to about a 10-inch round. Remove top sheet of paper. Using bottom paper, turn dough into baking container. If it breaks, reassemble in container. Working from center toward edge of pan, pat dough out to cover bottom and sides evenly and neatly. With small knife, trim excess dough off rim and flute edge with your fingers. It is not necessary to weigh down this dough while baking. Bake 30 to 40 minutes, or until edge begins to brown a little.

To bake tartlet and/or boat pastry shells, preheat oven to 350°F. Put small quantity of dough in each tin and pat dough out to line tins evenly. Place tins on jelly roll pan or baking sheet and bake 10 to 15 minutes, depending on size. Fill pastry shells as desired and leave in tins until serving time. Then carefully transfer from tins onto serving plates.

Makes 1 10- to 12-inch pastry shell or 12 tartlet shells, 3½ to 4 inches each

SPICY SWEET SHORT PASTRY

DO-AHEAD TIP: *Pastry dough can be prepared a day or two in advance and refrigerated. When ready to roll out, allow to soften a little at room temperature.*

- 2 cups whole wheat pastry flour
- 2 tablespoons finely ground almonds, or almond paste
- 1 teaspoon ground cinnamon
- ½ teaspoon ground ginger
- grated rind of 1 lemon
- 10 tablespoons cold unsalted butter, cut into ½-inch cubes
- 2 tablespoons light honey
- 2 tablespoons iced water
- 1 egg, beaten

To mix dough in food processor, put flour, almonds or almond paste, cinnamon, ginger, and lemon rind in processor bowl with steel blade in place, and activate processor briefly to blend. Add butter cubes all at once. Run machine on and off for about 5 seconds, just to break up butter *coarsely.* In measuring cup, combine honey and iced water (just stir a little; mixture won't completely blend), pour through food tube, and run machine on and off until dough roughly begins to mass together (only a few seconds). If dough can be gathered from bowl, remove. If it is still dry, cover bowl and add another 1 or 2 tablespoons iced water, 1 tablespoon at a time, through feed tube, running machine briefly after each addition. Turn dough onto unfloured work surface and quickly form into a ball. (Do not knead.) Wrap in plastic wrap and chill about 30 minutes in refrigerator to become more workable.

To mix dough by hand, combine flour, almonds or almond paste, cinnamon, ginger, and lemon rind in mixing bowl. Add butter cubes and quickly rub dry ingredients and butter between your fingers until mixture resembles coarse meal. In measuring cup, combine honey and iced water (just stir a little; mixture won't completely blend), add to bowl, and quickly gather dough into a mass. If dough is still dry, add more iced water, 1 tablespoon at a time. Turn dough onto unfloured work surface and quickly form into a ball. (Do not knead.) Wrap in plastic wrap and chill about 30 minutes in refrigerator to become more workable.

To bake pastry shell, preheat oven to 350°F. Have ready flan ring on jelly roll pan or baking sheet, or pie pan, or shallow round baking dish. Spread 24-inch sheet of waxed paper on work surface and dust with flour. (If tart is to be covered with lattice top, reserve one-third of dough, wrap in plastic wrap, and return to refrigerator.) Place dough in center of waxed paper and sprinkle with a little flour. Flatten dough a little with rolling pin and cover with another sheet of waxed paper. Roll dough between sheets of waxed paper to a round large enough to line baking container. With your fingers, shape dough firmly

(continued)

SPICY SWEET SHORT PASTRY—continued

against inside. Run rolling pin over top to trim off excess dough. Prick bottom of dough with fork in several places. Place sheet of waxed paper on top of dough and put dried beans or raw rice on top of paper. Bake 25 minutes. Remove weight and waxed paper.

To make tart with lattice top, leave oven set at 350°F. Fill pie as desired. (Spicy sweet short pastry is generally used with fruit fillings.) Roll out reserved dough between 2 sheets of floured waxed paper. Cut dough into ½-inch-wide strips long enough to span top of tart, and arrange in lattice (criss-cross) fashion. Press strips down at rim and pinch off excess. Brush top of pastry and edge with beaten egg. Bake until filling is cooked and pastry is lightly browned (usually 30 to 35 minutes).

Makes 1 10- or 11-inch tart shell or 1 8- or 9-inch tart shell with one-third of dough for lattice top

CRUMB CRUST

Not a dough, but a mixture for a pastry shell made with whole wheat bread crumbs, spices, and butter. It can be used in a pie pan for a cream tart or in a springform cake pan for a cheesecake.

DO-AHEAD TIP: *Crumb mixture keeps well in refrigerator or freezer.*

- ⅓ cup unsalted butter
- ¼ cup light honey
- 1 cup dry whole wheat bread crumbs
- ¼ cup wheat germ flakes (or additional bread crumbs)
- ¼ teaspoon freshly grated nutmeg
- ½ teaspoon ground cinnamon
- ¼ teaspoon ground ginger
- ¼ teaspoon mace

Preheat oven to 350°F. In small saucepan, combine butter and honey, and warm over low heat until dissolved. Combine all ingredients in food processor or mixer and mix well. Pat mixture in pie pan or springform cake pan. Bake crust before adding filling.

Makes enough to line a 9- or 10-inch springform cake pan (sides and bottom), or a 10- to 12-inch pie pan (bottom and sides)

COCONUT-CRUMB CRUST

DO-AHEAD TIP: *Coconut-crumb crust can be made in advance and stored in freezer.*

- **4 tablespoons unsalted butter, melted**
- **1 tablespoon light honey**
- **1¼ cups grated coconut**
- **½ cup dry whole wheat bread crumbs**

Preheat oven to 350°F. In small saucepan, combine butter and honey and warm over low heat until dissolved. Combine all ingredients in mixer or processor and mix well. Pat mixture into 10- or 11-inch pie plate or shallow round baking dish. Bake 10 minutes, remove from oven, and chill in refrigerator or freezer.

Makes 1 10- or 11-inch tart shell

BASIC CHOU PASTE (CREAM PUFF PASTE)

Pate a Chou

Cream puff shells can be made in any size, from ½ inch diameter, used as garnish in consomme, to a big 8-inch-diameter circle for a gateau favori. *One-inch puff shells are used for hors d'oeuvre fillings, and 2- to 3-inch cream puffs are nice for dessert, filled with various flavored pastry creams.*

DO-AHEAD TIP: *Baked cream puff shells can be frozen. Store in tightly sealed plastic bag. To use, thaw at room temperature and crisp in moderate oven; then fill.*

1 cup water

8 tablespoons light vegetable oil (e.g., safflower)

1 cup sifted whole wheat pastry flour

4 eggs

½ cup shredded almonds (optional)

To make chou paste (dough), combine water and oil in saucepan (about 1-quart capacity) and bring to a boil slowly. Remove from heat and add all flour to hot liquid at once. Return pan to low heat and stir with small whisk until mixture is smooth and comes away from sides of pan. Transfer dough to mixer or food processor. Add 3 eggs, 1 at a time, beating after each addition. Beat remaining egg in cup and add half of it to dough. Continue beating until dough is shiny. Let dough stand in refrigerator at least 30 minutes, or up to all day.

To bake puff shells, preheat oven to 350°F. Put dough in pastry bag fitted with plain tube with about ½-inch opening (#6 or #7). Pipe small balls of dough on unoiled baking sheet. For puff shells of 2- to 3-inch diameter when baked, pipe mounds of dough 1½ inches in diameter and about ½ inch high. Brush top of each mound with reserved beaten egg. Do not use too much egg; it should not drip down side onto pan or puff paste will not puff. If desired, sprinkle shredded almonds on tops. Bake puff shells 30 minutes. Reduce heat to 325°F. and bake another 30 minutes, or until puffs are firm to touch. Remove from oven and loosen from baking sheet with spatula.

To fill puff shells with a cream mixture, make a round hole in bottom of each, using point of small knife. Put filling in pastry bag fitted with plain round tube with ¼-inch opening. Pipe filling through hole. To fill puff shells with a thicker or textured mixture as for hors d'oeuvres, cut shells in half horizontally. Fill bottom half with stuffing, then replace tops.

Makes 18 to 24 cream puff shells, 2 to 3 inches in diameter

WHOLE WHEAT PUFF PASTRY

Pate Feuilletee

For successful puff-pastry-making: (1) The first time you try it, allow for plenty of time, patience, and a cool kitchen; (2) Never attempt to roll puff pastry in a warm room. The butter will soften and mix with the flour, and the layering objective will be lost; (3) After puff pastry is cut into desired shapes for baking, freeze it on the baking sheet. Puff paste bakes best when placed in the oven while frozen.

DO-AHEAD TIP: *Unbaked whole wheat puff pastry can be stored in the freezer but is best prepared and baked the same day.*

- **2 cups stone-ground whole wheat bread flour (do not use whole wheat pastry flour; it does not contain enough gluten to give elasticity to dough)**
- **⅓ cup plus 2 tablespoons ice-cold water or well-chilled skim milk**
- **2 teaspoons fresh lemon juice**
- **1¼ cups cold unsalted butter, cut into ½-inch cubes**

Place 1¾ cups flour in food processor. With machine running, add water or milk and lemon juice and mix until dough forms a ball, about 2 to 3 minutes. Turn dough out onto unfloured surface and shape into smooth ball. Using sharp knife, make deep crosscut on top of ball. Cover with plastic wrap and chill in freezer until firm, about 30 minutes.

Meanwhile, combine butter and remaining flour in large bowl and mix until smooth. Turn out onto surface. Form into 4-inch square using spatula. Cover butter with plastic wrap and chill in freezer until firm, about 20 minutes.

When dough and butter are chilled to equal firmness, but not frozen, transfer dough to lightly floured surface and roll into 12-inch square. Place butter mixture in center of dough and fold sides of dough over butter evenly, making sure ends meet in center. Pinch ends of dough together so there are no holes. Using rolling pin, make series of slight depressions in crisscross pattern over dough until square is flattened to 8 inches. Roll dough into rectangle. Fold as you would a business letter: top one-third toward center; with remaining one-third folded over top. *This is called a single turn.* Cover with plastic wrap and chill in freezer until firm, but not frozen, about 20 minutes.

Turn dough out onto lightly floured surface with open end toward you. Roll into large rectangle about ⅜ inch thick. Fold short ends so they meet at center of dough without overlapping. Fold dough in half at center. *This is called a double turn.* Cover with plastic wrap and chill in freezer until firm, but not frozen, about 20 minutes.

Repeat single turn, chilling in freezer until firm but not frozen, about 20 minutes. Repeat double turn *three* more times, chilling in freezer after each. Cover with plastic wrap and refrigerate.

Makes 1 pound

BASIC CREPES

DO-AHEAD TIP: *Crepes freeze well. Stack on round cake pan and enclose in tightly sealed plastic bag.*

- 1 cup whole wheat pastry flour
- 2 whole eggs
- 2 egg yolks
- 6 tablespoons light vegetable oil (e.g., safflower)
- 1½ cups milk, or reconstituted nonfat dry milk

Combine flour, eggs, egg yolks, oil, and ½ cup milk in mixing bowl. Beat with whisk until smooth. Add additional milk to bring batter to consistency of heavy cream. (It should just coat the back of a metal spoon.) Cover bowl with plastic wrap and let batter rest in refrigerator at least 1 hour, or all day.

To cook crepes, heat 7- to 10-inch saute pan. Arrange near pan the batter, some oil in a cup or sauce dish, wad of waxed paper, ladle, and metal spatula. If batter has thickened, add a little more milk to bring to heavy cream consistency. With wad of waxed paper, wipe pan with film of oil. Pan should be quite hot. For 6-inch-diameter crepe, ladle about ⅓ cup batter into pan. Tilt pan to spread batter evenly into a nice round crepe with all holes filled. Brown crepe on one side. Carefully turn it with the spatula and brown the other side (called the underside). Continue to cook crepes in this manner. Stack crepes on wire rack.

Makes about 16 crepes, 6 inches each, or 20 to 24 smaller ones

CAROB CREPES

DO-AHEAD TIP: *Crepes freeze well. Stack on round cake pan and enclose in tightly sealed plastic bag.*

- 1 cup whole wheat pastry flour
- ¼ cup carob powder
- ¼ teaspoon ground cinnamon
- 2 whole eggs
- 2 egg yolks
- 6 tablespoons light vegetable oil (e.g., safflower)
- 1½ cups milk
- 2 teaspoons light honey

Combine flour, carob powder, cinnamon, eggs, egg yolks, oil, and ½ cup milk in mixing bowl. Beat with wire whisk until smooth. Add more milk to bring batter to consistency of heavy cream. (It should just coat the back of a metal spoon.) Cover bowl with plastic wrap and let batter rest in refrigerator at least 1 hour, or all day.

To cook crepes, heat 10-inch saute or omelet pan. Arrange near pan the batter, some oil in a cup or sauce dish, wad of waxed paper, ladle, and metal spatula. If batter has thickened, add milk to bring to heavy cream consistency. With wad of waxed paper, wipe pan with film of oil. Pan should be medium hot. For 6-inch-diameter crepe, ladle about ⅓ cup batter into pan. Tilt pan around to spread batter evenly into nice round crepe with all holes filled. Brown crepe on one side. Slide spatula around edge of crepe to loosen; then slide spatula under crepe and carefully turn it. Brown other side (called underside) just slightly. Continue to cook crepes in this manner. Stack on wire rack.

Makes about 16 crepes, 6 inches each

SHORTCAKE DOUGH

DO-AHEAD TIP: *Flour and butter mixture can be prepared ahead and refrigerated or frozen. Add honey and milk when ready to bake.*

- 1¾ cups sifted whole wheat pastry flour
- 3 teaspoons baking powder (without aluminum salts)
- 4 tablespoons cold unsalted butter
- ½ to ⅔ cup milk
- 2 teaspoons light honey
- extra milk or melted butter to brush tops

To mix dough in food processor, sift flour again with baking powder. Combine flour mixture and butter in processor. Process until mixture has texture of coarse meal. In separate small container, combine ½ cup milk and honey and beat with fork until mixture is blended. Add to flour and butter mixture in processor and process until ingredients are just mixed. If mixture can be gathered into a mass of stiff dough, transfer it to lightly floured work surface. If it is too crumbly, add more milk, 1 tablespoon at a time.

To mix dough by hand, sift flour again with baking powder. Combine flour mixture with butter in mixing bowl. Quickly rub flour and butter between your fingertips until mixture resembles coarse meal. In separate small container, combine ½ cup milk and honey and beat with fork until mixture is blended. Add to flour and butter mixture and stir until ingredients form into a mass of stiff dough. If it is too crumbly, add more milk, 1 tablespoon at a time.

To bake, preheat oven to 400°F. Gently and firmly knead dough 2 or 3 times. Pat dough to desired thickness. Cut for biscuits or into large round or rectangle for cobbler topping.

For biscuits, pat dough to ½ inch thickness and cut into 1½- to 3-inch-diameter rounds with cutter. Place on oiled baking sheet or in muffin tins. Brush tops with milk or melted butter. Bake until lightly browned, about 12 to 15 minutes.

To bake biscuit dough in sheet pan, allow 15 to 20 minutes at 400°F. for ½-inch-thick dough.

For cobbler topping and other uses, bake according to specific recipe instructions.

Makes about 24 biscuits, 1½ inches each, or 12 biscuits, 3 inches each

PLAIN-COOKED BROWN RICE

DO-AHEAD TIP: *Plain-cooked brown rice freezes well. Steam to reheat.*

1½ cups long grain or short grain brown rice

1 egg, beaten

3½ cups water or stock (e.g., chicken, vegetable, or soy—3½ cups water with 3½ teaspoons tamari soy sauce)

Preheat oven to 350°F. Place rice in deep, heavy pot (about 1½-quart capacity). Add egg and stir mixture over moderate heat until all kernels are dry and separate. Add water or stock and stir over moderate heat until liquid comes to a brisk boil. Cover pot with firm-fitting lid and cook in oven 1 hour, or until tender, without disturbing rice. When cooked, fluff with 2 forks. Use as desired.

Yields 4½ cups

TABLE FOR COOKING VARIOUS QUANTITIES OF BROWN RICE (FOLLOW RECIPE PROCEDURE)

Raw Rice	Egg	Cooking Liquid	Vegetable Oil	Oven Temp.	Average Cooking Time	Cooked Quantity (not packed)
½ cup	½	1¼ cups	1 teaspoon	350°F.	35 minutes	1½ cups
¾ cup	½	2 cups	1½ teaspoons	350°F.	40 minutes	2 cups
1 cup	½	2½ cups	2 teaspoons	350°F.	45 minutes	3 cups
1½ cups	1	3¾ cups	1 tablespoon	350°F.	1 hour	4½ cups
2 cups	1	5 cups	1 tablespoon	350°F.	1 hour/ 10 minutes	6 cups

ASPIC

DO-AHEAD TIP: *Aspic can be made 1 or 2 days ahead and refrigerated. Do not freeze, or aspic will become cloudy. Reheat to liquefy.*

6 cups stock (e.g., chicken, vegetable, or soy—6 cups water with 3 tablespoons tamari soy sauce)

6 tablespoons tomato paste, or 4 medium-size ripe tomatoes, sliced but not peeled

1 tablespoon light honey

4 tablespoons unflavored gelatin

4 egg whites, beaten to soft peaks

Combine all ingredients in large saucepan and bring mixture slowly to a boil, stirring constantly with wire whisk. When mixture comes to a rolling boil, stop stirring, remove pan from heat, and let stand without disturbing it for 15 minutes.

Line large wire strainer or colander with damp cloth and place over another large container. Pour mixture through it. The strained mixture is clarified stock with gelatin which will set when chilled.

Yields 5 cups

PART IV

Holding Fruits for the Future

FREEZING FRUITS

Let's face it, fresh fruits lose something when they are processed, whether frozen and reconstituted, preserved, even cooked, or just pureed. Today, most of us can get fresh fruit year-round. But, when one is blessed with a bumper crop of homegrown fruit, as happens sometimes on our Italian farm, and there is the deep-freeze space in which to store it, then it's great to save some for tasty remembrances during the off-seasons.

One of the handiest ideas in freezing fruits, I think, is freezing fruit purees, even when freezer space is minimal. You might as well make a little extra when fruit is in season. Thawed frozen fruit purees don't have much appreciable difference from the fresh when used in ice cream, sherbet, sauce, or other types of puree use. In my apartment freezer are stashed all sizes of containers with quantities of fruit purees at this very moment – rhubarb, apple sauce, carob sauce, and kiwi – which will be used as sauce or flavoring, with some impromptu inspiration one of these days.

Guide for Freezing Fruits
Use only firm, ripe fruit.

APPLES. Freeze sliced apples, peeled and cored. First soak in salt water solution (½ cup salt to 1 gallon water) and drain. Put sliced apples in freezer containers. Cover with cooled syrup (1½ cups light honey, 3½ cups water, and 2 teaspoons ascorbic acid). Allow 1 inch headspace and cover tightly.

Apple sauce: Pack in freezer container with 1 inch headspace and cover tightly.

Apple juice: Pour into freezer container with 1 inch headspace and cover tightly.

APRICOTS. Put washed, peeled or unpeeled apricots, cut in halves and pitted, in freezer containers. Cover with cooled syrup (4 cups light honey, 4 cups water, and 1 teaspoon ascorbic acid). Allow 1 inch headspace and cover tightly.

AVOCADOS. Blend mashed ripe avocado with ascorbic acid (½ teaspoon to 1 quart). Put in freezer container with 1 inch headspace and cover tightly.

BANANAS. Mix mashed ripe bananas with lemon juice or ascorbic acid (½ teaspoon to 1 quart) to prevent discoloration. Pack in freezer container with 1 inch headspace and cover tightly.

BLACKBERRIES. Pack cleaned, whole blackberries in freezer containers. Cover with cooled syrup (2 cups light honey and 4 cups water). Leave 1 inch headspace and cover tightly.

BLUEBERRIES. Pack cleaned, whole blueberries in freezer containers, leaving ½ inch headspace. Freeze dry, unsweetened.

CAROB. Carob Sauce or Coating Carob (see Index) can be frozen. Pour into freezer container with ½ inch headspace, and cover tightly.

COCONUT. Coconut in chunks, shredded, or grated can be frozen dry. Pack in freezer containers or plastic bag and seal tightly.

CRANBERRIES. Freeze plain, whole. Put into freezer container or bags and seal tightly.

GOOSEBERRIES. Clean; remove stems and blossom ends. Freeze plain, whole. Put in freezer container or bags and seal tightly.

KIWI FRUIT. Strained, sweetened kiwi puree can be frozen. Allow 1 inch headspace and cover tightly.

MANGOES. Sweetened mango puree can be frozen. Allow 1 inch headspace and cover tightly.

PEACHES, NECTARINES. Cut peeled nectarines or peaches in halves or slices and pack in freezer containers. Cover with cooled syrup (2 cups light honey, 4 cups water, and 2 teaspoons ascorbic acid). Allow 1 inch headspace and cover tightly.

PINEAPPLES. Peel, core, and cut pineapple into spears, slices, or cubes. Pack in freezer container and cover with cooled syrup (3 cups light honey and 4 cups water). Allow 1 inch headspace and cover tightly.

Sweetened crushed pineapple can be frozen. Allow 1 inch headspace and cover tightly.

PLUMS. Cut in halves or quarters and remove pits. Pack in containers. Cover with cooled syrup (3 cups light honey and 5 cups water). Allow 1 inch headspace and cover tightly.

RASPBERRIES. Use cleaned, whole raspberries. To freeze dry, unsweetened, spread berries on jelly roll pan, freeze firm, pack in freezer container, allowing ½ inch headspace, cover tightly, and return to freezer. To freeze in syrup, pack in freezer containers. Cover with cooled syrup (4 cups light honey and 4 cups water). Allow 1 inch headspace and cover tightly.

RHUBARB. Rhubarb Puree (see Index) can be frozen. Pour into container, leave 1 inch headspace, and cover tightly.

STRAWBERRIES. To freeze dry, unsweetened, spread cleaned, stemmed, whole strawberries on jelly roll pan, freeze firm, pack in freezer containers, allowing ½ inch headspace, and return to freezer. To freeze in syrup, put whole berries in freezer containers and cover with cooled syrup (3 cups light honey and 4 cups water). Allow ½ inch headspace and cover tightly.

DRYING OR DEHYDRATING FRUITS

In the section on kiwi fruit, I described my green, red, and white Christmas snack bowl of dried kiwi, tomato, and banana or pear slices that is always such a hit. Dried fruits are delicious as a predinner appetizer or after-dinner mignardise or conceit. They can be prepared days ahead. And, when the refrigerator is overstocked with fruit, don't let it spoil. Slice and dehydrate it, and it will keep for months.

Today there are several compact home-style dehydrators to make the drying procedure as possible in an apartment as in the country, and very convenient in consideration of your time and attention, and space. Dehydration time varies according to moisture content of fruit, size of pieces, and system of dehydration. An explanation and guide are usually supplied with dehydration equipment. Dried fruits can be stored from 4 to 6 months in a sealed container in a cool, dry place (70° to 50°F.; not freezing).

To rehydrate dried fruit, steam briefly or soak in water or fruit juice for a few minutes.

FRUITS RECOMMENDED FOR DRYING

Always use good-quality, firm, ripe fruit.

Fruit	Preparation	Use
Apples	Peel, core, slice ¼ inch thick.	Dried snack. Rehydrate for use in apple sauce, pie, cobbler, dumplings, fritters, or as puree for various uses.
Apricots	Wash, halve, remove pits. To prevent discoloration soak in solution of 1 teaspoon ascorbic acid in 1 quart water until ready to dehydrate. Drain between paper towels.	Dried snack or hors d'oeuvres. Rehydrate for variety of uses.
Bananas	Use yellow or brown-flecked bananas. Peel and slice ¼ to ⅜ inch thick.	Dried snack or in cooked cereal. Rehydrate for use in banana bread, cakes.

(continued)

DRYING OR DEHYDRATING FRUITS

FRUITS RECOMMENDED FOR DRYING—continued

Fruit	Preparation	Use
Blueberries	Wash and stem. (When dried, they will look like raisins.)	Can be used like raisins. Rehydrate for use in muffins or pancakes.
Cherries	Wash and stem. Pit and dry whole, or halve and remove pits.	Dried snack. Use like raisins in cooking. Rehydrate for use in pie and sauce.
Coconut	Grate or cut into chunks. Because of high oil content, store in refrigerator.	Use in any way fresh grated coconut is used.
Figs	Wash, remove stems, halve or quarter.	Use dried or rehydrated as dried figs are normally used.
Kiwi Fruit	Peel, slice.	Dried snack or in cooked cereal.
Peaches/ Nectarines	Peel, halve, pit, and cut into 3/8- to 1/2-inch-thick slices. To prevent discoloration soak in solution of 1 teaspoon ascorbic acid in 1 quart water until ready to dehydrate. Drain between paper towels.	Dried snack. Rehydrate for use in cobbler, pie, dumplings.
Papaya	Halve, remove seeds, peel, cut into 3/8-inch-thick slices.	Dried snack or in cereal or yogurt.
Pears	Peel, core, cut lengthwise into 1/2-inch-thick slices. To prevent discoloration soak in solution of 1 teaspoon ascorbic acid in 1 quart water until ready to dehydrate. Drain between paper towels.	Dried snack. Slightly rehydrate for use in fritters.
Pineapples	Peel, slice lengthwise, remove core, cut crosswise into 1/2-inch-thick slices.	Dried snack. Slightly rehydrate for use in fritters, sauces.
Plums (sweet, except Italian)	Wash, halve, and remove pits. Cut into 1/4-inch slices. Do not peel.	Dried snack.
Plums (Italian)	Wash, halve, remove pits, flatten by pressing thumb against skin side.	Dried snack. Use in sauces, stuffing, or stewed.
Strawberries	Wash, stem, cut into 1/2-inch-thick slices.	Dried snack. Use in cooked cereal, or add to yogurt or ice cream.

INDEX

INDEX

C

INDEX

D

INDEX

H

I

K

L

INDEX

M

N

O

P

INDEX

INDEX